Smart STATES, *Better* COMMUNITIES

{ *How state governments can help citizens preserve their communities* }

By CONSTANCE E. BEAUMONT
with a preface by RICHARD MOE

NATIONAL TRUST FOR HISTORIC PRESERVATION

1785 Massachusetts Avenue NW
Washington DC 20036

202 / 588-6000

This publication was produced by the National Trust for Historic Preservation,
a private nonprofit organization with approximately 270,000 members dedicated to protecting
the nation's cultural heritage. The Trust was chartered by Congress in 1949.

The mission of the National Trust for Historic Preservation is to foster an appreciation
of the diverse character and meaning of our American cultural heritage and to preserve and revitalize
the livability of our communities by leading the nation in saving America's historic environments.

Book design by Brian Noyes of the National Trust for Historic Preservation
Production assistance by The Magazine Group, Washington, D.C.

ISBN 0-89133-356-8

Library of Congress Catalog Card Number: 96-70432

Acknowledgements

THE IDEA TO WRITE THIS BOOK CAME FROM NATIONAL TRUST PRESIDENT RICHARD MOE, whose enthusiasm for the creativity and hard work of those seeking to improve state policies is contagious. He thought that the innovations of different states—and the issues they've had to face—should be shared so the states could build upon the lessons learned by others. His leadership and guidance have been invaluable; his patience, much appreciated.

Ed Norton, the National Trust's vice-president for public policy, played a major role in the development of this publication. Throughout the past year, he offered many helpful suggestions and insights. He also provided encouragement during difficult moments.

Megan K. Bellue not only contributed the chapter on Rural Preservation but also assisted with the research for the entire book. In addition, she directed the photograph assemblage, managed the book's production, and assisted in countless other ways.

Other colleagues at the National Trust who were particularly generous with their time and who contributed in major ways are Julia Miller, Dwight Young, Peter Brink and Elizabeth Merritt.

Among those who reviewed early drafts and made constructive suggestions are Dan Costello, Courtney Damkroger, Paul Edmondson, Bridget Hartman, Shelley Mastran, Wendy Nicholas, Kennedy Smith, Liz Wainger, Carter Wilkie, Claudia Wu, and Carol Wyant. Russ Garman assisted with contracts for design, production, and printing. Brian Noyes designed the book and the cover. Jim Lindberg provided photographs. Theodore DeLony helped with research.

Outside the Trust, Wisconsin State Senator Brian Rude, Robert E. Stipe, Paul Bruhn, Professor E.L. "Roy" Hunt, and Frank C. Frantz read early chapters and made helpful recommendations for improving them. Suggestions offered by Bradford White, Dorothy Miner, and Stephen Dennis are appreciated as well.

Grant Dehart, director of Maryland's Program Open Space, contributed the case study on Maryland's easement program in the chapter on rural preservation. Ted Sanderson, deputy state historic preservation officer of Rhode Island, provided the case study on Rhode Island's programs. Harry K. Schwartz and Jim Sewell assisted with the chapter on tax incentives for historic preservation. And Jerold S. Kayden, associate professor at the Harvard Graduate School of Design, contributed a chapter on the issue of private property rights.

The patience and professionalism of Brenda M. Waugh, George L. Perikles, Mary Fran Miklitsch and Jeff Macharyas at The Magazine Group made it possible to complete the book's production on a tight deadline.

Still others outside the National Trust, too numerous to mention here, made themselves available for interviews, provided photographs, rushed information via fax and Fed-Ex, or helped in other ways.

* * *

This publication was made possible with generous assistance from Furthermore, the J.M. Kaplan Fund Publication Program.

Table of Contents

PART II:TRANSPORTATION AND ALTERNATIVES TO SPRAWL: FLIP SIDES OF A COIN

PART III: THE PROPERTY RIGHTS ISSUE AND STRATEGIES

APPENDIX

Preface

THERE IS A YEARNING IN AMERICA TODAY FOR A SENSE OF COMMUNITY. AT the same time, Americans are deeply anxious about seemingly intractable problems: government deficits, random violence, deteriorating schools, crime and drugs.

Interestingly, people seem to be saying that the solution to these problems lies in maintaining—or restoring—a sense of belonging. "If you have a community that's cohesive, if you have a sense of community," observes Keith Roark, former mayor of Hailey, Ida., "these and other problems can be controlled. If you don't, if you just have anonymous, impersonal settlements, it becomes much more difficult to solve these problems."

The physical character of our cities, towns, and suburbs is not the only influence on our ability to create a sense of community, but it is a major one. The way that our buildings are designed, the nature of our streets and highways, the length of time that our buildings stay in place, the existence of public gathering spaces for people to meet, the extent to which the concentration—or dispersal—of buildings encourages—or discourages—repetitive, face-to-face contacts through which people get to know one another—all these things affect what urban designer Alex Achimore calls the "habitat for community."[1] As Jane Jacobs, author of *The Death and Life of Great American Cities*, once observed, "Lowly, unpurposeful and random as they appear, sidewalk contacts are the small change from which a city's wealth of public life must grow."

The physical features of our built environment profoundly affect whether people have the time and the opportunity to get to know, and therefore trust, one another. They affect whether people develop enough of a personal attachment to the place in which they live to want to stay and get involved in community activities. They affect whether people take pride in their community and see it as something worth investing in. And they affect whether people feel comfortable in their physical surroundings, whether these surroundings foster positive interaction with others in the community. Winston Churchill once said, "We shape our buildings: thereafter they shape us." We could add: We shape our communities, and then they shape us.

Many thoughtful Americans have noticed the link between buildings and streetscapes, on the one hand, and the intangible ingredients that go into creating a sense of community on the other. "The destruction of things that are familiar and important causes great anxiety in people," the famous anthropologist, Margaret Mead, once said. Jerold S. Kayden, a nationally respected land-use attorney, notes that "bricks and mortar are material repositories of stability in an ever-shifting world. Precipitous change in our physical fabric that cuts the connective tissue between people and place may unwittingly upset our mental well-being." The late urban pioneer James Rouse once told a University of California audience: "I believe that many of the most serious problems of our society flow from the fact that the city is out of scale with people; that it is too big for people to comprehend; to feel a part of; to feel responsible for; to feel important in. I believe this out-of-scaleness promotes loneliness, irresponsibility, superficial values."

The physical features of our built environment profoundly affect whether people have the time and the opportunity to get to know, and therefore trust, one another.

In *Democracy's Discontent*, Michael J. Sandel has observed that there are "two concerns that lie at the heart of democracy's discontent. One is the fear that, individually and collectively, we are losing control of the forces that govern our lives. The other is the sense that, from family to neighborhood to nation, the moral fabric of community is unraveling around us. These two fears—for the loss of self-government and the erosion of community—together define the anxiety of the age."

In working together to improve a neighborhood—whether by rescuing an endangered landmark, reviving a Main Street, or cleaning up the debris around an abandoned house—people get to know each other. They engage each other and their government. They become involved in community affairs. An intangible but powerful by-product of such activities is a sense of civic pride that carries over into other areas. Success in making tangible improvements to one's neighborhood—in making the city or town beautiful—gives people a renewed spirit. It gives them a legitimate sense of control over their domain.

If the urban planner looks at the effects of zoning and land-use on the capacity of a community to support such vital activities as housing, commerce, transportation and recreation, the historic preservationist advocates the retention of places that unify and give meaning to a community, whether because these places are beautiful, historic, or simply comforting and familiar anchors in a world of sometimes bewildering, disorienting change.

As creatures of state government, local governments often look to the states for the tools and resources needed to preserve the buildings, the scenic vistas, and the countryside that people care about. An example of an issue that *only* the states can address is the mismatch between local political boundaries and developments with regional impacts. Many development projects being built today are so large that they affect towns for miles around, not simply the host community. Even though these projects can quickly wipe out the identity of neighboring towns, these towns often have no say whatsoever over the development.

The historic preservationist advocates the retention of places that unify and give meaning to a community.

So far only about ten of the fifty states have passed laws that create forums to mediate interjurisdictional land-use conflicts. It is noteworthy that in passing such laws, these states have also sought to avoid the extra costs—and taxes—that result from inefficient land use and haphazard development.

Many state policymakers—governors, legislators, agency heads and their staffs—have recognized the great influence that states have over the ability of local communities to preserve physical environments that bring people together and give them a sense of belonging. To cite a few specific examples of such influence:

- Today Portland, Ore., is a successful city renowned for a strong civic spirit thanks in no small part to the leadership that Governor Tom McCall showed in the early 1970s. By persuading the state legislature to pass a land-use planning law designed to contain urban sprawl, McCall made it easier for Portland to preserve a cohesive downtown widely recognized now as one of the most attractive in the country. The overall economic vitality of Portland's downtown has been essential to the success of local preservation activities in this city, both in the central business district and in the surrounding neighborhoods.

- Beautiful historic districts—College Hill in Providence, Lower Downtown in Denver, Brooklyn Heights in New York City—contribute to the "soul" and unique identity of these cities. Today there are more than 2,000 historic districts across the country thanks in large part to the efforts of state legislators decades ago.

More recent examples of leadership on the part of state lawmakers exist as well. In Wisconsin, Senate President Brian Rude has been a major force behind legislation aimed at enhancing communities. Proposals he helped shepherd into law today encourage the recycling of historic buildings and enable communities to create "heritage tourism" districts

BLAIR SEITZ

as a way to attract outside visitors and boost local economies. In Maryland, Governor Parris Glendening is encouraging state agencies to locate downtown both to avoid urban sprawl and to give historic communities an economic shot in the arm. In New Jersey, Assembly-woman Maureen Ogden helped preservationists to obtain $60 million in over ten years from the Green Acres Bond Program to finance the rehabilitation and reuse of historic buildings. In Massachusetts Senator Robert Durand and members of his Special Commission on Historic Preservation developed a comprehensive agenda for preservation programs in the Bay State and were instrumental in securing funds to restore older neighborhoods once thought hopeless. These examples underscore the bipartisanship of preservation: Rude and Ogden are Republicans; Glendening and Durand are Democrats.

This book describes these and other actions by state policymakers to support efforts of citizens to save what they value most about their communities. Besides presenting an array of preservation tools for states to consider, the book analyzes the strengths and weaknesses of various state policies and provides case studies to illustrate the practical application of such policies. Recognizing that the social, economic, and political climate of each state differs, the book avoids recommending a single model for historic preservation. Instead, it lays out a menu of choices in key areas: historic resource protection, tax incentives, funding, regulatory relief, state agency investments, community revitalization, rural preservation, transportation and alternatives to sprawl.

While offering this book as a resource for states, the National Trust is also working with the private sector at the state level. Through its Statewide Partners Program, the Trust is collaborating with nonprofit state preservation organizations in an effort to help them become stronger, more effective voices for preservation in their states. Through its Nation-

Communities— and states— should be shaped by choice, not chance.

al Main Street Center, the Trust has entered into partnerships with some 40 states to rejuvenate historic downtowns, create jobs, and recycle old buildings for new businesses.

While various subthemes emerge from the text that follows, the overriding theme is that political leadership on the part of state officials is a critical ingredient to the preservation of communities. Such leadership may come from someone like Oregon Governor Tom McCall, who educated the public about the importance of sensible land-use planning back in the early seventies, or from former Maryland Secretary of Transportation James Lighthizer, who directed the state highway department to redesign a road project after a citizen pleaded with him to halt the imminent bulldozing of old trees lining a small-town Main Street. What matters is that state policymakers recognize the profound impact of their decisions on community life and exercise the leadership necessary to ensure that the impact is positive. Whether we end up with "non-communities," or "bits and pieces of a city...splattered across the landscape," as James Rouse described the urban sprawl that has consumed so much of America, or whether we get more cohesive and satisfying communities, depends on state governments as well as others.

A single state lawmaker or agency director can make good things happen. So can a single individual who takes the initiative to talk to a state policymaker and engage him or her on these critical issues.

Communities—and states—should be shaped by choice, not chance. States can allow their communities to be shaped by the accidental collision of random economic forces, or they can give communities the tools they need to become what they want to be. That is what this book is all about.

We invite state governors, legislators, agency heads and their staffs to work with the National Trust and our state and local partners in preserving places that people value and in encouraging the use of historic town planning and urban design principles that could help make new settlements less impersonal and anonymous, places where a sense of community can take root and flourish.

Richard Moe, President
National Trust for Historic Preservation
September 1996

INTRODUCTION

2

Building the Preservation Constituency

The Experience of Massachusetts

In three years, Massachusetts has vaulted over many states to rank among the top five in terms of financial support for historic preservation. Behind the Bay State's success in making the robust sum of $30 million available for historic preservation in such a short period lies a politically astute approach to building public support for preservation, a broad definition of historic preservation, and a focus on making preservation relevant to ordinary people.

WHEN HISTORIC MASSACHUSETTS, INC. (HMI), ASKED ARTHUR BERGERON to serve on its board in 1992, Bergeron thought the position might be fun and interesting, but he did not see historic preservation as a particularly burning issue. "I liked old buildings. My wife and I would stop at local historical museums whenever we travelled," recalls the lawyer from Marlborough, "but frankly, I didn't really think of historic preservation as being terribly significant."

Bergeron nonetheless agreed to serve on the board, and a few weeks later found himself having a conversation with two other board members and HMI's executive director. The topic: How could HMI broaden the public constituency for historic preservation in Massachusetts? That preservation lacked a strong constituency in the Bay State was evidenced by the legislature's failure to approve a single dollar for the Massachusetts Preservation Projects Fund in the past several years. Created in the 1980s by the Massachusetts Historical Commission, this program had helped local communities complete some $4 million in rehabilitation projects around the state. Now, however, the program was simply not a priority for the legislature.

So Bergeron and his colleagues turned to State Senator Robert A. Durand for advice. A Democrat from Marlborough and chairman of the Senate Committee on Natural Resources, Durand recommended that HMI try to get a statewide commission created to focus on historic preservation and its relationship to other issues facing communities— economic development, neighborhood revitalization, and farmland preservation. The commission should include representation from the public, the Massachusetts House and Senate, and all the major state agencies. Durand offered to seek legislation creating the commission

Stanley Lowe (on far right) of Pittsburgh talks to neighborhood leaders from Massachusetts.

if HMI would give him proposed language. The HMI leaders followed up almost immediately. Within a month, Durand had secured the legislature's approval for the commission.

Soon thereafter, however, Governor William Weld vetoed the proposal. So in early 1993, HMI tried again. While the legislature approved the commission proposal a second time, the governor again vetoed it. Weld was listening to his economic development commissioner, who thought that historic preservation was "anti-economic development." Why approve a commission likely to come up with recommendations antithetical to economic development?, he reasoned.

So HMI went back to Durand and asked, "What do we do now?" The senator suggested expanding the commission to include five additional members, all to be drawn from real estate and development constituencies. This should allay the fears of the governor's staff that the commission was out to sabotage economic development, Durand thought. The idea worked. After the legislature approved the commission a third time, Governor Weld signed it in August 1993.

The purpose of the Special Commission on Historic Preservation—nicknamed the "Durand Commission" after its chairman—was to develop a comprehensive historic preservation policy for the Commonwealth of Massachusetts. The 24-member Commission included representatives from the state departments of transportation, economic affairs, environmental affairs, historic preservation, commerce and labor, and communities and development; six state legislators; five representatives from the real estate and development industry; and four representatives from the preservation community. State Representative Steven Angelo co-chaired the Commission with Senator Durand.

An Introduction to Stanley Lowe

"Preservation is about bringing the community together."

WHILE STILL THINKING ABOUT THE DIRECTION the Commission should take, Bergeron, who had become HMI's new board chairman, and HMI's new director, Marcia Molay, attended the National Trust for Historic Preservation's annual meeting in St. Louis in October 1993. Both still new to historic preservation, they were looking for fresh ideas for HMI's agenda. At a plenary session, they heard Stanley Lowe, then assistant director of the Pittsburgh History and Landmarks Foundation in Pittsburgh, Pa., talk about inner-city residents who were using historic preservation as a vehicle to attack neighborhood apathy and to develop a sense of pride in people who had lost their self-esteem. With the help of the Preservation Loan Fund Lowe administered, neighborhood residents were buying up bars that had become nuisances. They were hiring neighborhood youth to restore houses instead of submitting to the lure of gangs. They were working with bankers to bring needed capital into areas once redlined. They were helping lower-income people become better housed in historic homes. And they were sponsoring "Family Fun Days" and picnics to let children know someone cared about them. "Preservation is about bringing the community together," Lowe said. Lowe made it clear that historic preservation was not the preserve of wealthy landowners, but a cause that people from every background could enjoy and benefit from.

"Lowe's speech completely changed my life," said Bergeron afterwards. It convinced him and Molay that historic preservation was more than a pleasant activity; it could play a central role in sparking community pride in depressed urban neighborhoods. To make functional and beautiful neighborhoods out of areas that have been given up for lost—this was worth working on, Molay thought.

Bergeron and Molay left the St. Louis meeting excited about the idea of adapting Lowe's ideas to Massachusetts. If Lowe and his allies could restore hope and community pride in Pittsburgh's demoralized older neighborhoods, others should be able to do the same thing in the older cities of Massachusetts. Bergeron and Molay decided to try to develop a create a statewide program in Massachusetts akin to the initiative Lowe had created in Pittsburgh.

But this would take money, and they still didn't have any funding for preservation. HMI had won approval for a statewide commission, but the movement still lacked the constituency needed to get the Massachusetts Preservation Projects Fund reactivated. Moreover, Governor Weld had not yet even appointed the commission members.

A Conference and Hearings

TO GET THINGS MOVING, Molay suggested holding a major conference in Boston. Lest the conference draw historic preservationists only—thus not advancing the goal of building the preservation constituency—HMI reached out to real estate developers, bankers, mayors, and neighborhood development leaders, urging them all to attend. The conference drew about 300 people, almost half of whom came from fields unrelated to preservation. Guest speakers included Stanley Lowe and Richard Moe, president of the National Trust for Historic Preservation.

Meanwhile, news of the conference had prompted the governor to appoint the Commission members with Senator Durand as their chairman. HMI now worked with the Commission to get the study group out of Boston to hold six regional public hearings on a tight timeline. "These commissions can drag on and on and never produce anything of substance. You need to work fast," Durand cautioned HMI, which was now serving as the commission's staff since the legislature had not provided any funds to hire its own. Durand and HMI agreed that the hearings should hammer away at the point that historic preservation was concerned about people, job creation, neighborhood revitalization, downtown economic development, and other issues of general concern to communities.

The hearings took place between February and June 1994 in six towns represented by key senators in the legislature. To encourage public participation in the hearings, HMI notified over 7,000 preservationists and political and business leaders.

As at the Boston conference, HMI wanted to attract a broad spectrum of people, not just preservationists, to the hearings, for if no one else came, the goal of broadening the constituency would not be achieved. To make sure others did become involved, HMI sponsored "power breakfasts" before each hearing. "Every community has 'important' people, whether they are bankers or town council members or business people,'" explains Bergeron. "We looked at each state senator's district and identified the important people in that district. We figured that if we couldn't get these people to attend the hearings, we could at least get them to breakfast and engage them there in discussions about historic preservation." In each case, between 75 and 100 people came to the breakfasts. The hearings themselves were extremely well-attended.

To help these local civic and business leaders visualize the relevance of preservation to their own communities, Bergeron showed slides he had taken of local historic buildings: "I tried to illustrate certain themes, such as downtown revitalization and neighborhood preservation. I would show these people wonderfully restored houses sitting next to dilapidated 'dogs' of buildings to convey the power and potential of preservation as a tool for community revitalization. When people saw buildings that they knew on the screen, they suddenly became much more interested."

Following these presentations, the "important people" discussed local preservation issues, and near the end of the breakfasts, someone from each table rose and reported ideas generated to the group as a whole. Many of the more dynamic recommendations that later came out of the Durand Commission were born at these breakfasts.

Lest the conference draw historic preservationists only...HMI reached out to real estate developers, bankers, mayors, and neighborhood development leaders.

In the summer of 1994, HMI produced a draft report for the commission reflecting input from the breakfasts and hearings. "In writing this report, we tried to focus on how historic preservation relates to people," says Bergeron. "The question we wanted to answer was: 'What's in preservation for me?'" The focus of the Durand Commission report thus differed from that of preservation commissions in some states, which have focused on government's role and administrative matters.

In August of that year, the commission began circulating the draft. A few critics immediately began picking it apart. "I've participated in a number of these commissions," said Durand, "and this is how they die." To prevent that from happening, Durand called a meeting of the commission to resolve differences over the report's language. "We'll meet for however long it takes to get the job done," said Durand, who conducted two marathon meetings. By early September 1994, the commission had completed its report. (See sidebar.)

Meanwhile, in June of that year, Senator Thomas S. Birmingham, in whose district one of the hearings had taken place and who chaired the Senate Ways and Means Committee, managed to include a recommendation for $5 million for the Massachusetts Preservation Projects Fund in the state's capital outlay budget. The legislature approved this request, as did the governor. "Suddenly we not only had this money but also a sense that there really was a broader constituency for historic preservation," says Bergeron.

Since the approval of the $5 million,[1] the legislature has approved a second infusion into the Massachusetts Preservation Projects Fund of $10 million from a bond-financed open space preservation fund, and $15 million for historic parks and landscapes. In all, the Massachusetts legislature has approved $30 million for historic preservation projects, a phenomenal accomplishment for HMI and its preservation partners in just two years. This success also reflects the good will created by the many local rehabilitation projects that the Massachusetts Historical Commission assisted during the eighties.

"I thought that if they can restore these run-down areas, we can, too."

Pilot Projects for Community Revitalization

WITH THE HELP OF THE HISTORICAL COMMISSION and the availability of state funds, HMI has been able to move ahead with a pilot demonstration of what it calls the "statewide Stanley Lowe" program (officially, the Community Preservation Program) in three cities: Lawrence, Chelsea, and New Bedford. This effort got a jump-start in August 1994, when HMI hosted a statewide conference of urban leaders to hear Lowe and Pittsburgh Mayor Tom Murphy discuss the neighborhood rejuvenation activities that had taken place in their city. "When I saw their slide shows," recalls Mary Claire Kennedy, mayor of Lawrence, Mass., "I saw amazing similarities between Pittsburgh's old neighborhoods and ours. I thought that if they can restore these run-down areas, we can, too." Lawrence is an old, economically depressed city.

Mayor Kennedy and local leaders from Chelsea and New Bedford volunteered at this conference to participate in HMI's adaptation of Lowe's ideas. It was decided to focus on the rehabilitation of the historic Orange-Wheeler house in Lawrence as the catalyst for their first project. The house was decaying, but volunteer board members of HMI determined that it was structurally sound and capable of rehabilitation.

HMI helped a local community-development corporation to acquire an option to buy the house. After its rehabilitation is completed, it will be transferred and will serve as the headquarters for City C.O.R.E., a local branch of the national YouthBuild vocational and leadership training organization. A community policeman will live upstairs to provide extra security for the neighborhood.

Massachusetts Recommendations

MASSACHUSETTS' SPECIAL COMMISSION ON HISTORIC PRESERVATION emphasized assistance to private property owners and the relationship of preservation to other public goals. Among the Commission's more noteworthy recommendations:

- Adopt state enabling legislation to give local governments the option of abating local property taxes on rehabilitated historic structures (passed in 1996)
- Change regulations governing the location and construction of elementary and secondary schools to make it easier to preserve and reuse historic school buildings
- Reactivate and ensure compliance with a state policy that directs state agencies to reinforce downtowns by locating there as opposed to outlying areas
- Develop a Heritage License Plate Fund to support the preservation of local archives
- Support a statewide planning law that makes historic preservation an integral part of local comprehensive planning
- Disseminate information on planning and zoning techniques that encourage historic preservation and the retention of community character
- Develop a public information program to increase public interest and support for historic preservation
- Establish a training program for local building inspectors to improve their understanding of preservation issues and to ensure that their decisions not be detrimental to the preservation of historic resources (passed in 1996)
- Create a task force composed of preservationists, developers, municipal leaders, developers, and environmentalists to identify ways to balance environmental and historic preservation concerns when regulations are implemented to remove lead paint and asbestos and to clean up hazardous waste on urban sites
- Amend Massachusetts' Chapter 61A program, which allows working farms to be taxed according to their actual rather than potential land use, to include historic structures located on these farms as well
- Replenish the Massachusetts Preservation Projects Fund to provide brick-and-mortar funding for local preservation projects ($15 million was authorized by 1996)
- Adopt more flexible road design standards, as allowed under the federal Intermodal Surface Transportation Efficiency Act, to allow for greater preservation of local community character and historic resources
- Assemble and disseminate model local ordinances and planning and zoning laws to help communities preserve historic resources and community character
- Establish a heritage signage system identifying major heritage attractions along the state's highway system
- Establish "Immigrant Heritage Trails" to recognize the contribution that the Commonwealth's major nationality groups have made to the State's development
- Establish pilot vocational training programs to teach historic preservation techniques used in restoring or rehabilitating historic structures
- Develop a program to target state lending agency loans to historic preservation (implemented in 1996)

The Orange-Wheeler House, before rehabilitation and with work in progress, will serve as headquarters for City C.O.R.E. (a local branch of the national YouthBuild vocational and leadership training organization).

HMI tapped Andres Gonzalez, a neighborhood resident working on crisis intervention for troubled children, to coordinate the project. The 23-year-old former gang member was shot four years ago witnessing a dispute. "There I was, a young father lying on the ground asking a friend to take care of my child in case I died," Gonzalez says. "That got to me—and to my friends in the gang. We realized that while we were poisoning our neighborhood, little 'gang-member wannabes' saw us as role models. We got smart and quit the gang."

HMI sent Gonzalez and coordinators selected for four similar projects to Pittsburgh for a firsthand view of Lowe's work. "I was amazed by Stanley," says Gonzalez. "He took us around the older neighborhoods. Seeing how he worked with local banks, how he encouraged low-income people to take charge of their lives, how he raised his son…He gave us a lot of pointers. From Stanley I got the idea that [neighborhood revitalization] was definitely do-able."

Buoyed by the Pittsburgh experience, Gonzalez returned to Lawrence and set to work. He distributed fliers to neighborhood residents. "If you care about your neighborhood, please come to our meetings," they read. Fifteen people showed up. They formed the Orange-Wheeler Neighborhood Association, recruited more members, cleared debris from the alleys, and met regularly. The mayor sent city officials to the meetings to help solve problems as they arose. When local residents complained about drug dealers and prostitutes haunting the dark alleys, the city asked Massachusetts Electric to install lights and the city police to crack down. The association is tracking down absentee landlords and identifying those who will cooperate with the renewal effort. By enforcing building codes, the city is taking a harder line with landlords content to milk their properties while letting them deteriorate.

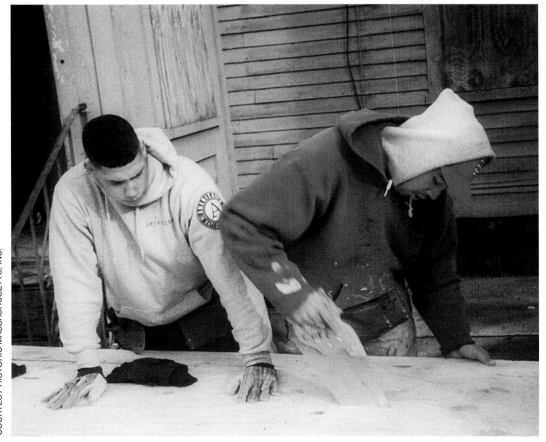

COURTESY HISTORIC MASSACHUSETTS, INC.

Project coordinator Andres Gonzalez (left) works on the Orange-Wheeler house with a member of Lawrence, Massachusetts's City C.O.R.E.

To assist in the Orange-Wheeler House's rehabilitation, the city obtained a $50,000 grant from the Massachusetts Preservation Projects Fund. The state community development office approved a city request for $750,000, matched by local banks. With these funds, Lawrence will be able to acquire and repair other dilapidated buildings in the neighborhood. "It doesn't make sense to invest in just one property," Kennedy says. "We need to do the whole block to protect our investment."

HMI hopes to stimulate as many as 40 "Stanley Lowe" projects throughout the state. Much work lies ahead in Lawrence, but the most important accomplishment—giving the neighborhood hope—has been achieved. And Gonzalez feels lucky to have a key role in the Lawrence effort: "A lot of people are depending on me for a lot of things. I'm gonna try my hardest to do this for my city and my people."

Lessons from Massachusetts

"I'm gonna try my hardest to do this for my city and my people."

BY STIMULATING THE CREATION OF A STATE COMMISSION with political clout, by bringing out local civic, business, and neighborhood leaders to the public hearings and power breakfasts, and by convening a statewide conference on neighborhood revitalization, HMI has travelled a long distance in a short time toward its goal of broadening the constituency for historic preservation in Massachusetts. A languishing fund has been turned into a $15 million resource for brick-and-mortar preservation projects throughout the state, and $15 million more has been reclaimed to restore historic parks. The Massachusetts Historical Commission's work in having distributed the MPPF funds to worthwhile projects during the eighties made it easier for HMI to demonstrate the project's potential to state legislators.

The reasoning behind Bergeron's strategies in Massachusetts holds lessons for preservationists in other states. "My operating assumption has been that government responds to people. It is futile to look to government for help until you have built a political constituency. This is the key to everything. Government simply does not spend money unless a lot of people want it to," observes Bergeron. "Our elected representatives are looking for ways to solve community problems, and communities are looking for ways to differentiate themselves from other towns, to preserve their uniqueness. Historic preservation helps achieve both of these objectives," he adds.

To "preservation purists" who favor investments in the better credentialed historic structures over more ordinary neighborhood buildings, Bergeron says: "The merit of a project lies in whether or not it builds pride in a neighborhood. Historic preservation is important to the extent that it's building America. If it's not doing that, it's not important.

Keys to Success in Massachusetts

- Create a broad-based, high-level commission that includes real estate and economic development representatives as well as community leaders
- Move quickly.
- Turn people out for public hearings. Make sure local civic and business leaders show up.
- Show what historic preservation can do for communities. In doing so, use visuals—photographs and slides.

"Historic preservation as an aesthetic movement is great, but if that's all it is, it shouldn't be funded by government. And it won't be. You might get 51 percent of the people in a country like France to fund an aesthetics-oriented program, but you won't in the United States. Ironically, through our constituency building approach, we may yet produce the kind of public constituency that exists in France for aesthetics."

PART I

Making Preservation Happen

CHAPTER 1

Protection for Historic Places

Protection for Historic Places

COMMUNITIES CHOOSE TO PROTECT HISTORIC PLACES FOR MANY REAsons. The protection of property values is one. "We saw the historic district ordinance as a tool for protecting and enhancing property values," comments a homeowner in the Brooklyn Heights (N.Y.) Historic District in explaining why he supported the ordinance.[1] "The historic district controls help ensure that the area's desirability will be maintained. They ensure long-term stability in property values." The design controls that accompany a historic district ordinance in Denver "protect my buildings from what my neighbors might do to adjoining properties," observes a developer who invested heavily in the Lower Downtown section of this western city. "If you make an investment here, you have a sense it will be in good company."

The stimulation of economic activity is another reason. This is particularly true in communities with enough historic resources to attract tourists…and the dollars they bring into a local economy. "Every study of travel motivations has shown that an interest in the achievements of the past is among the three major reasons why people travel," writes Arthur Frommer, author of the famous travel guide series. But the link between tourism and historic preservation "occurs only when a community preserves entire districts, not just isolated structures," he adds. "All over America we find cities that possess scattered historical structures, and yet they enjoy no tourism at all."[2]

The need for a healthy environment is a third reason. Making good use of limited resources, including those embodied in existing and historic buildings, can alleviate pressures to destroy forests for new timber or to consume prime farmland for new development. The demolition of existing buildings adds to waste disposal problems. According to some recycling experts, the debris from building construction and demolition can account for more than 20 percent of a municipality's solid waste. Because such debris is bulky and difficult to compact or burn, many landfills refuse to accept it.[3]

The desire for livable communities is a fourth reason. The human scale of many historic districts, the ease with which people can walk around in them, the comfort provided by familiar places—these and other attributes all contribute to that intangible but powerful asset known as "community livability."

Robert E. Stipe, one of the nation's foremost experts on historic preservation, suggests there are psychological reasons as well for protecting historic resources:

Dupont Circle Historic District, Washington, DC.

I have come to believe that the urge to preserve is less rooted in high-style cultural soil than in a more fundamental, even biological, need all of us have to try to reduce or moderate the pace and scale of change itself. What we are really trying to preserve, I think, is memory. It is an attempt to keep a mental grip on familiar and accustomed environments that make us feel comfortable and secure whether or not they are aesthetically pleasing or historically credentialed. The real issue is not whether we will have change, but how great it will be, how quickly it will happen, and how shattering its impact will be. Of course we value our National Landmark buildings, but we may equally value a single tree or even an undistinguished building in a known, comfortable environment.[4]

In short, there are compelling economic, social, environmental and even psychological reasons to protect beautiful and historic places.

All too often, however, communities lack the legal means to achieve these social goals. A few years ago, the historic Central Bank in Denver was destroyed by an out-of-town corporation. Because the city lacked adequate protection for its historic buildings in the central business district, the best efforts of the mayor, the city council, the chamber of commerce, the tourism bureau, and the local citizenry could not save this landmark. "Where there was once a magnificent commercial structure with understated grace, charm, and appropriate scale, there is now yet another pile of used brick, soon to be a parking lot. Almost everyone wanted it saved, but now it's gone," lamented a local resident.[5]

Ultimately, most historic preservation decisions are local. But as Wisconsin State Senator Brian Rude points out, "Without the necessary tools, citizens may not be able to compete against powerful forces that run counter to preservation. What we are trying to do in state government is to give people the tools they need to make historic preservation happen in their communities."

While numerous legal mechanisms exist to protect historic resources, we shall focus in this chapter on two especially important ones:

- state enabling laws that permit local governments to enact local historic district and preservation ordinances; and
- state laws intended to ensure that state agencies—and sometimes local government agencies and private developers as well—minimize harm to historic resources.

"What we are trying to do in state government is to give people the tools they need to make historic preservation happen in their communities."

State Enabling Laws

S TATE ENABLING LAWS—whether for zoning in general or historic preservation in particular—empower local governments to pass ordinances that protect historic resources from demolition, neglect, or inappropriate alterations. A typical preservation ordinance creates a local commission to regulate proposed changes to individual landmarks or buildings in a historic district. Changes considered harmful, such as the demolition of a landmark or the construction of a high-rise tower amid a small-scale historic neighborhood, may be denied outright or simply delayed to allow time for the exploration of better alternatives.

The first city in America to enact a preservation ordinance was Charleston, S.C., which created an Old and Historic District in 1931. In passing this law, Charleston exercised municipal powers assumed under the state's zoning enabling law. The second American city to enact a preservation ordinance was New Orleans. In contrast to Charleston, New Orleans acted pursuant to a state constitutional amendment passed by the legislature in 1936. This amendment allowed the Vieux Carre Commission to regulate development in

BRYCE LANKARD

A restaurant in the famed French Quarter of New Orleans.

New Orleans' famous French Quarter. It was not until 1956 that New York became the first state to provide general enabling authority to municipalities throughout the state to establish and protect local historic districts. Whether a local government acts pursuant to a state enabling law or constitutional amendment, the key point is that it may exercise only those powers conveyed by the state.

All kinds of questions may arise concerning a local government's authority to take certain actions. Can it temporarily stop the demolition of historic buildings to give city planners time to update local development rules? Can it protect the setting of a historic landmark in addition to the landmark itself? Can it protect an individual historic building that stands outside a historic district? Can it deal with the problem of "demolition by neglect?" Can it regulate non-historic buildings located inside historic districts? When these or other questions arise, as they often do, the scope and clarity of state enabling laws are critical. A local government's action may be overturned in court if it is shown that the municipality exceeded the authority provided under a state enabling law.

In exercising their powers to regulate private property, it is critical that state and local governments not only be fair and reasonable, but also that they comply with certain legal requirements. Their actions must, for example:

- promote a valid public purpose, such as the public health, safety, or general welfare;
- leave property owners with a reasonable economic use of their property; and
- honor citizens' rights to "Due Process" and "Equal Protection" under the law.

For over half a century, both federal and state courts have upheld the validity of local preservation ordinances that were enacted pursuant to state enabling laws meeting these requirements.

Court Decisions Upholding Preservation Laws

For over half a century, both federal and state courts have upheld the validity of local preservation ordinances.

THE MOST IMPORTANT JUDICIAL RULING bearing on historic preservation laws was handed down in 1978 by the U.S. Supreme Court in a now famous case, *Penn Central Transportation Co. v. City of New York*.[6] Penn Central had attacked New York City's landmark ordinance as unconstitutional because it prevented the company from building a 55-story office tower atop the historic Grand Central Terminal in Manhattan. The local landmarks commission determined that the tower, four times taller than the terminal, would overwhelm this Beaux Arts building. Said the commission: "The Terminal, in its setting, is a great example of urban design. Such examples are not so plentiful in New York City that we can afford to lose any of the few we have. And we must preserve them in a meaningful way—with alterations and additions of such character, scale, materials and mass as will protect, enhance and perpetuate the original design rather than overwhelm it." The Supreme Court ruled that New York's ordinance—and, by inference, comparable ordinances elsewhere—*was* constitutional and that it met the "public purpose" requirement:

> Because this Court has recognized, in a number of settings, that States and cities may enact land-use restrictions or controls to enhance the quality of life by preserving the character and desirable aesthetic features of a city...appellants do not contest that New York City's objective of preserving structures and areas with special historic, architectural, or cultural significance is an entirely permissible governmental goal.

* * *

> The [land-use] restrictions imposed [on Penn Central] are substantially related to the promotion of the general welfare...

An even earlier U.S. Supreme Court decision, *Berman v. Parker*, had upheld the principle that the government could regulate for the purpose of making communities more livable and beautiful:

> The concept of the public welfare is broad and inclusive...The values it represents are spiritual as well as physical, aesthetic as well as monetary. It is within the power of the legislature to determine that the community should be beautiful as well as healthy, spacious as well as clean, well-balanced as well as carefully patrolled.[7]

A long line of state court decisions interpreting the U.S. Constitution also recognizes historic preservation as a valid public purpose. One of the earliest such decisions came in 1941 from the Louisiana Supreme Court, which upheld local restrictions on private property—limits on the size of signs, in this case—in the historic French Quarter:

> Preventing or prohibiting eyesores in such a locality is within the police power and within the scope of this municipal ordinance. The preservation of the Vieux Carre [in New Orleans] as it was originally is *a benefit to the inhabitants of New Orleans generally* [emphasis added], not only for the sentimental value of this show place but for its commercial value as well, because it attracts tourists and conventions to the city, and is in fact a justification for the slogan, America's most interesting city.[8]

BRYCE LANKARD

It is buildings such as these, with their ornate iron work, that draw tourists to New Orleans.

Today, half a century later, millions of Americans flock to New Orleans, pouring money into the city's coffers every year. They do so in such large numbers *because* the French Quarter was protected and can still be enjoyed for its beauty and uniqueness.

In a more recent decision linking historic preservation to the general welfare, the Ohio Supreme Court upheld the Village of Hudson's preservation ordinance, finding that historic preservation is a valid public purpose in Ohio. In *Albrecht, Inc., v. Village of Hudson*, the Ohio Supreme Court stated:

> [I]t is our finding that there is a legitimate governmental interest in maintaining the aesthetics of the community and that, as such, aesthetic considerations may be taken into account by the legislative body in enacting zoning legislation... Moreover, we further find that the ordinance...also reflects a concern for the monetary interests of protecting real estate from impairment and destruction of value. We believe that these goals are includable under the general welfare aspect of the municipal police power and may therefore justify its reasonable exercise.[9]

Of course, one state does not bind other states. However, these decisions do provide helpful insights into certain legal principles that run through many state court decisions.

Suffice it to say here that historic preservation is on solid legal ground as a valid public purpose and has been found by courts on many occasions to advance the general welfare—a prerequisite for government regulation.

Reasonable Economic Uses and the "Takings" Issue

VERY OFTEN WHEN STATES are considering historic preservation legislation, someone raises the so-called "takings" issue. This issue and the concept of private property rights are discussed at length in Chapter 11, but a few words on the subject are in order here as well.

Preservation regulations rarely prohibit property owners from making a reasonable economic use of their land.

While preservation regulations may affect private property, they must leave property owners with a reasonable economic use of their property. If they do not, the regulations may be considered a "taking" of private property in violation of the Fifth Amendment to the U.S. Constitution or of similar provisions in state constitutions. When government "takes" property, it must pay the owner a fair price, or what the constitution calls "just compensation."

Sometimes landowners have argued that historic property designations or preservation regulations are an unconstitutional taking of private property. However, federal and state courts have generally rejected this argument, noting that preservation regulations rarely prohibit property owners from making a "reasonable economic use" of their land. In effect, the courts have often told property owners in so-called "takings" cases: Don't confuse your *speculative* hopes for *maximum* profits with your legal right to a *reasonable* economic use of your property. This, in essence, is what the U.S. Supreme Court said to Penn Central when the company argued in 1978 that the city's refusal to allow the 55-story tower was a "taking":

> ...the submission that [property owners] may establish a "taking" simply by showing that they have been denied the ability to exploit a property interest that they heretofore had believed was available for development is quite simply untenable.[10]

State courts, too, have made distinctions between property owners' dreams of reaping the highest possible profits and their right to *reasonable* economic benefits from private property. In a 1993 ruling on the United Artists Theater's challenge of Philadelphia's preservation ordinance, the Supreme Court of Pennsylvania stated:

[W]e hold that under the Constitution of Pennsylvania, the designation of a building as historic without the consent of the owner is not a "taking" that requires just compensation…[W]e have upheld as constitutional regulations that prevent the most profitable use of property…[T]his Court does not see the possibility that the owner is wholly deprived of any profitable use.[11]

In order to demonstrate an unlawful "taking" of property, property owners must establish one of two things: (1) that the law in question does not substantially advance a legitimate state interest; or (2) that the law has denied them the economically viable use of their property.[12] As noted above, the *Penn Central* decision confirmed that the first prong of the "takings" test is satisfied because historic preservation advances a legitimate state interest.[13]

Under the economic prong of the takings test, both the economic impact of the regulation on the property owner and the regulation's effect upon what the Supreme Court in *Penn Central* called "distinct investment-backed expectations" are relevant considerations.[14] The regulation's impact must also be substantial. The owner must establish that he is not capable of earning a reasonable return on his investment or that the regulation substantially interferes with the continued use of the property.[15] Thus, for example, in a recent Pennsylvania decision, *Pittsburgh Historic Review Commission v. Weinberg*,[16] the state supreme court ruled that the City of Pittsburgh's denial of permission to demolish a dilapidated historic house requiring substantial renovation did not result in an unlawful taking. The court found that the owners had failed to establish that they could not recoup their investment in the property by selling the property "as is" or that they had been "'deprived of any profitable use' of their property."[17] (*See also p. 38 on economic hardship provisions.*)

One of the most basic concepts underlying the American experiment in democratic government has always been…the idea that all citizens are to be treated equally before the law.

Due Process

THE THIRD BASIC LEGAL REQUIREMENT that government regulation must meet is that of "due process." The Fourteenth Amendment to the U.S. Constitution guarantees every citizen the right to "due process." In explaining what this means, Robert E. Stipe writes:

One of the most basic concepts underlying the American experiment in democratic government has always been a special sense of "fairness"—the idea that all citizens

Purposes of Historic Preservation Laws

STATE ENABLING LAWS for historic preservation vary widely, but virtually all of them reflect the desire of people to preserve their cultural heritage and quality of life. The language below comes from Minnesota's Historic District Act of 1971. The values it expresses exist in every state:

The spirit and direction of the state of Minnesota are founded upon and reflected in its historic past. In the effort to preserve the environmental values of the state, *outstanding geographical areas possessing historical, architectural and aesthetic values are of paramount importance* in the development of the state; in the face of ever increasing extensions of urban center[s], highways, and residential, commercial and industrial developments, *areas with an unusual concentration of distinctive historical and architectural values are threatened by destruction or impairment. It is in the public interest to provide a sense of community identity and preserve these historic districts* which represent and reflect elements of the state's cultural, social, economic, religious, political, architectural and aesthetic heritage.

are to be treated equally before the law. This sense of fairness and equality are what the Fourteenth Amendment and equivalent provisions in most state constitutions are all about. Without these words, the American Constitution—indeed, the grand adventure itself—would be meaningless.

The concept of fairness or "due process"…embraces two central ideas. One is that the process of *making* laws will be open to everyone. The other is that in *administering and enforcing* the law, the procedures employed will not only be open, but essentially neutral as well. In other words, laws will not be passed without the knowledge of citizens subject to them, and the procedures by which they are enforced will be impartial—applicable equally to all.

Nowhere are these concepts more important than in the passage, administration, and enforcement of historic district, landmark, and other preservation regulations of local and state governments. [18]

* * *

The practical implication of the Due Process requirement for preservation is that local governments must meet due process requirements in the drafting and administration of their historic preservation ordinances. Adequate and timely notice to property owners of pending designations of historic properties, public hearings, impartial and informed decisions based on objective criteria, adequate standards for approving or denying specific development proposals, written findings explaining local preservation commission decisions—these are just some of the safeguards that states should encourage local governments to provide in order to ensure fair treatment of property owners.[19]

In recent years, groups claiming to defend the rights of property owners have become very aggressive in arguing that various land-use restrictions violate federal or state constitutions. But the U.S. Supreme Court continues to cite the *Penn Central* decision approvingly, indicating that its legal principles remain the law of the land. State courts, meanwhile, continue to uphold properly drafted and administered local preservation ordinances.

Thus the courts in general continue to validate the efforts of citizens to preserve their heritage through the use of state-enabled preservation ordinances regulating private property.[20] Virtually every state has authorized its local governments to protect individual historic landmarks, historic districts, or both, through the enactment of local preservation ordinances. Today there are some 2,000 ordinances around the country.

> *Today there are some 2,000 local historic preservation ordinances around the country.*

The Basics of State Enabling Laws

WHAT MAKES FOR A GOOD STATE ENABLING LAW? Political, cultural, and geographical differences among the states vary too much to provide a single answer to that question or to offer a single model for state legislation in this area. It is possible, however, to draw ideas from statutes in different states. Let's examine issues addressed by various state laws in ways that historic preservation practitioners have found to be effective.

Rigidity vs. Flexibility

AT THE OUTSET, LAWMAKERS SHOULD CONSIDER whether it makes more sense for their state to have a detailed enabling law or one that is more general. There are good arguments on both sides.

The Detailed Approach. A detailed law is more likely to ensure that local governments draft preservation ordinances that include all of the provisions necessary to pass legal muster and to be most effective. By spelling out procedures and standards for municipalities to follow, a state can help local governments avoid legal problems. Such a law can also help to ensure that local ordinances address specific issues that might otherwise be ignored. Examples of such problems include "demolition by neglect," the need to protect the settings of historic sites, and the need for interim protection for resources nominated for landmark status, but not yet designated. Detailed laws are probably most useful to states with many small towns, the local governments of which may lack the staff or expertise to prepare local ordinances and who need guidance regarding specific issues. Such laws can also save local governments time and money that might otherwise be spent researching questions to which others have already found answers.

The General Approach. Some preservation law experts prefer short and simple state enabling laws. In their view, the more general approach gives local governments more freedom to tailor their ordinances to their own unique circumstances. This approach recognizes the wide differences that exist among communities and takes the view that communities

COURTESY KAEMPFER COMPANY

The once endangered historic Warner Building in Washington, D.C.

should be allowed to decide whether they want to regulate paint color, archaeological sites, and other matters. A detailed statute can be *too restrictive*, requiring municipalities to return to the state legislature if more flexibility is needed. Some experts believe that the more detailed laws can restrict the latitude communities might otherwise enjoy to be creative.

In summary, there is no perfect answer to the question of whether an enabling law should be detailed or more general. Lawmakers should consider this question in light of the special political, legal, and other circumstances of their state.

In the discussion below, we take a look at two specific state enabling laws—those of Maryland and Michigan—to illustrate specific issues that can arise. Neither law is perfect, and neither is intended as a recommended "model" here. But it is useful to ground legal discussions of preservation principles in real-world examples. Following this discussion of the Maryland and Michigan laws, we look at several issues that often arise in the context of historic preservation regulation.

Maryland

AN EXAMPLE OF A DETAILED STATE enabling law is that of Maryland, which was updated in 1995. Besides providing guidance to local governments on the basics—ordinance objectives, criteria for designating historic properties, etc. (*see sidebar*)—the Maryland statute has additional features not always found in state enabling laws. For example, it requires counties and municipalities to adopt design guidelines for rehabilitation and new construction in historic areas. The statute leaves the guidelines up to local governments to develop but requires that they be consistent with those recognized by the Maryland Historical Trust. The statute limits the authority of local preservation commissions to the review of any exterior changes that would affect the historic, archaeological, or architectural significance of designated sites or structures and specifically exempts routine property maintenance.

The Maryland statute also deals with specific problems that have plagued communities elsewhere. One is the difficulty encountered by small towns in finding people with the necessary qualifications to serve on preservation commissions. It is important to a local program's success that a commission have members with a good grasp of architecture, architectural history, urban design, and other relevant subjects. If a commission lacks such expertise, its decisions may be more vulnerable to the allegation that they are "arbitrary and capricious." By allowing counties and municipalities to draw a minority of the required minimum of five commission members from out of town, the Maryland law makes it easier for small towns to meet the special training requirements.

Another problem addressed by Maryland's law is the intrusiveness of utility wires in historic districts. Telephone wires, cables, traffic signals and other ganglia often mar the visual quality of historic districts. Maryland permits towns to require utility companies to bury these facilities, provided that the companies not be forced to pay more than half the cost of doing so. Special assessments may be levied on property owners in a historic district to recover the cost of burying these wires.

Whereas the enabling laws of some states ignore the importance of environmental *settings* of historic structures, the Maryland statute explicitly allows for the protection of settings in addition to that of the structures themselves. Settings are defined broadly and include "walkways and driveways (whether paved or not), trees, landscaping, pastures, cropland, waterways, and rocks."

In other states the authority of local governments to acquire and hold easements on historic properties as a means of protecting them is unclear. The Maryland statute clarifies this authority:

It is important to a local program's success that a commission have members with a good grasp of architecture, architectural history, and urban design.

Subject to any requirements of a county or municipal corporation governing the acquisition of easements, the commission may acquire easements in connection with individual sites or structures, or with sites or structures located in or adjacent to a locally designated historic district. Such easements may grant to the commission, the residents of the historic district, and the general public the right to ensure that any site or any structure and surrounding property upon which it is applied is protected, in perpetuity, from changes which would affect its historic, archaeological, or architectural significance.

(*For more discussion of easements, see pp. 43 and 181–188.*)

Michigan

ANOTHER STATE TO TAKE A DETAILED, prescriptive approach to enabling legislation is Michigan. Michigan preservationists see the amendments passed in 1992 (1970 PA 169, §5; MCL 24.281; MSA 3.560 [281]) as a major improvement to their enabling statute, which had not been substantially updated since its original enactment in 1970.

Like Maryland, Michigan seeks to keep local governments out of political and legal trouble and to ensure fairness to affected property owners. To ensure that local governments

States Providing Model Local Ordinances

A NUMBER OF STATES—Wisconsin, Pennsylvania, and Rhode Island, to name just a few—provide model ordinances to local governments to help them draft historic preservation laws. In general, these models recommend that local governments address questions such as the following:

- What is the purpose of the ordinance? To protect property values? To enhance the local economy? To preserve the community's heritage? To foster civic pride?
- What is important to the community and worth preserving? What criteria are used to evaluate the architectural or historical significance of buildings and sites and to determine whether they merit protection?
- What procedures are followed to designate historic landmarks and districts?
- How are key terms—e.g., "alterations," "demolition by neglect," "environmental setting"— defined?
- How does the community create a local preservation commission to review development proposals affecting historic resources?
- What powers does the commission have? Can it deny, or merely delay, requests to demolish or alter historic structures? What standards must it use in making these decisions?
- What qualifications must commission members have? How long may they serve?
- What rules exist to ensure that development proposals are adequately reviewed and that property owners are treated fairly?
- How does the ordinance ensure that property owners are not forced to bear financial burdens that are unreasonable?
- How can property owners appeal commission decisions they consider unfair? To whom do they appeal?
- What penalties exist for violating the ordinance?

meet "due process" requirements, the Michigan law sets forth specific rules for public hearings and requires written notices to property owners who might be affected by the creation of a district. After a district is established, the law requires local preservation commissions that reject proposals for exterior changes or demolition to state their reasons for doing so in writing. This forces these bodies to think carefully about their actions and to be disciplined in the exercise of their legal duties.

One noteworthy feature of the Michigan law is an appeals process that some state preservation leaders believe is simpler and more accessible for property owners. Under the new process, property owners must appeal local commission decisions first to the state historic preservation review board, rather than directly to circuit court.

To ensure that local governments meet "due process" requirements, the Michigan law requires written notices to property owners...

This system has several advantages, according to its proponents. The state review board is knowledgeable about historic preservation issues in general. In contrast to judges who may be preoccupied with other matters and sometimes poorly informed about historic preservation issues, the review board members tend to be experts on this subject. The system also provides an opportunity for full consideration of the issues in a forum not constrained by complex rules of evidence and allows for a more timely resolution of the matter at hand.

Property owners can file appeals without having to hire an attorney to represent them, although they may have legal representation if they wish and often do so. Under the prior law in Michigan, property owners unhappy with a local commission decision could only appeal directly to circuit court and were required to follow special procedures used in zoning appeal cases. But this meant that most property owners had to hire an attorney to rep-

Conditions for Special Merit Projects Used in Evanston, Illinois

EVANSTON, ILLINOIS, PERMITS THE DEMOLITION of historic structures to make way for projects of special merit but carefully circumscribes the conditions under which such projects may be approved. Under the Evanston ordinance:

A project shall not receive a Certificate of Special Merit unless the [city] Council determines that:

- The project is consistent with the [city's] comprehensive plan...;
- The project is necessary and in the public interest and will provide public and civic benefits, including but not limited to social or other benefits, that are significant to the community and particularly desirable at the location proposed. Such benefits that further the general welfare of the residents of the city...must substantially outweigh the loss of or the effect upon the affected Landmark or property, structure, site or object in a [historic] district. Such benefits shall not consist solely of monetary or economic benefits to the City or other parties arising from economic development, property taxes, or other financial returns.

Portland, Maine, has a similar "special merit" provision, but in addition, it requires that the special merit project be "of exceptional design...and compatible with the surrounding historic area." Approval by a super-majority of the planning commission is required for a special merit project.[21]

resent them, sometimes at considerable expense. It also meant long delays—as much as a year in many courts and possibly as many as three years in a busy court like Wayne County's, which handles cases from Detroit and nearby suburbs.

The state review board has delegated the responsibility of conducting the appeal hearings to the Hearings Division of the Michigan Department of State. "The members of the review board are not as accustomed as hearing officers to handling contested matters," explains Nicholas Bozen, director of the Hearings Division. "The Board decided it was better to have legally trained hearing officers handle these cases, people who have had experience dealing with attorneys and others who raise legal objections."

Once an appeal hearing is held, the hearing officer prepares a proposed decision for consideration by the review board at its next regular meeting. Copies of the recommended decisions are also furnished to each party involved and to the local preservation commission. If either party is dissatisfied with the proposed outcome, written exceptions may be filed with the board. However, when the board reviews a recommendation at a board meeting, parties are not permitted to address the board since they had that opportunity at the administrative hearing.

As the state review board decides cases that are written up, it establishes precedents and builds up a body of law at the state level. This provides guidance to local historic district commissions as they grapple with individual issues and contributes to consistency in decision-making among different local jurisdictions in Michigan.

An unusual, and somewhat controversial feature of the Michigan law is a provision intended to help local governments balance historic preservation with other community

An architectural intrusion such as that shown here can reduce adjoining property values. Historic district controls protect property owners against the devaluing effects of such intrusions.

KENNEDY SMITH

values. The law permits, but does not require, commissions to approve the demolition of a historic structure if preservation would be "a deterrent to a major improvement program that will be of substantial benefit to the community." Before approval of a "major improvement" project can be granted, property owners must have all necessary planning and zoning approvals, financing, and environmental clearances in place. This provision helps to avoid the all-too-common scenario of property owners (or public agencies) who promise to replace a historic building with a project of special merit but then lose their financing or change their plans. The community is then in the sad position of having exchanged a treasured landmark for a vacant lot.

If a property owner disagrees with the decision of the state review board, he may appeal that decision to circuit court. It is assumed that the local preservation commission or other interested party may also appeal but the statute is less clear with respect to such appeals. Preservation advocates differ over whether provisions allowing for "major improvements"—sometimes called "special merit" projects—are good or bad. Some believe that such provisions create loopholes big enough for a bulldozer to drive through. They point out that these provisions often lack adequate standards for determining what constitutes a "major improvement" or project of "special merit." Thus a "major improvement" project may simply be whatever the mayor wants.

Other preservationists believe that political pressures to approve "major improvement" projects are going to arise anyway and that communities should establish clear ground rules for evaluating them. If a landmark must come down, it should at least be replaced by a well-designed project that benefits the community in the long run and fits in harmoniously with existing structures.

One way to overcome the looseness of Michigan's "major improvement project" provision might be to add clearer standards for evaluating projects of special merit, such as those included in the ordinances of Evanston, Illinois, and Portland, Maine. (See sidebar.)

The Michigan law is not perfect. Some preservation law experts believe it could be still further improved by clearer standards to govern economic hardship cases. Moreover, as noted above, many preservationists think "major improvement" or "special merit" provisions are a bad idea because they can be interpreted to allow almost anything. But given the political realities in Michigan, state preservation leaders there are pleased with their revised law so far. In their view, the statute recognizes these realities and the fact that governments must balance historic preservation goals with other community objectives. The statute provides a more "people-friendly" appeals process for an expensive, intimidating, and frustrating legal gauntlet. And by emphasizing to local governments the importance of following good procedures and clear standards, the statute helps them avoid unnecessary conflicts with property owners in the first place.

* * *

If a landmark must come down, it should at least be replaced by a well-designed project that benefits the community in the long run.

Unanimous Approval for a State Enabling Law: A Case Study from Michigan

T HE REVISED MICHIGAN ENABLING LAW for historic preservation (see p. 27) was passed by unanimous votes in both the Michigan House and Senate, with the Michigan Historic Preservation Network having taken the lead in advocating its enactment. Given the difficulties that statewide preservation organizations in other states have experienced in obtaining even minor improvements to their enabling laws, it is worth examining how the Michigan Network was so successful.

Garnering Political Support

MICHIGAN HAD ENACTED ITS LOCAL HISTORIC DISTRICT ACT IN 1970, but by 1991, preservationists agreed that the law was out-of-date and in need of an overhaul. The law left communities uncertain as to whether they could enact interim development controls to protect historic buildings nominated to be historic landmarks, but not yet designated as such. For example, it was unclear whether local preservation regulations applied to publicly-owned buildings, such as fire houses. Its criteria for designating historic properties were vague. Its rules, procedures, and standards of conduct for local preservation commissions were weak. The law was generally full of loopholes, according to Jennifer Radcliff, president of the Network.

The Michigan Historic Preservation Network had already laid the groundwork for an effort to update the law by asking historic district commissions throughout the state to identify the changes they thought were necessary or desirable. Having analyzed the answers to this question, the Network formed a legislative task force in late 1991 and charged it with drafting an up-to-date enabling law and working for its enactment.

When State Representative Ilona Varga, a Democrat from Detroit, learned of the Network's efforts, she offered to sponsor the legislation in the Michigan House. State Senator John Schwarz, a Republican from Battle Creek, agreed to sponsor the legislation in the Senate. "My home town is 160 years old now," he says in explaining why. "We have buildings dating to the 1870s, buildings associated with the origins of the cereal industry. The more we can do to preserve our heritage, the better off we are."

Having secured bipartisan support for its initiative, the Network issued an "all points bulletin" urging its members to contact their representatives about the proposed law and to urge their support. "We made sure every state legislator heard from at least one or more constituents," says Radcliff. "We encouraged our members to write letters rather than making phone calls," she adds. "Letters meant the creation of a file, whereas phone messages got pitched at the end of the day." When the time came for public hearings on the proposed legislation, the Network encouraged preservationists from every region of the state to show up and testify or otherwise make their presence felt at the hearing.

The network tried to anticipate all possible objections to the legislation and to deal with them before, rather than after, the bill came up for debate in the House and Senate. "We met with anyone who had questions," says Radcliff. "We explained what the legislation asked of cities, what it required of homeowners. When we visited our legislators, we gave them one-page, five-point handouts explaining why historic preservation is good for Michigan. We explained how the bill would make local commissions more responsive and responsible," she adds. The network also made sure that a core group of some 15 legisla-

Michigan historic preservationists celebrate the approval of a new state enabling law for historic districts.

tors had a thorough understanding of the bill and could help answer questions concerning it.

This groundwork paid off well. With 50 representatives from both parties joining in cosponsorship, the legislation passed the House unanimously in April of 1992. In May, all 38 Michigan senators voted for the bill, and on June 18, 1992, Lt. Governor Connie Binsfeld signed it into law.

Special Issues

BESIDES REQUIRING LOCAL GOVERNMENTS TO INCLUDE SUCH BASICS AS "DUE process" requirements and standards for designating historic resources, state enabling laws can address special problems as well. Below are examples of provisions from around the country aimed at dealing with these problems. This list is by no means comprehensive. It is simply provided to give states a sense of the range of possibilities that exist.

Demolition by Neglect [22]

AN UNFORTUNATE BUT RATHER COMMON PROBLEM TODAY IS "demolition by neglect:" the intentional neglect of a property by a landowner deliberately seeking to evade preservation regulations. Under the demolition-by-neglect scenario, a property owner reasons that if his property becomes so deteriorated it must be demolished in order to protect the public safety, he will then be free to do whatever he wants. Occasionally, after intentionally allowing their property to deteriorate, property owners declare "economic hardship" as a defense against any local regulations requiring property maintenance, even though the hardship was self-inflicted.

An article by Allison Dyches explains why demolition-by-neglect is such a serious problem for many communities:

> Neglect not only causes the destruction of a historic structure, [but] also destroys the morale of the residents and the aesthetic character of their neighborhood. Dilapidated structures soon become havens for crime, which not only affects the safety of the neighborhood, but also lowers property values. The uncertainty about the future of individual neighborhoods is thus often reflected by a cycle of disinvestment by the owners who may be residents, investors, and lending institutions. Reluctance to invest limits both homeowners and investors in their ability to obtain the financing to purchase or rehabilitate existing structures, further reinforcing the cycle of disinvestment which fosters the demolition by neglect of individual buildings. [23]

Neglect not only causes the destruction of a historic structure, but also destroys the morale of the residents.

Every state should make sure that communities with preservation programs have the capacity to address this problem. A first step is to define demolition-by-neglect. In this regard, the Maryland statute provides a definition: "any wilful neglect in maintenance and repair of a structure, not including any appurtenances and environmental settings, that does not result from financial inability to maintain and repair the structure and that threatens to result in any substantial deterioration of the exterior features of the structure."

A second step is to allow for minimum maintenance requirements. In this regard, Virginia's enabling statute gives counties and municipalities the authority to "regulate, restrict, permit, prohibit, and determine…(b) [t]he size, height, area, bulk, location, erection, construction, reconstruction, alteration, *repair, maintenance* [emphasis added], razing, or removal of structures [in historic districts]." [24]

Michigan's statute allows local preservation commissions, upon a finding that a historic resource is threatened by such neglect, to require the property owner to repair "all conditions contributing to demolition by neglect" within a reasonable time. If the owner does not do so:

> the commission or its agents may enter the property and make such repairs as are necessary to prevent demolition by neglect. The costs of the work shall be charged to the owner, and may be levied by the local unit as a special assessment against the property. *The commission or its agents may enter the property* for purposes of this section upon obtaining an order from the circuit court.[25]

Rhode Island authorizes city or town councils to publish standards for the maintenance of properties in historic districts. In cases of demolition-by-neglect, such councils:

> may establish a reasonable time not less than 30 days within which the owner must begin repairs. If the owner has not begun repairs within the allowed time, the council shall hold a hearing at which the owner may appear and state his or her reasons for not commencing repairs. If the owner does not appear at the hearing or does not comply with the council's orders, the council may cause the required repairs to be made at the expense of the city or town and cause a lien to be placed against the property for repayment.

Some states do not explicitly authorize minimum maintenance provisions, but the ability of local governments to apply them may be inferred from general preservation enabling statutes. In an important federal case that addressed this issue, the U.S. Court of Appeals for the Fifth Circuit held in *Maher v. City of New Orleans* that "[o]nce it has been determined that the purpose of the…[preservation] legislation is a proper one, upkeep of buildings appears reasonably necessary to the accomplishment of the goals of the ordinance."[26]

Washington, D.C.'s historic Willard Hotel was threatened with demolition in the 1970s. Today this landmark is a source of civic pride. Hotel exterior appears opposite; restored hotel lobby, above; rundown interior prior to rehabilitation, below.

Eminent Domain: Some states explicitly permit local governments to use their "eminent domain" authority—the power to condemn private property for a public purpose—to save endangered historic landmarks that are being demolished by neglect. While municipalities generally prefer to avoid such expensive tools as condemnation, they occasionally use this authority when a property owner resists all reasonable entreaties and so neglects a historic structure as to invite its destruction and devalue properties all around it.

One example of eminent domain's application to historic preservation comes from Milwaukee, which used such authority in the city's historic Brewer Hill and King Drive area, a 24-block district near the downtown. After this area was designated as historic in 1985, the city condemned several boarded-up buildings and resold them to small developers for rehabilitation. The city also took advantage of state laws authorizing the use of "tax increment financing." Finally, the state helped this historic area by building a state office there, rather than at the suburban site originally selected.

Owner Consent

IN RECENT YEARS, the notion of inserting so-called "owner consent" provisions in state enabling laws has occasionally surfaced. Under such provisions, property owners are given the opportunity to veto the designation of their property as historic, which could have the effect of exempting them from land-use restrictions that might be included in a local preservation ordinance. There are serious questions about such provisions.

First, it should be understood that, like zoning, historic preservation laws are a type of land-use law. Although citizens are encouraged and even invited in many cases to participate in the development of overall local planning and zoning policies for their communities, local governments are not required to obtain the consent of individual property owners before zoning certain lands for residential, agricultural, or commercial purposes. This is so even though the designation of land for a specific purpose can have a major effect on the land's economic value. If property owners were permitted to prevent local governments from designating prime farmland for agricultural purposes, or floodplains as areas in which to avoid development, or aquifers as assets to preserve for safe drinking water, the entire concept of zoning would become meaningless. Communities could not plan effectively to preserve resources they value or to otherwise protect the health and safety of the people. Absent a system for protecting key resources, the economic value of communities as a whole can fall. With that decline, the values of individual properties may fall as well.

Once a community, acting through its elected representatives, determines that it wants to protect certain resources for valid public purposes, whether the resources be historic areas, high-quality soil, aquifers or something else, then the objectivity with which such resources are identified and designated becomes critical. To be credible, historic designations must be based on relevant factors, such as a building's historical significance, its architectural qualities, its cultural importance, etc. A property owner's desire to be exempted from regulations applied to other property owners in the same class is a subjective, not an objective, criterion for the designation of historic properties.

In addition to undermining the very idea of law itself by giving property owners veto power over public laws with which they do not want to comply, owner-consent provisions raise constitutional questions.

Laws are supposed to be rationally and uniformly applied. Legislatures delegate legal powers to local governments with the understanding that laws will be applied according to objective standards. Indeed, the whole idea of "equal protection," a right guaranteed under the U.S. Constitution, is that the law applies equally to everyone who is similarly situated.

A property owner's desire to be exempted from regulations... is a subjective, not an objective, criterion for the designation of historic properties.

For these reasons, courts have invalidated owner-consent provisions in regular zoning laws on the rare occasions that such provisions have appeared in them. Courts have found such provisions to be "standardless delegations of legislative authority." For example, in *Eubank v. City of Richmond*, the U.S. Supreme Court struck down an ordinance that established building setbacks upon the consent of two-thirds of the property owners on a given street:

> The statute and ordinance, while conferring the power on some property holders to virtually control and dispose of the property rights of others, creates no standard by which the power thus given is to be exercised; in other words, the property holders who desire and have the authority to establish the line may do so solely for their own interest, or even capriciously.[27]

In a more recent case, *Brodner v. City of Elgin*,[28] an Illinois court invalidated an owner consent requirement in a zoning ordinance, stating that "the adoption of a rezoning ordinance is a legislative act which constitutes the exercise of the police power" and that "[l]egislative authority may not be delegated to private individuals." The court said that the provision effectively conferred upon the property owner "the absolute discretion to decide that no rezoning shall ever occur" and that an owner could arbitrarily frustrate the City's efforts to adopt a comprehensive zoning plan in pursuit of the common good.

In May 1996, a California trial court struck down a state law allowing churches and religious institutions to exempt themselves from local historic preservation laws. In addition to ruling that the exemption violated the First Amendment, the court ruled that it "impermissibly delegates historically municipal functions relating to land use and planning law to private religiously affiliated organizations in violation of the California Constitution."[29] The statute had conferred on all religiously affiliated institutions the ability to avoid the application of local preservation laws to their property simply by objecting to the application of the regulation and stating in a public forum that they would "suffer substantial hardship" or that historic designation was likely to deprive the institution of the "reasonable use" of its property.

In a special analysis of this issue, Julia Hatch Miller, editor of the *Preservation Law Reporter*,[30] summarizes the problems with owner-consent provisions:

> Owner consent provisions in historic preservation ordinances raise serious due process and equal protection concerns. Such provisions undermine the police power objective of preserving historic property for the benefit of present and future generations. They also prevent the fair and uniform application of preservation laws by extending protection only to those properties whose owners have conferred their consent.
>
> Moreover, owner consent provisions appear to constitute an unlawful and standardless delegation of decision making authority. Such provisions, in effect, unlawfully delegate authority to individual property owners to decide whether or not a preservation law will apply. This authority should be reserved by the legislative body or delegated to an administrative body whose discretion is limited through the application of objective criteria.[31]

As the U.S. Supreme Court recognized in 1978 in *Penn Central Transportation Co. v. New York City*:

> [I]n recent years, large numbers of historic structures, landmarks, and areas have been destroyed *without adequate consideration of either the values represented therein or the possibility of preserving the destroyed properties for use in economically productive ways* [emphasis added].[32]

It is out of a concern that communities at least be given the *opportunity* to consider the possibility of preserving endangered historic resources that local historic designation exists in

Owner consent provisions... raise serious due process and equal protection concerns.

the first place. If resources cannot be identified, local governments and property owners alike may unwittingly destroy or endanger them. The impact of preservation regulations on property owners is an important, but separate issue. It, too, must be addressed, but in a context separate from the designation of historic properties and according to appropriate standards.

Economic Hardship

AS NOTED EARLIER IN THIS CHAPTER, the U.S. Constitution and most state constitutions protect landowners against the "taking" of their property without just compensation. The courts have generally held that if an owner retains a "reasonable economic use" of his or her land, a taking has not occurred.

A local preservation ordinance should include "safety valves" to deal with hardship cases when they arise, and most such ordinances do so. Thus the hardship question is typically addressed most directly at the local government level rather than by the state.

Nonetheless, some state enabling laws include provisions that seek to address this question by establishing a standard for hardship. The Illinois statute, for example, states:

> The denial of an application for a building demolition permit…or the denial of an application for a building permit to add to, modify, or remove a portion of any building…or the imposition of any regulation solely by reason of the provisions of this Division…shall not constitute a taking or damage for a public use of such property for which just compensation shall be ascertained and paid, unless the denial of a permit application or imposition of a regulation, as the case may be, deprives the owner of all reasonable beneficial use or return.[33]

In a forthcoming article on this subject, *Preservation Law Reporter* Editor Julia Hatch Miller offers some general guidance for policymakers seeking to deal with the economic hardship question. According to Miller, administrative relief, not simply recourse to the courts, should be provided for property owners on economic hardship issues for several reasons:

- The availability of administrative proceedings helps to avoid litigation. Such proceedings offer an opportunity for communities and property owners to hammer out the issues and resolve them in a less formal, and inherently less expensive, forum that is not hindered by complex rules of evidence and procedural limitations. Hardship provisions allow communities to address fundamental issues of fairness on an individual basis.

- The existence of economic hardship reviews helps to assuage concerns expressed by property owners over the potentially adverse impact of historic preservation regulation. Hardship provisions provide assurance to property owners that relief is available in the event that the impact of a regulation proves to be unduly harsh.

- The existence of hardship review also enables communities to put together alternative plans to save an endangered historic resource. Such plans can combine various types of relief—tax incentives, zoning variances, exemptions from parking requirements, and so forth.

- Finally, consideration of hardship concerns at the administrative level can enhance the ability of localities to protect historic properties if their actions are challenged in court. Courts generally afford review boards considerable deference in reviewing administrative decisions. Under most administrative review acts, judicial review is limited to the record made at the administrative hearing and a decision must be upheld if supported by "substantial evidence" or if there is a reasonable basis in the record for the decision.

North Carolina's "demolition delay" provision prevented the building's owner from tearing down the Henry Porter House (photos opposite page), one of Raleigh's oldest structures. A solution was arranged during the delay period that was agreeable to all parties.

It is beyond the scope of this publication to deal exhaustively with the complex issue of economic hardship, but state historic preservation offices are urged to make sure that local preservation commissions are aware of the issue's importance to the success of a preservation program. Many states regularly sponsor education and training workshops for local commission members and include sessions specifically dedicated to the economic hardship issue.

Other Issues

Interim Protection: Many states permit local governments to provide interim protection to buildings that have been nominated, but not yet designated, as state or local historic sites. Such authority addresses the problem of property owners who race to demolish historic buildings at the very mention of a preservation ordinance or landmark designation that might affect their property.

Interim development controls are typically enacted by local governments as protective measures to allow time for the completion of a local comprehensive plan or to guide development. In a paper on this subject, Robert H. Freilich, a noted land-use attorney, observes that "the authority of a local government to enact interim development ordinances may be found in specific enabling legislation, implied authority under the zoning enabling act, and through informal techniques of administrative processing. Once authority has been established to enact interim zoning controls, the validity of the controls depends on the reasonableness of the approach. In particular, the duration of the ordinance is of critical importance. When no specific statutory limitations exist, the courts determine reasonableness of the time period on a case-by-case basis. A primary determinant appears to be complexity and scope of the plan being prepared."[34]

Interim development controls are typically enacted to allow time for the completion of a local comprehensive plan.

North Carolina's interim protection can last up to six months, giving communities time to complete the evaluation of historic properties in an orderly way. Other states allow interim protection of up to two years and permit its extension when necessary. It is important, however, that communities use these interim periods to work diligently on their revised plans or development rules.

Transfer of Development Rights: At least 22 states, including California, Colorado, Maryland, New York, Washington[35] and Delaware, authorize the "transfer of development rights (TDRs)." Under this concept, a property owner may sell or transfer the right to develop land on which a historic landmark sits—the "sending" site—to a parcel elsewhere in town—the "receiving" site. By selling unused development rights to someone who can use them on the receiving site, and by committing to maintain the landmark, the property owner receives money he might have made by destroying the landmark, but the landmark is saved and the community benefits. The transfer of development rights can help churches and other nonprofit property owners who do not pay taxes and who therefore cannot take advantage of property tax abatement or other incentives. It is important, however, to ensure that development transferred to the "receiving zone" fits in with what is already there.[36]

Tax Assessment: Many states seek to address financial impacts by requiring tax assessors to consider the effect on property values of preservation regulations when they appraise historic properties for tax purposes. An example of such a policy can be found in Idaho's enabling law:

> The local historic preservation commission shall give notice of such [historic] designation to the tax assessor of the county in which the property is located. The designation and any recorded restrictions upon the property limiting its use for preservation purposes *shall be considered* [emphasis added] by the tax assessor in appraising it for tax purposes.

(For more on preservation tax incentives, see Chapter 3.)

Historic District Gateways: Virginia allows local governments to regulate new development adjoining roads that lead into historic districts. Such authority can help municipalities negotiate with out-of-state chains, which often insist on the same cookie-cutter designs on every highway. Virginia's "gateway preservation" provision grew out of concerns that insensitive development might mar the entrance to Monticello, Thomas Jefferson's home near Charlottesville.

Penalties: State enabling laws should allow for the effective enforcement of local preservation ordinances. If penalties and fines for violating an ordinance are too small, a developer may simply treat them as a cost of doing business and ignore the law. If the penalty is too severe, a judge may be reluctant to apply it. In recent years, several states have added provisions to their enabling laws authorizing local governments to compel property owners who willfully and illegally destroyed historic landmarks to restore them (or pay for a new structure resembling the demolished one). Texas enacted just such a law after the owners of the historic cigar factory infuriated the citizens of San Antonio by demolishing the structure without giving the city a chance to save it. A law enacted in June 1996 by the Wisconsin legislature states that "whoever intentionally demolishes a historic building without a permit issued by a city, village, town or county or without an order issued [pursuant to state requirements] shall be fined an amount equal to two times the fair market value of the historic building and the land upon which the building is located immediately prior to demolition and may be imprisoned for not more than nine months."

Requirement for Local Preservation Ordinances: Wisconsin law requires every city in the state with properties on the National or State Register of Historic Places to adopt a historic preservation ordinance by December 1995. The content of the ordinance is entirely up to the municipality. As of Winter 1996, many municipalities were in the process of preparing ordinances and still others had enacted them. However, 125 local governments had not complied with this requirement as of January 1996.[37]

Training of Local Preservation Commissioners. Increasingly, states have recognized the "front line" role played by local historic preservation commissioners who administer preservation ordinances. Most commissioners are citizens serving in a volunteer capacity on local preservation boards. These people do not necessarily have professional training in historic preservation law. A number of states now impose special requirements aimed at making sure that commission members receive good information or training in preservation issues. Some state statutes require commissioners to attend a certain number of educational conferences each year to improve their knowledge and understanding of preservation issues.

Coordination between Land-Use and Historic Preservation

WHILE MOST STATE HISTORIC PRESERVATION enabling laws deal with changes to a building's physical appearance, very few—the laws of Idaho, South Dakota and Iowa are exceptions—authorize local preservation commissions to review changes in a building's *use*.[38] But the way land and buildings are used can be critical to historic preservation.

Many communities have historic preservation ordinances that, when looked at in a vacuum, *appear* to offer good protection for historic resources. But such ordinances are often completely undermined by the local government's land-use, transportation, and economic development policies. A cluster of low-rise historic buildings in a downtown may be designated as a historic district and theoretically protected by the local preservation ordinance, but the zoning ordinance may permit new high-rise development in the area. In such situations, which are surprisingly common, the local government creates a built-in conflict

Wisconsin law requires every city in the state with properties on the National or State Register of Historic Places to adopt a historic preservation ordinance.

between property owners, historic preservationists, and the community. Similar conflicts arise when a locality designates a historic district for protection but the public works department plans a new road widening for the district that will inevitably destroy its unique character. Most visitors to San Francisco are probably not aware of the fact that many of the beautiful historic buildings that draw them to the downtown exist today because the city undertook to resolve land-use/preservation conflicts in 1985, when it "downzoned" certain historic areas.[39]

To encourage local governments to make general land-use policies supportive of, or at least consistent with, local historic preservation goals, several states have enacted laws requiring localities to include a historic preservation element in their local comprehensive plan. Such a plan is a legal document explaining how a community plans to grow and develop.

Rhode Island's Comprehensive Planning and Land Use Regulation Act,[40] passed in 1988, requires every locality in the state to revise (or enact for the first time) a comprehensive land-use plan that is consistent with ten state planning goals, one of which is the protection of historic and cultural resources. Every local plan must contain a natural and cultural resources element that "include[s] policies for the protection of the historic and cultural resources of the municipality and the State. The policies and implementation techniques must be identified for inclusion in the implementation element" of the plan. Each plan must articulate the community's policies with respect to preservation and development. It must also spell out a five-year implementation program identifying specific actions to be taken, the cost of these actions, and the timetable for carrying them out.

A variant of the Rhode Island approach to preservation planning comes from Florida, whose Local Government Comprehensive Planning and Land Development Regulation Act[41] requires every local government to prepare a local comprehensive plan. Although Florida does not require municipalities to include historic preservation elements in their plans—such elements are optional—three of the mandated elements—those for housing, land use, and, if the municipality lies on the coast, that for coastal management—must include preservation values. A community's land-use map designating growth and conservation areas must identify all state or federally-designated historic sites. Sites not yet designated do not have to be included in the map.

Every local plan must contain a cultural resources element.

The Florida Division of Historical Resources reviews and approves the local preservation plans submitted in the mandatory land-use, housing, and coastal management elements. These plans cannot be mere vague generalizations; they must outline specific, measurable goals and provide budgets and timetables for accomplishing the goals. In reviewing plans, the Division makes suggestions, offers technical assistance, and provides exemplary plans from other communities.

The effectiveness of preservation planning requirements such as those mandated by Rhode Island and Florida depends largely upon the assertiveness of local preservation advocates and their effectiveness in making sure that preservation values find their way into local comprehensive plans. In the past, the preservation movement has probably not paid as much attention to planning issues as such issues warrant. As Julia Hatch Miller, editor of the *Preservation Law Reporter*, observes in an insightful article on this subject:

> The need for comprehensive preservation planning is highlighted by the fact that many communities have never developed a clear set of policies to define local interests in preservation, design quality, commercial development, or neighborhood conservation. In fact, many jurisdictions have comprehensive plans that directly conflict with preservation objectives. For example, some plans establish strong priorities for economic growth through new construction, without imposing design controls or density restrictions to insure compatible development in historic areas. Without a

comprehensive plan that addresses local preservation needs, the likelihood of complementary zoning and preservation laws is remote.[42]

When preservation-development conflicts are litigated, the content of a local comprehensive plan can either support or undermine historic preservation objectives. Hailey, Idaho, and Lawrence, Kansas, are just two examples of cities that have used their plans in court to help fend off development projects that threatened to undermine the economic viability of their older downtowns. (*See case study, Chapter 10.*) Courts often look for consistency between a local zoning action and a local comprehensive plan; when they do, what the plan says (or does not say) about historic preservation can prove to be critical.

(For further discussion of other land-use planning issues as they relate to historic preservation, see Chapter 10, Alternatives to Sprawl.)

Easements

MARYLAND AND SOME OTHER STATES treat the question of easements in their state enabling statutes for historic preservation. Other states address easements in separate legislation. Easements are one of the most important tools for protecting historic resources, particularly in an era when concerns about private property rights are paramount. Easements are voluntary, non-regulatory preservation tools.

Under the easement concept, property owners donate or sell easements to qualified easement holding organizations. In doing so, they agree to permanently forfeit certain property rights—e.g., the right to demolish or alter a property without approval from the easement holder—in exchange for money, tax benefits, or both. This agreement is recorded with the deed and binds all future owners as well. The value of the easement is the difference between the property's fair market value before and after the easement is donated or sold.

Easements are one of the most important tools for protecting historic resources.

A historic home in the Browne's Addition Historic District of Spokane, Washington.

JOHN EVANS

As Robert E. Stipe explains in *The American Mosaic: Preserving A Nation's Heritage*, easements hold certain advantages for communities over the outright acquisition by a local government of a historic property to ensure its preservation:

> [It]is important to understand that there are different degrees of ownership or dominion over property held by government or anyone else, however acquired. All or part of a property can be owned. If, for example, a historic property were to be acquired for permanent use as a museum, then lawyers would say that the fee simple or fee, representing the entire bundle of property rights, would be needed.
>
> However, as an alternative to acquiring all ownership rights, it will often be just as effective to obtain only those actually needed to preserve a property. For example, there is no reason to buy the entire bundle of ownership rights if all that is needed is the single right to control its exterior appearance. There are several advantages to this approach. One is that buying specific or limited rights is usually cheaper than buying all of them. Another is that they can be tailored to individual situations, unlike regulations that must apply equally to everyone similar situated. A third is that such restrictions can go beyond the permissible limits of regulations; for example, they may have effect inside the building to save an important interior, where regulations might not. A fourth is that the owner or seller of rights is paid for what is given up. This is not the case with regulations where no compensation is made.[43]

The Maryland Historical Trust holds 400 easements on historic properties involving more than 9,500 acres.

Some states allow conservation easements for the protection of natural resources but are unclear as to whether historic resources may be similarly protected. Florida is an example of a state that acted in the early 1980s to make sure that easements for historic preservation purposes were clearly permitted by the state's easement law. Any city or county government or qualified nonprofit historic preservation organization in Florida may be the recipient of an easement on a historic property.

While many states both allow and encourage the use of preservation easements, Maryland has been one of the most active states in acquiring historic preservation easements to protect historic properties. The Maryland Historical Trust holds 400 easements on historic properties involving more than 9,500 acres. Other easement holding organizations in Maryland have preserved thousands more acres of historic rural landscapes and Civil War sites.

Under Section 170 of the Internal Revenue Code, owners of historic properties who donate easements may qualify for a charitable deduction. (See Chapter 6, pp. 181–188.)

State Laws to Consider Historic Resources

W HILE VIRTUALLY EVERY STATE HAS AUTHORIZED LOCAL GOVERNMENTS to enact preservation ordinances, thereby giving communities the *opportunity* to provide substantive or procedural protection for historic resources, over 30 states have enacted laws intended to protect historic resources by requiring state agencies and, in some cases, local government agencies, to consider or minimize harm to historic resources caused by their actions. While some of these laws also provide substantive protection as well, they tend to emphasize *processes* for balancing historic preservation and other public values against each other. In addition, these laws often give citizens an opportunity to voice their opinions on a specific preservation-development conflict. While procedural laws require that consideration be given to the impact of particular state (or local) actions on historic resources, they do not guarantee that such resources, even the most significant ones, will be protected.

These state statutes generally mirror federal laws, such as the National Historic Preservation Act, enacted during the sixties to protect historic places and the natural environment. At that time, federal urban renewal and highway projects were wreaking havoc on urban neighborhoods. Horrified at this damage, the public rose up and demanded that federal agencies, at the very least, consider the potential impact of their actions before plowing ahead with them.

Congress responded to this outcry by enacting three laws that have since become prototypes for state laws.

The first law was the *National Historic Preservation Act of 1966* (NHPA), which contains two features relevant to our discussion:

- a National Register of Historic Places, or an honor roll of historically, architecturally, and otherwise culturally significant sites, structures, and objects; and
- "Section 106," a requirement that federal agencies give the national Advisory Council on Historic Preservation an opportunity to review and comment on federally-licensed and assisted projects affecting historic resources listed on, or eligible for, the National Register. The agencies must consider these comments before carrying out their projects.

The second law was the *National Environmental Policy Act* (NEPA), enacted in 1969. This law requires federal agencies to evaluate the effects of *major* federal actions that "significantly" affect the "human environment." When they determine that a project *will* have a major effect, they must prepare an "environmental impact statement" (EIS) and show that they have explored alternatives to harmful effects.

The third law was the *Department of Transportation Act*, enacted in 1966. Aimed primarily at the damage caused by federal highways, Section 4(f) of this statute prohibits the U.S. Secretary of Transportation from approving any federally-aided transportation project that *uses* land from a historic site unless there is *no prudent and feasible alternative* and *all possible*

Federal Prototypes for State-Level Section

Section 106 of the National Historic Preservation Act of 1966, 16 U.S.C. § 470f

The head of any Federal agency having direct or indirect jurisdiction over a proposed Federal or federally assisted undertaking in any State and the head of any Federal department or independent agency having authority to license any undertaking shall *prior to the approval of the expenditure of any Federal funds* on the undertaking or *prior to the issuance of any license*, as the case may be, *take into account the effect of the undertaking* on any district, site, building, structure, or object that is included in or eligible for inclusion in the National Register [of Historic Places]. The head of any such Federal agency shall afford the Advisory Council on Historic Preservation...a reasonable opportunity to comment with regard to such undertaking.

Section 4(f) of the Department of Transportation Act of 1966, 49 U.S.C. § 303 (c)

It is the policy of the United States Government that special effort should be made to preserve the natural beauty of the countryside and public park and recreation lands, wildlife and waterfowl refuges, and *historic sites*.

* * *

The Secretary may approve a transportation program or project...requiring the use of publicly owned land of a public park, recreation area, or wildlife and waterfowl refuge of national, State, or local significance, or land of an historic site of national, State, or local significance (as determined by the Federal, State, or local officials having jurisdiction over the park, area, refuse, or site) only if:

(1) *there is no prudent and feasible alternative* to using that land; and
(2) *the program or project includes all possible planning to minimize harm* to the park, recreation area, wildlife and waterfowl refuge, or historic site resulting from the use.

National Environmental Policy Act of 1969, 42 U.S.C. § 4332

The Congress, recognizing the profound impact of man's activity on the interrelations of all components of the natural environment...declares that it is the continuing policy of the Federal Government...to use all practicable means and measures...in a manner calculated to foster and promote the general welfare, to create and maintain conditions under which man and nature can exist in productive harmony, and fulfill the social, economic, and other requirements of present and future generations of Americans.

planning to minimize harm to the site has taken place. This statute goes beyond the procedural requirements of Section 106 and NEPA by providing substantive protection for historic resources. It requires the Secretary to make specific findings, supported by substantial evidence, that Section 4(f) requirements have been met. The Secretary can be sued if a decision under Section 4(f) is not supported on substantive grounds.

In passing these three laws, Congress took the view that the Federal Government should be a *guardian*, not a destroyer, of the nation's historic and natural resources.

Like Congress, many state legislatures have taken note of the damage that state-funded projects, too, can do to irreplaceable resources and have enacted their own versions of these

106, 4(f) and NEPA Laws

* * *

In order to carry out the policy set forth...it is the continuing responsibility of the Federal Government to use all practicable means, consistent with other essential considerations of national policy, to improve and coordinate Federal plans, functions, programs, and resources to the end that the Nation may:

(1) fulfill the responsibilities of each generation as trustee of the environment for succeeding generations;
(2) assure for all Americans safe, healthful, productive, and aesthetically and culturally pleasing surroundings;

* * *

(4) preserve important historic, cultural, and natural aspects of our national heritage, and maintain, wherever possible, an environment which supports diversity and variety of individual choice;

* * *

The Congress authorizes and directs that, to the fullest extent possible...all agencies of the Federal Government shall:

* * *

(C) *include in every* recommendation or report on proposals for legislation and other *major Federal actions significantly affecting the quality of the human environment, a detailed statement by the responsible official* on:

   (i) *the environmental impact of the proposed action,*
   (ii) any adverse environmental effects which cannot be avoided, should the proposal be implemented,
   (iii) alternatives to the proposed action,
   (iv) the relationship between local short-term uses of man's environment and the maintenance and enhancement of long-term productivity, and
   (v) any irreversible and irretrievable commitments of resources which would be involved in the proposed action should it be implemented.

Prior to making any detailed statement, the responsible Federal official shall consult with and obtain the comments of any Federal agency which has jurisdiction by law or special expertise with respect to any environmental impact involved. Copies of such statement and the comments and views of the appropriate Federal, State, and local agencies...shall be made available...to the public.

federal statutes. These state laws are sometimes referred to as "state 106," "state 4(f)," or "state-NEPA" laws.

State Registers of Historic Places

WHETHER ONE OF THESE PROCEDURAL LAWS comes into play often depends on whether a building or site has been identified as historically significant by the state, federal or local government. Today most states have State Registers of Historic Places, official listings of resources important to their history and culture. Like the National Register of Historic

Places, state registers may include archaeological sites (underwater and under land), landscapes, artifacts and objects as well as historic buildings and districts.

Listing on a state register can have any of several consequences:

- It may trigger a requirement that a state or local agency review the effects of its actions and mitigate them if they threaten to harm a designated historic resource.
- It may open the door to financial benefits, such as state tax incentives, grants, or loans available for the rehabilitation of historic properties.
- It may serve as a planning tool and help state and local governments develop land-use, financial, or capital improvement policies that enhance the prospects for saving historic resources while minimizing threats to their future.
- It may serve as an educational tool that makes the public more aware of its heritage.

Some state historic preservation offices produce publications on properties listed on the National Register of Historic Places. New York State is an example. Thus the public has easy access to this information.

State Procedural Laws

Section 106: A state-level "106" law works something like this. In planning a project, state officials observe that historic sites will be affected. State officials are legally obligated to evaluate the impact of their project and, when appropriate, explore ways to mitigate any harm. They send their evaluation to the state historic preservation office for its review and comment. The office may concur with the evaluation and sign off on the project, or it may recommend that the agency explore other options. The agency must consider these recommendations, but not necessarily accept them. If the agency feels it cannot accept them, it so certifies and proceeds with its original plans. Almost 40 states have "state 106" laws.

Often a state law will specify a time period during which this review-and-consultation process must occur. In Alaska it is three months; in Arizona, 30 days. During this time, the agency proposing the project may not move forward until it has carried out its obligations.

Sometimes the state preservation office and agency in charge of the project will meet face-to-face and negotiate a compromise. If this compromise results in a written agreement, it may obligate the agency to avoid or minimize harm to the endangered resource. In this case, the procedures mandated by the state 106 law can result in substantive protection. In some cases, the agreement may require the agency to record a historic site slated for demolition through photographs or architectural drawings.

> *Sometimes the state preservation office and agency in charge of the project will meet face-to-face and negotiate a compromise.*

In general, the obligation to comply with the state process falls on state agencies, not on private parties. However, if a private individual or company is under contract with or licensed by the state, it, too, may be subject to the requirements. Some state 106 laws only apply to state-owned properties or state-sponsored projects, while other states require compliance for state-issued permits as well. In some states, the obligations fall on local as well as state governments. In Minnesota, the University of Minnesota, cities, towns, counties and school districts must all comply. These entities may not alter designated historic sites without first obtaining written approval from the Minnesota Historical Society.

New Jersey's "state 106" law has two main provisions. First, it creates a New Jersey Register of Historic Places and a Historic Sites Council to oversee the protection of sites listed on the register. Council members are appointed by the governor and represent a variety of professions. The law also requires any state, county or municipal agency involved in a project that will encroach upon a listed site to obtain approval from the Commissioner of Environmental Protection. The law also gives citizens an opportunity to make their views known at public hearings.

The New Jersey statute states:

> The State, a county, municipality or any agency or instrumentality of any thereof shall not undertake any project which will encroach upon, damage or destroy any area, site, structure, or object included in the [New Jersey] Register of Historic Places without application to, and the prior written authorization or consent of, the Commissioner of Environmental Protection. The Commissioner should solicit the advice and recommendations of the Historic Sites Council in connection with any such application and may direct the conduct of a public hearing or hearings thereon prior to granting or denying authorization or consent. The failure of the Commissioner to authorize, consent or deny any such application within 120 days of application therefore should constitute his consent thereto.[44]

Unlike the federal Section 106, which protects properties *eligible* for the National Register as well as those actually listed, the New Jersey law shelters only state-listed properties. But the New Jersey statute provides stronger protection than the federal law in that the Commissioner has the power to deny projects under certain circumstances.

Although the law usually covers only the actions of public agencies—state, county or municipal—it can govern private actions as well if a public agency delegates certain public functions to a private entity. For example, if an agency delegates the responsibility to build roads or other public infrastructure associated with a large development project, the project's impact on the designated historic property may be subject to review.

Charles Scott of New Jersey's historic preservation office says the recommendations of the Historic Sites Council are usually followed and gives the law a "B+." As with many laws, however, politics can and does influence the outcome in certain cases. This is particularly true of road projects, which are often controversial and frequently affect historic resources.

State-level Section 4(f): While over 40 states have "state 106" laws, only a handful—e.g., Florida, Connecticut, Minnesota, South Dakota, New Mexico and Kansas—have Section 4(f)-type laws. Depending upon the political context, these laws may be stronger than Section 106-type laws.

A good example of a state-level 4(f) law is the Kansas Historic Preservation Act, which states:

> The state or any political subdivision of the state…shall not undertake any project which will encroach upon, damage or destroy any property included in the national register of historic places or the state register of historic places or the environs of such property until the state historic preservation officer has been given notice and an opportunity to investigate and comment upon the proposed project. If the state historic preservation officer determines that such proposed project will encroach upon, damage or destroy any historic site, such project shall not proceed until: (a) the governor…or the governing body of the political subdivision…has made a determination…that there is **no feasible and prudent alternative** to the proposal and that the program includes **all possible planning** to minimize harm to such historic site resulting from such use…[45]

The Kansas attorney general has interpreted this law to apply to local zoning decisions as well as to state agency actions. One unusual feature of the statute is the "buffer zone" protection it provides to historic structures through its reference to "environs." In other words, development projects on lands immediately surrounding historic resources may be subject to review under the law.

"SEPAs" or State "NEPAs": A "SEPA" is a state environmental policy act modeled after the National Environmental Policy Act (NEPA). At least 17 states and Puerto Rico have SEPAs

The law gives citizens an opportunity to make their views known at public hearings.

ED VIDLER

Main Street in East Aurora, N.Y. Local residents turned out in record numbers at public hearings in 1995 to protest the construction of a sprawling commercial development on the edge of town for fear it would destroy their downtown. The residents won this battle with the help of New York's State Environmental Quality Review Act.

while still others have limited environmental review requirements established by statute, executive order, or other administrative directives.[46] Under a "SEPA," a state agency assisting a project—whether through a loan, permit, or license—must first determine whether the project will have an effect on the environment and then whether the effect is significant or minor. An agency's approval of a large shopping center or a major highway is likely to have a significant effect; its approval of minor building alterations is not.[47] In the latter instance, the agency may simply file a "negative declaration" and be done with the matter. While focussing primarily on natural resources, SEPAs usually shelter historic resources under their umbrellas as well. Moreover, their very breadth can complement the narrowness of state 106 laws and address problems untouched by the latter.

If the effect is significant, the state agency must prepare a draft "environmental impact statement (EIS)." Some states—California and Massachusetts, for example—call these statements "environmental impact reports" (EIRs) to distinguish them from the federal "EIS."

This describes the effects on environmental and (if covered) historic, cultural, and archaeological resources. The EIS then explores ways to minimize the harmful effects. Once the draft EIS becomes public—and most SEPAs require that these statements *do* become public—the agencies involved hold public hearings. These give citizens an opportunity to learn about a project and to voice their opinions on it. The agency then prepares a final EIS, which is supposed to reflect public input, and makes a final decision on how to proceed.

New York's "State Environmental Quality Review Act," or SEQRA,[48] requires agencies to consider the effects of their actions on "local community character" as well as on historic and archaeological resources and the environment. The New York law also applies to local government agencies. In fact, the vast majority of reviews that take place under this law are municipal actions such as rezonings.

Although state and local agencies sometimes ignore their SEPA responsibilities, they can be taken to court for doing so. If a court agrees with a citizens' complaint that the agency

Maryland's "state 106" law was used to help preserve these historic buildings at Camden Yards, the Baltimore Orioles' ballpark. This project is a national model for integrating historic buildings into a new construction project and for making a massive public facility and traffic generator fit in sensitively with the surrounding neighborhoods. The Maryland Historical Trust reports that the Maryland Stadium Authority, a state agency, and the lead project architect worked cooperatively and creatively with the Trust to retain as much as possible of the area's historic fabric.

failed to follow correct procedures, it can send the agency back to the drawing board with instructions to do things right. Under some SEPAs, citizens may seek "substantive enforcement." If a court finds their case persuasive, it may order the agency not to approve a project that would irreparably harm a historic or natural resource. In many states, the courts have developed a solid body of case law interpreting SEPA requirements, many of which are stronger than their federal NEPA counterpart.

Although the legal burden of preparing the EIS (or EIR) technically falls on the "lead" public agency in charge of reviewing the project, as a practical matter, this chore is sometimes handled by the developer advocating the project. Under those circumstances, there may be a temptation for the EIR to minimize a project's environmental impacts. Citizens should be alert to this situation, conduct their own independent research, if warranted, and get credible rebuttal information into the record. This can be expensive, however, which is why a preservation organization must have a broad base in order to be effective. Such a base helps the organization draw on available professional expertise and raise money to pay for technical experts on such matters as traffic, historic preservation, water quality, fiscal and economic impacts of development, and so forth.

Advantages of State Laws to Minimize Harm

WHILE THESE PROCEDURAL LAWS are sometimes weaker than state-authorized local ordinances, which often provide outright prohibitions against the destruction of historic resources, state preservation laws nonetheless have several benefits for preservation.

Time and A Forum for Negotiation: One benefit is the *time* they provide. At a minimum, these laws require state agencies—and in many cases, municipalities—to slow down and consider the effects of their actions before causing irreparable damage to historic resources. A second

A Basis to Deny the Rezoning

"FOR COMMUNITIES WHO DON'T UNDERSTAND the state environmental policy act, they see this three-ring binder report produced by the developer, and they're snowed," says Susan A. Benz, an East Aurora resident who played a key role in her village's fight to prevent its historic main street from being deadened by sprawl. "The developer will often try to persuade the village board that a project has "no significant impact" and therefore doesn't warrant a full environmental review. In East Aurora, Benz and others insisted that the village board require that the developer conduct a thorough review of the project. And in the end they won. The village board ultimately voted against a rezoning that would have paved the way for the sprawl-type development on East Aurora's edge.

While local zoning laws usually provide the public with an opportunity to comment on a project, a SEPA such as New York's requires a factual finding on each of several specific environmental factors: traffic, wetlands, the local economy, local community character, historic and archaeological resources, etc.

Because the New York statute[49] provides for a public review and comment period, the "Save Historic East Aurora" organization was able to get its experts' studies into the public record.

"What it all boils down to," observes Benz, "is a battle between the experts. Ultimately the village board can decide whatever it wants, so long as it has a rational basis for its decision. We gave the board a rational basis to deny the rezoning."

Washington's Environmental Policy Act

A PHILOSOPHY AKIN to that expressed in this preamble to Washington State's Environmental Policy Act[50] suffuses many SEPAs:

> [I]t is the continuing responsibility of the state of Washington and all agencies of the state to use all practicable means, consistent with other essential considerations of state policy, to improve and coordinate plans, functions, programs, and resources to the end that the state and its citizens may:
>
> (a) Fulfill the responsibilities of each generation as trustee of the environment for succeeding generations;
>
> (b) Assure for all people of Washington, safe, healthful, productive, and aesthetical and culturally pleasing surroundings;
>
> (c) Attain the widest range of beneficial uses of the environment without degradation, risk to health or safety, or other undesirable and unintended consequences;
>
> (d) *Preserve important historic, cultural, and natural aspects of our national heritage*;
>
> (e) Maintain, wherever possible, an environment which supports diversity and variety of individual choice;
>
> (f) Achieve a balance between population and resource use which will permit high standards of living and a wide sharing of life's amenities; and
>
> (g) Enhance the quality of renewable resources and approach the maximum attainable recycling of depletable resources.[54]

benefit is a *forum for negotiation*. By mandating that public agencies take a good, hard look at what they are doing, these laws enhance the prospects for finding alternatives that may have been overlooked. This combination—time and a negotiating forum—can be invaluable.

Controversies over the impacts of state-assisted projects often involve citizens, who may be at a distinct disadvantage when pitted against powerful, heavily financed developers or state agencies advocating projects capable of destroying historic areas. The procedural requirements of these laws give citizens time to develop arguments for preserving an endangered site; time to educate the media—and through it, the general public—about the issues at stake; and time to conduct economic, architectural, traffic or other studies on the feasibility of alternatives to demolition; time to locate and enlist professional experts—creative architects, engineers, retailers, historians or other professionals—who may come up with innovative compromises that no one imagined possible. It also provides time to organize grassroots efforts aimed at broadening the public debate when appropriate.

Protection Against Public Agency Actions: Another advantage of these laws is that they apply to public agencies that are not covered by federal laws and are sometimes exempted from local preservation laws that apply to private property owners. They thus fill a major gap in the protection of historic resources. This can be helpful when there is a need to mitigate damage likely to be caused by a public agency—a local public works department's plan to widen a road through a historic neighborhood, for example.

Protection Against Segmented Project Budgets: Although the federal Section 4(f) law protects historic resources threatened by federally-financed transportation projects, many highway projects are state financed. Moreover, state transportation departments sometimes segment the financing of projects in order to evade the federal 4(f) requirement. For example, they might allocate federal funds to road projects that do not harm historic areas and state funds to sections that cut through such areas. A state-level review process can prevent such piece-mealing from evading review altogether. The process cannot necessarily prevent the segmentation, but it adds a measure of review for the segmented sections.

A Handle on Sprawl: Increasingly, communities with vibrant downtowns are coming to recognize that large, sprawl-type developments on the edge of town can destroy the historic downtown's economic vitality. Such developments often shift the local economic center of gravity away from the downtown to the exit of a major highway. In doing so, they enervate the downtown, leaving historic buildings under-used, vacant, and vulnerable to demolition. SEPAs can sometimes give citizens a handle for preventing this scenario. This, in fact, is precisely what East Aurora, N.Y., did in 1995 with the help of New York's State Environmental Quality Review Act (SEQRA). In East Aurora, an economic analysis made possible by the SEPA revealed that a 249,000-square-foot shopping center on the outskirts of the village was likely to displace as many as 65 percent of the historic Main Street's businesses. This and other information brought to light during the SEQRA review resulted in the village's rejection of the project and a recommitment to its Main Street.

While most SEPAs include historic resources in their definition of the environment to be protected, a few do not. But even if they do not, through their mandated reviews of a project's impact on environmental quality generally, they can sometimes help to combat poorly planned, or unplanned development, which can damage historic downtowns and neighborhoods.

An environmental impact statement (EIS) requires government agencies to disclose in writing the anticipated impacts of a project and to develop a record against which they can be held accountable. Without the EIS, citizens may have no record to work with, and thus no way to counter government activities that may harm historic resources without giving due consideration to alternatives.

Disadvantages

Lack of Substantive Sanctions: The main disadvantage of these state laws is that very often, they merely invoke procedural requirements. In this sense, they resemble a stop sign at an intersection. State officials must stop, look, and listen before making decisions. After doing so, agencies may proceed in any direction they wish. So long as a state or local agency complies with these requirements, it can do whatever it wants, even tearing down a landmark. Often the end result is merely a delay in the day of reckoning.

Lack of Coverage for Some Private Developments: Another disadvantage is that some of these laws only apply to state-sponsored projects or state-owned historic properties, and they may not cover private development, even if state permits are required. Since most development in America is privately financed and executed, this is a big gap. In communities lacking local preservation ordinances or zoning, historic resources may be left unprotected altogether.

Political Pressures on Weak Preservation Agencies: Political pressures that often accompany large development or highway projects can also pose problems. State preservation offices often have less political clout and money than other state agencies, especially economic development and transportation departments with direct access to the governor via cabinet status. As a result, the ability of state preservation officials to use these procedural laws may depend heavily on the negotiating skills of their personnel and the political savvy of their directors. Large, controversial projects backed by powerful political and financial interests can put a state preservation official in a difficult position. In such cases, the preservation sympathies of the governor, if any, and the access of the preservation office to the governor—can be crucial.

* * *

State officials must stop, look, and listen.

In the final analysis, one should remember that a law's existence on the books is one thing, its enforcement is another. These procedural laws are rarely self-executing. They work best—some would say only—when state or local preservation advocates speak out and participate in the negotiating process that the laws invoke. As William Pencek, deputy director of the Maryland Historical Trust, says, "These laws work best when there is a local advocacy group working for preservation. It can't be just a bunch of egghead bureaucrats waxing poetic over the cultural significance of a historic resource. There's got to be a local constituency making sure that elected officials understand that the outcome matters to the community."

Historic areas such as this one in Portland, Maine, receive protection from local preservation ordinances.

ALISON HINCHMAN

Minnesota Environmental Rights Act Helps Save Landmark Hotel in Hibbing

Minnesota has one of the stronger state environmental policy acts. Its law not only protects natural resources in the environment but also historic buildings and sites. Additionally, the law includes a strict, substantive standard limiting the demolition of historic resources unless there is no feasible and prudent alternative. The case study below illustrates the difference this law, combined with the help of the state preservation office, made to citizens in Hibbing, Minn., who fought to save a historic building that embodied the soul of this small community.

WHEN THE ANDROY HOTEL opened in downtown Hibbing, Minnesota, in 1921, its promoters boasted such innovations as a dishwasher, a long-distance telegraph service, and an electric coffee urn. Rooms went for $1.50 a night. Women used a separate entrance.

For nearly six decades, the Androy held sway as the finest hotel on the Minnesota Iron Range. Celebrities like President Coolidge, Tyrone Power, and Guy Lombardo stayed there when they came to town. Wedding receptions, balls, power luncheons—all of Hibbing's important social and business activities took place here.

But by the mid-seventies, competition from motels and a decline in the Iron Range's mining-based economy had taken their toll on this downtown landmark. Banks took the property back from its owners in 1977. Unable to find new owners, the bank turned the hotel over to the city in 1985.

By 1990, the Androy looked pitiful. Its roof leaked. Paint on the ballroom walls was peeling. Bursting pipes had caused water damage. Icicles hung from the ballroom ceiling.

Tired of worrying about the Androy, the city council voted in early 1991 to tear the structure down and replace it with a parking lot.

News of the council's decision stunned Maria Magdalena Reynolds, a local resident. Putting pen to paper, she wrote a letter to the local newspaper. "How can we destroy such a historically important building?" she asked.

A few days later, Gene Nicolelli, the only council member to vote against the demolition, called Reynolds and other city residents to apprise them of an upcoming town meeting at which they could discuss the matter further with the council. Two hundred and fifty people, including Reynolds, showed up for this event. Speaker after speaker stood up to urge the council to save the four-story, Italian Renaissance building. At one point during this emotional evening, someone pleaded with the Council, "Give us the keys. We'll go in and clean up the hotel if you're worried about its condition."

The council relented and offered a one-month stay of execution to let those who wanted to save the Androy to come up with a plan for its restoration. Reynolds and others formed the Androy Project Committee and swung into high gear. They developed a fundraising plan and presented it at the next council meeting. But the council again voted to raze the hotel. Soon thereafter, the city signed a contract with a demolition company from southern Minnesota to demolish the historic landmark.

Minnesota Environmental Rights Act

A WEATHER-RELATED DELAY in the demolition gave the committee time to explore the possibility of a legal challenge to the city's decision. A committee member recalled a presentation on the Minnesota Environmental Rights Act (MERA, see sidebar) by an attorney at a recent

The historic Androy Hotel in Hibbing, Minn. (Exterior, above; interior views before and after rehabilitation, below).

workshop held by the Minnesota Historical Society. The group contacted the attorney, Mark Anfinson, to see if he might represent them in a legal challenge to the city's decision.

A Minneapolis lawyer with a background in preservation law, Anfinson agreed with the committee that the MERA might help save the building. At least it could give local preservationists more time to strike a better deal with the city council, he reasoned. He also liked the Androy: "It had a broad-shouldered presence in the downtown. Its demolition would have been the equivalent of removing a person's two front teeth."

The committee now faced the challenge of quickly raising funds to cover legal and other expenses. It sold T-shirts designed by a local artist—he depicted the Androy with the caption 'Preserve Your Heritage'—for $10 apiece. Another successful fundraiser was a huge barbecue at a nearby lake. "Many contributors were elderly people who had fond memories of the hotel," recalls Reynolds. "When I went to the post office, many of them would grab me and say, 'Keep up your work.'"

But time was short. With the demolition contract already let, it was just a matter of the weather's clearing up before the contractor would demolish the hotel.

Minnesota Environmental Rights Act [51]

THE LEGISLATURE FINDS and declares that each person is entitled by right to the protection, preservation, and enhancement of air, water, land, and other natural resources located within the state and that each person has the responsibility to contribute to the protection, preservation, and enhancement thereof. The legislature further declares its policy to create and maintain within the state conditions under which human beings and nature can exist in productive harmony in order that present and future generations may enjoy clean air and water, productive land, and other natural resources with which this state has been endowed. Accordingly, it is in the public interest to provide an adequate civil remedy to protect air, water, land and other natural resources located within the state from pollution, impairment, or destruction.

* * *

"Person" means any natural person, any state, municipality or other governmental or political subdivision or other public agency or instrumentality, any public or private corporation, any partnership, firm, association, or other organization, any receiver, trustee, assignee, agent, or other legal representative of any of the foregoing, and any other entity, except a family farm, a family farm corporation or a bona fide farmer corporation.

* * *

Natural resources shall include, but not be limited to, all mineral, animal, botanical, air, water, land, timber, soil, quietude, recreational and *historical resources. Scenic and esthetic resources shall also be considered natural resources when owned by any governmental unit or agency.*

"Pollution, impairment or destruction" is any conduct by any person which violates, or is likely to violate, any environmental quality standard, limitation, rule, order, license, stipulation agreement, or permit of the state or any instrumentality, agency, or political subdivision thereof which was issued prior to the date the alleged violation occurred or is likely to occur or any conduct which materially adversely affects or is likely to materially adversely affect the environment; provided that "pollution, impairment or destruction" shall not include conduct which violates, or is likely to violate, any such standard, limitation, rules, order, license, stipulation agreement or permit solely because of the introduction of an odor into the air.

Under the MERA, when an endangered site is truly historic, and is threatened with impairment or destruction, then the court may deny protection only if the defendant demonstrates that there is "no reasonable and prudent alternative to destruction…in light of the state's paramount concern for the protection of its historic and other natural resources." Those seeking to save an endangered resource must be able to show two things—

- an endangered site is truly historic; and
- there is a feasible and prudent alternative to its destruction

—in order to persuade a judge to impose a temporary or permanent restraining order, i.e., a temporary delay or an outright ban, on a proposed demolition.

In this case the preservationists succeeded in obtaining a temporary injunction. This was obtained on an emergency basis, by means of affidavits and other submissions describing the Androy's value and by arguments of the attorneys at a hearing. At that point, demolition was imminent. The judge gave the preservationists less than a month to prepare for the full-blown trial—much less time than is usually allowed in litigation.

* * *

Any person residing within the state, the attorney general; any political subdivision of the state; any instrumentality or agency of the state or of a political subdivision thereof; or any partnership, corporation, association, organization or other entity having shareholders, members, partners or employees residing within the state may maintain a civil action in the district court for declaratory or equitable relief in the name of the state of Minnesota against any person, for the protection of the air, water, land, or other natural resources located within the state, whether publicly or privately owned, from pollution, impairment, or destruction…

* * *

…[W]henever the plaintiff shall have made a prima facie showing that the conduct of the defendant violates or is likely to violate said environmental quality standard…the defendant may rebut the…showing by the submission of evidence to the contrary…

* * *

The defendant may also show, by way of an affirmative defense, that there is *no feasible and prudent alternative* and the conduct at issue is consistent with and reasonably required for promotion of the public health, safety, and welfare in light of the state's paramount concern for the protection of its air, water, land and other natural resources from pollution, impairment, or destruction. *Economic considerations alone shall not constitute a defense hereunder.*

* * *

In any action maintained under this section the plaintiff shall have the burden of proving that the environmental quality standard, limitation, rule, order, license, stipulation agreement, or permit is inadequate to protect the air, water, land, or other natural resources located within the state from pollution, impairment, or destruction. The plaintiff shall have the burden of proving the existence of material evidence showing said inadequacy of said environmental quality standard, limitation, rule, order, license, stipulation agreement, or permit.

Help from the State

LOCAL PRESERVATIONISTS AND ANFINSON had to scramble to locate expert witnesses who could help them at the trial. The Minnesota Historical Society helped them out. Testifying as an expert witness on this case, Charles Nelson, the Society's chief architect, validated the local preservationists' assertion that the Androy was not just "any old building;" it was considered important enough to be placed on the National Register of Historic Places, the list of the nation's most important buildings. Nelson made the point that historic structures are not arbitrarily or casually listed; their listing must be backed up by solid research. With his years of experience in the adaptive reuse of historic buildings, Nelson was also able to persuade the judge that the Androy had a realistic economic future if it were rehabilitated.

On the second day of the trial, it was evident that the preservationists were likely to prevail. The city backed away from its decision to raze the Androy and agreed to transfer ownership of the property to the Androy Project Committee for a nominal sum.

Nelson's expertise, and the Historical Society's willingness to go to bat for Hibbing's preservationists in the first place, were critical to this outcome. Having gotten a reprieve, the committee was able to locate a developer willing to restore the Androy. Richard Brustad, a partner with the Brighton Development Corporation in Minneapolis, presented a plan to renovate the building for mixed uses: senior housing on the upper floors, shops on the ground floor. The city liked this plan and bought it.

Again, the Historical Society helped out. Nelson reviewed the developer's architectural plans to expedite federal approval for historic rehabilitation tax credits. He also helped to cut through the red tape surrounding the state's allocation of low-income housing tax credits—another tax incentive that helped to make the project economically feasible. Finally, the state played a role through its authorization of tax increment financing. (The Society is currently working to get the state TIF laws amended to specifically target historic areas for TIFs.)

In May 1995, a beautifully restored Androy Hotel reopened to the public. Elderly residents now occupy the upper-floor apartments. A catering service and a copy shop have filled the ground-level space. And instead of being a drag on the city's coffers, the hotel (not counting the small businesses inside it) contributes $59,000 a year in property taxes.

"It's getting to be the hub of the community again," says Nicolelli. "It's hosted quite a few weddings. The local service clubs are using it again. The Androy is reclaiming its prominent place in the city's life." Brustad observes that the hotel's restoration has stimulated neighboring property owners to fix their places up. A drug store that had left the city for an outlying mall is even returning to the downtown.

"I belong to a nice dancing club in town," says Reynolds, "and we celebrated New Year's Eve in the hotel this year. It was one of the most gorgeous New Year's Eves I've ever attended. With a beautiful Christmas tree, lights, music—for me, it was absolutely fantastic."

The Androy, six years ago a symbol of the city's failure, is now a symbol of hope for Hibbing.[52]

CHAPTER 2

Money for Historic Preservation

The restoration of the Davis administration building in Wichita was made possible with funds from the Kansas Heritage Trust Fund.

CHAPTER 2

Money for Preservation

W HILE MANY STATE LEGISLATORS LIKE THE IDEA OF preserving beautiful historic buildings, when faced with such urgent needs as road repairs, crime prevention, and health care, preservation may be seen as a frill. Given the current competition for public dollars, preservationists must be able to do three things to succeed in this area:

- explain preservation's relevance to goals that state legislators consider essential, like job creation, economic development, deficit reduction, and the like;
- ensure that preservation programs that do receive state support produce tangible, visible public benefits; and
- find a source of money not already claimed.

Evidence demonstrating historic preservation's relevance to such essentials as job creation abounds, but the extent to which it is assembled and packaged effectively varies widely. One of the most effective presentations of preservation's economic benefits was made in 1995 by the Preservation Alliance of Virginia in a little booklet, *Virginia's Economy and Historic Preservation: The Impact of Preservation on Jobs, Business and the Community*. In explaining preservation's importance to Virginia's tourism industry, a leading source of jobs in the state, the booklet observes that:

> Historic preservation visitors stay longer, visit twice as many places, and spend, on average, over two-and-a-half times more money in Virginia than do other visitors. The economic impact of Colonial Williamsburg alone on Virginia's economy is *over half a billion dollars a year*. The result: visitors coming to see Virginia's vast inventory of historic sites add their dollars to Virginia's economy.[1]

When the booklet came out, the Alliance made sure every member of the Virginia General Assembly received a copy.

There appears to be no correlation between a state's population and its commitment, as measured in dollars, to historic preservation. Some of the nation's most populous states, such as California and Texas, have provided only token financial support for preservation in recent years. Smaller states, including New Jersey, Florida, Colorado and Vermont, have all done better when dollars for preservation are measured on a per-capita basis.

If population size does not determine a state's monetary commitment to historic preservation, other factors do. Among the most important are:

- leadership—whether from a governor, a state legislator, or private citizens;
- bi-partisan political support;
- diverse and broad-based coalitions;
- well-organized grassroots lobbying;
- effective statewide preservation advocacy organizations;
- compelling evidence of preservation needs; and
- public awareness of preservation's economic and social benefits.

This chapter examines how preservation advocates have garnered public and political support for funding historic preservation, what sources of state funds have been tapped for preservation, and what ingredients account for successful state preservation funding programs.

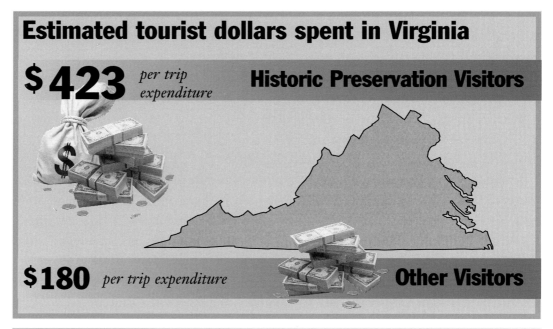

Estimated tourist dollars spent in Virginia

$423 *per trip expenditure* **Historic Preservation Visitors**

$180 *per trip expenditure* **Other Visitors**

What Virginia Visitors Come to See	% Visitation By First Time Visitors	% Visitation By Repeat Visitors
Historic Preservation	73 %	36 %
Discount Centers	30 %	29 %
Shopping Centers	32 %	25 %
Beaches	20 %	13 %
Theme Parks	13 %	7 %
Golf Courses	4 %	4 %

Historic Preservation Visitors are those visiting Historic Buildings and Sites, Museums and Civil War sites.

INFORMATION FROM PRESERVATION ALLIANCE OF VIRGINIA

Green Acres Bonds for Preservation in New Jersey

SINCE 1961, THE STATE OF NEW JERSEY HAS OPERATED AN OPEN-SPACE BOND PROgram known as "Green Acres," and the voters have approved eight bond issues totalling more than one billion dollars. To date, the program has helped to rescue hundreds of historic buildings and has saved more than 300,000 acres of farmland and open space from being paved over for new development.

The Green Acres Bond Program provides grants and low-interest loans to cities, towns, and nonprofit organizations to acquire land for open space, parks, playgrounds, athletic fields, and swimming pools. It also helps to underwrite the rehabilitation of historic buildings. As the loans are repaid, the principal and interest replenish a revolving "Green Trust Fund," enabling the program to make even more loans. To raise this money in the first place, the state of New Jersey sells bonds to investors. Green Acres loans to municipalities are repaid to the state at two percent interest over 20 years.

Background

ALTHOUGH NEW JERSEY HAD LOST OVER HALF of its entire stock of historic buildings to urban renewal, highways, neglect and other causes by the mid-1980s, not a dime of the millions of dollars raised by the Green Acres Program went into historic preservation before 1987. The seed for a change in that situation was planted in October 1986, when an article entitled "State of Ruins" appeared in the *New Jersey Monthly*. Depicting the sorry state of New Jersey's historic sites, author Tom Dunkel wrote:

> Consider the Dey Mansion in Wayne. Twice used by General Washington as his headquarters in 1780…Don't bet Washington would still sleep here. Buckets are strategically placed in the attic to catch rainwater…

> Consider that there are only six original Dutch Colonial barns left in Bergen County. They used to number in the thousands.

> Consider…the George Inness House in Perth Amboy, which the internationally renowned landscape artist occupied from 1864 to 1867…It serves as an all-purpose junkyard for [an] auto repair business.

Tom Dunkel noted the irony in the state's spending $10 million on tourism to lure people to New Jersey while letting important historic sites, a major tourist attraction, deteriorate.

Dunkel noted the irony in the state's spending $10 million on tourism to lure people to New Jersey while letting important historic sites, a major tourist attraction, deteriorate.

Galvanized by Dunkel's article, Assemblywoman Maureen Ogden, a Republican from Millburn who chaired the state assembly's Environment and Natural Resources Committee, and Assemblyman Rodney Frelinghuysen, a Republican from Harding who chaired the Assembly's Appropriations Committee, held public hearings to identify historic preservation funding needs. The outcome: a bond issue proposal sponsored by Ogden, Frelinghuysen, and the President of the Senate, John Lynch, a Democrat from New

Brunswick, to provide capital funds for historic sites and structures. This was a bipartisan effort.

Governor Thomas Kean suggested hitching historic preservation and cultural centers to the open-space-bond wagon by folding funding for preservation into the popular Green Acres Program. This idea was incorporated into the "Green Acres, Cultural Centers, and Historic Preservation Bond Act" that appeared on the ballot in November 1987. New Jersey voters approved this $100 million bond by a margin of two to one.

The proposal included $25 million for a Historic Preservation Bond Program, with $22 million dedicated to brick-and-mortar grants and $3 million set aside for a revolving loan fund for historic sites. The New Jersey Historic Trust, a state-chartered nonprofit organization affiliated with the state Department of Environmental Protection, established the new bond program (see Appendix C) in 1988 and began making grants for preservation projects around the state. Early projects included:

- rehabilitation of a Greek Revival mansion in Jersey City as a community center;
- roof repairs on the Hoboken Terminal, a magnificent public building and a landmark in transportation history dating to 1907; and
- restoration of "Old Barracks," a structure built in 1758 to house British colonial troops and now used as a living history museum in Trenton. The site attracts 30,000 visitors annually, 17,000 of them children.

The money went quickly, however, and by 1992 the preservation cupboard was almost bare again. This was not surprising. A 1990 survey conducted by the Historic Trust had revealed the need for nearly $400 million to stabilize and rehabilitate New Jersey's historic buildings.

With Assemblywoman Ogden again taking the lead, the New Jersey Assembly authorized a second bond issue in 1992, the "Green Acres, Clean Water, Farmland and Historic Preservation Bond Act." This proposal called for $345 million, with historic preservation again slated to receive $25 million. Despite the existence of a full-fledged taxpayer revolt in 1992, the voters approved the bond issue by a margin of three-to-one.

Since 1960, New Jersey has lost over 600,000 acres to new development.

Reasons for Success

HOW DID THE BOND'S PROPONENTS manage to garner the largest vote ever for the Green Acres program when New Jersey voters were often antagonistic toward state government and fed up with taxes?

First, people could see that they were getting something for their money. With Green Acres signs posted on rescued open spaces and parks all over the state, the program enjoyed a high degree of visibility. People knew about it and understood how it benefitted their communities directly.

Second, despite the program's success in saving more than 300,000 acres of farmland from new development since 1961, the threat of sprawl to the state's quality of life seemed imminent and real. As Richard Bagger, former chairman of the Historic Trust and now a state assemblyman, puts it, "There is a feeling in New Jersey that we are just teetering on the brink, from having a very good living environment to being swallowed up by sprawl." As a promotional flier for the 1992 bond issue pointed out, new development was claiming some 30,000 acres of open space each year. Since 1960, the state has lost over 600,000 acres to new development.

Most important, Green Acres advocates campaigned hard for the bond issue. After Governor James Florio asked E. James Ferland, CEO of New Jersey's Public Service Electric and Gas Company, to head the "New Jersey Coalition for a Clean and Green Tomorrow," a broad array of organizations lined up behind him. Coalition backers included such diverse interests as the recreation and park association, business and industry, the lake associations, the Chamber of Commerce, Preservation New Jersey and the AFL-CIO.

Ferland agreed to spearhead the campaign because, as James Shissias, PSE&G's general manager for environmental affairs, points out, "It's important for New Jersey to remain attractive as a place to do business. It's hard to imagine a favorable business climate unless the state is an attractive place to live and recreate. To the extent that the bond issue can provide for a higher quality of life in the future—and we're convinced that it can—that's a plus for us."

Led by PSE&G, other corporations, nonprofit organizations, and individuals contributed a total of $182,000 for the "clean and green" campaign. This enabled PSE&G to retain a public relations firm, Kohm Associates of Morristown,[2] to develop a comprehensive campaign strategy aimed at garnering public support for the bond. Elements of the strategy included:

- a public opinion poll to survey voter attitudes and determine the best way to present the bond issue to voters;
- a campaign kick-off at a park attended by the governor;
- 250,000 copies of a promotional brochure;
- op-ed pieces, letters-to-the-editor by prominent citizens, press releases, editorial endorsements, and interviews with the media;
- newspaper ads and 30-second spots on cable television;
- sample endorsement resolutions for municipalities to adopt;
- endorsements by organizations such as the New Jersey League of Municipalities and the New Jersey Association of Counties; and
- joint press releases by business and labor groups.

The public opinion poll confirmed Governor Kean's hunch that the clean water and open space elements served as the bond's engine and that historic preservation could benefit from a ride on this quality-of-life train. Whereas 78 percent of those polled said it was "very important" to sell bonds to clean up the state's water and 61 percent said that it was important to preserve farmland and open spaces, only 32 percent considered it "very important" to preserve historic places.

With the message to the public defined, the Coalition urged its members to make a pitch to their respective memberships. More than 200 articles were written to promote the ballot initiative to different interests.

In November 1995, New Jersey voters provided $10 million more for historic preservation grants when they approved yet another bond issue. This one, known as the Green Acres, Farmland and Historic Preservation, and Blue Acres Bond Issue, was sponsored by Assemblywoman Ogden with support from Governor Christine Todd Whitman. It will provide a total of $340 million for the acquisition of coastal areas prone to flooding, open spaces, farmland protection easements, and historic preservation. More people—68.1 percent—voted yes on the bond issue than on the three other questions put to the public on the 1995 ballot.

A bumper sticker used to promote Green Acres bond funds in New Jersey.

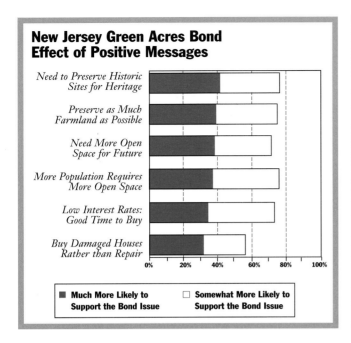

**New Jersey Green Acres Bond
Effect of Positive Messages**

*Need to Preserve Historic
Sites for Heritage*

*Preserve as Much
Farmland as Possible*

*Need More Open
Space for Future*

*More Population Requires
More Open Space*

*Low Interest Rates:
Good Time to Buy*

*Buy Damaged Houses
Rather than Repair*

■ **Much More Likely to
Support the Bond Issue**

☐ **Somewhat More Likely to
Support the Bond Issue**

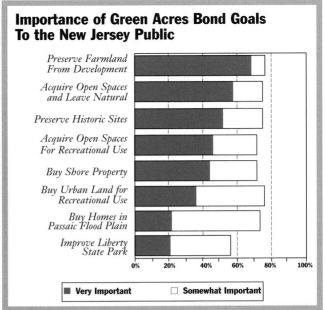

**Importance of Green Acres Bond Goals
To the New Jersey Public**

*Preserve Farmland
From Development*

*Acquire Open Spaces
and Leave Natural*

Preserve Historic Sites

*Acquire Open Spaces
For Recreational Use*

Buy Shore Property

*Buy Urban Land for
Recreational Use*

*Buy Homes in
Passaic Flood Plain*

*Improve Liberty
State Park*

■ **Very Important**   ☐ **Somewhat Important**

Since 1987, then, when historic preservation was first included in a Green Acres bond issue, voters have approved an impressive total of $60 million for historic preservation in the Garden State.

We need to preserve historic places so we and our children can understand our heritage.

Update

IN THE 1995 CAMPAIGN, the Public Service Electric & Gas company again played a key role and underwrote the New Jersey Coalition for a Clean and Green Tomorrow. This time, the greatest obstacle to success was voter backlash to big government and budget deficits. This problem was exacerbated by the general lack of interest shown by the public in the 1995 elections. The Coalition retained Holt & Ross, Inc., a public relations firm in Far Hills, N.J., to help organize the campaign. In addition to using some of the same techniques that had been used in previous campaigns (public opinion research, issues advertising, media relations, organization of grassroots support and special events involving high-profile, credible spokespeople), the firm created a World Wide Web page on the bond issue, which served as an innovative vehicle for getting the message out to potential voters.

Information recently released on the 1995 Green Acres bond reveals that historic preservation has risen in importance in the public's view. As the chart above shows, farmland preservation was seen as "very important" by 68 percent of those polled; open-space acquisition, by 58 percent; and historic preservation, by 52 percent.

When the effectiveness of different messages used to promote the bond with the public was tested, about three-quarters of the voters said they would be more likely to support the bond issue when presented with the following statements:

- With New Jersey's population continuing to grow, we must preserve as much open space as possible. (77 percent)
- We need to preserve historic places so we and our children can understand our heritage. (76 percent)
- Since interest rates and land prices are now fairly low, this is a good time for the state to acquire open spaces. (76 percent)

■ Too much farmland is being lost to housing development and the state should spend money to preserve as much farmland as possible. (75%)

Commentary

WHILE THE GREEN ACRES program has proven tremendously successful, it costs about two and a half times more than it would if it were funded without borrowed money. Though the bonds seem like a painless tax, they will eventually have to be paid back by children growing up today. Governor Whitman has asked Ms. Ogden to chair the Governor's Council on New Jersey Outdoors, a body charged with assessing the state's open space needs and finding a less expensive, yet stable funding source to meet them.

One of the program's disappointments has been the hesitancy of older cities to participate. While the cities need parks, they don't have the money to maintain them or to remove the graffiti and drug dealers who sometimes take over these areas. Ms. Ogden has proposed an Urban Heritage District Act that would address these problems by diverting half of the state's six percent tax on retailers located in the district into a special maintenance fund for urban parks. To critics who argue that the state can't afford to lose the money thus diverted, Ms. Ogden replies: "That's shortsighted. If you improve a whole urban area, you will generate more money for the state in the long run."

Despite these problems, the Green Acres Program enjoys great popularity. "As the nation's most densely populated state," explains Harriette Hawkins, executive director of the New Jersey Historic Trust, "we have great pressures on our remaining open space. The public values open space, parks and farmland as refuges from urban sprawl. Because these areas represent an increasingly precious commodity, the Green Acres program has a solid base of public support." The program is a nice, "happy face" sort of thing that people like.

"The public values open space, parks and farmland as refuges from urban sprawl."

Advice from Maureen Ogden

MOST HISTORY ADVOCATES don't like to push aggressively for public funding, but they must compete for public funds like everyone else. They have to be at the table. While I share the belief of preservationists that our cause is exemplary, every cause must sell itself in the public arena.

The selling point for preservation comes with tourism, job creation, and revitalization of urban areas. In New Jersey, tourism is a $20 billion dollar industry, and visiting historic sites and structures is becoming an increasingly important component.

Today elected officials at local, state and national levels are looking at almost every issue in terms of dollars and cents. While recognizing the paramount importance of conserving our irreplaceable heritage, one must not overlook the economic rationale for historic preservation.

New Jersey Assemblywoman Maureen Ogden watches while Governor Christine Todd Whitman signs the History Task Force Bill.

Behind New Jersey's success in funding historic preservation lie several factors. First, the sense of urgency created by the article in the *New Jersey Monthly* got the attention not only of the public but also of state officials in a position to do something about the crisis. Second, the skills of a key state legislator and the high esteem in which her colleagues held her enabled her to serve as an effective champion for preservation. Third, the existence of a funding vehicle with a long history of strong popular support provided a train for the preservation funding proposal to ride. Preservation benefitted not only from the public's enthusiasm for open-space preservation but also from corporate support for this program. Finally, the high visibility provided by signs on sites saved all over the state has made the New Jersey bond program something the public can see, touch and feel.

Postscript

ALTHOUGH BRICK-AND-MORTAR preservation projects have enjoyed strong financial support in New Jersey through the Green Acres Program, the state contributes very little to the operating expenses of the New Jersey Historic Trust and the state Department of Natural and Historic Resources. These agencies barely scrape by and have virtually no funds to pass on to local governments for historic resource surveys and other preservation planning activities. Only 13 of the state's counties had completed historic surveys by the end of 1994, and less than a quarter of New Jersey's communities have enacted local ordinances to protect historic districts.

Under a proposal sponsored by Ms. Ogden and signed into law in January 1996, the state will issue a special license plate for history. Motorists who want the plate will pay $50 for the plate ($15 more than the cost of the regular plate); renewal is $10. After the program's start-up costs are repaid, proceeds will go into a dedicated Historic Preservation License Plate Fund that will provide grants for historic preservation as well as the interpretation and operation of historic sites. The new plate will go on sale in Fall 1996.

In the hope of building stronger public support for historic preservation, the New Jersey Historic Trust recently funded a study of the economic impact of historic preservation. The research is being conducted by Rutgers University.

Florida: A Focus on the Grass Roots

F LORIDA BEATS ALL OTHER STATES IN FUNDING HISTORIC PRESERVATION. Since 1985, the Sunshine State has appropriated $82.3 million in general revenue funds for local preservation projects. When bond-financed monies are included, this total rises to more than $250 million. This commitment surpasses that of the entire federal government for preservation in all 50 states.

But it wasn't always that way in Florida.

"Before 1984," recalls George W. Percy, director of Florida's Division of Historical Resources, "we had asked the state legislature with some regularity for a lump sum—three million or so—for historic preservation for the state. But we never got any action. The general line was always, 'This is a bad year for preservation. Other things—schools, prisons, what have you—rank higher on our agenda'."

Tarpon Springs, Florida, City Hall, is now used as a community center.

GEORGE COTT

After getting nowhere for several years in a row, Percy suggested taking a different tack, one that emphasizes grassroots involvement by the state legislators' own constituents and tangible projects with strong community support. This thinking resulted in the creation of Florida's "Special Category Grants Program" in 1985. The results of the new approach proved dramatic: The legislature approved $1.3 million for brick-and-mortar preservation projects that first year, and in the ten years since, it has never approved less than $1.4 million. (See table below.)

The mechanics of this grant program, which provides grants ranging from $50,000 to $250,000 for brick-and-mortar preservation projects, are straightforward while the process for selecting projects to fund is politically savvy.

Each spring, between April 1 and May 1, the Florida Division of Historical Resources invites other state agencies, local governments, and private nonprofit organizations to nominate historic preservation projects worthy of state funds. The division staff reviews the applications for completeness over the summer, and in the early fall, the state's Historic Preservation Advisory Council evaluates and ranks the applications. This 12-member council includes citizens from around the state who have experience and an interest in historic preservation.

In ranking applications, the Council asks such questions as:

- How significant is the historic building or site? How endangered is it?
- Is the proposed rehabilitation work appropriate?
- Is the grant applicant administratively and financially capable of carrying out the project?
- Will the project benefit the public? Will it help the local economy?
- Is there strong local support for the project?

The Council forwards its recommendations to the Florida Secretary of State, who folds them into his or her departmental budget request to the state legislature. The Secretary has the authority to delete or add projects but usually accepts the Council's recommendations.

The process weeds out "turkeys" for which support might later prove embarrassing to a politician.

Getting into the Secretary of State's budget request to the legislature is like winning the Good Housekeeping Seal of Approval. The careful screening of projects—first by the division staff, then by the expert advisory panel—and the requirement for evidence of strong community support reassure the state legislators. The process weeds out "turkeys" for which support might later prove embarrassing to a politician.

"The projects are rated according to very specific criteria," says Joan Jennewein, a Tampa preservation leader who has served on the state's advisory council. "So you really do get projects that involve the most historically and architecturally significant buildings. You also get projects that have the most meaning to communities." The council emphasizes geographical distribution in its selections. "We try to reach as many legislators' districts as possible," adds Jennewein.

Special Category Grant Funds for Historic Preservation in Florida

1985–86	$1,300,000	1991–92	$ 2,926,587
1986–87	$8,154,000	1992–93	$ 1,412,718
1987–88	$9,386,529	1993–94	$ 8,965,832
1988–89	$7,758,070	1994–95	$12,220,277
1989–90	$6,613,988	1995–96	$11,994,001
1990–91	$8,854,574		

Historic preservationists meet during Florida's "Preservation Day."

The "Pink Book"

PROJECTS RECOMMENDED FOR INCLUSION in the Secretary of State's budget make it into the so-called "Pink Book." This is a compendium of "Special Category" projects recommended for funding and is published each year by the historical division. Its purpose is to help those who lobby the legislature in behalf of the projects.

"If you're going to lobby for a quarter of a million dollars, you can't just go to your state representative and say, 'I want money' and give vague answers when asked what it's for," says Percy. "The Pink Book shows legislators what the projects look like. It provides information on how they were selected and who selected them. It shows where the projects fit within the state's overall budget."

At this point grassroots preservation organizations take over and lobby their state legislators. The historical division does not lobby, but it does make sure that the grassroots preservationists understand the legislative and appropriations processes. "We tell the local people about the legislature's committee structure and composition, the legislative process, the timing, etc.," says Suzanne Walker, Florida's deputy director of the historical division. "But the real lobbying is done by the local people. A Sarasota legislator doesn't care what a bureaucrat from Tallahassee thinks."

A centerpiece of this lobbying process is Preservation Day, an event cosponsored by the historical division and the Florida Trust for Historic Preservation in Tallahassee, the state capital. The number of people who show up for this event varies, but busloads of constituents often pour in. Armed with their "Pink Books," they fan out, meet with their state representatives and senators, and make the pitch for the recommended projects. Preservation Day includes a special reception held in a convenient, popular location for legislators. The Florida Trust prints the reception invitations, but it's the local constituents who follow up and personally urge their representatives to attend.

The strength of this grassroots approach is that it involves many people from a community telling their legislator that something is important to them. One of the things they are saying is, "This is how we want our community to look. We look to our representatives in Tallahassee to support our efforts."

Preservation Day

IN FACT, THE MOST IMPORTANT LOBBYING actually occurs through face-to-face meetings with legislators in their home districts—and through individual letters and phone calls. "Preservation Day" reinforces the spirit of those involved. "I love the process," says Kathy Monahan, community affairs administrator for the city of Tarpon Springs, Fla. "It helps build a preservation network. You meet other people working on similar projects and who are in the same boat. You learn what's going on around the state. It makes you feel you're part of a movement that's doing important work."

In June 1995, when word leaked out that Governor Lawton Chiles was planning to veto the $11.9 million approved earlier by the legislature for Special Category grants that year, an elaborate phone and fax "tree" set up by the state's preservation activists sprang into action. On one day alone, the governor's office received over a thousand phone calls from Floridians asking him not to veto the preservation and museum grants. At the end of this rapidly mobilized blitz, the governor decided not to veto the grants after all.

Florida's Other Funding Sources

T HE SPECIAL CATEGORY GRANTS PROGRAM is not Florida's only source of preservation money. The state has three others.

One is Florida's Historic Preservation Matching Grants Program, which provides grants of up to $50,000 for small preservation projects. Eligible activities include historic resource surveys and architectural feasibility studies. What's unusual about this program is that it has a dedicated source of funding: fictitious name registration fees. These are fees paid to the Florida Department of State by private entrepreneurs whenever they register the names of their unincorporated businesses with the state. Between 1990 and 1995, $1.5 million annually went into the matching grant program. In 1995, the annual allocation from the fees rose to $2 million.

> *"People are frightened about how quickly Florida's landscape is changing."*

Another source of money for preservation in Florida is fees from trademark renewals, limited partnerships, and other business transactions. These now generate $1.5 million annually for the Museum of Florida History Trust Fund, which makes grants for historical museums.

Finally, Florida has a $3 billion bond program, Preservation 2000. Created in 1990, this program authorized $300 million annually for ten years for the acquisition of large ecologically, archaeologically, and historically significant lands that are endangered. However, since one Florida legislature may not require future legislatures to fund specific programs, Preservation 2000 must be reauthorized each year. Its reapproval record thus far is six for six.

The legislature approved this program after public opinion polls revealed that 80 percent of Floridians favor environmental preservation. "People are frightened about how quickly Florida's landscape is changing," says Monahan.

Half of Preservation 2000's $300 million annual allocation goes into a program known as "CARL": Conservation And Recreation Lands; the remainder is split among five state agencies, with 10 percent, or $30 million annually, dedicated to the Florida Communities Trust, and 1.3%, or $3.9 million annually, earmarked for the Florida chapter of the Rails to Trails Conservancy.

The debt service on the Preservation 2000 bonds as well as brokerage and other costs incurred in floating the bonds are funded by Florida's "Documentary Stamp Tax" revenue. When people buy homes in Florida, they pay a fee for the filing of official documents needed for closings. At the same time, home sellers pay another tax.

While CARL emphasizes the acquisition of imminently endangered, ecologically important lands by the state to ensure their permanent protection, it also helps rescue significant archaeological and historic sites. Among sites assisted by CARL are the Key West Custom House, where the court of inquiry following the sinking of the battleship *Maine* in 1898 was held, and the DeSoto winter encampment of 1539. CARL also pays for archaeology and historic preservation staff who survey, evaluate, and help manage sites on lands purchased by the CARL program.

The Florida Communities Trust, meanwhile, awards grants on a competitive basis to local governments for the acquisition of parks and historic sites when such projects advance the goals of a local comprehensive plan. By law, all Florida municipalities must prepare such plans, the land-use, housing, and coastal zone management elements of which must include historic preservation objectives. Under the Florida Communities Trust program, towns with fewer than 10,000 people need not provide matching funds; larger communities must simply provide "some level" of match.

Reflections from George W. Percy

George W. Percy, director of Florida's Division of Historical Resources, shares his views below on the best way to promote historic preservation:

HISTORIC PRESERVATION HAS BEEN very successful during the last 25 years. Many of the movement's goals have been achieved. But in other respects, the movement is floundering and showing signs of weakness. Local preservation ordinances are under attack. Property owners are angry about regulation. Historic preservation is not well integrated into local land-use decision-making processes. There is substantial public apathy. There is a lack of broad-based public support. The preservation movement has devoted a lot of attention to historic preservation tools, but not much to making preservation seem more relevant to the lives of people.

We need better public information programs, initiatives that encourage appreciation on the part of the general public, not just historic preservationists. One of the preservation movement's great weaknesses is that it has become over-professionalized. We expect people to act on professional motives. But most people who own property don't think that way; they think in personal terms. We've got to put preservation onto a more personal level.

Preservation is best done by community consensus. People have to want to do it. You can't make them do it. Preservation does better as a community movement when it's achieved through consensus.

Our Special Category Grants Program personalizes preservation. It activates people to work together toward a concrete goal surrounding a particular historic building or site. Yes, you have to go back to the legislature every year, and some people see that as a drawback. And no, the program doesn't provide a dedicated revenue source. There are no guarantees. But I see these features as a strength. It means people have to remain energized.

It's best to think of historic preservation in personal, consensus terms rather than in scientific or statistical terms. Many people can listen to statistics or to the discussion of a preservation problem and say, "Well, that's a shame." But most won't take action unless it becomes a personal issue for them. In the national fight against "Disney's America" in the Northern Virginia Piedmont, networks were activated. Without that network, without those personal links, nothing would have happened. If a person lives in Miami and hears of a preservation problem in Pensacola, he may think it's a shame, but he won't become as personally involved as he would if a Miami landmark were threatened. The same thing is true with money for preservation; the process of getting it must be made relevant to people's lives.

The Politics of Florida's Preservation 2000

HOW HAS PRESERVATION 2000 managed to receive funding six years in a row during a period of cutbacks in other state programs?

"Floridians overwhelmingly support this program," says Audrey Ordenes of the state chapter of The Nature Conservancy. But she quickly points out that evidence of this support is not left to chance. A network of grassroots supporters can and does mobilize quickly during the legislative session if the program is threatened with cutbacks. "We are working to get legislators 'invested' in the program, so we prod local organizations to stage events with legislators. We inform local groups of lands about to be saved so they can arrange such events. We send out press releases. We get quotes from legislators on how wonderful the program is."

Advocates point to the program's economic benefits, noting that tourism, the state's largest industry, depends heavily on the quality of its natural environment and historic sites. A March 1995 study conducted for the state's tourism division revealed that many tourists were no longer returning to Florida due to its over-commercialization and disappearing green spaces. CARL advocates have used this study to underscore the urgency of saving endangered sites for economic as well as environmental reasons.

CARL advocates also make sure that legislators are kept abreast of the program's activities and public benefits. "We mail them pictures of saved sites. We invite them to special events celebrating a site's acquisition. These activities are a big part of advocacy," says Ordenes. The advocates also work closely with the media, arranging for meetings between program supporters and editorial boards, press releases, and letters-to-the-editor.

"Localizing the campaign is important," adds Melva McFie, The Nature Conservancy's communications director in Winter Park, Fla. "We don't talk to people about wilderness lands they've never seen, but about places they pass by every day. We do the same thing with newspapers. When I talk to an editor, I make sure I have a list of sites in the newspaper's market area. We also place a high priority on identifying grassroots activities. We've ransacked the best networking lists to find people who participate in phone trees. We have 700 people on our list now. That's a significant force." McFie also maintains a quarterly newsletter that features important projects funded by Preservation 2000. It is mailed to a well-selected list of state legislators and media representatives.

> *"Localizing the campaign is important. We don't talk to people about wilderness lands they've never seen, but about places they pass by every day."*

Around the Country

AS PRESERVATION ADVOCATES IN OTHER STATES HAVE DISCOVERED, A WIDE variety of funding sources can be tapped for historic preservation:

- general appropriations
- bond issues
- lotteries
- taxes on something else (real estate, mortgage registration fees, gambling, cigarettes, hotels/motels, and limited partnerships)
- license plate revenues
- linked deposits
- litigation proceeds

The challenge is to find a source of money that is not already claimed, and, as noted earlier, to help state lawmakers understand how investments in historic preservation can help to address other needs. Described below are examples of states that have used non-traditional funding sources for preservation.

Lottery Funds in Arizona

B Y A TWO-TO-ONE MARGIN, Arizonans approved a ballot-box initiative, Proposition 200, in 1990 that committed $20 million annually in state lottery funds for the "Arizona Heritage Fund." Historic preservation's annual share of this dedicated source of revenue is $1.7 million. This program is the result of a major campaign involving a broad-based coalition of diverse interests—environmentalists, preservationists, sportsmen, fishermen, park advocates and the League of Women voters; bipartisan political support; and a public opinion poll showing that 79 percent of Arizonans favored using lottery revenues to protect their heritage.

As in New Jersey, historic preservation benefitted from its alliance with the broader, "quality of life" movement in Arizona and from the sense of urgency surrounding the need to save rapidly vanishing resources. Fliers promoting the fund highlighted a number of alarming facts that underscored how quickly Arizona was losing its heritage. For example, they observed that "90 percent of our ecologically important riparian areas have been lost or seriously degraded."[3] The fliers also emphasized that the proposal would not add to the tax burden and that the preservation of Arizona's tourism and recreation industries, which respectively generated $5.6 billion and $2.6 billion annually, depended on the preservation of the state's scenic beauty and historic sites. "Arizona...has over 15,000 historic sites and 40,000 prehistoric cultural resources," said one flier. "If well protected, these sites would attract the many travelers interested in history and ancient cultures."[4]

A Gambling Tax in Colorado

W HILE MANY CITIZENS, preservationists included, have serious reservations about the long-term effects of gambling on a community, taxes on gambling have created a large pot of money for preservation in Colorado.

The Town Hall in Silverton, Colorado, seriously damaged by fire in 1992, has been restored with help from funds raised by the state's gambling tax.

JAMES LINDBERG

In 1990, Coloradans approved an amendment to the state constitution permitting gambling in three mountain towns: Central City, Black Hawk, and Cripple Creek. A year later, the state legislature enacted the Limited Gaming Act, which dedicates 28 percent of all tax revenues generated by gambling to historic preservation. Of the money thus raised, 20 percent is earmarked for preservation activities in the mountain towns; 80 percent, for preservation activities elsewhere in the state. In 1995, gambling generated a total of $10.6 million for preservation in Colorado.

Under this program, municipalities, nonprofits and even private individuals or companies may apply to one of three funding pools: a General Funding Pool, which provides grants ranging from $5,001 to $100,000; Mini-Grants, which offer grants of up to $5,000; and the Emergency Funding Pool, which provides funds to help save imminently endangered historic sites. The grants may be used to acquire and rehabilitate designated historic properties or sites, educate the public about historic preservation, or survey and plan for the protection of historic buildings and districts.

Grant agreements between the state and private individuals or for-profit businesses include "recapture" provisions. If a grant recipient uses the money to rehabilitate a property but then sells it within a year, the state recaptures 100 percent of the grant. Each year thereafter, the recaptured percentage drops by 20 percent.

The program is popular and has enabled the Colorado Historical Society to support hundreds of projects so far, including some that use preservation to address serious community issues. For example:

- In Denver, a $100,000 grant is helping to restore the historic Las Pazs Pool Hall to house a community-focused youth project. An economic development effort involving the African American community, the project involves the creation of a recreational facility for youth in the community.

- In Burlington, a $100,000 grant is helping to rehabilitate the historic Winegar Building, now a vacant, deteriorating building located on a prime corner in the downtown. When renovated, the building will house a ground-floor restaurant, a small museum with Kit Carson memorabilia, and an upper-floor bed and breakfast. It is expected to generate a $26,000 increase in local property and sales tax revenues and ten new full-time jobs.

- In Silverton, a $177,500 grant is helping the town restore its most significant structure, the historic Town Hall. A National Historic Landmark seriously damaged by fire in 1992, the building's restoration has served as the rallying point for a community revitalization effort in this historic mining community.

- In Grand Junction, a grant is helping to restore the historic train depot. This mixed-use project is aimed at revitalizing a two-block area surrounding the train station. It includes a 400-seat, upscale restaurant and an outlet for miniature train collectors. Over 1,000 high-school students volunteered for this project, scraping paint, scooping up pigeon droppings, and removing damaged roof tiles.

Over 1,000 high-school students volunteered to save the historic train depot, scraping paint, scooping up pigeon droppings, and removing damaged roof tiles.

The Rhea-Applegate House's spectacular rehabilitation was made possible with grants awarded by the New Jersey Historic Trust.

A Mortgage Registration Tax in Kansas

TAXES PAID WHEN HOUSES are bought and sold help to support a statewide Heritage Trust Fund authorized by the Kansas legislature in 1990. The law allowed the state to raise Kansas' mortgage registration tax by one penny—26 cents for every $100 of mortgage registered instead of 25 cents—and to dedicate the added revenues to historic preservation.

GARRY W. STONE

HARRIETTE HAWKINS

The Fund generates between $500,000 and $600,000 annually and supports small rehabilitation and planning projects. Grants range from $5,000 to $75,000, with the average around $45,000. Grantees must match them on an 80–20 basis. Small towns are exempted from this requirement, however, as it is very difficult for them to meet it.

Kansas' historic preservation department has simplified the grant application process and eased some of the program's earlier requirements, which were modeled after National Park Service rules. For example, the state has done away with a requirement that people or organizations receiving grants sign 15-year covenants. Now it simply requires them to agree to maintain an assisted property for at least five years. If the property owner sells the property before then, he must return all or a portion of the grant to the state.

Like Colorado's grant program, Kansas' is popular. It puts the state preservation department in the positive position of being able to assist property owners. The fund has generated good will and favorable publicity for the department, which arranges for local ceremonies when grant agreements for local projects are executed. Public officials, civic leaders, and the public are invited to these events and are thus exposed to historic preservation's contributions to local communities.

A Real Estate Transfer Tax in Arkansas

ARKANSAS LEVIES A REAL ESTATE transfer tax to support its state heritage fund. Under this program, $2.20 for every $1,000 worth of real estate sold goes into a state grant fund for natural and cultural resources. The program has generated $42 million since 1987. Of this, slightly over $4 million has been dedicated to preservation projects. The state preservation office currently receives about $600,000 annually from this source and uses the money to support local community revitalization projects. Among other activities, the fund has provided "model business grants" to help Main Street businesses upgrade their appearance and even improve their merchandise displays.

Tax Increment Financing in Texas

Texas permits localities not only to levy hotel taxes but also to designate a percentage of these taxes to historic preservation activities that help to improve a city's appeal to tourists.

TAX INCREMENT FINANCING (TIF) is a mechanism many states authorize to help local governments fund areas specially designated for redevelopment. Depending on the state's enabling legislation, TIF can be used to pay for physical improvements in a downtown—e.g., new sidewalks, the undergrounding of utilities, a parking garage—as well as for the administrative costs of downtown revitalization programs. Here's how the TIF works: The community assesses the property values within the TIF district at the outset of a program. The sum of these values becomes the baseline. To the extent that tax revenues generated as a result of the local revitalization program exceed the baseline, they can be plowed back into the program instead of reverting to the city's general revenues. Alternatively, the local government may decide to float bonds to pay for the revitalization activities, with the extra taxes generated by revitalization used to pay off the bonds.

Many local Main Street revitalization programs have used TIF. (*For more information on the Main Street Program concept, see Chapter 7.*)

The Texas state enabling law permits localities not only to levy hotel taxes but also to designate a percentage of the revenue thus raised for historic preservation activities that help to improve a city's appeal to tourists. In Galveston, the Galveston Historical Foundation received $123,000, or 33 percent of the city's hotel tax revenues, in 1995 for tourism-related preservation activities. The Foundation has used these funds to pay for the printing of brochures, advertising, press releases, and the salaries of public relations professionals. The Foundation's promotion of preservation activities has generated two million dollars worth of publicity for the city.

Lottery-Funded Grants in Iowa

I OWA HAS A LOTTERY-FUNDED GRANTS PROGRAM, the Resources Enhancement and Protection Act (REAP). Passed by the state legislature in 1989, the act authorized $200 million over ten years for activities aimed at protecting the state's natural and historic resources. Such activities include historic building renovations, soil conservation, open-space preservation, heritage education and park acquisition.

Twenty-eight percent of the REAP monies goes toward open-space preservation; 20 percent, toward soil and water enhancement; 15 percent, for city parks and recreation; nine percent, toward state land management; and five percent, toward historic preservation. In 1996 the legislature appropriated $8.5 million for REAP, of which $425,000 went into matching preservation grants. The legislature is expected to approve $10 million in 1997 for REAP. Private individuals as well as nonprofit organizations and local preservation agencies are eligible for REAP grants.

As in New Jersey and Arizona, a broad coalition of diverse interests—environmentalists, farmland preservationists, historic preservationists, sportsmen, fishermen, and the League of Women Voters—teamed up to push for this program's enactment in the first place. Here, too, the public's concern over the rapid loss of Iowa's resources—nearly half of the state's legendary topsoil has been lost—propelled the REAP program into law. Since the program began, the state has saved over 18,000 acres of farmland and open space.

Nearly half of Iowa's legendary topsoil has been lost.

Litigation and Real Estate Proceeds in Alabama

I N 1992, A FEDERAL COURT found the Transcontinental Gas Pipeline Company guilty of violating provisions in the National Historic Preservation Act and slapped the company with a $14 million fine. Under an agreement worked out with the state, $9.5 million of this was earmarked for the Alabama Historical Commission; $4.5 million, for the state attorney general's office to enforce activities related to environmental and cultural resource protection laws.

Since then, the Commission has dedicated $4 million of the $9.5 million to preservation projects in the ten counties affected by the gas pipeline and $5 million to a small grants program, the Alabama Cultural Resources Preservation Trust Fund. Interest earnings on the $5 million have helped to fund local projects since 1993.

In 1991, the Alabama legislature enacted a law permitting the Historical Commission to buy and sell property and to invest the proceeds in stocks and bonds. Under previous law, the Commission could purchase and rescue historic properties but could not resell them without following cumbersome state regulations governing the disposal of "surplus" property. Earnings from investments made under the new law sustain a flexible revolving fund: HELP ("Historic Endangered Landmarks Program").

The HELP program enables the Commission to rescue endangered historic properties by buying them, placing protective covenants on them and then selling them to the highest bidder. The program is not large, but it has helped to save about 14 properties, mostly in small towns and rural areas that lack formal preservation organizations. By maintaining a county-by-county, statewide inventory of endangered properties, the commission can monitor the status of these properties and facilitate their purchase and restoration by private entities. Approximately 300 endangered sites are listed in the inventory.

HELP also operates a small emergency fund that allows the state to provide funds for the stabilization of imminently threatened properties. The state has used this fund to make emergency repairs on a property, even without having legal control over it, in cases involving property owners who are unable or unwilling to make necessary repairs. The emergency fund usually requires matching funds.

Litigation Proceeds in Virginia for an Environmental Foundation

Virginia used settlement funds from legal disputes to establish a permanent foundation, the Virginia Environmental Endowment.

V IRGINIA HAS USED SETTLEMENT FUNDS from legal disputes to establish a permanent foundation, the Virginia Environmental Endowment, that makes grants for environmental and preservation projects.

The endowment dates to 1977, when a court fined the Allied Chemical Corporation $13.2 million for polluting the James River with Kepone. Rather than directing Allied to pay this fine to the government, the judge urged the corporation to explore ways to make the fine benefit the people of Virginia. The result: Allied capitalized the Virginia Environmental Endowment (VEE) with $8 million. Since 1977, Virginia courts have imposed fees on other corporate polluters and channelled this money into the endowment.

The VEE now makes grants annually to support environmental projects. Although the endowment favors organizations concerned with the natural environment, it has funded public policy and public education projects benefitting historic preservation. These have included a series of op-ed articles on environmental issues for Virginia's print and broadcast media, research into Virginia laws affecting the environment, and efforts to provide appropriate balance to debates over private property rights and the public interest.

Preservation North Carolina's successful revolving fund has helped restore hundreds of buildings, including the Griffen House in Washington County.

A Revolving Fund in North Carolina

THE HISTORIC PRESERVATION FOUNDATION of North Carolina in Raleigh, provides the best known and most experienced model of a statewide revolving fund for historic preservation. The Foundation capitalized this program in 1977 with a private foundation grant of $35,000. Since then, the Foundation has rescued 245 endangered historic properties, all of which are under protective covenants. The Fund operates by purchasing properties—or more often, by purchasing options on them—then placing covenants on the buildings and reselling them. The program favors options over outright purchases because options require less money and often accomplish the same objectives as a full purchase.

State Income Tax Check-Offs in Illinois and Nebraska

ILLINOIS TRIED USING STATE INCOME tax check-offs to raise money for historic preservation but was disappointed in the results. The program generated only $40,000 its first year. Under the authorizing state statute, a cause to which state taxpayers may dedicate their taxes must generate at least $100,000 annually in order to remain on state tax forms. Due to insufficient time to publicize the preservation check-off option and a $10-per-person limit on donations, preservation failed to meet this requirement.

The check-off concept is currently being examined in Nebraska, where a historic preservation task force created by the state legislature has recommended that taxpayers be permitted to voluntarily check off a contribution of $1 or $2 for historic preservation purposes. It is hoped that this concept will experience greater success here and that the monies thus raised will sustain a Nebraska Heritage Trust fund.

Preservation North Carolina has rescued 245 endangered historic properties, all of which are under protective covenants.

Heritage Areas in New York

A NUMBER OF STATES HAVE CREATED SO-CALLED "HERITAGE AREA" programs as a way of linking historic preservation to local economic development. A heritage area is a grouping of buildings, parks, trails, neighborhoods or other historic places that relate to a specific historical or cultural theme—e.g., labor and industry, transportation, social reform movements, maritime trade, immigration and the like.

One of the first states to create heritage areas was New York, whose Office of Parks, Recreation and Historic Preservation established an Urban Cultural Parks Program in 1977. With financial and technical assistance from the state, and in partnership with the private sector, 22 New York communities have created 15 cultural parks. Now called the "Heritage Area System," the program provides funds to local communities for the interpretation of heritage areas and for the rehabilitation of historic structures. The money comes primarily from New York's Environmental Protection Fund (EPF), which was created by the state legislature in 1993 to provide a permanent revenue source for parks, open space acquisition, and historic preservation. In Fiscal Year 1996-97, the EPF made $8 million available to municipalities and nonprofit organizations. Of this, $4.5 million was earmarked for parks; $2.7 million, for historic preservation and Heritage Area System projects; and the balance, for other state and local projects.

One of the most successful heritage areas is Rochester, New York's Urban Cultural Park, which features a laser, light and sound show with music and theatrical lighting to illuminate a 96-foot waterfall and the massive walls of the Genessee River Gorge. The city has created an interpretive center at Rochester's "High Falls" so the public can learn about Rochester's development during the 1800's as a milling and manufacturing center. Besides the spectacularly beautiful waterfall, the cultural park includes: the Brown's Race Historic District, where the Brown brothers built a 1,300-foot-long raceway to attract industry to the area in 1816; an atrium next to the gorge where local groups can host banquets, receptions, dances, meetings and "happy hours;" the Triphammer Forge, an archaeological site; a restored water wheel; a microbrewery; and a number of renovated warehouse buildings. Small businesses, offices, and restaurants have moved into historic buildings in the district, which the city has actively promoted. Several corporations, including the Rochester Gas and Electric Company, have supported this city-state partnership aimed at urban revitalization.

The heritage area concept pioneered by New York has generated such widespread interest around the country that a number of states are developing heritage area programs. Pennsylvania and Massachusetts have longstanding programs while Maryland has a new one. *(For more information about heritage areas, contact the New York State Office of Parks, Recreation & Historic Preservation, Empire State Plaza, Bldg., #1, Albany, NY 12238; or the National Center for Heritage Development, P. O. Box 33011, Washington, D.C. 20033-0011. Tel: 202/588-6204 or -6000.)*

An Environmental Bond Issue in New York

O N AUGUST 1, 1996, New York Governor George E. Pataki signed legislation authorizing a $1.75 billion environmental bond act intended to preserve open spaces, clean up waterways, and pay for other environmental projects. If the bond is approved by voters in November 1996, $200 million of this money will be available to purchase land to protect the state's water supply, restore state parks, and rehabilitate historic sites.

New York voters rejected two similar environmental bond issues in 1990 and 1992, and it would be hard to predict the outcome of this one. Governor Pataki has announced his intention to campaign aggressively for the bond proposal.

In Vermont, an unusual coalition of historic preservationists formed in 1987 to work together.

Vermont's Housing and Conservation Trust Fund

T HE VERMONT HOUSING AND CONSERVATION TRUST fund uses real estate transfer taxes and the state's bonding authority to pay for farmland preservation, open space conservation, historic preservation and affordable housing. The combination of these goals reflects the creation of an unusual coalition of historic preservationists, farmland preservationists, and affordable housing advocates that formed in 1987 to work together. Between 1987 and 1996, the Vermont legislature has approved $95 million for the grants and loans provided through this program. *(For more information on this program, see Chapter 6 on Rural Preservation).*

Various Sources in Florida

Preservationists in Florida have tapped various nooks and crannies in state law for preservation funding. Besides benefitting from the Special Category Grants and CARL programs discussed earlier (see pp. 71–76), historic preservation has used other funding sources as well. The Florida Historic Preservation Trust Fund receives monies not only from the Special Category Grants Program but also from a variety of sources, including fees paid by developers to mitigate environmental damage and proceeds from parimutuel betting events. An important feature of this Fund, according to E.L. "Roy" Hunt, a preservation law expert at the University of Florida, is that money unspent at the end of each fiscal year does not revert to the state's general fund, as is true elsewhere. Such a "use it or lose it" situation often makes state officials feel pressured to commit funds quickly before the beginning of a new fiscal year lest they lose the benefit of these funds.

Commentary

The provision of a stable revenue source for historic preservation is an essential ingredient of any well-rounded state program. But a prerequisite for state funding is a recognition that the preservation of historic sites and districts confers economic benefits on the state. As noted at the outset of this chapter, evidence that historic preservation contributes to job creation, economic development, and tax revenues abounds.

In many states, tourism is a top generator of jobs and revenues, and in virtually all of these states, historic sites figure prominently. As Arthur Frommer, the famous travel writer and author of Frommer *Guidebooks*, has observed, "Every study of travel motivations has shown that an interest in the achievements of the past is among the three major reasons why people travel. The other two are rest or recreation and the desire to view great natural sights."[5] Frommer adds: "Tourism does not go to a city that has lost its soul."[6] He could easily have said the same thing about states. As we saw earlier in this chapter, New Jersey and Arizona have recognized the link between well-preserved historic sites and the health of their tourism industries, and they have committed state funds to the preservation of these sites.

Forty states now have "Main Street" programs that emphasize the rehabilitation of historic buildings in older downtowns as an economic development tool. Wisconsin's Main Street Program, one of the most successful, has generated more than 4,700 new jobs, over 900 new businesses, and about 1,200 rehabilitation projects since it began seven years ago.[7]

These are just a few of countless examples of returns on investment from state-funded preservation programs.

The states that seem to be leaders in funding historic preservation have not simply recognized the link between historic preservation and economic development; they have also focused on the speed at which they are losing an irreplaceable heritage. In New Jersey, the state had lost over half of its entire stock of historic buildings to urban renewal, highways, neglect and other causes before expanding the Green Acres Program to embrace historic preservation. In Nebraska, a new report discloses that of the state's 5,000 recorded archaeological sites, 87 percent have been seriously damaged or destroyed.[8]

Thus a sense of loss, the need to move quickly, and a recognition of the opportunities preservation offers for economic development are all providing the impetus for states to commit funds to historic preservation.

CHAPTER 3

State Tax Incentives

State Tax Incentives

I N 1990, BUILDINGS ON THREE OF THE FOUR CORNERS OF SPOKANE, WASH-
ington's Carnegie Square sat completely vacant. Their windows were broken or boarded up. Suspicious fires occurred periodically, drug dealing regularly. The old Buena Vista apartment building provided a roost for a
thousand pigeons. The Square, named after the historic Carnegie Library that
faces it, looked sad and seedy.

Today, these historic buildings have been completely rehabilitated and are now
fully occupied. The once tawdry looking area has become a vibrant urban neighborhood. A bagel bakery, a fabric shop, and several other businesses have moved
in. One renovated building, a wallflower on the real estate market for seven years,
now has three tenants clamoring to lease space in it. The library building, now
used for commercial purposes, will pay $7,084 annually in property taxes to the
city starting in 2005. That's $6,174 more a year than it would have contributed
had it not been rehabilitated and reused.

Ron Wells, the local developer who renovated three of the Square's buildings,
credits Washington's historic preservation tax incentives with the turnaround:
"These incentives made all the difference in the world. They were crucial during
the early years of this project, when normally it's so difficult to generate a positive
cash flow."

Under Washington State's "Special Valuation for Improvements to Historic
Property" program, local governments have the option of abating property taxes
on rehabilitated historic structures for ten years. Spokane is one of 29 localities
that have chosen to do so.

Wells has completed 25 rehabilitation projects during the last 17 years. He has
elected to do most of these projects in Washington, rather than nearby Idaho
where he once lived, because of the incentives. "Idaho offers no incentives. After
we rehabbed one building there, the property taxes jumped from $3,000 to
$22,000. The taxes stayed at $3,000 following our rehab of a comparable building
in Spokane. Without the incentives offered by the state and adopted by the city
and county, this turnaround at Carnegie Square would not have occurred."

After local citizens suggested at a recent city council meeting that Spokane
withdraw from the state program on the grounds that it shifts a heavier tax burden onto other taxpayers, Teresa Brum, the city's historic preservation officer,
pointed out that assessed values on 43 historic buildings rehabilitated with the aid

**Spokane's old
Carnegie Library
has been
rehabilitated and
adaptively reused
with the help of
Washington
State's historic
preservation tax
incentives.**

of the incentives will jump from $8,053,800 to $36,021,066 in the 11th year. Over a third of these buildings were vacant—or about to become so—before their owners decided to rehabilitate them. The $28 million these owners spent to renovate the buildings generated $235,344 in sales tax revenues for the city, according to Brum.

Sadie Charlene Cooney, Spokane County Assessor, believes that in the long run, historic properties rehabilitated with the help of the Special Valuation program provide a net gain to the city: "If you are going to have historic preservation in your community, you must offer incentives to encourage it. If you want to entice businesses into your community, you must make it attractive."

BLAIR SEITZ

Rationale for Incentives

THIRTY SEVEN STATES[1] NOW OFFER TAX INCENTIVES to encourage property owners to maintain and renovate old and historic buildings. While each incentive program differs, most fall into one of two categories:

- state enabling laws permitting municipalities to offer *local property tax abatement;* or
- state income tax *credits.*

Although each state has its own reasons for offering preservation tax incentives, many states might agree with those given by Florida in a brochure promoting a constitutional amendment authorizing such incentives in 1992:

> The [property tax exemption] program is designed to encourage private investment in historic properties, neighborhoods, and traditional commercial districts. If the exemption is effective, the level of this investment will be substantially increased over that which would have occurred without the exemption. At the end of the exemption period, the fabric of the community will have been improved and the community will experience a substantial increase in property tax revenue over that which would have been generated otherwise. The improvement of declining commercial areas and neighborhoods has a beneficial effect on the entire community—preserving tangible links with its roots, improving its image and fostering civic pride, and improving its overall economic well-being.

Interest in preservation tax incentives has grown significantly in recent years. Many preservationists believe it is easier to get properties listed on national, state or local historical registers if a state offers incentives. Even if the incentives are not actually used, their mere existence on the books can significantly enhance the prospects for protecting historic buildings. Increasingly, communities feel they must be in a position to offer "carrots" as well as "sticks"—tax breaks as well as land-use regulations—in their local preservation programs. Communities need ways to alleviate competitive disadvantages sometimes experienced by owners of historic properties.

Preservation incentives can help to level the playing field upon which older cities and towns, major repositories of historic buildings, compete with new development being built ever further away from city and town centers. Through road construction, water and sewer

JOHN EVANS

(Opposite page) A historic street in Pennsylvania. (This page) Carnegie Square in Spokane, Washington. This once dilapidated corner building now bustles with businesses. Washington's preservation tax incentives were instrumental in the Square's rehabilitation.

line extensions, and tax subsidies, states frequently add to the many advantages that new suburban development already has in its favor—vast expanses of land for free parking, a predisposition among lenders to finance new construction, and the lack of such requirements as lead paint removal and contaminated site clean-up. Richard J. Roddewig, a leading expert on historic preservation economics, observes that the private marketplace never operates independently of government action and policy:

> Banking laws, the Internal Revenue Code, real property taxes, building codes, zoning regulations—all of these aspects of government regulation profoundly affect the real estate development process, and all of them fundamentally affect the cost, character, and amount of real estate investment. Government policy must be scrutinized continually for its effect on preservation. The danger in the current determination to foster private sector investment is that some types of economic enterprises will be given unfair "most favored investment" status. Preservationists must make sure that investment in the renovation and continued use of historic buildings is not slighted.[2]

A well-designed incentive program can make the difference in whether a historic building is preserved or destroyed. A poorly designed program can give the illusion that the state favors private-sector investment in historic preservation but provide little, if any, real stimulus to preservation.

This chapter discusses general issues that states need to consider in shaping successful tax incentive programs. It examines two state programs in greater detail: one offering local property tax abatement; the other, a state income tax credit. Finally, we identify elements important to the success of a state preservation tax incentive program.

Property Tax Abatement or Income Tax Credits?

IN CREATING A PRESERVATION TAX INCENTIVE PROGRAM or fine-tuning an existing one, states must answer a variety of questions. Is it better to offer state income tax credits or local property tax abatement? If the state requires taxpayers to invest a certain amount of money in the rehabilitation of a historic property, will this shut out low- or middle-income people? How can the state make incentives generous enough to be meaningful but not overly so? How does the state guard against program abuse? How will incentives affect the state's budget? Other taxpayers? How can the state ensure that incentives benefit the public at large and not just a few property owners?

In general, property tax relief seems to be more effective than state income tax credits as a preservation incentive. In an essay on preservation economics, Roddewig explains why such relief is so important. While his analysis focuses on commercial buildings, it also applies to residential structures:

> The property tax is one of the largest single expense items for owners of new and old buildings alike. Thus it is a logical place for the government to intervene...Owners of older landmark buildings may devote substantially more than 14 percent of their total operating income to real estate taxes.

> Without a doubt, the American system of assessing the value of, and levying the property tax on, historic structures is a significant threat to the continued use of many income-producing landmark buildings across the country. Few preservationists understand why parking lots are so often more profitable than the older buildings they replace. If they would investigate the differences in assessed valuation of and property taxes on the historic building and on the subsequent parking lot, they would quickly understand.

Through road construction, water and sewer line extensions, and tax subsidies, states frequently add to the many advantages that new suburban development already has in its favor.

The American real property tax system assesses the value of the underlying land as well as the value of the improvements on a piece of property. In the case of small, older landmarks on downtown parcels, the value of the underlying land may be substantially greater than the value of the improvements.[3]

If the land underneath a historic building is zoned for high-rise construction, it will probably be more valuable than the building itself. This will encourage the owner to tear it down and build new. It may also make it difficult for prospective buyers to obtain financing to renovate the structure.[4]

In many areas of the country, local property taxes are considerably higher than state income taxes. This is why property tax abatement enabled by state government is often a superior incentive to a state income tax credit. If such abatement is predictable and substantial, it can be particularly helpful as a cushion against the uncertainties that typically accompany commercial building renovation. Another factor in favor of property tax relief is that property owners almost always pay property taxes, whereas they may not have sufficiently high incomes to be taxed by the state. Some states do not even impose income taxes.

In some areas of the country, however, the opposite is true: Property taxes are relatively low and state income taxes are high. Property tax relief is therefore less meaningful; state tax relief, more so. A few states, such as Maryland and North Carolina, offer both types of incentives. What works best depends on the "highness" or "lowness" of local property and state income taxes, so these tax rates are among the first factors a state should consider.

If a state wants to permit local governments to offer property tax abatement for historic structures, it must determine whether its constitution allows this. Some state constitutions prohibit such abatement on the grounds that taxes for any given class of property must be uniform, and all real estate is generally considered one class. The constitutional principle is that property owners should be treated equally, with no disproportionate benefits or burdens for individual taxpayers. Citizens in several states, including Texas, Georgia, and Florida, have overcome this legal barrier by amending their state constitutions to permit property tax abatement for historic properties. In these three states, voters approved the amendments by referendum. In New Mexico, however, the state attorney general declared such tax abatement unconstitutional, prompting the state to offer an income tax credit instead.

Another question to settle is what types of historic properties should be eligible for the incentives. Many states have chosen to focus on owner-occupied residential structures because these properties cannot take advantage of the federal 20 percent rehabilitation tax credit. (See sidebar, p. 103.) Illinois now allows owner-occupied housing condominiums and cooperatives as well as single-family houses to qualify for the state's "homeowner's assessment tax freeze." Louisiana allows duplexes as well as condominiums to participate. Since many historic residential properties are located in multi-unit buildings, it makes sense to include condominiums.

If the land underneath a historic building is zoned for high-rise construction, this will encourage the owner to tear it down and build new.

Minimum Investment Requirements

ANOTHER QUESTION IS WHETHER TO REQUIRE A MINIMUM INVESTMENT. How much money should a property owner have to invest in the rehabilitation of a historic structure in order to qualify for the incentive? Some states—e.g., Arizona—do not require taxpayers using the incentives to make any improvements to a property at all. In their view, the public benefits if historic property owners simply commit to maintaining historic buildings for

Why Provide Tax Incentives?

by Harry K. Schwartz

The following text, excerpted from an article by Harry K. Schwartz, explains why preservation tax incentives are important and offers two proposals for making state income tax credits more effective. Mr. Schwartz is Of Counsel to the law firm of Shulman, Rogers, Gandal, Pordy & Ecker, P.A., of Rockville, Md. During the past two years, he has conducted in-depth research into preservation tax incentives. The complete article, "State Income Tax Incentives for Historic Homeownership," appeared in the June 1996 of **Preservation Law Reporter**. *Reprinted with permission.*

OVER THE DECADES SINCE WORLD WAR II, a combination of social and economic forces, abetted in no small measure by government policies and programs, has produced a steady outmigration of population and business activity from large and small urban areas. In 1991, there were over nine million vacant year-round housing units in the U.S.—in other words, about one in every 12 homes.[5] Left behind in the surge to the suburbs and exurbs is an enormous (but dwindling) inventory of sound housing stock and older commercial buildings, much of which has historic or architectural importance, or both.

The economic benefits of reclaiming these buildings and the existing infrastructure which supports them have been persuasively recited elsewhere.[6] It is certainly arguable that in a truly efficient capital market, uninfluenced by government subsidy and policy bias, investment would naturally flow to the rehabilitation and reuse of these buildings. However, the capital markets for real estate have been extensively tampered with by government at all levels. Investment decisions have been greatly influenced by substantial subsidies provided for sprawl, particularly in the form of highway construction, and the demolition of existing building stock through the well-intentioned, but ultimately catastrophic bulldozing of established urban centers and neighborhoods under federal urban renewal and highway construction programs. The result has been a spiralling cycle of blight, crime, and decline in urban tax base and services.

Tax incentives cannot reverse demographic trends, restore fiscal solvency to cities and towns, fight crime or improve education. What they can do is provide, at the margin, a salutary corrective to the institutionalized bias toward the suburbanization of population and business activity. In addition, where incentives are linked to the appropriate rehabilitation and reuse of buildings of historic or architectural value, the social benefits of historic preservation—both tangible and intangible—can be realized.

* * *

Two Modest Proposals. State income tax incentives for historic homeownership can be made both more effective and more equitable by adopting two programmatic initiatives contained in the federal historic homeownership tax credit legislation: the Historic Rehabilitation Mortgage Credit Certificate, and the developer pass-through provision.

Historic Rehabilitation Mortgage Credit Certificates. Tax credits do not work well for persons with moderate incomes; they do not work at all for persons with modest incomes. Lacking sufficient state tax liability to use the credit, such persons are effectively excluded from the benefits of state homeownership income tax credit programs.

That is not an equitable result. Families with incomes below $50,000, for many of whom homeownership is a viable option, simply do not owe enough state income tax to make effective use of a tax credit. In order to remedy this gap in coverage of the credit, and make it more useful to taxpayers of moderate means, state laws should permit persons who cannot use the credit to convert it into a mortgage credit certificate which could be used to obtain an interest rate reduction on their home mortgage loan.

Persons entitled to the credit would be able to elect to receive in lieu of the credit a Historic Rehabilitation Mortgage Credit Certificate in the face amount of the credit to which that person is entitled. The election would be made at the time of the receipt by the taxpayer of the final approval of the historic rehabilitation project.

The taxpayer would then transfer the certificate (evidencing a right to claim a credit in an amount equal to the applicable percentage of the qualified rehabilitation expenditures) to the mortgage lender in exchange for a reduced interest rate on the home mortgage loan. The mortgage lender would be permitted to reduce its own state income or franchise tax liability by the face amount of the certificate. The lender would then be required to apply the benefit of the reduction in its state tax liability to "buy down" the interest rate on the mortgage using a formula approved by the state. Where state law provides for recapture of a credit in the event the homeowner sells the building within a specified period, such recapture would not apply to a lender using a mortgage credit certificate.

Mortgage credit certificates could be used by homeowners who are rehabilitating their homes "in place." Upon completing the rehabilitation and securing the certificate, the property could be refinanced at a lower interest rate obtained through the certificate. However, the certificates could also be used by homeowners purchasing a newly rehabilitated home, where state law provides for a developer pass-through.

Developer Pass-Through. The most efficient way to carry out historic rehabilitation of housing stock, both for lower-income as well as more affluent homebuyers, is through non-profit and for-profit developers. Rehabilitating a historic building in accordance with the Secretary of the Interior's Standards is not an easy matter for the uninitiated. For any significant volume of rehabilitation to take place (without placing intolerable burdens on the State Historic Preservation Officers), a knowledgeable, professional industry of historic preservation developers and contractors will have to come into being.

But, unfortunately, the state tax credit laws now in place were not drafted to accommodate a situation in which a developer acquires a historic building, rehabilitates in accordance with the Secretary's Standards, and sells it to a homebuyer. These laws tend to require that the person who performs the rehabilitation and the person who claims the tax credit as the owner-occupier of the residence be the same.

If, however, the developer were permitted or required to pass through the credit to the homebuyer, the program would become far more effective. It would enable non-profit developers, using the Mortgage Credit Certificate, to acquire deteriorated historic housing and rehabilitate it to provide homeownership opportunities for lower-income persons. It would provide a stimulus to speculative rehabilitation for more affluent homebuyers. And, given the superfluity of vacant historic housing in most urban settings, it would accomplish these objectives without displacing low-income residents.

Conclusion. Although state income tax credits for historic homeownership are not now widely used, a number of states presently provide such incentives. Some are more generous than others, and have had more success in spurring rehabilitation activity. However, all such incentives are severely limited by the fact that many taxpayers do not have enough state income tax liability to make effective use of the credits for substantial rehabilitation. In addition, lower income persons are unable to make any use of the credits.

These problems could be addressed by adopting a Historic Rehabilitation Mortgage Credit Certificate program. Such a program would permit homeowners and homebuyers to convert state income tax credits that they cannot use into certificates which can be used to lower the interest rate on their home mortgages. In addition, provision should be made to permit non-profit and for-profit developers to pass through the historic rehabilitation tax credit to the homebuyer. This would greatly facilitate the rehabilitation of historic buildings for homeownership by lower income as well as more affluent homebuyers.

a certain period of time. Washington and Louisiana, on the other hand, stipulate that property owners invest a substantial sum of money in the renovation of historic buildings: an amount equal to 25 percent of the property's total value. In Florida, rehabilitation expenses must equal 50 percent of the property value. In Georgia, renovations made on commercial buildings must increase property values by 100 percent.

Several states have eschewed the minimum investment requirement—sometimes called the "substantial rehabilitation test"—used for the federal rehab tax credit. Under that test, a taxpayer's rehabilitation expenses must exceed the greater of $5,000 or an amount equal to the property's "adjusted basis"—that is, the price originally paid for the property and the cost of any previous improvements, minus depreciation and the value of the land. Except in extremely depressed areas or outside of metropolitan areas, a person must invest considerably more than $5,000 to pass this test. Most states with minimum investment requirements have opted for a lower bar. One reason is that they want to encourage the rehabilitation of owner-occupied residential properties—the federal credit applies only to "income-producing" properties like rental housing or commercial projects—and it is often very difficult for a homeowner to spend enough money on a renovation to equal the "basis" of the building. Another reason is that many properties warrant only minor renovations and the state does not want to encourage more work than is really necessary.

If a state calls for a large minimum investment, it may prevent lower-income people from using the incentives. This does not mean that low- or middle-income people will fail to benefit from the incentives—tax base improvements brought about by restored neighborhoods frequently benefit lower-income people along with the rest of a community—it simply means that they cannot personally use the incentives. If a city's middle or upper-middle class

has fled to the suburbs and the city wants to bring it back to help pay for city services, and if the building stock in certain neighborhoods is so rundown that it needs major improvements, it may make good sense to set a high threshold for the tax incentives.

New Mexico, which allows property owners to take a state income tax credit on 50 percent of their rehab expenses, has no minimum investment requirement. Robyn Powell of the state's historic preservation office thinks that the absence of a high minimum expenditure requirement opens the program to wider use by middle-class households: "Most of the projects we approve range from about $2,000 to $10,000. Some are as small as $200. People can bite off one project at a time—window replacements, for example—and then come back to us later with a roof project or something else." The state has not had the resources to conduct a formal analysis of the program, but Powell believes that most of its users are middle-income people working on smaller projects.

Because of a $25,000 cap on the amount of rehabilitation expenses against which the credit may be claimed, however, the New Mexico program has not induced developers to carry out large-scale projects on major buildings, even though there are some important projects that the state would like to encourage.

One way to make it easier for people with more modest incomes to meet minimum investment requirements is to give them more time to complete rehabilitation work. Utah gives homeowners claiming its 20 percent credit three full years to meet the state's $10,000 "sub rehab" test. Washington State allows property owners two years to meet its requirement that rehabilitation expenditures equal 25 percent of the property's value. Harry K. Schwartz, a Maryland-based attorney who has analyzed state tax credit programs, suggests that states permit taxpayers with incomes below a certain level to convert credits into a

COURTESY GEORGIA HISTORIC PRESERVATION DIVISION

Even modest houses, such as this one, can take advantage of Georgia's property tax abatement for historic rehabilitations.

mortgage credit certificate that could be used to obtain lower interest rates on their home mortgages from private lenders. (See p. 94 for more details.)

Size of Incentive

ANOTHER ISSUE IS THE GENEROSITY OF THE INCENTIVE ITSELF. How big should it be? How long should it last? The incentive should be generous enough to motivate property owners to make investments in preservation that they might not otherwise make, but it should not be so large that it shifts an undue tax burden onto other taxpayers. Arizona allows a reduction of up to 50 percent in property tax assessments on historic properties. Georgia, Illinois and Florida permit taxpayers to exclude from their assessments the entire value of any improvements made for a certain period of time. In other words, property taxes are frozen at the level they were before the property owner undertook the rehabilitation. The freeze can last as few as five years, as in Louisiana and Montana, or as many as ten years, as in Washington and Maryland.

States can decide whether to apply property tax abatement statewide or to limit its use to areas whose governments opt to adopt such abatement. Arizona and Georgia make the property tax abatement available on a statewide basis. Communities in these states do not have the ability to opt out or to tailor the program to their circumstances.[7] In most "local option" states, cities or counties that elect to offer abatement have the freedom to work out the details of their own programs. Illinois is a hybrid: every taxing district, including school districts, is required to provide the abatement unless it opts out.

Controls

TO ENSURE THAT THE PUBLIC AS A WHOLE, not just individual property owners, benefits from the tax incentives and that the rehabilitation work for which incentives are granted leaves a building's distinctive architectural features in place, most states attach several conditions to the incentives. Some common requirements:

- adherence to rehabilitation standards promulgated by the U.S. Department of the Interior;
- agreements requiring property owners to maintain properties in good condition for as long as the abatement or credit is claimed. If property owners sell their property, they may be required to transfer this obligation to future property owners through provisions in sales contracts;
- filing of an annual certification that the property continues to be maintained; and
- holding a property open to the public for a limited number of days each year.

If these conditions are too onerous, however, they may discourage property owners from using the incentives. In California, for example, few people took advantage of property tax breaks authorized in 1972 because of requirements for public viewing and 20-year covenants. It was not until after 1984, when the legislature removed these conditions, that people began using the incentives more widely.

What can a state do if a taxpayer violates the terms of an agreement with the state? Arizona imposes a penalty of up to 50 percent of the total amount by which taxes were reduced or 50 percent of the property's market value, whichever is less. An additional 15 percent penalty may be imposed if a property owner fails to notify the tax assessor that the property no longer qualifies as historic. Most programs provide some means for the state to recapture foregone tax revenues if a property owner violates the terms of an agreement or sells a property before the "recapture period" expires.

The rehabilitation of this house in Georgia was encouraged by property tax abatement available to historic homeowners.

Several states—Kentucky, New Jersey, and Minnesota—do not offer special incentives for historic properties, but incentives provided to encourage the preservation of older properties generally may also be used by historic property owners. Under Minnesota's new "old house" law, local governments are required to offer partial property tax abatement on houses over 35-years-old and full abatement on houses over 70 years old. This benefit is generally limited to houses valued at less than $150,000.

Kansas recently enacted a Neighborhood Revitalization Act permitting local governments to offer tax rebates for renovation projects in designated areas. Under this program, Topeka and Atchison County provide 95 percent rebates on the assessed value of property improvements over a 10-year period. To encourage new investment in central business districts, Mississippi extends the same seven-year property tax abatement available to historic structures to new buildings located downtown.

Fiscal Impacts

HOW MUCH OF AN IMPACT do preservation incentives have on state budgets? And what can states do to keep these impacts under control?

Unfortunately, few state historic preservation offices have had the resources to pay for analyses of their incentive programs. Many states offering property tax abatement on a local-option basis do not require localities to report on the extent to which incentives are

Patsy Clark's restaurant in the Browne's Addition Historic District of Spokane, Washington, has been rehabilitated with the help of Washington's preservation tax incentives.

JOHN EVANS

used. For this reason, observations concerning the usage and effectiveness of many incentive programs are largely anecdotal.

One state that did analyze the effectiveness of its incentives is Washington, whose Department of Revenue released an evaluation of the state's Special Valuation program in 1993. Under this program, owners of historic properties may have their property taxes frozen for ten years at the level they were before substantial renovations were made. The study found that relatively few property owners—122 at the time of the study—took advantage of the program, but that their projects had a generally positive effect on both state and local tax bases. When sales and business-and-occupation taxes were taken into account, the 122 projects would eventually produce a net gain of $10 million for state and local governments over the life of the incentives, according to the study. Although $3 million in property tax revenues would be foregone over the life of the special valuations, over $13 million would be gained from these tax revenues as a result of the new economic activity stimulated. An additional $5–6 million in property tax revenues would be gained before the 122 exemptions expire in the year 2001, bringing the total net revenue gain up to as much as $16 million between 1983 and 2001, the study found.

To control the negative fiscal impact of tax incentives, several states have imposed caps of various kinds. Colorado limits its 20 percent credit to the first $50,000 of rehabilitation expenses. It also restricts the value of a credit taken in any one year to $2,000 plus 50 percent of the remaining taxes owed during that year. Indiana taxpayers may only apply their state's 20 percent credit to the first $100,000 of rehabilitation expenditures, and the total value of credits taken statewide may not exceed $450,000 in any one year. If the limit is reached, property owners "queue up" for credits available the following year. So far, it appears that Indiana need not have worried about the drain on its coffers as a result of the tax incentives. In 1995, only $250,000 of the $450,000 available in credits was claimed. One theory is that although many people are aware of the program, state income taxes are so low that people do not see the credits as a sufficient incentive to complete the paperwork and comply with rehabilitation and other requirements. This is so even though property owners may carry forward the unused portion of the credit for up to 15 years.

Other limitations on the use of incentives include the exclusion of certain rehabilitation activities and restrictions on properties eligible for incentives. Wisconsin excludes all cosmetic work done on the interior of a property. New Mexico excludes minor repairs and partition alterations. Oregon and Arizona limit eligibility to properties listed on the National Register of Historic Places.

Although state preservation tax incentives—especially state income tax credits—are less widely used than one might expect, they are nonetheless regarded as important historic preservation tools, particularly in local historic districts subject to special regulations. Robyn Powell of the New Mexico State Historic Preservation Office speaks for many when she says: "When property owners object to the regulations that accompany historic districts, we are able to respond by pointing out that if you do 'X', you may also qualify for this tax credit. It is useful to have something to offer people when you are trying to get a local preservation ordinance passed."

Program Administration

A TAX INCENTIVE PROGRAM SHOULD BE "USER-FRIENDLY." Paperwork should be as simple as possible and yet adequate to yield information the state needs to guard against abuses or misunderstandings. Utah and several other states minimize red tape by allowing property owners who claim both the federal and state rehabilitation tax credits to use the same application forms for each program.

Over $13 million would be gained as a result of new sales and business-and-occupation taxes as well as new economic activity stimulated.

To minimize uncertainty about the incentives, several states require renovation plans to be "pre-approved" before the actual work begins. Such a requirement helps to avoid difficult situations created when projects are denied incentives after an owner has gone to considerable expense.[8]

Several states provide technical assistance to property owners to help them avoid mistakes that might disqualify their projects, such as making alterations that violate Interior Department standards. Utah's Division of History staff makes on-site visits to homeowners. These visits give the Division an opportunity to educate homeowners about appropriate materials and techniques to use in rehab. The state does a lot of "hand-holding."

But such technical assistance can make a program very labor intensive and, therefore, more costly to administer, requiring some states to charge for assistance provided to property owners. Utah has not had to charge application fees for its services because the state legislature has provided adequate administrative funds. Other states have had to charge fees, however. Colorado permits local governments to participate in the administration of its tax credit program, and they are allowed to charge fees to cover administrative costs.

With small staffs and limited budgets, many state preservation offices do not have the resources to promote the incentives aggressively. In states where Certified Local Governments—i.e., local governments certified by the National Park Service as having preservation programs that meet NPS standards—administer the incentives programs, these municipalities can help to publicize the incentives. Many states advertise the incentives through their own newsletters or participation in conferences or workshops—either on their own turf or that of other interest groups such as realtors, municipal leagues, tax assessors, planners, and historic preservation commissioners. Still other states work with the general media to publicize their programs.

Uncooperative local tax assessors can render a well-intentioned program meaningless.

One of the biggest challenges is getting local tax assessors to cooperate. A common complaint is that assessors who are unaware of, or even hostile to, the goals of the incentives can make a program difficult to use and defeat a state legislature's objective of encouraging preservation. Wisconsin's historic preservation staff has met with the statewide assessors association to educate assessors about the program's goals.

In summary, to be successful, a state tax incentive program should not only offer meaningful incentives, but it should also be well-administered. Excessive red tape, delays in processing applications, uncertainty about the incentives, lack of public awareness, onerous conditions or uncooperative local tax assessors can render a well-intentioned program meaningless.

Property Tax Abatement in Washington State

IN 1985, THE WASHINGTON LEGISLATURE ENACTED A PROGRAM KNOWN AS "SPECIAL Valuation for Improvements to Historic Property." The goal, as state lawmakers wrote in the statute, was "to encourage maintenance, improvement, and preservation of privately owned historic landmarks as the state approaches its Centennial year of 1989."

Normally, when a property owner completes a major renovation, the value of his property suddenly zooms upward, triggering a corresponding increase in his property taxes. The Special Valuation program prevents this from happening by excluding the value of a building's rehabilitation from its assessed value for a period of ten years. In the eleventh year, the increase in property values attributable to the rehabilitation is once again included in the assessment on which taxes are based.

If, for example, a historic building is worth $100,000 and its owner spends $50,000 on its rehabilitation, the property may now be worth $150,000. Instead of handing the owner a tax bill based on an assessment of $150,000, the tax assessor excludes the value added due to the rehabilitation and calculates taxes as if the value of the property were only $100,000.

As with most tax benefits, certain requirements go with the special valuations. The property owner must agree to keep his building in good condition for ten years. He must obtain the approval of a local preservation board before making any alterations. And he must hold the property open for public view at least once a year—unless its exterior is already visible to the public. The penalty for violating this agreement is severe: all back taxes that would otherwise have been paid—plus interest on those taxes—and a penalty equal to 12 percent of the back taxes and interest.

Rehabilitation expenses must equal at least 25 percent of a property's assessed value and owners must complete work in 24 months. Only properties listed on either the National Register of Historic Places or a local historic register can qualify. Unlike many state programs, Washington's does not require compliance with the U.S. Department of the Interior's rehabilitation standards; compliance with local standards, which vary from town to town, is mandated.

The special valuation program exists only in communities whose local governments have chosen to provide it. Localities may limit the program to residential or commercial properties only, or they may make both types eligible. Since the program began, 19 cities and ten counties have chosen to participate.

Originally set to expire at the end of 1991, the program has now been extended permanently. The extension was made after a study conducted by the state Department of Revenue refuted a state legislator's charges that the Special Valuation program conferred tax

Federal Tax Incentives

INCOME-PRODUCING BUILDINGS that are listed on the National Register of Historic Places (or located in a historic district and certified as contributing to the district) may qualify for a 20 percent rehabilitation tax credit under the Internal Revenue Code. "Income-producing" buildings include structures used for rental housing, offices, commerce and industry but not for owner-occupied residences. Income-producing buildings constructed before 1936 that are not listed on the National Register of Historic Places may qualify for a 10 percent rehabilitation tax credit.

To qualify for the credits, the rehabilitation work must be considered "substantial." That is, a property owner must spend at least $5,000 or an amount that exceeds the adjusted basis of the building (purchase price, minus cost of land, plus improvements already made, minus depreciation already taken), whichever is greater, over a 24-month period.

The federal historic preservation tax incentives program is jointly administered by the U.S. Department of the Interior and the Department of the Treasury. State historic preservation officers are involved in the review of tax credit projects.

For more information, contact the appropriate state historic preservation office listed in the Appendix. Or contact the National Park Service, U.S. Department of the Interior, P. O. Box 37127, Washington, D.C. 20013-7127.

breaks on rich people who did not need them, gave developers an incentive to do things they would do anyway, forced middle-income taxpayers to compensate for tax revenues lost due to the incentives, and would cost the state $7,781,000 in revenues over ten years. Among this study's major conclusions:

- The Special Valuation program would produce a net revenue gain of $10 million for state and local governments.
- Prior to being rehabilitated, 82 percent of the buildings participating in the incentives program were either partially occupied, vacant, or completely abandoned. After rehabilitation, they were almost all fully occupied.
- Over 70 percent of the property owners surveyed believed that their rehabilitation projects inspired other renovation activity in their neighborhood.

Since the Washington study is one of the few thorough analyses conducted by any state on its incentive program and addresses questions that frequently arise when state legislatures consider preservation tax incentives, its major findings are presented in the sidebar below.

The Special Valuation program appears to be more important to commercial and rental housing projects than to renovations of single-family houses. Homeowners find it difficult to meet the program's "substantial rehabilitation" test, which requires renovation expenses to equal 25 percent of the property's assessed value.

Teresa Brum, Spokane's historic preservation officer, sees Special Valuation as the most important tool available locally for encouraging developers to restore vacant or dilapidated historic properties: "Developers repeatedly tell me they wouldn't do these projects without the Special Valuation. This is more so for commercial than for residential properties. The commercial projects are riskier. Developers need the extra incentive to take on the risk of carrying them out."

Prior to being rehabilitated, 82 percent of the buildings were partially occupied, vacant, or abandoned.

Spokane's preservation office, whose future has been clouded during the last several years due to lack of funding, is exploring the possibility of increasing the application fees for Special Valuation, currently a flat $250, to one-half of one percent of the cost of rehabilitation. Thus a $2 million project would generate a fee of $10,000 rather than $250. The extra funds would be used to add staff to provide better, more timely technical assistance to developers using the program. Developers with whom Brum has spoken support the idea.

Bruce Lorig, a Seattle-based developer who has rehabilitated at least six historic buildings, also sees Washington's abatement program as a powerful incentive: "Property taxes are a significant part of your operating expenses, so without them, you might be able to lower your operating expenses by as much as 15 percent. That's a significant number. The tax incentives have helped projects succeed when they might otherwise have failed." In all six of the projects he has completed, Lorig took previously empty buildings and converted them into productive uses.

In Seattle, almost 80 rehabilitation projects have been completed with the help of Special Valuation since the program began in 1985. Many of these have resulted in the production of low-income housing units whose developers can combine the property tax abatement with federal tax credits available for both the rehabilitation of historic buildings and the creation of low-income housing. "Washington's tax incentives have been very instrumental in encouraging the rehabilitation of historic buildings," says Karen Gordon, historic preservation officer for the city of Seattle. "There is no way that we could offer grants that would help as much."

Findings of the Washington State Study [9]

Methodology. The evaluation of Washington State's "Special Valuation for Improvements to Historic Property," conducted between October 1990 and October 1991, was based on the program's first six years of operation (1986–1991). To launch the study, the state Department of Revenue contacted tax assessors in each of Washington's 39 counties. All counties responded, with nine reporting a total of 122 projects participating in the historic property tax abatement program. The department then calculated the tax revenue generated over time by the specially valued properties.

In the study's second phase, the Department of Community Development sent questionnaires to all 122 property owners receiving special valuations and followed up with telephone interviews. Eighty-two property owners, or 67 percent, responded. Those who did not, the department concluded, were mostly third-party lenders who had no knowledge of the initial owners' investment decisions.

DOES WASHINGTON'S "SPECIAL VALUATION FOR IMPROVEMENTS TO HISTORIC PROPERTY" program stimulate new investment? Or does it simply reward property owners for making investments they would have made anyway? Where did most of the activity stimulated by special valuations take place? In wealthy or rundown neighborhoods? Did the property tax exemptions result in a net gain, a net loss, or a wash for state and local governments? To what extent did non-historic property owners get saddled with the burden of compensating for tax revenues lost due to the exemptions? Here's what a study released in 1993 found in answer to these questions:

- 62 percent of the historic buildings rehabilitated under the special valuation program were located in blighted or rundown neighborhoods.
- Prior to rehabilitation, 82 percent of the buildings were either partially occupied, vacant, or completely abandoned; after rehabilitation, they were almost all fully occupied.
- Over 70 percent of the property owners surveyed believed that their rehabilitation projects inspired other renovation activity in their neighborhoods.
- When sales and business-and-occupation taxes were taken into account, the 122 projects participating in the Special Valuation program would produce a net gain of $10 million for state and local governments.
- Although $3 million dollars in *property* tax revenues would be foregone over the life of the special valuations, over $13 million would be gained from *sales and business-and-occupation* tax revenues resulting from the rehabilitation activity.
- An additional $5–6 million in property tax revenues would be gained before the 122 exemptions expire in the year 2001, bringing the total net revenue gain up to over $15–16 million between 1984 and 2001.
- About $12 million in property tax liability would be shifted from historic property owners to other taxpayers during the 10-year special valuations for the 122 properties. This sum represents 00.04392 percent of the $28 billion in property tax revenues collected statewide. In more practical terms, this means that the owner of a $100,000 home in King County would have had to pay an extra $2.47 a year in property taxes as a result of the special valuations.
- Because the special valuation program does not involve a means test, the study could not determine the wealth of those using it. Clearly, the 122 historic property owners had the financial credibility to obtain financing for their projects. Special valuation helped to provide that credibility for many owners, wealthy or not.

Rehabilitation Tax Credits in Wisconsin

F ROM THE EARLY TO MID-EIGHTIES, HISTORIC PROPERTIES USED COMMERCIALLY enjoyed generous tax benefits throughout the country. Under federal law, taxpayers could claim a 25 percent tax credit for rehabilitating such properties. (This was reduced to 20 percent in 1986. See sidebar, p. 103.) But there was no comparable incentive for people to renovate historic houses that they lived in themselves. In an effort to stanch the deterioration of historic houses in old city neighborhoods—and thus the decline of the neighborhoods themselves—many preservationists turned to state government for help. Among the states that responded was Wisconsin, whose legislature voted in 1987 to permit homeowners who rehabilitate and occupy historic houses to claim a state income tax credit of 25 percent of renovation expenses.

Surprisingly, this seemingly generous benefit went virtually unused during its first few years of existence. In their desire to protect the tax credit against abuse and the state budget against a revenue drain, the program's creators loaded the credit down with three provisions that effectively sunk it.

The first and most problematic provision was a minimum investment requirement that many homeowners found virtually insurmountable. The requirement was an amount equal to the "basis" of the property. The basis is the purchase price of the property, minus depreciation and the value of the land, plus the value of any improvements. Say, for example, that a homeowner paid $100,000 for his home—of which $15,000 represented the value of the land[10]—and previously made $20,000 worth of improvements. This would mean the homeowner would have to spend at least $105,000 on rehabilitating the property. A hefty sum for most homeowners.

Surprisingly, this seemingly generous benefit went virtually unused during its first few years of existence.

The second provision that proved unworkable was a restrictive covenant intended to prevent taxpayers from claiming the credit and then destroying the distinctive features of their property—or selling it to someone who might. The covenant required homeowners to commit not only themselves but also anyone else who bought the rehabilitated property to maintain it according to U.S. Department of Interior standards for 20 years. Breaking this agreement would mean forfeiting the entire credit.

The third provision to create problems was a $10,000 cap[11] on the amount of the credit. While this provision, by itself, may not have presented a major hurdle, when combined with the above two requirements, it put off many would-be-users of the tax credit. In order to take full advantage of the credit, a person would have had to own a property valued at under $40,000, sign a covenant that might lower his property value by more than the $10,000 maximum credit, and go through a substantial amount of paperwork. Thanks, but no thanks, homeowners said upon reading the fine print.

At the recommendation of the State Historical Society of Wisconsin and others, the legislature corrected these problems in 1991 by lowering the minimum investment requirement and eliminating the restrictive covenants. The $10,000 cap on the credit remains in place. Now, homeowners need only spend $10,000 on a rehabilitation project, and they can spread this expenditure out over two years. They can even spread it out over five years if their project involves discrete phases of work.

A system for recapturing the tax credits has replaced the old covenants to guard against taxpayers who might claim the credit and later violate the terms of their agreement with the state or sell prematurely. Under the new rules, if a homeowner continues to own and maintain his property for five years, he retains the full credit. If he sells within one year of taking the credit, he forfeits 80 percent of its value; within two years, 60 percent; within three years, 40 percent; within four years; 20 percent.

In making these major changes, the Wisconsin legislature also did some fine-tuning. For example, it eliminated interior cosmetic work, such as kitchen remodeling and wallpaper changes, from the list of expenses eligible for the credit. The state reasoned that exterior improvements that help to revive historic neighborhoods—or even interior alterations essential to a structure's proper functioning, such as electrical or heating repairs—could warrant special tax treatment; purely cosmetic interior changes, however desirable to homeowners, could not as they provided no tangible public benefit. One of the arguments made in the first place to justify the credit was that well-maintained historic houses in attractive neighborhoods rank among the state's major tourism attractions, and such attractions confer an economic benefit on the state as a whole.

In contrast to other states, Wisconsin allows homeowners to install artificial siding on their homes and still claim the credit, provided that the new siding matches the house's appearance exactly, that the siding is not covering obvious signs of water damage, and that the property owner leaves the original wood siding and house trim in place. "We know that a lot of people are going to be installing siding anyway as a way to reduce maintenance costs. This way, we can control the siding's appearance and make sure that the original siding isn't destroyed so that some future owner can restore it," explains James A. Sewell, the preservation architect at the state historical society who administers the program. The policy allows homeowners who need to remove lead-based paint, but who do not now have the money to do so, to make exterior improvements they can afford while leaving future owners the option of restoring the original siding.

Applications for the credit must be submitted to the state before renovation work begins. This "pre-approval" requirement is intended to avoid the problem of taxpayers who spend a lot of time and money on projects, present their work to the state for review, only to have it denied.

Historic farm buildings, such as the picturesque old red barns that dot the Wisconsin landscape, can now qualify for the credit if they, or the farmsteads in which they are located, are determined to be eligible for the state register of historic places. There is a separate program of property tax abatement for archaeological sites, and this credit can help offset the cost of fences or other measures taken to protect a site from harm.

The popularity of Wisconsin's historic homeowners tax credit has grown significantly since 1990, when it had virtually no takers at all. In 1995, 43 taxpayers completed projects costing a total of $1,250,000. While these numbers represent substantial growth in the program, the $312,500 in state income taxes foregone as a result is not even a blip in the state's total budget of $16.2 billion for the same year.[12] Property tax revenues attributable to the renovation work stimulated by the credit have undoubtedly increased, but no one has calculated the extent to which they have offset the $312,500.

Sewell thinks the legislative changes made to the credit in 1991 have greatly enhanced the program's attractiveness: "The minimum investment requirement is now low enough for average homeowners doing periodic maintenance to meet it. Our earlier threshold, which mimicked the federal tax credit's 'substantial rehabilitation test,' was simply too high."

One side benefit of the Wisconsin program is that it gives homeowners inexperienced in rehabilitation work access to state architects with a solid knowledge of good rehabilitation techniques.

One side benefit of the Wisconsin program is that it gives homeowners inexperienced in rehabilitation work access to state architects with years of experience and a solid knowledge of good rehabilitation techniques and products. "Homeowners often plan their projects based on advice from contractors with no experience in rehab work," says Sewell. "We are usually able to help them save money and avoid big mistakes," says Sewell. "Tuckpointers, for example, often propose to use hard mortar that can harm a building permanently. Many of them don't know that less damaging soft mortar even exists. The tax credit program gives us a chance to point these things out to homeowners by requiring that the work be done correctly. They, in turn, require their contractors to do a better job. In a way, we are educating contractors through their customers."

The program is helping to bring working class people back to the city.

Sewell says that households of relatively modest means are using the program along with those who are more wealthy: "We've seen rehabilitation projects on smaller homes in old Milwaukee neighborhoods with large minority populations. People are moving into blighted areas of Evansville and Janesville and rehabilitating once beautiful homes with rotting porches. The program is helping to bring working class people back to the city." Sewell sees revitalized neighborhoods as a tangible product of the program and believes that by encouraging as few as one or two rehabilitation projects in a historic district, the state can indirectly inspire an entire neighborhood to make improvements. "We now have neighborhoods that are starting to come back economically as well as physically," he says.

State Income Tax Incentives Versus Grants: Which Are Better?

By James A. Sewell

Preservation Architect, Wisconsin Historical Society

James A. Sewell is senior preservation architect for the Wisconsin Historical Society and has administered the state's grant and tax incentives programs for over 20 years. Having had exposure to both types of programs, he has discovered that each has its advantages and disadvantages. Sewell explains below.

T*ARGETING OF RESOURCES.* GENERALLY, GRANTS HAVE AN ADVANTAGE OVER TAX CREDits in this respect. They allow you to set criteria and fund those projects that you deem most important to advance the cause of historic preservation. In this way, grants better harmonize with strategic planning efforts. Tax incentives, on the other hand, can be aimed at specific resources, such as owner-occupied houses, but even then they are hit and miss. Even when certain property types are targeted, specific properties and specific geographical regions may not benefit. Moreover, some resources, such as archaeological sites, are difficult or impossible to reach.

Program users. The clear advantage here is with grants. They allow you to fund projects statewide, and let you decide what kinds of owners can qualify. They allow you to emphasize certain types of owners, such as residents of deteriorated neighborhoods, church congregations, or nonprofit organizations. Tax credits limit program users to those with sufficient tax liability to make them worthwhile. Low-income owners, tax-exempt organizations, and units of government are effectively excluded from participating. Even if you are able to narrow down the types of owners who qualify, such as owners of historic homes, you are only able to assist those who walk through the door.

Quality of work. Again, grants have the edge. Grants allow you to select projects that can meet your program standards and objectives. Poorly conceived projects can simply be rejected. On the other hand, tax credits can attract bad projects that the state preservation office must then try to bring into conformance with the standards, usually at the cost of large amounts of staff time. The higher a program's minimum investment requirement, the more likely a project is to violate state standards intended to ensure that the architectural distinction of a historic structure is kept intact. That is because the more you force an owner to spend, the more likely he is to do unnecessary work and to engage in wholesale replacement of important building elements—windows and siding, for example—that should be left alone.

Budget control. Grants are more predictable, budget-wise. With grants, you know in advance what the impact will be on the state budget. This impact is based on the amount of money budgeted for a program. With tax incentives, all you can do is make an educated guess. Moreover, program usage may vary with economic conditions—interest rates, for example—making it hard to predict what the budget impact will be from year to year.

Administration. Both programs have advantages. Grants allow you to predict your administrative costs. With grants, there is a predictable relationship between the number of grants issued and the staff time required to administer the program. You can predict and control the amount of staff time the program will consume. You can also set yearly staff priorities. With incentives, it's hard to know in advance how much staff time will be needed to admin-

The more you force an owner to spend, the more likely he is to engage in wholesale replacement of important building elements.

Grant programs, live from hand-to-mouth, year-to-year.

ister the program properly. You might have high program usage one year, low usage the next. The worst situation is having a program that becomes so popular that your staff can't handle the work load. On the other hand, tax credits generally require less administrative time per project. You do not have to monitor a recipient's hiring procedures and collect auditable records, as you do with grants. This can consume a large amount of staff time. With tax credits, applicants are responsible for their own contracting and financial records.

Public Relations: A major advantage of grants is that they offer more opportunities for the state to generate positive publicity for historic preservation. You can make press announcements when grants are awarded, when construction begins, and again when important projects are completed. You can require a grant recipient to acknowledge the grant in its publicity and its project sign. It is generally harder to find such opportunities with projects assisted by incentives. Grants also have more public appeal, particularly in Wisconsin, where taxpayers are suspicious of government in general and of the tax system in particular.

Program continuity. Tax credits have an advantage in this area. Grants represent on-line budget items. To create and perpetuate a grants program, a state must commit financial resources to the program every year. When money becomes scarce, grant programs become "unfunded," as happened with federal development grants in the eighties. Tax programs, on the other hand, don't show up on the budget. The costs show up as foregone revenues, rather than direct budget expenditures. Tax incentives tend to continue from year to year and are less likely to be eliminated. To terminate an ongoing incentive program takes affirmative, often unpopular action on the part of a number of legislators. Grant programs, on the other hand, live from hand-to-mouth, year-to-year.

* * *

JAMES LINDBERG

Elements of a Successful State Tax Incentive Program

- Incentives generous enough to motivate property owners to invest in preservation opportunities, but not to provide unnecessary giveaways.
- Simplicity of administration—for both program administrators and property owners.
- Minimal paperwork that is nonetheless adequate to yield information that guards against abuse and gives the state the data it needs.
- Minimum investment requirements appropriate to the state's goals. Lower requirements favor small projects by lower-income people; higher requirements, major projects by larger developers.
- Technical assistance to help property owners perform high-quality work, avoid pitfalls, and save money.
- Controls over the fiscal impact, whether through caps on incentives, restrictions on types of historic properties eligible, or limitations on rehabilitation activities.
- Good promotion and explanatory materials.
- Outreach and education for tax assessors, whose cooperation and understanding are critical.
- Certainty for property owners.
- Well-defined and appropriate rehabilitation standards.
- Good coordination with other relevant programs—e.g., federal tax credits for rehabilitation, low-income housing tax credits, etc.

A historic Main Street (below) and a contemporary "sprawlscape" (opposite).

BLAIR SEITZ

- Reasonable and appropriate penalties for the violation of contracts with the state.
- Elimination of tax incentives for sprawl-type development that undermines the goal of urban and historic building conservation.
- Administrative review of projects at the early planning stage of any eligible project so that property owners do not incur unnecessary expenses or make changes that might disqualify their projects for the tax incentives.

Making the Case for Tax Incentives: What Works

- *Selection of sponsors.* Pick state legislators who hold power, whether through committee assignments or leadership positions, who are respected by both political parties, and who have a good track record for getting bills passed. If the Speaker of the House or President of the Senate is really committed to getting incentives, he or she may be a good sponsor. If not, you are better off with someone willing to devote time and attention to this issue. It is important to get bipartisan sponsors and also members from both urban and rural districts.
- *Broad-based support.* Line up the major historic preservation organizations in the state in support of the legislation, but reach out to other constituencies, too: the state board of realtors, league of municipalities, county government associations, general contractors, homebuilders, unions, etc.
- *Strategic approach.* Take a strategic approach in organizing public testimony for the incentives. Include property owners, realtors, elected officials, local tax assessors, and others with direct, personal knowledge of preservation issues. Select articulate people to testify at public hearings. Work to ensure that different, but complementary, points of view are brought out in the hearings. These might include the catalytic effects of investment in deteriorated neighborhoods or potential for improving a community's overall tax base. Make sure someone covers every hearing at which the legislation might be discussed.
- *Comparables.* In describing tax incentive programs in other states, use comparables. If you live in Oklahoma, don't talk about New York's program. And if you live in New York, don't talk about South Dakota's.
- *Information materials.* Prepare brief, readable fact sheets outlining the benefits of tax incentives that can be left behind with state legislators following face-to-face meetings with them. Make sure these sheets address misconceptions or common concerns regarding the proposed incentives. Be careful and conservative in presenting economic data. If numbers are overstated or inaccurate, the entire case will be suspect. Present a combination of hard facts and figures and emotional arguments (civic pride, beautiful cities, etc.)
- *Narrowcast as well as broadcast.* You can have a great letter-writing campaign, but sometimes the interest of a handful of key legislators will do as much good.
- *Relationships with legislative aides.* Legislative staff members are often as important to the passage of legislation as the members themselves. Develop good relationships with them.
- *Contacts with agency staffs.* Do not neglect approaching key state administrators, such as budget directors, fiscal aides to the governor, etc.

- *Tap board talent and contacts.* Find out who on your board or in your network knows—or has contributed to—whom. Get these people to open doors and make key contacts for you.
- *Economic benefits of historic preservation.* Have ready good information on the economic benefits of historic preservation.
- *Show legislators restored historic buildings.* If possible, invite legislators to events in historic buildings so they can see first-hand the value of rehabilitation.
- *Peer to peer contacts.* If your state representative does not serve on a tax-writing committee, ask him or her to contact members who do in your behalf.
- *Tap talent outside the preservation community.* The Georgia Trust for Historic Preservation worked with Georgia Power on the development of a computer model to illustrate how taxing bodies would actually derive a net increase in tax revenues as a result of an abatement program proposed. The Utah Heritage Foundation turned to a leading economic guru—a respected economics professor at a local university—for testimony on the value of proposed tax credits.
- *Thank you's.* Always be sure to thank legislators who work in your behalf. Even if your legislation did not get enacted, these thank-you's are still important.

The Georgia Trust for Historic Preservation worked with Georgia Power on the development of a computer model.

State Tax Incentives for Historic Preservation

State	Property Tax Abatement	State Income Tax Credit	Usage	Comments
Alabama	Yes. Commercial. Properties assessed at 10% of appraised values (vs. 20% for non-historic properties). No time limit on the abatement.			
Alaska	Yes. Local option.		Never used. No local government has opted to use the abatement.	
Arizona	Yes. Available statewide. Owner-occupied residential. Reduction of up to 50% in property tax assessment. Owner must sign 15-year agreement to maintain property; can renew for 15 more years. Annual certification of compliance with agreement required. Property must be on National Register. No minimum investment required, but if rehab carried out, must comply with Interior standards. Penalty: lesser of 50% of total amount by which property taxes were reduced or 50% of property's market value. (Arizona also allows commercial properties to be taxed at 1% (vs. 25%) of property value for 10 years.		439 residential projects approved in 1995. Cumulative total since program's inception in 1979: 1,975. 5 commercial projects approved in 1995. Cumulative total since program's inception in 1993: 28 properties.	
Arkansas				
California	Yes. Local option. Owner-occupied residential & commercial. Assessments may be reduced by up to 50%. No minimum investment unless locality requires one. Owner signs 10-year contract to maintain &, if necessary, rehabilitate structure. If property is rehabbed, must comply with Interior Dept. Standards. Penalty: up to 12.5% of property value.		Incentive enacted in 1972, but little used until legislature removed requirements for public access and 20-year contracts in 1984. As of April 1996, 35 localities participate, but many have only 1 or 2 projects. With 42 projects, San Diego has highest rate of participation.	Legislation offering credits for seismic upgrading pending
Colorado		20% of rehab expenses of up to $50,000. Residential and commercial. Tenants with 5-year leases also qualify. Minimum investment:	Average credit: $19,941.	

State Tax Incentives for Historic Preservation (continued)

State	Property Tax Abatement	State Income Tax Credit	Usage	Comments
Colorado (continued)		$5,000. Cap: $50,000 per property; for any tax year, reduction in taxes limited to $2,000 plus 50% of remaining taxes owed that year. Carry forward term: 5 years. Interior standards apply. Properties designated by national, state or local governments qualify. Pre-approval of rehab plans required. Fees: $250 to $1,000. Certified local governments may administer.		
Connecticut				
Delaware				Statewide legislation under consideration. Operating pursuant to home rule powers, Newark freezes property tax assessments at pre-rehab levels for rehabbed historic residences. Freeze for 5 years; phased out over next 5 years.
Florida	Yes. Local option. Constitutional amendment authorizing local abatement approved in 1992. Owner-occupied residential & commercial. Localities may exempt up to full value of improvements. Value of improvements must equal 50% of property's assessed value. Exemptions do not apply to school taxes. Term: up to 10 years, but locality determines. Nationally or locally designed properties may qualify. Interior standards apply to both exterior & interior renovations.		As of August 1995, 13 of Florida's Certified Local Governments had adopted tax incentives and 51 projects in those communities had been started. Coral Gables was most active, with 17 projects initiated and two completed.	Florida also has Community Contribution Tax Incentives, whereby corporations may receive credit equal to 50% of donation to approved community development or historic preservation projects. Businesses eligible to receive credits of up to $200,000 a year.

State Tax Incentives for Historic Preservation (continued)

State	Property Tax Abatement	State Income Tax Credit	Usage	Comments
Georgia	Yes. Statewide. 8-year freeze; 2-year phaseout, with property taxes returning to normal in 10th year. Owner-occupied residences & commercial. Minimum investment: rehab must increase property's market value by 50% if owner-occupied residential; by 75%, if mixed use; by 100%, if commercial.		151 projects approved in 1995. Cumulative total approved between 1991 and 1994: 662 projects involving $54 million in private expenditures. Program used primarily by homeowners.	Georgia also permits local governments with preservation ordinances to exercise "local option" & provide property tax freezes on income-producing landmark historic structures. As of June 1995, only two jurisdictions had adopted this program: Atlanta & Cobb County.
Hawaii				
Idaho				Local assessors may consider restrictions on historic properties in assessments, but not used.
Illinois	Yes. Mandatory for all taxing districts, including municipalities, school districts, & airport authorities unless they opt out. Owner-occupants of condos, co-ops, and single-family residential qualify. 8-year freeze; 4-year phaseout; for total of 11 years of abatement. Minimum investment: 25% of property's market value. National Register or locally designated properties qualify. Interior standards apply.		89 rehab projects representing 151 housing units certified in 1995. Cumulative number of projects approved since 1983, when program began: 531; cumulative total of residential units: 631.	
Indiana		20% of rehab costs up to $100,000. Commercial, rental housing, barns & farm buildings qualify. Minimum investment: $5,000 over 2 years. Per-project cap: $20,000. Statewide cap on total amount of credits permitted annually: $450,000. State Register properties qualify. 15-year carry forward period. Pre-approval of work required. No fees. Interior standards apply.	3 projects approved in 1995 for total fiscal impact of $250,000.	

State Tax Incentives for Historic Preservation (continued)

State	Property Tax Abatement	State Income Tax Credit	Usage	Comments
Iowa	Yes. Local option. 4-year freeze on increased valuations attributable to rehab; 4-year phaseout.		5 projects approved in 1995. Cumulative total approved since 1990: 21 projects.	
Kansas				Kansas Neighborhood Revitalization Act of 1994 allows tax rebates for community revitalization projects in designated areas. Percentage and length of rebate are up to local government.
Kentucky				5-year freeze on property tax increases attributable to improvements made to residential properties at least 25 years old in designated "neighborhood improvement zones"
Louisiana	Yes. Local option. 5-year freeze; renewable for 5 more years. Owner-occupied residential (including condominiums & duplexes) and commercial. Minimum investment: 25% of assessed value for residential over 2 years; no minimum for commercial.			
Maine				
Maryland	Yes. Local option. 10-year freeze.	10%. Owner-occupied residential & commercial. Minimum investment: $5,000 for owner-occupied residential; greater of $5,000 or "basis" for commercial/rental housing. Carry forward term: 15 years. Unused portion of credit transferrable to new owners if property sold.		Maryland also allows owner-occupants of rehabilitated historic structures to receive a state tax deduction of 100% of the costs of rehab.
Massachusetts				Legislation pending

State Tax Incentives for Historic Preservation (continued)

State	Property Tax Abatement	State Income Tax Credit	Usage	Comments
Michigan				Legislation under consideration.
Minnesota				Local governments required to offer partial abatement on houses over 35 years old & full abatement on houses over 70 years old. Limited to residential properties valued under $150,000 unless located in lower-income areas.
Mississippi	Yes. Local option. Abatements up to 7 years. Commercial and residential. (New buildings in central business districts also qualify.)		Only one community, Canton, MS, participates in the abatement program.	
Missouri				No special historic benefit, but abatement available in blighted areas.
Montana	Yes. Local option. Abatement up to 5 years. Owner-occupied residential.		Local option little used, but figures not available.	
Nebraska				Restrictions on properties encumbered by easements must be taken into account by tax assessors.
Nevada	Yes. Local option.			
New Hampshire				
New Jersey				State allows 5-year deferrals of property tax increases attributable to rehab on homes at least 20 years old

State Tax Incentives for Historic Preservation (continued)

State	Property Tax Abatement	State Income Tax Credit	Usage	Comments
New Mexico		50% of rehab costs of up to $25,000. Commercial, owner-occupied and rental residential, & archaeological. Tenants with 5-year leases may also qualify. Minimum investment: none. Per-project cap: $25,000 or 50% of amount spent on rehab. State Register properties qualify. Carry forward term: 4 years. Interior standards apply. Pre-approval required.	In 1993, $919,208 in rehab expenses on 14 projects approved. Maximum allowable tax credit claim against state in 1994: $117, 881.	
New York				Legislation pending
North Carolina	Yes. Local option.	5%. Commercial. Can be piggybacked on federal 20% rehab credit.	Separate records not kept for state credit, but SHPO assumes 122 federal rehab credit projects reviewed & sent to National Park Service in 1995 also used state credit.	
North Dakota				No special historic benefit, but improvements exempt for 3 years on properties at least 25-years-old
Ohio				Tax assessors must consider any reduction in property values attributable to easement restrictions
Oklahoma				Attorney general declared property tax abatement for historic structures unconstitutional in 1980. Local Development Act passed in 1992 allows tax increment financing

State Tax Incentives for Historic Preservation (continued)

State	Property Tax Abatement	State Income Tax Credit	Usage	Comments
Oklahoma (continued)				and other tax incentives in targeted areas, including historic districts.
Oregon	Yes. Statewide. Residential & commercial. 15-year freeze on pre-rehab value of historic properties listed on National Register. Rehab is mandatory. Program terminated in 1994 but reactivated with changes in Sept. 1995.		Figures on revised program not yet available. Under special assessment program in operation between 1975 and 1994, 1,320 properties participated in program. Annually, an average of $13.5 million in frozen property value was approved for special assessments between 1976 & 1991. In 1991, 200 properties (largest ever) entered program. Statewide, cumulative total valuation of exempt (non-taxable) historic properties totalled $168 million in FY 1991, or less than 2/10 of 1% of total statewide taxable value of $94.32 billion in 1991.	
Pennsylvania				
Rhode Island		10%. Owner-occupied residential. Minimum investment: $2,000. Maximum credit allowable per year: $1,000. Unused credits may be carried forward as long as property maintained. Interior work ineligible. State Register properties qualify.		

State Tax Incentives for Historic Preservation (continued)

State	Property Tax Abatement	State Income Tax Credit	Usage	Comments
South Carolina	Yes. Local option. 2-year freeze; for next 8 years, property taxed at 40% of post-rehab assessment or pre-rehab assessment, whichever is greater. Nationally or locally designated properties qualify. Minimum investment: 50% of building's appraised value over 2 years.			
South Dakota	Yes. 8 year freeze on increased valuations due to rehab.			
Tennessee				Tax assessors required to consider reduction in property values attributable to easement restrictions. Property tax exemptions for historic properties declared unconstitutional in 1985
Texas	Yes. Local option. Residential & commercial. Partial or full exemption from property taxes allowable. Details of abatement program up to participating municipalities. School taxes never exempted. Constitutional amendment authorizing abatement approved in 1977.		18 cities participate	
Utah		20%. Residential. Cap: none. Minimum investment: $10,000 over 3 years. Interior standards apply. No fees for applicant; state approved money for program administration.	38 projects approved & completed in 1995; 141 projects costing $12.6 million approved between January 1993 and December 1995. 495 housing units created. Average project cost: $89,691. Average credit: $17,938. Total value of credits approved statewide: $2.5 million.	

State Tax Incentives for Historic Preservation (continued)

State	Property Tax Abatement	State Income Tax Credit	Usage	Comments
Vermont				State allows 5-year property tax exemption for rehabilitated residential properties located on land unoccupied for 2 preceding years. In addition, since Vermont's income tax is calculated as a percentage of the federal income tax, federal rehabilitation tax benefits also result in a reduction at the state level.
Virginia		25%. Enacted in 1996, credit will begin at 10%, then increase by 5% a year until rate reaches 25% in year 2000. State register properties eligible. Interior standards apply.	Assessors must consider reduced property values attributable to easements	No special historic benefit, but substantial improvements on buildings at least 25-years old may be exempted from property tax assessments for up to 10 years.
Washington	Yes. Local option. Residential & commercial. 10-year special valuation. Minimum investment: 25% of building's assessed value prior to rehab.		19 cities & 10 counties participate. $10 million net benefit to state estimated to occur between 1985 and 2001 from sales & business-and-occupation taxes; up to $16 million benefit when property values taken into account.	Historic properties may also be taxed according to their current, rather than "highest and best" use.
West Virginia		10% (credit expires in 1996 unless renewed). Commercial and residential.	Little usage.	

State Tax Incentives for Historic Preservation (continued)

State	Property Tax Abatement	State Income Tax Credit	Usage	Comments
Wisconsin		25%. Owner-occupied residential properties & some farm buildings. Per-project cap: $10,000. Minimum investment: $10,000 over 2 years; extendable to 5 years. Also a 5% credit for commercial properties. Can be piggybacked on federal 20% credit. Minimum investment: expenses equal to building's basis.	Between 1992 and 1995, total of 100 projects representing $2.7 million approved. 43 residential projects completed in 1995. Value of work completed: $1.25 million (up 50% over 1994 & 300% over 1993). Budgetary impact: $312,500. Average project cost: $29,070.	
Wyoming				
District of Columbia				Historic properties may be assessed according to their actual, rather than "highest and best" use.

CHAPTER 4

Removing Regulatory Barriers

Removing Regulatory Barriers

WHILE MANY STATES CAN ENCOURAGE HISTORIC PRESERVAtion by providing grants or loans to help finance the rehabilitation of historic structures, others may not feel they are in a position to do so for budgetary reasons. These states can still help simply by providing relief from regulations that may be inappropriate or counterproductive. In fact, the removal of regulatory barriers to preservation can sometimes have as much of a positive effect on the bottom line of a rehabilitation project as a grant or loan.

David Brown, director of the Preservation Alliance of Virginia, has observed that "the greatest threat to historic preservation is the general bias in public policies favoring suburban construction over urban reinvestment. You see this in building codes, environmental regulations, housing policies, transportation decisions, and school requirements set by state governments as well as by the Federal Government. The cumulative effect of all these policies makes it difficult to make preservation pay. Taken together, these policies put preservation on a very unequal footing with suburban development."

Regulations governing the clean-up of contaminated urban sites, requirements for public school construction, and building codes are just three examples of many state regulations that pose special challenges for historic preservation. This chapter looks at how Minnesota, Maryland, and California have addressed problems such regulations aim to solve, but in a way that allows historic buildings to continue to serve useful functions.

Milwaukee Road Depot and Train Shed in Minneapolis.

Reclaiming "Brownfields" in Minnesota

I N 1993, FIVE HISTORIC BUILDINGS ON THE OLD MARQUETTE BLOCK IN THE ST. Anthony Falls Historic District of Minneapolis sat empty and deteriorating. The buildings were in such a state of disrepair that they faced almost certain demolition if nothing were done to restore them. When the Minneapolis Community Development Agency issued a request for proposals to redevelop the block, Richard Brustad, a partner with the Minneapolis-based Brighton Development Corporation, went down to take a look. He determined that the buildings were still salvageable. In fact, if they were combined with compatibly designed new townhouses, they would form a nice centerpiece for a downtown housing project, he and his partners concluded. There was just one problem: the adjoining surface parking lots had once been used for a gas station, an auto repair shop, and a dry cleaners. This meant that the soil underneath the buildings was possibly contaminated.

Such a site is sometimes called a "brownfield:" a previously productive industrial or commercial property now contaminated and unused due to uncertainty over who bears responsibility for cleaning up the pollution.

Some 100,000 brownfields exist across the country. Many of them occupy prime locations near waterfronts and downtowns in older cities and towns, where historic buildings are concentrated. Although many brownfields are large industrial properties once used as railroad yards, mills, or manufacturing plants, others are smaller sites located in old urban neighborhoods. Sites once used as dry cleaners, paint shops, photo processing plants, printers or gas stations are just a few examples of places that can become "little brownfields" if pollutants happen to have seeped into the soil. When left vacant and unused, these properties attract illegal dumping, arson, and vandalism.

In 1980 Congress enacted the Comprehensive Environmental Response, Compensation, and Liability Act (CERCLA) and created the "Superfund" to pay for contaminated site investigations and clean-ups. Sometimes called a "polluter pays" law, CERCLA and many comparable state statutes require property owners to clean up contaminated sites or be held liable. Increasingly, however, these laws are seen not only as ineffective in getting the brownfields cleaned up, but also as inadvertently contributing to their continued dereliction as well as to the proliferation of sprawl on "greenfields" at the outer fringes of suburbia. As Ted Mondale, a Minnesota state senator and leader in the effort to reclaim brownfields, observes, "When a developer has to spend $5 million to develop a brownfield but only $3 million to develop a greenfield, you don't need a fancy calculator to figure out where the developer will go."

"When a developer has to spend $5 million to develop a brownfield but only $3 million to develop a greenfield, you don't need a fancy calculator to figure out where the developer will go."

Liability Issues

CERCLA AND MANY OF ITS STATE CLONES hold present, past, and future owners of a contaminated site potentially liable for its clean-up, regardless of whether the owner contributed to the contamination. Even if the activities that caused the contamination occurred before certain environmental laws existed, the owner may still be liable. This focus on land ownership, rather than fault, causes many people—developers, lenders, insurers and property owners—to shy away from doing *anything* to improve and recycle brownfields. Terry J. Tondro, a law professor at the University of Connecticut, explains why:

> [T]he lender's inquiry is focused exclusively on whether the land is contaminated, not whether the potential borrower is the culpable party. The liability for cleaning up the property extends to all the costs of restoring it to a pollution free state, even if a particular contaminant was not known to be harmful to human health or to the environment at the time of its disposal. This means that, after cleaning a site to a pristine state under [current]…knowledge and regulations, should we five years from now become newly aware of the dangers of a particular substance, of a significantly lower threshold of exposure, or of a previously unknown location of a contaminant on the site, the borrower, and perhaps its lender, would be liable for cleaning up the substance and correcting any newly perceived damage it may have caused. Once a party's fingerprints are on the title to the property, liability seems to last forever.[1]

In many states the story of the Marquette Block at St. Anthony Falls would have ended with the Brighton Development Company's looking at the property but moving on. Minnesota, however, has a program that led to a very different outcome: the rehabilitation of the five historic buildings; conversion of the surrounding land into a mixed-use project with street-level stores, 20 upper-floor apartments, and 20 new townhouses; and most important, the cleaning up of the site. The new project, scheduled to open in late 1996, is expected to enliven the St. Anthony Falls Historic District, provide convenient downtown housing, and return an "orphaned" site to the tax rolls.

Minnesota's Voluntary Investigation and Clean-up Program

Once a party's fingerprints are on the title to the property, liability seems to last forever.

IN AN ATTEMPT TO HELP PROPERTY OWNERS and others interested in urban redevelopment clean up polluted sites without the fear of Superfund liability, Minnesota enacted the Land Recycling Act in 1992.[2] Cosponsored by State Senator Ted Mondale and Representative Jean Wagenius, this statute was the first of its kind in the nation. It created the VIC program—for <u>V</u>oluntary <u>I</u>nvestigation and <u>C</u>lean-up—administered by the Minnesota Pollution Control Agency (MPCA). The program accomplishes its overall goal of reclaiming brownfields in several ways:

- It provides assurances against legal liability to people who voluntarily investigate site contamination and clean it up to MPCA's standards. The law extends this liability protection to other parties associated with the brownfield as well, such as owners, developers, lenders and their successors.
- It allows the MPCA to approve partial clean-up plans when property owners who are not responsible for the pollution want to develop just a portion of a larger site. Clean-ups under VIC must meet standards similar to those of the Superfund, but the former are often much less expensive because uses planned for the site are known, thereby allowing for "risk-based assessments," and the process of identifying a clean-up method is streamlined.

VIC thus helps buyers and sellers of possibly contaminated land resolve legal and financial clouds over brownfields while expediting their clean-up. Potential buyers willing to invest in a site's reclamation are able to get assurance from an independent third party that if they restore a site to the satisfaction of the authorities, they will not have to worry about future liability.

"Before the VIC program, redevelopment projects would just come to a standstill," says Linda Donaldson, a partner at the Brighton Development Corporation. "Nobody could get answers to anything. Who was responsible for what? How contaminated was the land? How could you clean it up? And if you did clean it up, how could you get the liability assurances necessary to obtain financing for your project? None of this was clear."

The VIC program addressed these and other questions by arranging for professional experts to define clearly the amount of site investigation needed and, when appropriate, to approve a property owner's clean-up plans. If an owner completed an adequate investigation and removed whatever pollution was on the site, the MPCA would issue a letter saying so. MPCA thus removed the uncertainty clouding a brownfield's future. The agency's letters cleared businesses, including buyers, sellers, bankers, insurers, and private developers, of future liability if they performed site investigations and clean-ups approved by the MPCA. The letters reassured both buyers and sellers that the MPCA would not refer the site to the state or federal Superfund programs. Only sites that pose an immediate threat to drinking-water wells and sites where hazardous wastes were mishandled after 1980 are ineligible for action under VIC. As a fee-for-service program, VIC recovers more than 95 percent of its costs, so environmental benefits are achieved with minimal public funding.

An Action-Oriented Program

"Before the VIC program, redevelopment projects would just come to a standstill."

VIC IS AN ACTION-ORIENTED PROGRAM that removes road-blocks to redevelopment, according to Donaldson: "It creates a process that has a beginning and an end. It eliminates all the finger-pointing that used to go on."

"Our program is unique," says Deborah DeLuca, VIC's supervisor. "We offer a whole menu of liability assurances depending on what is appropriate for any given site. We tailor our responses to the individual situations brought before us. Many states don't offer such a menu."

In the case of the Marquette Block at St. Anthony Falls, the Brighton Development Corporation hired an environmental consultant to investigate the extent to which the site was contaminated. Once the contamination was identified—a fuel tank and residue from a former dry cleaners were found—Brighton retained a company and got rid of it. A letter provided subsequently by the VIC program certified that no further action was necessary. This letter was critical to Brighton's ability to obtain financing for the renovation of the historic buildings and the construction of the new townhouses.

In contrast to the purist approach of the federal Superfund and other state statutes, Minnesota's law takes the position that some clean-up is better than no clean-up at all. Contaminated sites are not always required to be made pristine, just clean and safe enough for the particular new use to which they are put.

In 1995, the MPCA and U.S. Environmental Protection Agency's Region V Office executed a "Brownfield Addendum" to its "Superfund Memorandum of Agreement." Under the addendum—one of the first of its kind in the nation—VIC participants would be assured that EPA would not get involved if VIC approved their projects.

Besides dealing with the liability problems surrounding brownfields, Minnesota has also acted to address the financial issues. Under Minnesota's Livable Communities Act, passed in 1995, the state's Tax Base Revitalization Account will contribute $7 million annually to the clean-up of brownfields in the Twin Cities area. An additional $4 million annually is available statewide for grants to cities and redevelopment authorities for clean-up projects through the Contamination Clean-up Grant Program administered by the Minnesota Department of Trade and Economic Development.

"What we do is to provide written assurances against legal liability, so that people who voluntarily investigate a site's pollution and clean it up to our satisfaction will feel they have a green light to proceed with redevelopment," says DeLuca. "Our program evolved from a recognition that urban sites were sitting idle while developers fled to the greenfields. There they destroyed wetlands and other natural resources. Meanwhile, the cities lost jobs."

Minnesota is seen as a leader among the states for its efforts to reclaim brownfields. Since VIC's inception eight years ago, over 700 sites have entered the program and 4,000 acres of industrial and commercial land have been put back into productive use. More than half of these have been cleared for financing, sale, or redevelopment through the issuance of liability assurances. About 11 percent of the 700 sites have involved or affected historic properties.

National Recognition

IN 1994, THE VIC PROGRAM RECEIVED an "Innovation Award" from the Ford Foundation and John F. Kennedy School of Government at Harvard for its success in recycling brownfields. Commenting on the award, *Boston Globe* columnist Thomas Oliphant contrasted Minnesota's program with that of other states and the Superfund, which, he said, "essentially rope anyone, no matter how tenuous the past or present connection to the site, to the liability dispute. The purpose is commendable in slogan form—'let the polluters pay'—but the reality is that nothing happens...Minnesota is proving that blame is an obstruction as well as an abstraction and that what counts is effecting clean-ups, followed by job-producing redevelopment. Every site that comes alive again in these neighborhoods in and near cities takes that much pressure off green spaces and wetlands further out in the relentless path of development."[3]

In Mondale's view, cleaning up polluted sites is the best return on investment government can make today. "If you look at the core cities in this country," he says, "you can see that we need more than just housing programs and short-term benefits for residents. We need to revitalize and reweave the communities that we have abandoned. Critical to that is bringing jobs back into these core areas. Without the remediation of polluted sites, that just can't happen. We in Minnesota have made a commitment to clean up the urban industrial sites of the past. We believe our region will reap many benefits by having stronger, more sustainable communities."

Urban sites were sitting idle while developers fled to the greenfields.

Postscript

THE MINNESOTA VOLUNTARY INVESTIGATION AND CLEAN-UP PROGRAM has also been critical to the future of the Milwaukee Road Depot and Train Shed in Minneapolis (see photo, p. 126), which is listed in the National Register of Historic Places. For years this depot's future was clouded by the presence of oil that had leaked underground. With VIC's help, the Minneapolis Community Development Agency has been able to analyze the problem and identify a new technology for removing the oil. This should help clear the way for the site's redevelopment. With the contamination problem solved, a major developer has signed a letter of intent to create two new ice skating rinks inside the train shed frame.

Around the Country

ALTHOUGH MINNESOTA STANDS OUT AS A LEADER in the reclamation of brownfields, other states, too, have passed laws or created programs to facilitate the redevelopment of polluted sites. Delaware, Illinois, Indiana, Massachusetts, Missouri, New Jersey, Ohio, Oregon, Pennsylvania, Rhode Island and Virginia are among these states.

Delaware's law authorizes tax breaks and exempts new owners from future liability if they restore any of some 100 brownfields.[4] Pennsylvania's Land Recycling Program, administered by the state Department of Environmental Protection, limits future liability on sites where clean-ups meet certain standards and provides grants and loans to help finance environmental assessments and site clean-ups.

A New Jersey law approved by Governor Christine Todd Whitman in January 1996 permits owners of brownfield sites in "environmental opportunity zones" that are adequately cleaned up to qualify for a ten-year property tax exemption. Rhode Island, whose urban corridor contains nearly 200 contaminated sites, enacted an Industrial Property Remediation and Reuse Act in 1995. Among other things, this law exempts landowners from liability for contamination if they did not contribute to a site's pollution.

Postscript

FOR A MORE DETAILED DISCUSSION of the "brownfield" liability issues affecting historic preservation, readers may wish to refer to two articles that appeared on this subject in the Preservation Law Reporter, *published by the National Trust for Historic Preservation. The first is entitled "Environmental Liability Issues for Preservation Organizations;" the second, "Environmental Liability Issues for Preservation Organizations as Property Owners." Both were written by JoAnna J. Barnes, Esq., and appeared in the February 1992 and November 1992 issues, respectively, of PLR. Other insights into this issue appear in "Reclaiming Brownfields to Save Greenfields: Shifting the Environmental Risks of Acquiring and Reusing Contaminated Land," an article by Terry J. Tondro in the* Connecticut Law Review, *Volume 27, Number 3, Spring 1995.*

Historic Schools

STATE REQUIREMENTS GOVERNING THE SIZE AND LOCATION OF PUBLIC SCHOOLS can be a major barrier to the preservation of historic school buildings. "These requirements are very difficult for virtually any existing urban school on a small site to meet," says Daniel Fogarty, deputy director for the Indiana State Historic Preservation Office. "We are seeing the abandonment of one historic school building after another. They are putting up big new facilities on the edge of town." Myrick Howard, president of Preservation North Carolina, echoes this concern: "Our Department of Public Instruction has promulgated ridiculous standards for school buildings. Its requirements for the number of acres, parking places, and other matters make it all but impossible to continue the use of older school buildings. The construction of new school buildings out in the suburbs plays a critical role in promoting residential sprawl in outlying areas at the expense of older communities."

One factor in the problems is the size of the school site. Guidelines promulgated by the Council of Educational Facility Planning, an organization based in Scottsdale, Ariz., recommend the following acreage requirements for schools:

- 10 acres of land plus one acre for every 100 elementary school students. Thus a school with an enrollment of 200 students would require 12 acres;
- 20 acres of land plus one acre for every 100 middle school students. A school with 500 students would therefore require 25 acres;
- 30 acres of land plus one acre for every 100 high school students. A school with 1,000 students would require 40 acres; and
- 50 acres of land plus one acre for every 50 post-secondary school students. A school with 4,000 students would require 130 acres.

The Council's guidelines assume that most schools will be built in suburban areas and call for large school sites that often exceed what historic schools can meet. "Expansiveness is taken for granted" in most suburban and rural areas, say the guidelines.[5] Although states are not required to adopt these guidelines, when they do, that can put pressure on small towns and cities alike to abandon still-serviceable historic school buildings for new "school sprawl" in outlying areas.

School construction principles discussed in the *School Renovation Handbook: Investing in Education*, another guide used by some states, also favor building new schools over renovating older ones. One rule of thumb discussed in this guide is that "the decision to modernize or renovate a school is probably questionable if the cost of modernization exceeds 50 percent of the cost of a new project."[6]

Those who set criteria for school sites may wish to reexamine the need for the acreage requirements in light of states' community revitalization goals.

"We are seeing the abandonment of one historic school building after another."

Maryland's Pro-Preservation Policy

O NE STATE THAT DOES NOT USE THESE GUIDELINES, precisely because they encourage the abandonment of existing schools, is Maryland. The state stopped using the standards sometime during the 1970s. In recent years, Maryland's pro-preservation policy has become more pronounced.

In a 1991 memorandum to school superintendents, Yale Stenzler, executive director of Maryland's Public School Construction Program, said that the state would consider the effect of proposed school construction projects on sprawl, which he defined as development that is "isolated from already-developed areas, and which does not utilize existing or planned infrastructure." His memorandum said that sprawl development "unnecessarily harms the environment, is wasteful of public infrastructure investment, and is not cost effective. Therefore we will seek to avoid budgeting for [school] projects that contribute to sprawl development."[7]

Governor Parris N. Glendening's strong stand against urban sprawl has moved the state even further in the direction of preserving and rehabilitating older schools. The Maryland State Public Construction Program encourages the renovation of existing schools—and additions to them—over the construction of new schools. Among the criteria promulgated by the department in early 1996 for the review of local funding requests are the following:

- Projects must be consistent with the local government's plans for growth, development, redevelopment, revitalization, preservation, conservation, and protection.
- Projects should not be located in agricultural preservation areas, rural areas, or resource conservation areas unless other options are not viable and the project's development will have no negative effect on future growth and development in the area.
- Projects should encourage revitalization of existing facilities, neighborhoods, and communities.
- Projects should not encourage "sprawl" development.
- Projects should be located in developed areas or in a locally-designated growth area.

Maryland uses a funding formula for renovation projects based upon a percentage of the cost of new construction. The State's formula allows 50 percent of the cost of new con-

A historic school that contributes to local community identity and a contemporary school that could be anywhere. Like most modern schools, the latter is surrounded by asphalt and not easy for students to walk to.

Views of Maryland's Director for Public School Construction

Yale Stenzler, executive director of Maryland's Public School Construction Program, has received praise from historic preservationists for his support of recycling older schools. Stenzler's position, set forth below, has played an important role in the reclamation of Maryland's historic schools.

WE HAVE OVER 1,200 PUBLIC SCHOOLS IN MARYLAND that serve students and citizens in their neighborhoods and communities. These older buildings can be renovated and revitalized to provide for the most up-to-date educational programs and services. If we can provide revitalized schools in our existing neighborhoods and communities, it will encourage individuals and their families to stay in these areas. They will use the existing roads, parks, libraries, and other public facilities. State and local resources can be saved if we do not have to continually build new infrastructure outside of these existing areas.

struction for renovating a school that is between 16 and 25 years old; 60 percent if the school is 26 to 40-years-old; and 85 percent if the school is 41 years or older. Schools younger than 15-years-old may not receive any state money for renovations. In other words, if it costs $100-per-square-foot to build a new school, the state would allow $50-per-square-foot for a building 16-to-25 years old; $60-per-square-foot for a building 26-to-40 years old; and $85-per-square-foot for a building 41 years or older.

Prior to December 1995, the state would only pay for renovation projects that replaced an existing building system—electrical or mechanical, for example—that was already in existence. Under Glendening's new policy, the state will pay for the cost of adding new improvements, such as air conditioning, new wiring for computer systems, and the like. As the governor announced in a recent speech, "I have changed the focus of the Maryland Public School Construction Program to emphasize the renovation of existing schools in older neighborhoods instead of building new schools in new communities. Now we will provide older communities with schools that have state-of-the-art information technology and computers, so that young families will know they can live in an older community and still have access to the best possible public education."

The extent to which Maryland has shifted its emphasis away from new schools in outlying areas and toward the rehabilitation of older schools in urban areas can be seen in the fact that in Fiscal Year 1991, 66 percent of the state's school construction funds went into new construction while only 34 percent went into renovations or additions to existing schools. By Fiscal Year 1997, the percentages had shifted: only 18 percent of the state's funds went toward new construction while 82 percent went into renovations or additions.

In an editorial praising Maryland's emphasis on improving older schools, the *Baltimore Sun* observed: "For decades now, the public's tendency to move farther from the [urban] core has been encouraged by state-of-the-art schools built on the fringes. The state should not neglect school needs in already settled growth areas. Also, renovating or rebuilding a school in an older community may not be enough to convince someone to remain in that neighborhood instead of moving farther out. But it will help older communities' chances of retaining young families. The premise here isn't so much "build it and they will come," as Kevin Costner's character was urged in the baseball movie, "Field of Dreams," but rebuild it and they may stay."[8]

The Church Hill Elementary School in Queen Anne's County, MD, is being renovated with the aid of Maryland state funds. Built in 1916, the school will be made more energy-efficient and accessible to people with disabilities.

Winthrop, Maine, Battles State on School Site Standards

IN SEPTEMBER 1993, GLADYS RICHARDSON WAS OUT WALKING WITH A FRIEND ON Route 202, a busy high-speed state highway separating the village of Winthrop from the countryside. As they approached Annabessacook Road, a narrow country road along which was an entrance for a proposed new high school, it suddenly dawned on Richardson that no student would be able to walk to the new school without risking life and limb. "I never gave a second thought to the issue of the new high school until that day in September," Richardson says. "But in the five minutes it took me to walk from my house to Bob Barrows Chevrolet, my eyes were opened. Even though I have travelled that stretch of road hundreds of times in a car, the impact of walking on and crossing Route 202 with traffic passing at 55 miles an hour was a shock to me."

A few years earlier Richardson had attended a lecture given by Andres Duany, the Miami-based leader of the "new urbanism" movement. Duany had criticized public policies that have made it virtually impossible for school children to walk to school any more. He had lamented the widespread loss of beautiful, well-designed, historic schools in which whole communities took pride. He had derided the disposal of such buildings for the construction of nondescript schools on the outskirts of town that resembled warehouses and sometimes even jails. The impact of Duany's lecture, coupled with Richardson's own reactions during the walk on Route 202, prompted her to make an issue of the plans for a new school.

At the time, elementary and high school students were housed in a cluster of three buildings located in the heart of Winthrop. The Adell Building, a historic structure built in 1929, was centered between the elementary and high schools. Everyone agreed that Adell was overcrowded and needed renovations, but when the town asked the Maine Department of Education for help with additions and renovations, it was told no. "It has been the Department of Education's position for several years that the current site is too small for further expansion of the buildings," a state official wrote Winthrop. The state's policy is to pay for new construction but not for renovations, unless they are affected by an addition. Furthermore, the state requires elementary schools to have at least five acres plus one acre for every 100 students. It requires high schools to have at least 15 acres plus one acre for every 100 students. With elementary and high school populations of 582 and 305, respectively, the current site would need almost 30 acres for any addition. It had only 17. Thus the official wrote, "[I]t would be difficult for me to recommend to the Commissioner and State Board of Education a school construction project at the existing site of the high and grade schools...You may develop an addition to the existing schools as a locally funded project which, of course, would not be eligible for state subsidy."[9]

Upon receiving this information from the state, Winthrop's town leaders decided to close the Adell School and build a new school on a tract of land which has access from Route 202 and Annabessacook Road.

After doing a little research, Richardson and a group of other concerned citizens decided to put an ad in the local newspaper in May 1994. The ad read:

As residents of Winthrop…we are united in our opposition to the proposed new high school on Annabessacook Road for a variety of reasons, including the following:

(1) it disrupts the integrity of our traditional New England village, which urban planners across the U.S.A. are now referring to as *the model* for new development;

(2) it will force up the tax rate and make it even more difficult to adequately fund academic and other programs such as athletics and the arts;

(3) its location is unsafe for vehicle and walker access, and

(4) high school students, who now provide an invaluable service as volunteers in the grade school, may cut back or stop due to transportation and time constraints.

We *will support* solutions that are sensible, economical, and community-oriented to meet the educational needs of students and faculty.

In July 1994, Richardson and like-minded residents of Winthrop formed <u>C</u>itizens <u>H</u>aving <u>O</u>ther <u>I</u>deas <u>C</u>oncerning <u>E</u>xcellence in <u>O</u>ur <u>S</u>chools (CHOICES), a grassroots organization dedicated to preserving but upgrading the Adell School in town. Between July and September 20, 1994, the date scheduled for a vote on a bond issue to finance the new schools, CHOICES hammered away at the following points at public hearings, in letters-to-the-editor, and in fliers distributed to Winthrop citizens.

- Planners nationwide are rediscovering that what works best is a community where people can walk or bike to work, shops, and school. Small New England towns, exactly like Winthrop, are cited as ideal. National acclaim has been given to "new towns" designed on the concept of what we already have in Winthrop. Why destroy what other people are discovering to be the model?

- The current high school site keeps students in town where they are connected to the flow of life, seeing and being seen by neighbors and passersby. There are already strong pulls for teens to be isolated and not part of anything except their own world. Busing students out of town to an isolated site breaks important ties in their identification with the town of Winthrop. They might as well be in another town.

- The current school enables students and staff who live nearby to participate in after-school activities without being dependent on a car or bus.

GLADYS RICHARDSON

The Adell School in Winthrop, Maine.

- Winthrop's village should be the preferred location for a mixture of activities generally associated with the typical New England village. Efforts should be directed towards maintaining and improving this area. Historically significant buildings should be renovated instead of replaced.

CHOICES also pointed out that renovating the Adell School would cost only about half as much as building the new school.

That September, Richardson and a core group of some 25 volunteers conducted a telephone survey asking Winthrop residents where they stood on the school issue. The survey

Historic Schools in North Carolina

One state that has promoted the construction of new schools while letting existing ones deteriorate is North Carolina. Below are excerpts from an article that appeared in the Spring 1996 issue of North Carolina Preservation. *J. Myrick Howard, executive director of Preservation North Carolina, takes the Department of Public Instruction to task for such a wasteful policy. Unfortunately, the kind of policy followed by North Carolina is common to many states.*

NORTH CAROLINA'S OLD SCHOOL BUILDINGS represent the state's most endangered historic architecture. By the North Carolina Department of Public Instruction's (DPI) count, more than 1,000 school buildings in North Carolina are slated for replacement. This loss of the state's built heritage is not necessary to provide quality education for its children.

In 1993 I visited two schools in Japan, a country whose public education far outperforms ours. Both schools would have fallen far short of meeting DPI's facility standards, and yet the parents and their communities were proud of the schools and quality education was taking place within. Tearing down old school buildings and replacing them will not solve North Carolina's educational problems.

Three issues concerning our historic school buildings need to be addressed by state and local officials.

- The failure to maintain existing schools.
- The misguided policy of replacing schools rather than rehabilitating them.
- The community consequences of school abandonment.

DPI's guidelines are very specific: schools in Categories IV and V are not to be maintained except for matters of health and safety. The intent of this policy seems clear: let the older schools decay in order to win support for the construction of new schools. This policy is short-sighted, wasteful and wrong.

I have visited many North Carolina schools after their abandonment and witnessed the lack of basic maintenance. Roofs leaking because the gutters were never cleaned out. Wet basements where the outside drains were clogged with leaves. Broken windows repaired with cardboard. With North Carolina's schools (old and new), the most sensible program is continued maintenance and routine upfitting of buildings to keep them in good condition and to meet modern needs.

* * *

The state of North Carolina does not have the resources to replace every school that DPI wants to replace—nor should it...

To let a fine school building fall into disrepair because state guidelines specifically direct an end to its maintenance is exceedingly poor stewardship of public resources...

Many well constructed, handsome, serviceable older school buildings are being vacated by school systems across the state. Local school boards maintain that they are compelled to replace them because of DPI's guidelines, although DPI officials maintain that the guidelines are not binding on local boards. DPI's's guidelines require large acreage and large classrooms (for smaller classes), and specify construction details that quickly eliminate older build-

revealed widespread opposition to the new school, two to one. In making the calls, CHOICES recorded the names and phone numbers of the people who opposed the new school. On September 20, 1994, when local citizens voted on the proposed bond issue, CHOICES called these people and reminded them to vote. The proposal to build the new school lost, 816 to 1,596.

On April 1, 1996, the Winthrop town council voted, five to two, to issue a bond to raise funds to renovate the Adell school. Inasmuch as the state has shown little interest in helping with the renovation, it appears the project will have to be carried out entirely with local funds.

Historic school buildings all over North Carolina are threatened, but the Swain School now serves as elderly housing.

ings (such as no more than eight steps between stair landings).

Last year a new code for existing buildings, which makes rehabilitation more practical, was adopted [by the state]. Instead of embracing it, DPI tried tirelessly (and unsuccessfully) to get itself exempted from the new code.

* * *

Besides the enormous waste of tax dollars and public resources, there are many community reasons for seeing existing school buildings renovated and maintained in continued school use. The rehabilitation of existing buildings provides numerous benefits to the community:

- Rehabilitation projects help revitalize communities. An abandoned school building can become a haven for crime and a drain on a neighborhood.
- The infrastructure supporting the building (read sanitary and storm sewer systems, electrical and natural gas supplies, sidewalks, parks, etc.) is already in place.
- Rehabilitation projects, which are more labor-intensive than material-intensive, result in more local jobs and sales than new construction projects.
- Rehabilitation is less wasteful than new construction and prevents demolition, which adds thousands of cubic feet of waste into already cramped landfills.
- The quality of historic construction is far better than typical current construction. Rehabilitated historic buildings are likely to have lower long-term maintenance costs than new ones and will long outlast their modern counterparts.
- Rehabilitation and maintenance is likely to achieve and maintain greater community support than new construction.

* * *

The [North Carolina Department of Public Instruction] should consider a program which incrementally upgrades and routinely maintains the public's investment in its school buildings across the state, and [the department] should re-examine the feasibility and the public policy implications of rehabilitating—rather than replacing—existing schools.

Building Codes

VIRTUALLY ALL BUILDINGS BUILT TODAY MUST COMPLY WITH REGULAR building codes. Updated periodically to reflect the latest advances in construction techniques and materials, these codes can present problems for historic buildings built many years ago, long before such newer techniques and materials existed. A historic building may be perfectly safe today, but local code inspectors may not be able to document its safety as easily as that of a new structure for which modern codes provide clear safety standards for various building features. The newer codes may assign little or no value to archaic materials and methods, even though the buildings in which they are embodied have stood the test of time. Building officials thus have limited information regarding the fire resistance or structural capacity of archaic materials.[10]

Problems with code compliance typically arise when a property owner decides to build a major addition, change the way a historic building is used, or rehabilitate a structure that has been closed for some time. In many of these cases, the entire structure, not just the section being renovated, must comply with the latest code. If the cost of full compliance is very high, the property owner may decide he cannot afford to make the changes and as a result may choose to demolish the building or simply neglect needed repairs, leaving the building vulnerable to loss by fire or some other misfortune. Alternatively, the owner may make the changes, but then the cost is passed on to the building tenants in the form of higher rents.

The cost of comparable rehabilitation projects can vary by as much as a million dollars from one state to another simply because of building code differences, the attitudes of code officials, or the interpretations these officials give to the codes.[11] States with special code provisions for historic buildings, administered by well-trained building inspectors, can encourage the reuse of older buildings. Such codes can reduce construction costs, save developers time, or do both. The bottom line: They make rehabilitation projects more economical.

Model Codes

SINCE IT IS EXPENSIVE AND COMPLICATED to write building codes, most states simply adopt and apply one of four model codes promulgated by professional organizations comprised of engineers, architects, and others. The major codes are:

- Uniform Building Code, published by the International Conference of Building Officials (ICBO) and used heavily throughout the west and mid-west;
- Standard Building Code, published by the Southern Building Code Congress (SBCC) and used primarily in the southeast;
- BOCA National Building Code, published by the Building Officials and Code Administrators (BOCA) and used widely in the northeast; and the
- Life Safety Code, published by the National Fire Protection Association. In contrast to the above-mentioned codes, the Life Safety Code focuses primarily on fire safety and is applied throughout the country.

The renovation of Sacramento's historic city hall was helped by the California Historic Building Code.

In recent years, all of these code-writing organizations have added special sections to their codes to give local building inspectors more flexibility in evaluating the safety of historic buildings. Many state and local governments have adopted these provisions, but many others have not.

In addition to the building codes that address life safety issues, a model code known as ANSI—published by the American National Standards Institute—exists to deal with the accessibility of buildings for physically disabled people. This code is less flexible than the Americans with Disabilities Act and allows for few exceptions to prescriptive requirements. It can present a major barrier to the reuse of existing buildings, particularly upper-floor space in historic structures that many communities would like to convert into badly needed housing.

Vintage Cars and Preservation

By ROBERT E. MACKENSEN

The State Historical Building Code makes it possible to have both sensitivity and safety.

CALIFORNIA'S LOVE AFFAIR WITH VINTAGE CARS is legendary. We are seduced by their beauty, their craftsmanship and their authenticity. We would be horrified by any local, state or federal laws that required the installation of dual air bags, anti-lock braking systems, quartz-iodine headlights or any...noticeable alterations to the historic vehicle. It is universally acknowledged that such alterations would devalue the resource, even though it must also be acknowledged that their incorporation [into the vehicle] would tend to increase the level of safety of the car. In spite of this, the state—recognizing the importance of passing these historic vehicles on to the next generation as unaltered as possible—grants them a special license and, with few restrictions, sets them loose on the states' streets and roads.

The State Historical Building Code makes it possible to have both sensitivity and safety. Society has established a whole hierarchy of levels of "safety," and recognizes that each is reasonable for a given set of circumstances. And so society avails itself of the use of myriad types, sizes and qualities of airplanes, boats, cars or habitations. Most of us will happily board and experience a "horseless carriage" in spite of its limitations. Yet it would be hard to argue that a vintage car out on California roads is "safer" than a vintage building which, despite its imperfections, has been rooted to the ground for a half-century or more.

Robert E. Mackensen is executive director of California's State Historical Building Safety Board, the agency responsible for administering California's State Historical Building Code.

California's State Historical Building Code

IN ADDITION TO THESE EFFORTS by the major code-writing groups, several states have sought to alleviate code problems for historic buildings. Among the earliest to take action in this area was California, which today has one of the more successful programs for solving code problems encountered by historic buildings.

The state turned its attention to this issue in 1975, when the legislature enacted the State Historical Building Code. The code went into effect in 1979. For the first six years, however, it was little used as it was advisory only. Local governments had the option of applying it in their jurisdictions but were not required to do so. Few local governments applied the code because local jurisdictions feared problems with liability issues of interpretation.

In 1985, the California legislature made use of the historic code mandatory. Today a building inspector may not prevent a property owner from using this code.

The purpose of California's historical building code[12] is to protect the state's architectural heritage by providing alternative regulations for the rehabilitation of historic structures. It mandates that reasonable code alternatives be applied when the standard code might threaten or destroy a building's historic features. The code applies to all state-owned buildings and to all historic buildings listed individually or included in historic districts designated by the federal, state, or local governments. Buildings declared eligible for historic designation by the state historic preservation office are covered as well.

The code does not allow a reduced level of safety for building occupants; it simply permits more flexibility in the path pursued to achieve public safety. It is thus considered a "performance" code. A "performance" code requires a building to provide a reasonable level of safety for its occupants but allows flexibility in the use of building designs, materials, and construction systems. As Robert E. Mackensen, executive director of California's State Historical Building Safety Board, explains, "The performance-based historic code says, 'Close the books and start relying again on common sense, experience, and good judgement.'" In contrast, a "prescriptive" code requires the use of specific materials and methods, leaving little room for professional judgement. Local code officials often prefer prescriptive codes because they tend to put matters in terms of black and white.

The code sets forth a comprehensive body of regulations dealing with such issues as structural soundness, fire protection, plumbing, mechanical and electrical systems. It requires that reasonable alternatives be applied when standard code requirements threaten historic structures. For example, it is possible for fire escapes to qualify as building exits provided they are in good condition.

The code also provides alternatives for complying with handicapped-accessibility requirements. For example, the historic code allows existing doors as narrow as 29½ inches wide whereas the standard code requires doors to be 36 inches wide. It also permits alternate entrances when the historic building's geometry dictates, whereas the standard code requires access to the front entrances to buildings.

The code exempts historic buildings from California's stringent energy code but not from seismic upgrading requirements. With respect to the latter, the code calls for the least intrusive modifications consistent with a reasonable level of life safety protection. As Mackensen notes, "A building's ability to resist an earthquake is a key factor in its continued viability." He considers it an "indefensible misuse" of the historic code to propose an inadequate level of seismic protection just to save money. "It is a misreading of the Cali-

"The performance-based historic code says, 'Close the books and start relying again on common sense, experience, and good judgement.'"

DON RIVETT

Sacramento's Memorial Auditorium

SACRAMENTO'S HISTORIC MEMORIAL AUDITORIUM, a stunning building modeled after a Byzantine basilica, is currently taking advantage of California's State Historical Building Code.

Constructed in 1927 to honor Sacramentans who died for their country in World War I, the auditorium is the city's only major public building (except for the State Capitol) dating from the early 20th century that remains completely intact. For 60 years, the building hosted Sacramento's most important civic events—high school graduations, concerts, basketball games, ballets, and Governor's inaugural balls—and became a veritable repository of community memories. But in 1986, concerns over the building's ability to withstand an earthquake prompted the city to close the building. A ballot-box initiative calling for the preservation of the building's interior and its multiple uses won approval in 1992. Renovation plans approved by the city in 1994 are now under way.

Since the auditorium could not comply with handicapped-access and other code requirements, the flexibility allowed by the State Historical Building Code, which addresses Americans with Disabilities Act issues as well as basic construction matters, has played a crucial role in its preservation.

The auditorium is scheduled to reopen in early 1997. Says Robert Rakela, a member of the citizens advisory committee created by the city to oversee the building's renovation: "It's like seeing your great grandmother's Model T sitting in the garage. All you have to do is put gas in the tank, air in the tires, and then you can drive away. It's a piece of jewelry just waiting to be polished."

fornia Historical Building Code to interpret it as a license to merely 'paint the cracks,' " he says.

The State Historical Building Safety Board in the Office of the State Architect administers the code. Composed of representatives from the architecture and construction industry, state agencies and local governments, the Board advises individuals as well as state and local governments on code matters and interprets and enforces the code provisions. The Board evaluates projects brought to its attention on a case-by-case basis, applying professional judgement to individual problems. The law gives the Board officials the latitude necessary to exercise the judgment required to retain the viability of historic structures. In general, property owners with code problems are supposed to discuss them first with local code officials. If disputes arise, owners may appeal to the State Historical Building Safety Board, which will act on cases involving issues of statewide interest.

Analysis

SINCE 1985, USAGE OF CALIFORNIA'S Historic Building Code has grown dramatically, to the point where Californians now rank it as one of their most important historic preservation tools.

Mackensen sees the code as the most valuable historic preservation incentive that California has: "It is the key to cost-effective rehabilitation. Changing things like doors, windows or railings, just to conform to current codes, not only damages the integrity of the historic resource, but unnecessarily drives up rehabilitation costs."

The code has helped to preserve historic buildings in San Diego's historic Gaslamp District, "Old Sacramento," and in dozens of other historic areas. Features of the California code have been adopted by several other states, including Washington, Oregon, and Arizona.

Richard LaVoie, a Sacramentan who instigated a ballot-box initiative to save his city's historic Memorial Auditorium, says the state's historic building code has been "absolutely vital" to the preservation of historic buildings. "Two arguments are usually given in this country for not preserving historic buildings," he says. "The first is money. People say they can't afford to preserve and renovate if they are forced to bring their building entirely up to modern codes. They say, 'Give us a way to preserve so that we don't have to spend an absolute fortune on rehabilitation expenses.' The second issue is safety. People say old buildings aren't safe. California's historical building code addresses both problems."

The education of building inspectors and planning officials remains an ongoing challenge because they routinely deal with prescriptive codes. However, the number of appeals from local property owners to the California State Historical Building Safety Board has fallen dramatically as more architects and building inspectors have used the code and come to understand it.

An opinion rendered by the California state attorney general in 1976 held that "government officials are not liable for injuries resulting from enforcement or use of the State Historical Building Code." This opinion, which remains valid today, has reassured code officials otherwise concerned about liability lawsuits. In the nearly 20 years since the code has been in use, there have been only a handful of legal challenges, none of them successful.

The code is occasionally attacked for tolerating unsafe conditions. Mackensen responds to such attacks by noting that "anything less than the 'perfect' building may be perceived by some to pose a compromise with health and safety. Thus, even the rise and run of a stairway, if not in compliance with the latest code, could fall into this category. Yet we know that buildings legally remain open and in operation for generations, although they are clearly out of compliance with the most modern building codes."

"Give us a way to preserve so that we don't have to spend an absolute fortune on rehabilitation expenses."

Wayne Donaldson, a San Diego-based architect who specializes in historic preservation, believes that California's historic building code is "without a doubt, our best preservation tool in California. The unique value of the code is that it is performance-oriented rather than prescriptive, and it is mandatory. It simplifies matters for architects and developers throughout the state." He adds that "the code has permitted a wide range of historic buildings to be preserved, from adobe structures built in the 1700s on up to shortly after World War II. The code has helped us preserve such important buildings as the Ferry Building in San Francisco, the San Luis Rey Mission in Oceanside, even the Golden Gate bridge, which the state highway department once wanted to widen."

Massachusetts' Article 32

MASSACHUSETTS, ANOTHER STATE TO ACT early on building code problems, added "Article 22" to the State Building Code in 1979. Like the California Historic Building Code, the Massachusetts statute is mandatory for local governments.

Article 22, which has since been renamed Article 32, accomplished several things:

- It set forth performance standards for existing buildings;
- It created specific "compliance alternatives," or ways for historic buildings to compensate for code deficiencies through other means;
- It gave precedence to local historic district laws over the state building code insofar as exterior building features are concerned when the two regulations conflicted; and
- It generally exempted historic buildings from complete code compliance so long as existing hazards were corrected and the building remains as safe after rehabilitation as before.

The compliance alternatives are laid out in a special section of the code, "Appendix F."[13] They compare the fire ratings of archaic construction systems with the ratings of comparable modern systems. For example, a modern fire suppression system might compensate for the old wood-frame construction of a three-story historic mansion converted to professional offices. Appendix F helps architects and building inspectors alike in that it gives them an easy way to clearly determine what measures need to be taken to provide adequate safety and what materials or techniques can be substituted for others. Appendix F helps to overcome the problem created by the omission of historic construction techniques in the evaluations of building concepts tested by the Underwriters Laboratory.

Massachusetts' 1979 law also created two categories of historic buildings: "totally preserved" and "partially preserved." Examples of the former include landmarks such as the Old North Church that are open to the public. These are given broad exemptions from the state's standard building code. Partially preserved buildings are structures of less historical importance that nonetheless qualify for the National Register of Historic Places; these are subject to Article 32.

Wendall C. Kalsow, an architect with the Boston-based firm of McGinley Hart and Associates, which specializes in historic preservation, finds Massachusetts' Article 32 user-friendly and helpful: "Rather than saying, here are 200 pages of requirements for your renovation project, the code instead asks how will the building be used and then offers simple and clear solutions. Article 32 is also available to existing buildings that are not designated as historic. This is important, because there are many buildings important to the historic fabric of a community that are not official landmarks. As a whole, Article 32 translates into a higher comfort level for building inspectors who are afraid of liability problems."

"Rather than saying, here are 200 pages of requirements for your renovation project, the code instead asks how will the building be used and then offers simple and clear solutions."

Around the Country

O THER STATES TO TACKLE BUILDING CODE issues affecting historic buildings include Georgia, Connecticut, North Carolina, Ohio, Washington, New York and Wisconsin. Wisconsin's alternative building code resembles the Massachusetts code in that it permits the use of alternative building materials and construction techniques, provided they accomplish the same general purpose as those prescribed for newer buildings. The code also permits the state's Department of Commerce, which administers the program, to grant variances to code provisions if a property owner can demonstrate that alternative techniques are adequate.

Georgia's "Uniform Act for the Application of Building and Fire Related Codes to Existing Buildings," adopted in 1984, also resembles the Massachusetts code except that local governments have the option of adopting the Georgia alternative. The Georgia code grew out of a "Building and Fire Codes Task Force" organized by the Georgia Trust for Historic Preservation. The task force included representatives from the Georgia State Fire Marshall's Office, the Georgia Department of Community Affairs, Legal Counsel of the State Legislature, the Institute of Government of the University of Georgia, the Georgia Chapter of the American Institute of Architects, the Georgia Power Company, and local building and fire officials, and developers. Following the code's adoption, the Georgia Trust and the university sponsored a series of educational workshops for local code inspectors to acquaint them with the code. The state's largest communities and those with many historic properties have adopted the code, known as "Article 3." These include Athens, Atlanta, Augusta, Columbus, Macon, and Savannah. The code is seen as helpful to the rehabilitation of mixed-use projects—apartments over stores—in downtowns. Many communities have not adopted the Georgia code, however.

The code is seen as helpful to the rehabilitation of mixed-use projects— apartments over stores— in downtowns.

Although Texas does not have a special historic building code, its Main Street Program, which operates out of the Texas Historical Commission, has actively promoted educational workshops on this subject. Presentations on preservation code issues are made at conferences sponsored by Texas A & M University each year for building inspectors.

In New Jersey, the Center for Urban Policy Research at Rutgers University in New Brunswick has conducted an in-depth analysis of the Massachusetts, New York (Subchapter E), and Georgia historic building codes for the New Jersey Department of Community Affairs. At this writing, New Jersey is considering amending its building code to foster the rehabilitation of old and historic buildings.

The Future

IT SHOULD BE NOTED that all of the major building codes provide for some consideration of historic buildings in their sections on existing buildings. Each of the model codes has adopted separate provisions for existing buildings. As noted earlier, ICBO publishes the *Uniform Code for Building Conservation*, the SBCCI publishes the *Standard Existing Buildings Code*, and BOCA includes *Chapter 34*, which provides a quantitative method for determining alternate means of achieving fire safety.

According to Marilyn E. Kaplan, a New York-based architect who has written extensively on this subject, major efforts are underway to convert many of the model codes into true "performance-based" documents. The major barrier to this goal in the past has been the lack of available tools for design professionals and code officials to scientifically and quantifiably evaluate the performance of alternate systems. The recent development of computer fire models, which enable experts to predict the performance of a building in a fire, may expedite progress in this area.

Finally, a long-discussed effort to eliminate the three separate model codes is finally reaching fruition, Kaplan reports. The three model code organizations have collaborated with the International Code Council, established in 1995, to move toward a single model code for the U.S.

Postscript

READERS INTERESTED IN LEARNING MORE about this subject may want to refer to an Information Sheet published by the National Trust for Historic Preservation: Safety, Building Codes and Historic Buildings *(updated in 1996), by Marilyn E. Kaplan. See Appendix A.*

CHAPTER 5

State Agency Investments

152

State Agency Investments

IN *SAVE OUR LAND, SAVE OUR TOWNS*,[1] AUTHOR THOMAS HYLTON MAKES the point that state agencies in Pennsylvania often work at cross purposes with each other, wasting enormous amounts of money in the process:

Here's just one example: The state Department of Agriculture spends millions of dollars annually to preserve farmland by purchasing development rights from farmers. Meanwhile, the state Department of Transportation spends other millions expanding highways into prime agricultural areas, highways that promote the development of that farmland.

What do we really want? Farmland preservation or farmland development?

Here's another example: The state Department of Community Affairs spends millions of dollars in attempts to revitalize cities, while, at the same time, the Department of Environmental Protection enforces rules that encourage the development of virgin land instead of older urban areas.

Does Pennsylvania really want to revitalize its cities? You have to wonder.[2]

This problem is hardly limited to Pennsylvania. In many states, the investments of one state agency commonly undercut those of another.

This building in a downtown Rutland (VT) historic district is occupied by the regional offices of several state agencies.

An Interdepartmental Task Force in Maryland

ONE APPROACH TO THIS PROBLEM of the right hand not knowing what the left hand is doing is that taken recently by Maryland Governor Parris N. Glendening's administration. "It simply makes no sense to spend hundreds of millions of dollars on new infrastructure and facilities while we allow existing, underutilized investments to deteriorate," says Glendening. In November 1995, the governor announced the formation of a high-level task force charged with examining the effects of state agency policies on existing communities.[3] Known as the Working Group on Revitalization and Directed Growth, the task force includes representatives from the Maryland departments of transportation, housing and community development, economic development, general services, planning, natural resources, environment, and human resources. The participants are state agency officials just below cabinet rank—high enough up in the bureaucracy to have influence and access to the cabinet, but not quite as busy as cabinet secretaries.

Since December 1995, the group has organized two retreats for the governor's cabinet. Both focused on urban disinvestment problems and opportunities for the state to alleviate them. The working group holds informal, ad hoc meetings, expanding and contracting the number of participants as meeting agendas warrant. The goal is to target state resources in a more coordinated way and to eliminate inconsistencies between different state investments.

As part of his policy of promoting "smart growth," Glendening has directed every state agency to consider whether its decisions, policies, and programs encourage urban revitalization or promote urban sprawl. He has said he wants his cabinet to focus on these issues every third or fourth meeting so that this effort will be sustained. Glendening has also asked each cabinet secretary to designate a senior-level agency director to serve as a "point person" for this interdepartmental effort and as a conduit for interagency communication.

Tangible outcomes of Governor Glendening's policy thus far include:

- a new policy for the state's public school construction program to emphasize renovation of existing schools in older neighborhoods instead of building new schools in new communities (*see Chapter 4*); and
- rewriting of the Maryland Department of General Services' guidelines for locating state agencies.

> *Governor Glendening has directed every state agency to consider whether its decisions, policies, and programs encourage urban revitalization or promote urban sprawl.*

Under these new guidelines, the state will retain its emphasis on economy but will give 20 bonus points to areas designated by local governments for urban revitalization in its scoring system for evaluating possible locations for state agencies. Among the older communities in which the state has recently decided to locate state offices as a result of this policy is Cumberland, Md. The state plans to build a 40,000-square-foot office building in the middle of Cumberland's downtown. The first major construction project in the city's downtown since World War II, the office building will help to animate the town's street level through the inclusion of ground-floor retail shops. Previous state office requirements—e.g., free parking, wiring, etc.—have worked against older communities by encouraging state agencies to locate in outlying areas.

An Urban Coordinating Council in New Jersey

A CONCEPT AKIN TO MARYLAND'S Working Group on Revitalization and Directed Growth is being used in New Jersey, where Governor Christine Todd Whitman has directed her cabinet to form an "Urban Coordinating Council" with representatives from every major department. The council is dedicated to using state resources to their best advantage to revitalize cities. Governor Whitman has asked her cabinet officials to report to her periodically on the steps their agencies are taking to implement the comprehensive state plan for growth that New Jersey approved in 1992. Hundreds of citizens participated in shaping this plan, and it is generally very supportive of historic preservation values.

Despite pressures from developers to do otherwise, Governor Whitman has supported funding for the state planning office and has made strong statements in favor of better land-use planning in New Jersey. "New Jerseyans support planning," she told the State Planning Commission in February 1996. "They know that without it, we surrender our future to little more than the random will of those who stand to reap short-term benefits at the expense of New Jersey's long-term well-being…How land is used affects virtually everything that happens in a state as densely populated as ours: the health of our cities, the vitality of our farms, and the stability of our neighborhoods and towns."

A Cabinet Committee on State Planning Issues in Delaware

NEW JERSEY'S NEIGHBOR, Delaware, has also received strong gubernatorial support for better land-use planning and historic preservation. In 1995, Governor Thomas R. Carper signed legislation that, among other things:

- makes historic preservation a mandatory, rather than an optional, element of county comprehensive plans for growth and development;
- modifies guidelines affecting the location of state-assisted schools and libraries to discourage urban sprawl and to enable children to walk to school;
- authorizes counties to create districts from which—and to which—development rights may be transferred in order to preserve farmland, open spaces, and other environmentally sensitive resources; and
- limits the state's obligation to provide financial assistance or infrastructure improvements for land-use or development actions that are inconsistent with state plans and policies.

With respect to this last policy, the Delaware Department of Transportation announced in May 1996 a decision to withhold a highway access permit for a superstore outside the historic town of Lewes, Del., on the grounds that the development project would necessitate road improvements that were neither in the state's budget nor in its plans.

Governor Carper reactivated a Cabinet Committee on State Planning Issues in 1994 and approved the creation of an Office of State Planning Coordination in 1996 to help ensure that state agency investments support Delaware's goals of rejuvenating cities, preserving farmland, and encouraging more compact new development.

Simply by locating in a downtown, state agencies can give historic areas an economic shot in the arm.

Location of State Offices Downtown

SIMPLY BY LOCATING IN A DOWNTOWN INSTEAD OF ON THE URBAN PERIPHERY, state agencies can give old and historic areas an economic shot in the arm and avoid contributing to urban sprawl. Several governors have issued executive orders directing state agencies to do exactly that. In addition, several state legislatures have passed laws requiring state agencies to locate in historic buildings when this is practical and makes good economic sense.

One of the first governors to provide leadership in this area was former Massachusetts Governor Michael Dukakis, who issued an executive order in 1977. "State government can help to stimulate the revitalization of [the] downtown centers [of older cities and towns]," declared the order, "by focusing public investment such as roads, schools and offices in these areas, thereby encouraging a needed resurgence of private investment in these same areas…[I]t is hereby declared to be the policy of the Commonwealth to take every possible step to foster economic growth and development in downtown centers, thereby helping to reverse the deterioration and decay of such areas and to restore economic vitality to the downtown centers and the state as a whole."[4] Among other actions, this policy caused the Massachusetts Registry of Motor Vehicles to cancel plans to move to the outskirts of Worcester and to occupy a rehabilitated building in downtown Worcester instead. In a decision that reinforced the point of this executive order, Governor Dukakis refused to provide curb cuts for a regional mall proposed by the Pyramid Development Company outside Pittsfield, Mass. His reasoning: the outlying mall would harm downtown Pittsfield.

In Vermont, a succession of governors, Republican and Democrat alike, have supported the state's policy of reinforcing town centers by locating state offices there. While Governor Richard Snelling had informally encouraged the Vermont Department of State Buildings to locate several courthouses in downtowns, Governor Madeleine Kunin formalized this policy in 1985 with an executive order directing the department to give priority to locating state government activities in historic and other existing buildings when appropriate.[5] Vermont's current governor, Howard Dean, has reinforced Kunin's policy.

The Oregon Dept. of Transportation office, located in downtown Portland, Ore., pursuant to an executive order aimed at strengthening the urban core.

COURTESY LIVABLE OREGON

Today Vermont has located state agencies in new or existing buildings in downtown Burlington, Rutland, Middlebury, and White River Junction. Plans to locate state agencies in downtown St. Albans, Newport and Springfield are underway. Although most of these projects have involved new office structures, their proximity to historic buildings has benefitted historic preservation. When people visit state offices, they patronize nearby businesses in historic buildings. This economic activity makes it easier for historic property owners to maintain and upgrade their property. In the Springfield project, the state is renovating the historic Jones and Lampson manufacturing plant, which once fabricated machine tools. When renovated, the plant will house district and superior courts.

John Zampieri, commissioner of the Vermont Department of State Buildings, says that while it is sometimes harder to find suitable office space downtown because of parking and other requirements, the state consciously seeks to concentrate economic activity downtown, make good use of public transit, and avoid the consumption of natural resources—e.g., trees for lumber—needed for new construction. He also believes that the continuity provided by three successive governors—Snelling, Kunin and Dean—for this "pro-downtown" policy has helped to produce positive results.

In 1994, former Oregon Governor Barbara Roberts consolidated 230 state transportation department employees previously scattered throughout several suburban locations into one downtown office located a block away from a light rail stop. In explaining the consolidation and a companion executive order directing all state agencies to give preference to downtown locations when leasing office space, (see sidebar) Roberts said:

> The order will apply to small cities as well as larger communities like Portland. It will mean that the state of Oregon will be putting its rent payments toward the support of strong urban centers and in support of development that makes use of transit, bicycling and walking as well as driving. Last year the agencies of state government entered or renewed over 40 leases totaling 200,000 square feet of facilities. If that were all office space, it would be the equivalent of ten floors of a typical downtown office building. That kind of change and turnover happens every year. We can use that normal, ongoing state expenditure to focus a stream of investment into Oregon's downtowns. This is one way the state can act in partnership with communities as we seek to rebuild and renew the downtowns of Oregon and encourage compact, livable cities rather than suburban sprawl.

This Executive Order was issued at the recommendation of a "Good Development Task Force" created by the Oregon Main Street Program to answer the question: How could state government use its money, its incentives and its regulations to reinforce its already clearly stated land-use and transportation goals? The policy enunciated by the executive order was seen as a way for the state government to "put its lease payments where its mouth is."

The Oregon transportation agency is not located in a historic building, but it is in a historic area and the activity it generates benefits businesses in historic buildings nearby. The state did not provide any special parking facilities for the employees. According to Brian Scott, president of Livable Oregon, "The employees grumbled about this at first. Now they love the location. There is a lot of activity in the area and the employees can choose from among a zillion places to have lunch instead of having to drive somewhere."

Vermont has located state agencies in new or existing buildings in downtown Burlington, Rutland, Middlebury, and White River Junction.

* * * *

Historic Buildings for State Offices

A T LEAST SIX STATES—Texas, Florida, New York, Arizona, Minnesota, and Connecticut—have enacted laws requiring state agencies to give first consideration to historic buildings when seeking new office space. California has an executive order to the same effect. For the most part, however, these policies have been ignored.

The Texas law has been little used primarily because the specifications for office space set by the state General Services Commission (GSC) are often difficult for historic buildings to meet. The specifications typically call for such features as dropped acoustical ceilings, carpeted floors, wiring and large numbers of parking spaces. Unlike some cities, which have sometimes agreed to waive parking requirements on the grounds that many downtown trips occur by foot and public transit as well as by car, the GSC's parking requirements are based on principles more applicable to auto-oriented suburbs than to more compact downtowns.

Attitudes seem important, too. When Texas Main Street, a state agency within the Texas Historical Commission at Austin, sought to locate in a historic structure built in 1872, the GSC discouraged the agency from doing so on the grounds that it would cost $1.1 million to rehabilitate the building. The project would be too expensive and too much trouble, the GSC suggested. The Main Street agency persisted, raised some private money, found that it could rehabilitate the building for $340,000—not $1.1 million—and successfully renovated the building, which the agency now uses for its offices. State employees housed elsewhere, mostly in monolithic high-rises with no character, often tell the Main Street staff they wish they were located in a building like theirs, which is located in a pleasant, human-scale area.

Florida's law states that "each state agency of the executive branch, in seeking to acquire additional space through new construction or lease, shall give preference to the acquisition or use of historic properties when such acquisition or use is determined to be feasible and prudent compared with available alternatives." Enacted in 1990, the law has not been used even once. Florida's Division of Historical Resources believes that state agencies should be encouraged to *consider* historic buildings when looking for space, they should not be forced into doing so if these buildings do not meet their requirements. However, the division has encouraged *local* government agencies to reuse and occupy historic buildings by awarding grants for rehabilitation to local governments through Florida's Special Category Grants Program. (*See Chapter 2.*) George W. Percy, the division director, estimates that between 200 and 300 courthouses, city halls, and other historic buildings have been rehabilitated and reused by local agencies as a result of these grants.

In Minnesota and Arizona, despite similar laws on the books requiring state agencies to consider space in historic buildings, little use has been made of this policy.

It appears that unless the governor, an agency head, or someone else with influence is willing to promote the implementation of these laws, they tend to languish. It may be appropriate for preservation advocates to examine the specifications included in bid invitations for office space to determine which ones are truly necessary and which ones present artificial barriers to the recycling of historic buildings by state agencies. In this regard, parking requirements would be a prime candidate for scrutiny, for such requirements are often based on the parking needs of suburbs and do not reflect the alternatives to driving that exist in a compact downtown where historic buildings tend to be concentrated.

Oregon Governor Roberts' Executive Order[6] Directing State Agencies to Locate Downtown

OREGON'S BENCHMARKS FOR LIVABLE COMMUNITIES set targets for reducing communities' reliance on the single-occupant automobile, and encouraging the development of areas of mixed housing, employment and retail in which walking is convenient and pleasant. The best examples of this kind of mixed use are in Oregon's downtowns.

In addition to assisting local governments to plan for mixed use development, the state should support existing mixed use centers with its own business activity. The rental payments for leased state office space, and the retail and service trade generated by state workers, represent significant economic stimulus for the communities in which they are located.

Siting state facilities in downtowns and other central areas, particularly those well served by transit, assures that state services and programs are accessible to more Oregonians, particularly those who are dependent on transit. Enabling and encouraging both state workers and clients of state offices to conduct business by transit, walking and other methods in addition to the single-occupancy vehicle aids communities in their efforts to reduce vehicle miles traveled, traffic congestion and air pollution. Siting and retaining state facilities in these central locations is in the long term best interest of the State of Oregon...

IT IS HEREBY ORDERED AND DIRECTED:

1. State facilities, and state agencies' use of space, shall serve to strengthen Oregon's cities and their central districts by conserving existing urban resources, using existing infrastructure and services, and encouraging the development and redevelopment of central business districts and other mixed-use centers.

2. The process for meeting state agency office needs and, where practical, other facility needs shall give preferential consideration to locations within the central business districts of cities...The director of the Department of Administrative Services may identify special program needs that justify locating offices outside central business districts, but such offices shall be located conveniently close to transit in communities that have transit service. Other areas of mixed use development that are highly accessible to the public, have a fully developed pedestrian circulation system, have high quality transit service (in those communities with transit service), and are designated as urban centers in the applicable comprehensive plan may also be given priority consideration.

3. Site selection shall take into account the need for co-location of agencies or activities in common or adjacent space in order to improve public service and accessibility, effect economies of operation...

4. The director of the Department of Administrative Services shall develop policies to implement this order. The directors of state agencies shall cooperate with the Department in implementing this order and give the Department early notice of changes which affect space requirements.

5. No office space shall be located outside the areas described in paragraph 2 of this order without the direct approval of the director of the Department of Administrative Services.

6. In assuring that office space is acquired in the most cost-effective manner feasible...the director of the Department of Administrative Services shall give due regard to the value of the accessibility and central location of the areas described in this policy.

7. The director of the Department of Administrative Services shall submit a written report to the Governor, the Speaker of the House, and the President of the Senate on July 1, 1995 and annually thereafter, detailing siting decisions and describing how those decisions conform to the requirements of this order.

CHAPTER 6

Rural Preservation

CHAPTER 6

Rural Preservation

By MEGAN K. BELLUE

OLD STONE FENCES IN NEW ENGLAND. RED BARNS IN WISCONSIN. Civil War trenches in Georgia. Adobe churches in New Mexico. Historic trails in Wyoming. Windmills in south central Pennsylvania. Together with farms, scenic vistas, small towns and natural features of the landscape, these and countless other man-made elements contribute to the "soul" of the countryside and give it a special identity.

Stewart L. Udall has observed that we need small towns and rural areas as "slow-lane refuges where people overwhelmed by urban stress can find quietude and peace of mind...[W]e need the diversity they provide, as a reminder of the lifestyles and values of an older, perhaps saner, America."[1]

But the countryside has become increasingly threatened today by a combination of forces: suburban sprawl, insensitive development, inappropriately located roads, tax policies and economic forces that make it increasingly difficult to make a living in rural areas. Between 1970 and 1990, the Chicago metropolitan area grew by 46 percent while its population increased by only four percent. The Cleveland urban area expanded by 33 percent in that same period while its regional population declined by eleven percent.[2] Between 1982 and 1992, Michigan lost 854,000 acres of farmland—about ten acres every hour to new development.[3] Similar statistics describe growth patterns all across the country. Behind these figures lies the homogenization of America's rural landscape.

Samuel N. Stokes, an author of *Saving America's Countryside*, recommends a collaborative approach to rural preservation: "Rural conservation should integrate natural resource conservation, farmland retention, historic preservation, and scenic protection...While there may be good reasons in some instances for those concerned with protecting wildlife habitat, for example, to organize separately from those concerned with preserving farmland or historic buildings, joining forces make more sense. Seemingly different concerns are often, in fact, closely linked. The windbreak, which is designed to prevent soil erosion, also provides habitat for wildlife and is a scenic element in the landscape. The historic farmhouses and barns prized by the local historical society are far more interesting if they are still used by farm families and surrounded by active farmland."[4]

Farmland in Lancaster County, Pa.

163

Several states have responded to the disappearing landscape by enacting programs to protect farmland and open spaces. Through a combination of techniques—the purchase of development rights, conservation easements, barn preservation grants, special taxation and land-use policies, even honor awards—states are applying creative large- and small-scale solutions in this area. Three states—Pennsylvania, Vermont and Maryland—stand out for their innovations in rural preservation. This chapter examines Pennsylvania's use of purchased development rights, Vermont's Housing and Conservation Trust Fund, and Maryland's conservation easements to preserve Civil War battlefields. This chapter also considers, in less detail, more modest, but still effective programs such as Oklahoma's Centennial Farm and Ranch awards and the "BARN AGAIN!" initiative of North Dakota. In many of the more successful rural preservation programs, public-private partnerships play an integral role. Non-profit land trusts, for example, often work hand-in-hand with state agencies and complement the role of government.

While recognizing certain states for their successes, we emphasize the importance of making sure that state policies in other areas do not undercut their rural preservation efforts. As we shall see in Pennsylvania, for example, shortcomings in the state's land-use policies have seriously "eroded" the Commonwealth's progress in saving farmland. Rural preservation cannot be approached without looking at broader policy questions, including and especially land-use and taxation policies.

Lancaster County's beautiful countryside is internationally known but is now threatened by the type of sprawl development under construction here.

ED WORTECK

Farmland Preservation in Pennsylvania

ETWEEN 1960 AND 1975, THE COMMONWEALTH OF PENNSYLVANIA LOST 2.7 MIL-lion acres of farmland; between 1975 and 1985, the state lost another 900,000 acres. This was the equivalent of losing an area the size of Pittsburgh every six months.[5]

By the mid-eighties, it had become apparent to many Pennsylvanians that they were losing their farmland too fast. In an attempt to address this problem, farmland preservation advocates proposed a $100 million bond issue in 1987. Approved by voters by a margin of two to one, the referendum not only provided the initial funding for Pennsylvania's farmland preservation grant program, but it also sent state legislators a message: The public wanted farmland preserved.

The following year, the Pennsylvania Farm Bureau and other organizations persuaded the state legislature to create a comprehensive state farmland preservation program. When added to earlier preservation laws, the "Pennsylvania Agricultural Conservation Easement Purchase Program" approved in 1988 provided a well-rounded farmland protection program for the Commonwealth.

For the most part, Pennsylvania's program is voluntary. It offers communities several important tools, including:

- agricultural security areas;
- agricultural zoning;
- purchase of development rights;
- grants for farmland preservation; and
- property tax and fee assessment relief for farmers.

Program administration. The Pennsylvania farmland preservation program is administered by the State Agricultural Land Preservation Board. This is comprised of 17 members—county farm representatives, state officials, and state legislators—appointed by the governor and high-ranking members of the legislature. This board, which is staffed by the Pennsylvania Bureau of Farmland Preservation, establishes the general program criteria within which county programs operate. Local administration occurs through county agricultural preservation boards, which counties must establish if they wish to participate in the state program. So long as the counties operate within the state's guidelines, they may run their programs as they see fit. Counties are not required to follow state guidelines for farmland preservation activities that they pay for entirely out of their own funds.

The public wanted farmland preserved.

Agricultural Security Areas

THE FIRST STEP IN THE PROGRAM is the creation of Agricultural Security Areas (ASAs) at the local level. These must be created before any of the state's other program elements can be implemented. ASAs are created by municipal governments—usually townships—acting in response to petitions from landowners. An ASA must be at least 250 acres, or 500 acres for the county to buy development rights.[6]

ASA designation provides three major benefits for farmers.

First, the designation invokes the state's "right to farm" law, which protects farmers against local ordinances that might interfere with normal farming activities and against "nuisance" lawsuits. For example, a garden-variety zoning law might prevent early-morning farming chores through restrictions on allowable business hours. Like similar laws in other states, Pennsylvania's "right to farm" law addresses an increasingly common conflict: As suburban development encroaches on agricultural land, farmers who have tilled the soil for many years suddenly find suburbanites living next door. These new neighbors consider certain aspects of farming—the noise of a tractor or the smell of fertilizers, for example—as "nuisances" and sue the farmer to stop them. The law prevents these neighbors from suing if the farm was there before they arrived.

The second benefit of an Agricultural Security Area is extra protection against a government's use of condemnation proceedings to acquire farmland for a public purpose—e.g., a road or sewer line extension. Such protection is not absolute, but it does add four extra layers of review to the process of condemning land. The condemnation of farmland in an ASA may occur only if alternative solutions are completely infeasible.

The third benefit is that landowners in ASAs are eligible to sell development rights in exchange for cash, with the understanding that the landowners will agree to the permanent protection of their farmland.

Township governments must reassess their ASAs every seven years to determine whether the conditions that enabled these areas to qualify for ASA status in the first place still exist. If not, the designation may be cancelled. Townships may also decide whether individual landowners can withdraw from the program. Land may be added to the ASA any time after its creation so long as at least ten acres are added.

As of March 1996, 64 of Pennsylvania's 67 counties had created Agricultural Security Areas covering 2.7 million acres of farmland.

Although ASAs may or may not be accompanied by mandatory zoning regulations—this is up to municipalities—these areas can create a powerful but intangible effect *if* they contain large, contiguous blocks of farmland. The ASAs give farmers confidence that an agricultural area will continue to be used for farming for a long time. This sense of permanency helps to stabilize the farming community. If farmers believe that their neighbors will soon sell out to developers, they are less likely to invest in the improvement of their farms. However, when ASAs are small and scattered, as is sometimes the case, they do not inspire such confidence.

As of March 1996, 64 of Pennsylvania's 67 counties had created Agricultural Security Areas covering 2.7 million acres of farmland.[7]

Agricultural zoning

PENNSYLVANIA'S ACT 284, PASSED IN 1978, allows municipalities to create "agricultural zones" for the "protection and preservation of agricultural land." Such zoning is stronger than the agricultural zoning found in many states in that it limits rural residential development much more strictly. Local governments throughout the country have zoned land for agricultural use, but these zones often permit the carving up of farmland for low-density housing development. These districts are agricultural zoning in name only, according to some experts.[8]

The agricultural zoning ordinances of some Pennsylvania townships require that persons buying land in an agricultural zone be notified that agriculture is the primary economic activity and that landowners may be subject to inconvenience or discomfort arising from farming practices—e.g., noise, odors, dust.

So far only a few municipalities in Pennsylvania have adopted true agricultural zoning.[9] York and Lancaster Counties lead the state in the creation of agricultural zones. Whereas participation in an ASA is completely voluntary, compliance with agricultural zoning is mandatory for landowners once a township chooses to create such a zone. Agricultural zones have teeth; ASAs do not.

Purchase of Development Rights

THE MOST IMPORTANT OF THE VOLUNTARY elements in Pennsylvania's program is the purchase of development rights (PDRs).

The PDR concept works like this: A farmer agrees to forfeit certain rights that he may have to sell or develop his land for a use more lucrative than farming—a shopping center or housing subdivision, for example. (The local zoning code must already allow such land uses or the farmer may not have a legal right to them.) An appraiser assesses the real estate market, determines what price the farm could bring in the market place and compares that price to the value of the farm under development restrictions. The difference between those two amounts provides the basis for the value of the development rights, which the state then buys from the farmer. For example, if the farmland is worth only $1 million when used for agriculture but $1.5 million if turned into a shopping center, the state pays the farmer $500,000 in exchange for the forfeited development rights.

How does the state make sure that future owners of the land will continue to preserve it for agriculture as well? After the state buys the development rights, it places a "conservation easement" on the property. The easement, which is recorded on the property deed, permanently prohibits the land from being used for anything but agriculture. This restriction applies to the farmer's heirs and to all future owners.

Under this arrangement, the farmer gets the cash he wants, while the state and the local community enjoy the farmland's permanent preservation. The program is popular with farmers because the decision to sell development rights and place easements on the land is completely voluntary.

In determining whether to buy development rights, the state and the county agricultural land preservation boards ask several questions:

- Is the property within a designated Agricultural Security Area of at least 500 acres, at least 50 of which are contiguous?
- What is the quality of the soil?
- Is at least half of the farm devoted to crops, pastures or grazing?
- Is the land actually being used to produce a reasonably sized harvest?

The cost of development rights varies widely. Near Philadelphia, for example, the per-acre cost can be as high as $16,000. Overall, however, the cost is closer to $2,500 per acre. As of July 1996, Pennsylvania has purchased development rights on 80,000 acres on more than 600 farms. Interest among farmers is high, and the program demand far exceeds the money allocated by the state to fund it. Some 1,000 applications by landowners to sell development rights on over 100,000 acres are currently pending before the county farmland preservation boards.

As of July 1996, Pennsylvania has purchased development rights on 80,000 acres on more than 600 farms.

Grants

TO HELP COUNTIES DEVELOP their own purchase-of-development-rights programs and acquire easements, the state provides matching grants. In awarding these, the state asks such questions as: How strong is local interest in farmland preservation, as measured in part by the county's success in raising matching funds? How intense are local development pressures on farmland?

In 1996 the state grant program received a record-high level of funding: $31 million. The dedicated revenue source for these grants is Pennsylvania's two-cent per-pack cigarette tax. This tax has produced about $20 million a year for the program since its enactment in 1993. The remaining $10 million for the 1996 round of grants came from money still left over from the 1987 $100 million bond. The bonds are being repaid out of general revenues.

Additional Protection

RELIEF FOR FARMERS FROM CERTAIN TAXES and fees complements Pennsylvania's Agricultural Security Areas and Purchase of Development Rights-Easement program.

Tax breaks. Under the state's Clean and Green Act of 1974, farmers are allowed to pay property taxes based on the value of their land as it is actually used rather than according to its fair market value, which may be considerably higher. This usually lowers property taxes substantially, often by as much as 50 percent. Act 207, a related law passed in 1980, requires that farmland be appraised at its "use value" when inheritance taxes are calculated. If property heirs use the land for purposes other than farming within seven years of the original owner's death, they must pay a penalty. Inheritance taxes have caused farmers in many parts of the country to sell out for development.

Fee mitigation. Act 71, passed in 1976, gives farmers relief from potentially costly fees for infrastructure improvements. When a municipality extends water and sewer lines, it usually charges property owners a fee based on how many linear feet the line runs through their property. For the average property owner, this formula makes sense. For farmers with thousands of feet of water and sewer lines running through their property, the fee can be prohibitive. Under Act 71, farmers are assessed only for the road frontage of their house. One illustration of this program's value: An Allegheny County township extended sewer lines through three farms and assessed them $130,156. Due to Act 71, these farmers simply paid a standard hook-up fee.

Analysis

> *The Pennsylvania Municipalities Planning Code neither complements nor backs up the state's farmland preservation efforts.*

ALTHOUGH THE PENNSYLVANIA PROGRAM varies in quality from one county to another, overall, it is one of the nation's strongest farmland preservation initiatives. Some 80,000 acres of farmland have been permanently protected through easements. Although Maryland leads the nation in having protected farmland through easements, Pennsylvania's program started later than Maryland's and is catching up. Maryland has protected 175,000 acres of land through easements.

While the public strongly supports Pennsylvania's farmland preservation efforts, and the state's program is exemplary, the Pennsylvania Municipalities Planning Code neither complements nor backs up these efforts. Pennsylvania's enabling law for local planning and zoning has been criticized for not providing the tools that cities and towns elsewhere take for granted. According to Ron Bailey, planning director for Lancaster County, Pa.:

- Efforts to plan and manage growth on a regional basis in the state are often defeated by the fact that each of the state's 2,000 municipalities must zone for every conceivable type of land use. Even if it makes more sense for certain land uses to be concentrated in one part of a region, rather than allowed in every township within a county, the law does not permit this.
- Local plans and zoning ordinances are not required to be consistent, as is the case in many states. Even if all the municipalities within a county adopted a comprehensive plan that directed new growth into concentrated areas, where public ser-

vices could be provided most efficiently and at least cost to taxpayers, and away from fragile rural areas vulnerable to development, if a developer wanted to construct a project contrary to the plan, he could easily do so. Pennsylvania courts have interpreted the law in such a way as to make local comprehensive plans relatively meaningless here.

- Even if local planning efforts aimed at protecting rural areas are well under way, a municipality may not impose interim development controls to protect such resources on a temporary basis until the plan is completed. Such controls are permitted in other states.

- Counties can adopt zoning and subdivision controls, but if an individual municipality within the county doesn't like the rules, it can supersede the county's regulations.

Pennsylvania needs a clear, comprehensive and coordinated policy for dealing with land-use issues affecting rural and urban areas, according to Robert Freeman, a former state representative who oversaw a comprehensive analysis of the Commonwealth's policies affecting land-use.[10]

So the picture in Pennsylvania is mixed. On the one hand the state has created a $100 million farmland protection program that has achieved impressive results, but on the other hand, the state's land-use policies have often worked at cross purposes with farmland protection goals.

Lancaster County, Pennsylvania

LANCASTER COUNTY IS ONE OF THE MOST FERTILE areas in the nation today. It produces $800 million a year in farm products, more than any other non-irrigated county in the United States. The spectacular beauty of Lancaster's farms, the attractive small towns that dot the landscape, and the uniqueness of Plain Sect communities such as the Amish are also the magnet for thousands of tourists every year. "Agriculture is really the foundation of our half-billion-dollar-a-year tourism economy," says Tom Daniels, director of the Lancaster County Agricultural Preservation Board.

In some respects, Lancaster County's farmland preservation program represents a national model. In fact, the county program, which dates to the early 1980s, did provide the model for Pennsylvania's statewide program. County residents place a high value on farmland preservation, as a 1995 poll published by the *Lancaster New Era* revealed. According to the poll, Lancastrians ranked farmland preservation as the second highest priority for county government. Only fighting crime ranked higher.

The tool seen by local experts as the most effective technique for protecting farmland in Lancaster County is agricultural zoning. Agricultural zoning ordinances have been adopted by 39 of Lancaster's 41 townships, each of which has independent planning and zoning authority. A typical "ag zoning" ordinance allows one building lot for every 25 acres of land, with a maximum lot size of two acres. For example, if a farmer owns 100 acres, he may build four structures on his property. Those four building lots take up at most eight acres if each lot is at the maximum of two acres each. This leaves 92 acres for farming.

Several townships have enlarged their agricultural zones. Alan Musselman, former director of the Lancaster Farmland Trust, says agricultural zoning is one of the most important ingredients to success because such zoning limits the development of farmland.

Twelve of the county's independent townships have also adopted "Urban Growth Boundaries (UGB)." Under the UGB concept, the township determines how much land it will need for various purposes—economic development, housing, open space, etc.—and then draws a line around that acreage. New development may occur within the boundary but not outside

Pennsylvania needs a clear, comprehensive and coordinated policy for dealing with land-use issues.

it. But because the Commonwealth of Pennsylvania has not granted municipalities the statutory authority to mandate UGBs, the townships have worked out their own arrangements on a voluntary basis. Lancaster County's UGBs have reasonably strong political support but do not have the strength of UGBs in Oregon or Washington States. (*For a more complete discussion of the UGB concept, which was pioneered in Oregon, see Chapter 10.*)

Lancaster has also used farmland preservation tools available from the state, such as the purchase of development rights, to preserve farmland. The county spends about $3 million a year to purchase between 15 and 20 easements. Its efforts have been augmented by the Lancaster Farmland Trust, a local nonprofit organization. As of August 1996, the Lancaster County Agricultural Preservation Board and the Lancaster Farmland Trust had purchased—or acquired through donations—easements on more than 22,000 acres of farmland. But about twice as much money is needed, according to Daniels. As of July 1996, the board faced a backlog of about 150 easement applications, which meant a waiting list for farmers of about ten years. "We are the victims of our own success," says Daniels. "Unfortunately, our long waiting list means that some people will drop out, especially with today's farm economy."

> *The boards simply do not have the staff or the resources to analyze proposals for superstores whose square footage may exceed the size of an entire small-town downtown.*

So as is the case with Pennsylvania as a whole, Lancaster County's farmland preservation efforts are exemplary, but other factors—new development pressures, in this case—have made the task difficult. The county has protected an impressive 320,000 acres, over half the county, through effective agricultural zoning. Twenty-two thousand acres have been protected by easements—18,000 of which have been secured by the county's agricultural preservation board, 4,000, by the Lancaster Farmland Trust. But the county has lost 92,500

Countertrends in Lancaster County

WHILE LANCASTER'S PROGRAM is one of the more creative agricultural protection efforts in the country, the county faces daunting development pressures. In recent years national retail chains have moved in and flooded the county's small townships with proposals for superstores widely considered to be vastly out-of-scale for the small towns near which they would locate. While the county's local township boards are comprised of dedicated citizens who volunteer time to their communities, the boards simply do not have the resources to analyze proposals for superstores larger than an entire small-town downtown.

In Ephrata, a small town in Lancaster County that has worked hard to protect and revitalize its beautiful Main Street, approval for a 200,000-square-foot Wal-Mart was recently granted. The project was so controversial that public hearings attracted hundreds of residents, many of whom spoke against the project at hearings lasting well into the night.

The township's three-member board of supervisors had initially conditioned its approval of the store on the developer's agreement to pay for road improvements needed to mitigate some of the traffic the development is expected to create. However, Wal-Mart appealed the conditions, one of which sought to ensure safe passage for Amish people who do not drive cars, to Lancaster County Court. The township then backed down because of the lawsuit. If the Pennsylvania Department of Transportation approves a highway access permit for this project, as expected in Fall 1996, the project will go forward. This development, coupled with others like it that are being approved, will dump thousands of cars a day on Lancaster's already crowded roads. "Already at risk from development pressures on farmland," says Randolph Harris of the Historic Preservation Trust of Lancaster County, "Lancaster's Amish community may be further burdened with threats to personal safety from this increase in traffic."

acres of farmland since 1959. Approximately 4,800 acres of land have been approved for development every year since 1980. This translates into 68 square miles of developed land over a ten-year period to accommodate approximately 60,000 people. In contrast, the city of Lancaster, much of which is historic, accommodates about 60,000 people on only seven square miles.[11]

"Pennsylvania desperately needs a state planning program," says Daniels. "The southeast areas of the state in particular face enormous growth pressures. We need a better way to deal with regional planning issues."

Susan Shearer, assistant director of Preservation Pennsylvania, agrees: "Pennsylvania clearly needs the tools to plan in a more rational and regional way to protect valuable farmland, natural resources, and our historic towns." She reports that conservation, heritage, and related groups have recently joined together to form a group called "10,000 Friends of Pennsylvania," a statewide alliance committed to a land use agenda that "limits sprawl and manages growth to promote economic vitality without threatening what we value. Our hope is that it does not come too late for Lancaster County."

Sprawl development in Lancaster County, Pa., threatens the county's heritage as well as the basis for the county's tourism industry.

BLAIR SEITZ

C.B. JOHNSON

A Housing and Conservation Trust Fund in Vermont

PICTURES OF ROLLING GREEN HILLS AND SMALL TOWNS WITH WHITE STEEPLES often come to mind when someone mentions Vermont. This image is still the reality in most of Vermont, even though some of the same development pressures that have chewed up the countryside elsewhere in America are present here, too. While Vermont's well-preserved countryside and cohesive small towns contribute to the quality of life in this state, they also underlie important sectors of the Vermont economy. As Governor Howard Dean has pointed out, "Vermont's land-use patterns and rural character are critical to our economic health…[F]rom travel and tourism to small business development, Vermont's quality of life and its economy [are] tied to our ability to steward our land resources wisely."[12] According to a 1989 report by the Governor's Commission on the Economic Future of Vermont, tourism "draws its strength from Vermont's natural physical endowments…and from the state's agricultural heritage which has created the bucolic countryside appreciated by urban dwellers. Visitors come [to Vermont] for many reasons, but primarily they come because they like what they see."[13] Agriculture contributes more than $500 million a year to the Vermont economy, ranking only behind manufacturing and tourism. The tourism industry brings in more than $2 billion and accounts for more than 32,000 jobs. In a state whose total population is under 570,000, these figures are significant.

Vermont has worked hard to preserve the settlement patterns that distinguish this state from so many others. In this regard, one of Vermont's most effective programs has been the Housing Conservation Trust Fund. This program is unusual, if not unique, in that it combines affordable housing, historic preservation, farmland preservation, and open-space conservation goals that are normally treated separately in other states.

Background

WHILE VERMONT HAD TAKEN STEPS AS EARLY AS 1970 to protect its countryside through the enactment of a state land-use law (see Chapter 10), when a new wave of rampant land speculation took hold in the mid-eighties, it became clear to many Vermonters that more direct intervention was needed. In just two years, the cost of housing had risen by 50 percent and the state had lost 10 percent of its farms. Houses were becoming unaffordable to native Vermonters. The rural landscape was being carved up for development. The same development pressures threatening the countryside were also contributing to rapid inflation in housing prices.

Advocates of farmland preservation, historic preservation, open-space conservation, and affordable housing had long been working independently to advance their respective goals, but these groups were essentially competing for little bits of funding. The idea of joining forces and working together was discussed at a meeting convened in 1987 by the Vermont Land Trust, a nonprofit organization that purchased endangered farms and other lands and resold them with restrictive easements to protect them permanently from development.

Villages surrounded by countryside, such as the one shown here, typify much of the Vermont landscape.

C.B. JOHNSON

A historic barn in Vermont.

Participants in these early discussions included representatives not only of the Land Trust but also of the Vermont Natural Resources Council, the Nature Conservancy, the Preservation Trust of Vermont, Vermont Legal Aid, the Burlington Community Land Trust, and several community action organizations. Madeleine Kunin, then governor, had encouraged the groups' idea of forming a broad-based coalition. "We realized we all had the same interests in this overheated development climate. Land prices were rising rapidly as the economy overheated," explains Paul Bruhn, executive director of the Preservation Trust of Vermont. "This was hurting both low-income housing and rural conservation efforts."

With funds provided by the participating organizations, the coalition hired Steve Kimbell, a professional lobbyist, to draft legislation proposing a housing and conservation trust fund. In testifying before legislative committees, the coalition made sure that representatives from each of the diverse interests involved—farmers, land conservationists, historic preservationists, low-income housing developers and affordable housing advocates—appeared to make a statement. Legislators took notice of the fact that groups sometimes at odds with each other were now working together in unison. "It was hard for legislators not to fund something that brought together groups they kept saying were at odds," recalls Kimball.[14]

The coalition approach worked. Within six months, the state legislature approved creation of the Housing and Conservation Trust Fund to assist in the preservation of farmland, natural and recreational areas, historic buildings and affordable housing. The Fund was initially capitalized with $3 million in state funds, but the very next year, the legislature approved a $20 million appropriation as well as a proposal to dedicate proceeds from the state's real estate transfer tax to the Fund.

To administer the program, the legislature created the Vermont Housing and Conservation Board (VHCB), a nine-member board comprised of five governor-appointed citizens and four state officials responsible for agriculture, natural resources, housing and community development. The Board is unusual in that, although it is a creature of the state, it is not burdened with civil service, procurement, and other regulations that often cause state agencies to move slowly. The legislature recognized that in the world of real estate and land development, one often must act quickly in order to be effective. Thus the Board was given the ability to act creatively, flexibly, and fast. "We're the only state agency that can write a check in three days," says Gustave Seelig, the VHCB's executive director.[15]

What the Housing and Conservation Trust Fund Does

THE BOARD PROVIDES FINANCIAL AID—e.g., grants, loans, loan guarantees—to municipalities, nonprofit organizations, housing cooperatives and qualified state agencies to help them preserve working farms, open spaces, recreational areas such as trails, historic buildings, and affordable housing. Funds awarded by the Board may be used for a variety of purposes: the purchase of development rights, options to buy land, conservation easements, the outright purchase of land or buildings, the rehabilitation of historic properties, and the rehabilitation or construction of low-income housing. In addition, the Board provides money for feasibility studies that will help individual projects go forward. Real estate appraisals, engineering and environmental studies, energy assessments, marketing analyses and other pre-development work—these are all eligible activities so long as they advance the Board's program goals. Finally, the Board also assists the Vermont Department of Agriculture and land trusts with capacity-building funds to develop and manage farm and conservation projects.

The Board consciously seeks to maintain the cohesiveness of Vermont's small towns.

The Board's purchase of development rights program is focused on maintaining Vermont's working farms. Development rights purchased with Board-approved funds enable farmers to realize the equity in their land without having to develop it. Farmers can then reinvest in new farming equipment or repair old (often historic) barns. By emphasizing the conservation of blocks of working farms, the Board helps local communities retain a critical mass of productive farmland, thereby helping to stabilize farm-related economic activity in certain areas and to reduce the potential for conflict between farmers and their nonfarming neighbors.

In funding affordable housing projects, the Board favors projects that recycle historic buildings. A large percentage—nearly 30 percent—of housing projects have involved historic structures. The Board also encourages housing projects that reinforce, rather than destroy, Vermont's compact settlement patterns. The Board consciously seeks to preserve the countryside and to maintain the cohesiveness of Vermont's small towns.

Easements on farmland often protect historic buildings. When providing funds for farmland retention, the state asks property owners to notify the state historic preservation office if they plan to alter or demolish historic buildings. If so, state representatives may visit the property owner to discuss the proposed changes and offer advice for making the alterations fit in with the historic structure's character. Beth Humstone, chairperson of the Vermont

JOEL GARDNER

The historic Shelburne Farm in Shelburne, Vt.

Housing and Conservation Board, says the Board tries to be sensitive to farmers' needs. "They may choose not to participate in the program," she adds. "It is important that the farmers not feel that their hands are too tied. On the other hand, we do look favorably on projects that achieve more than one of our goals, such as historic preservation *and* agriculture, or historic preservation *and* housing."

In the Board's Single-Family Assistance Program, downpayment assistance loans of up to $2,000 are made to low- and moderate-income people to help them buy "limited equity" homes.

The Board's decisionmaking process is designed to provide significant financial assistance quickly when a need is identified. The Board meets and makes decisions on applications about ten times a year. Applications are usually reviewed and decisions are made within five weeks of submission. Through deed restrictions or other mechanisms, applicants are required to ensure any funds awarded will provide a lasting benefit for the public.[16]

Here are some examples of projects funded by the Vermont Housing and Conservation Board in 1995:

- a $186,000 grant for the purchase of development rights and an archaeological easement on a dairy farm in Addison County, Vt.;
- a $217,500 grant for the acquisition of a historic barn complex and 391 acres for the Shelburne Farms conservation area; and
- a $105,491 grant for the acquisition of development rights on a farm in Springfield, Vt., to protect a prehistoric archaeological site as well as the farm.

Private Land Trusts

A MAJOR STRENGTH OF THE VERMONT PROGRAM lies in its partnerships with the nonprofit sector, especially land trusts. While the Board was set up to be flexible and to act fast, the private nonprofit land trusts can sometimes act even more quickly. They also contribute private matching funds to projects sponsored by other nonprofits. According to Darby Bradley, director of the Vermont Land Trust, the state initially provided most of the money for farm conservation projects. Now the state provides only one of four dollars, with the rest coming from either private donations or the federal government.

Results

THE VERMONT HOUSING AND CONSERVATION TRUST FUND has produced impressive results during its tenure. Between 1987 and June 1996, the Fund had committed about $95 million in grants and loans to more than 501 projects. Given Vermont's tiny population, this is a remarkable achievement. When private contributions and matching funds are added to the financial assistance provided by the Fund, the projects funded represent more than $280 million of investment. These projects have resulted in the protection of 105,700 acres of land and the creation or protection of 4,024 units of affordable housing. Seventy-two of 247 housing projects involve historic resources. The Fund's total investment in these projects was $11.2 million, of which $1.2 million was for historic preservation. Twenty-five out of 162 farms have historic easements.

In summary, the Vermont Housing and Conservation Trust Fund is exemplary. The Fund's architects recognized that land speculation and development pressures threatened affordable housing, working farms, historic preservation and open-space conservation, and thus the Vermont Housing and Conservation Board combines each of these public

Vermont's Barn Preservation Grants

"FROM HOP HOUSES TO SHEEP SHEDS" is how barn preservation grant program director Mary Jo Llewellyn describes the variety of buildings eligible for the state's barn grants, a program created in 1992 to help property owners repair, or prevent the deterioration of, historic barns. Barns are seen as an important element in the Vermont countryside and are one of the features that tourists—so important to the state's economy—see as unique.

Vermont's Barn Preservation Grant Program is the only one of its kind in the U.S., although Wisconsin is considering a similar program. Its name notwithstanding, the Vermont program awards grants for all types of agricultural buildings, not just barns. Now in its fourth year, it has provided grants for 48 projects.

Under the program, the state historic preservation office makes matching grants of up to $7,500 (or 50 percent of project costs, whichever is less) to help property owners repair agricultural buildings or carry out maintenance activities that will obviate the need for subsequent repairs.

If a property owner sells his farm within a year of completing a grant project, he must repay the entire grant. This repayment requirement is phased out progressively over five years, so that if the owner sells after five years, he does not have to pay any money back.

Some non-agricultural uses—e.g., seasonal gift shops or hay storage for a neighbor—are permitted, but others, such as converting a barn into a house, are not.

Property owners are encouraged to have a well-defined plan for routine maintenance and long-term preservation of the building. The state gives priority to restoration projects that involve local landmarks, preserve historic building features on a barn, or that preserve important examples of certain building types. Buildings are considered local landmarks for various reasons: a silo may serve as a common reference point when people give directions; a farmstead may be the home of the original family in a town; or a community may simply feel a strong attachment to a building.

Grant projects must comply with the rehabilitation standards of the U.S. Department of the Interior and the property must be listed on the National Register of Historic Places.

The program is simple and popular. The demand for grants far exceeds the state's ability to provide them. In 1996, the state received 77 applications requesting a total of more than $500,000. It was able to fund only ten projects, as the program receives only about $50,000 each year.

values in its programs. The state legislature remains committed to the program and has outshone many other states with far bigger populations in its accomplishments in rural preservation.

Around the Country

Rural New York

A "RURAL NEW YORK GRANT PROGRAM" has been established in New York to provide grant support for local land conservation, environmental advocacy, land-use planning and historic preservation activities. The program seeks to protect the built and natural environment of villages and rural areas, to strengthen local groups and institutions, and to enhance the long-term economic viability of New York's rural communities. Grants of up to $5,000 are available to local governments, nonprofit organizations, and unincorporated groups working in the public interest. The program has become quite popular since its creation in 1993 as it not only provides a flexible source of funding for a wide variety of activities but also because it provides a network and means of communication for otherwise isolated advocates of rural preservation.

The program is jointly administered by four nonprofit organizations: the Land Trust Alliance of New York, the New York Planning Federation, the Open Space Institute, and the Preservation League of New York State. *(See Appendix B.)* The Rural New York Program was founded by the J. M. Kaplan Fund and has received support from the Botwinick-Wolfensohn, Andy Warhol, and Margaret L. Wendt Foundations.

There are smaller-scale projects through which a state can promote the conservation of rural landscapes.

Centennial Farms in Oklahoma

F OR STATES THAT LACK THE RESOURCES necessary to carry out major programs such as those undertaken by Pennsylvania or Vermont, there are smaller-scale projects through which a state can promote the conservation of rural landscapes. The Centennial Farm and Ranch Program of Oklahoma is one such example.

The Countryside Institute

THE COUNTRYSIDE INSTITUTE WAS CREATED IN 1990 with the mission of developing more effective methods for balancing economic development with conservation of natural and cultural resources. The Institute sponsors exchanges—both within the United States and internationally—between professionals and others interested in rural preservation so that they can learn from the tools and techniques used in other areas. Through its Glynwood Center in Philipstown, N.Y., the Institute supports the efforts of community leaders, both public and private, who seek information and training in rural conservation matters.

For more information, contact The Countryside Institute, Glynwood Center, P.O. Box 157, Cold Spring, N.Y. 10517. For information about TCI's exchange programs, contact The Countryside Exchange Program, The Countryside Institute, P. O. Box 73265, Washington, D.C. 20009.

Maryland's Conservation Easements: Preserving Civil War Sites

By H. Grant Dehart

Maryland leads the nation in the protection of historic landscapes through the use of conservation easements, a non-regulatory preservation tool. In this case study, Grant Dehart explains how the state protected 2,507 acres of land surrounding the Antietam National Battlefield, the site of one of the most important battles during the Civil War.

THE ARMIES OF THE NORTH AND SOUTH BEGAN FIGHTING AT DAWN ON September 17, 1862 in the Valley of Antietam Creek. By nightfall, 23,100 men and boys lay dead or wounded, making this the bloodiest single day of the Civil War. To commemorate this ferocious battle, Congress designated the Antietam National Battlefield in 1890. Today one can visit this historic site in Washington County, Md., about 60 miles north of the District of Columbia.

Historians estimate that the Antietam battleground encompassed roughly 8,000 acres. The boundary established by Congress encompasses 3,250 acres. Of these, 1,046 are owned outright by the federal government; 1,434 are in private ownership restricted by scenic easements held by the U.S. Department of the Interior; and 700 are privately-owned outright.

Now, over 130 years after the famous battle that earned a place for the tiny town of Sharpsburg in the history books, Antietam finds itself at the forefront of preservation as one of the most successful State efforts to protect Civil War sites in the nation. This success grew out of a philosophical dispute between some private landowners and preservationists over how to preserve the historic rural setting of Antietam.

Given a stagnant economy and distance from major population centers, few development pressures built up in the Antietam area prior to the mid-eighties. In fact, property owners had preserved the land around Sharpsburg so well that historians called Antietam a "time-capsule" battlefield. In contrast to Gettysburg, Fredericksburg and many other Civil War sites, Antietam remains relatively unchanged from the time of the war. Visitors can walk the fields and go back in time, imagining the events of the battle unfolding around them, without the distractions of fast-food franchises, observation towers or other modern intrusions at the borders. The historic character of Sharpsburg itself remains remarkably intact.

But by the late eighties, Antietam faced the specter of suburban sprawl emanating from the Washington-Baltimore corridor. Farms west of the battlefield were being subdivided and developed for high-priced homes located on prominent hill-tops or behind stone fences built prior to the Battle of Antietam. In 1989 the National Trust for Historic Preservation listed Antietam among America's Eleven Most Endangered Historic Places.

By the late eighties, Antietam faced the specter of suburban sprawl.

The Antietam National Battlefield near Sharpsburg, Md., site of the bloodiest single day of the Civil War, was threatened by sprawl before it was saved by easements arranged by the Maryland Open Space Program.

Background of Controversy at Antietam

WHEN MEMBERS OF THE FEDERAL ADVISORY COUNCIL on Historic Preservation came to Antietam in June 1989 to explore ways to protect this battlefield, they were greeted by a demonstration of placard-carrying citizens, a long line of farmers on tractors bearing signs opposing zoning restrictions and battlefield park expansion, and representatives of the media. Fearing the imposition of new restrictions on the use of their land, Sharpsburg residents and farmers had organized under the name of Save Historic Antietam with Responsible Policies (SHARP). Fearing that some of their property rights might be taken away, they had enlisted the support of an outside organizer to express their opposition to ideas under consideration by Washington County, the National Park Service and others for preserving the area.

Prompted by a public outcry over Washington county's decision to allow a shopping center and other commercial development on the historic Grove Farm, where President Lincoln visited wounded Union troops shortly after the battle, county officials established a citizen's advisory committee to find a way to prevent incompatible development on the private lands surrounding the battlefield and to explore tourism development, which was seen as a more benign economic use for the area than residential development. After meeting regularly for a year, the committee recommended several options for protecting the land visible from the battlefield. These included new zoning restrictions on development and increased tourism. The recommendations drew almost immediate fire. The controversy intensified when rumors surfaced that the Park Service might expand the battlefield boundaries.

Partly in response to this demonstration, Washington County commissioners rejected proposals to limit development of agricultural land and to develop tourism facilities, but they enacted a historic district and adopted limited protection for trees in the area. The Park Service, meanwhile, called for an expansion of the battlefield's boundary. (Congress later blocked this proposal.)

Zoning for Preservation in Rural Areas

MANY BELIEVE THAT LOCAL GOVERNMENTS need to take a stronger role in guiding growth to appropriate areas for development and away from farmland or open space that serves important economic values and preserves community character. Local governments invite eventual conflicts over land use when they zone farmland for new residential or commercial uses. Development rights created by government can be taken away by changing zoning regulations to prevent land uses that conflict with agriculture, as several counties in Maryland have done. However, in rural communities like Washington County it is not easy to lower property owner expectations of value in their land.

Any successful rural preservation strategy needs to assess the political and economic climate for success using alternative methods. Each community is different. Preservationists should not try to import methods that may not match the local situation. Zoning restrictions, historic district regulation, or nominations to the National Register of Historic Places may not be implementable in some rural areas. The tools may occasionally cause a community backlash that will defeat efforts to try other means. The approach used by the State of Maryland at Antietam has been a pragmatic one, tailored to the economics, politics and public attitudes in this unique community.

The local perspective

MANY FARMERS IN THE SHARPSBURG AREA feel a sense of pride in the fact that they and their ancestors have preserved the farmland intact since the Civil War. They share the

Any successful rural preservation strategy needs to assess the political and economic climate for success using alternative methods.

desire of preservationists and the government to keep the Sharpsburg area as it is and oppose major new development in the area. But they feel frustrated over inferences in some national media that they or their families are not good stewards of their historic property.

Because most area farmers lack outside sources of income, they see the economic value of their land as their primary asset. The fair market value of their land is often the collateral for mortgage loans used for new agricultural buildings or home improvements, farm implements, college education for their children, or, in years of drought or poor farm product markets, even basic expenses to continue farming, such as seed, fertilizer or property taxes. Many of these farmers, by necessity, consider the value of their farms as their only means of retirement when they are too old to continue farming. This value is directly influenced by zoning or other land use restrictions. The farmers may appreciate history, but may not believe they can afford it if this means sacrificing the value of their primary investment.

The Antietam Strategy—easements instead of regulation

A CONSERVATION EASEMENT IS A LEGAL CONTRACT between a landowner and an easement-holding organization (typically a non-profit land trust or government conservation agency). In granting an easement, the landowner retains all interest in the property except the rights that the owner willingly forfeits, such as the right to subdivide, demolish, or alter historic buildings. In so doing, the landowner typically reduces the market value of the property. He may continue to live on the property and generally use it as he or she sees fit. The easement is recorded with the property deed records and any land restrictions imposed by the easement bind future landowners permanently as well.

Conservation easement purchases or donations have many advantages over other preservation techniques in rural areas, especially for Civil War site preservation.

Many of these farmers consider the value of their farms as their only means of retirement when they are too old to continue farming.

In early 1989, following the endeavors of Save Historic Antietam Foundation (SHAF), the Conservation Fund, the County and other local preservation groups, the Maryland Environmental Trust (MET) became involved in preserving the land around Antietam through the Rural Historic Village Protection Program, funded by a Critical Issues Fund grant from the National Trust for Historic Preservation.[17] This was a collaborative interagency program designed to protect farmland and rural open space surrounding ten small historic villages in Maryland with donated or purchased conservation easements. Because the state easement programs have protected over 175,000 acres of farmland and open space though voluntary easements, with little or no public opposition, easements became the preferred preservation method for the program. The agencies steered clear of the heated controversy over the historic overlay zone in order to maintain good relations with the landowners.

Current progress—The Antietam Strategy

AFTER FOUR YEARS OF CONTENTION over how Antietam would be preserved, a solution emerged to put an end to the raging public debate over property rights. In February 1992, Governor William Donald Schaefer established by executive order a Maryland Civil War Heritage Commission, the first of its kind in the nation. It is chaired by former Secretary of Transportation O. James Lighthizer, a former Anne Arundel County Executive, state legislator and adjunct professor of Civil War history. Committees were established to pursue preservation alternatives around Antietam, South Mountain and Monocacy battlefields, building on the concept of MET's Rural Historic Village Protection program. The Antietam committee, including Civil War historians, state officials, farmers, and representatives of local land trusts, identified properties outside of the Antietam National Battlefield boundary that were of highest significance because of the activities that took place on or near them in 1862, the degree to which they were threatened by development, or the potential impact of new growth on the overall character of Sharpsburg if not protected.

With enactment of the Intermodal Surface Transportation Efficiency Act (ISTEA) and the adoption of a Memorandum of Agreement between the Maryland Department of Transportation and Department of Natural Resources to use future Program Open Space (POS) real estate transfer tax funds to match federal Transportation Enhancement funds, a substantial new block of funds for easement purchases became available. One of ISTEA's principal features is the Transportation Enhancement Program, under which each state must use ten percent of its federal transportation funds on enhancement projects, such as greenways, archaeological research, roadside beautification, scenic easements and historic preservation. With the support of Secretary Lighthizer and Secretary Torrey Brown of the Department of Natural Resources, $6.4 million in ISTEA funds and $6.4 million in POS funds were committed toward land and easement acquisition in Civil War and greenway sites.

Representatives of the two departments worked with property rights advocates in Sharpsburg and convened a group of about 30 landowners surrounding Antietam to discuss the purchase of their development rights under this innovative funding mechanism. The discussion ended with several farmers speaking in favor of selling easements to the state on a voluntary basis, keeping the land in private ownership. No one objected to the strategy.

The first ISTEA/POS-funded purchases in the fall of 1993 protected the Grove Farm, used by President Lincoln in his meeting with General George McClellan and his officers on October 3, 1862. The farm's house, Mt. Airy, served as the former headquarters of Major General Fitz John Porter and later as a field hospital for wounded troops. This historic farm had been subdivided into four large parcels: a five-acre lot for construction of a new American Legion hall, 40 acres with an approved subdivision plan for 10 homes acquired by SHAF, 20 acres rezoned for a retail shopping center and motel site, and the 30-acre site of the Mt. Airy house and farm buildings. The five- and 20-acre parcels were purchased by the State Highway Administration, with plans to place conservation easements on the properties before resale for continued agricultural use. An easement was purchased from the owners of Mt. Airy to protect the house, farm buildings and surrounding land. By 1994, all four parcels of this historic farm were permanently protected. This prompted Governor Schaefer and the departments to hold a dedication ceremony attended by more than 100 citizens and dignitaries.

Maryland has protected 19 properties at Antietam by purchasing easements or the whole title on 2,507 acres.

As of July 1996, Maryland has protected 19 properties at Antietam by purchasing easements or the whole title on 2,507 acres with $6 million in state and federal funds. When added to the MALPF's purchases of easements on five farms near the battlefield totaling 1,210 acres, the state has protected more land around Sharpsburg than exists within the Antietam National Battlefield boundary. Negotiations continue with six property owners for easements on an additional 840 acres of land. These jointly funded easements will be held and managed in perpetuity by the Maryland Environmental Trust. Of the 30 property owners identified for preservation by the Antietam Committee, only four have refused to negotiate easements, and three have rejected the price offered for their easements. Seventy-six percent of those contacted around Sharpsburg have sold property or easements to the state or have contracted to sell easements.

In addition, the state has purchased two farms and seven easements on Civil War battle sites at Fox's, Turner's and Crampton's gaps on South Mountain in Frederick and Washington Counties, where General Lee's and General McClellan's armies engaged on September 14, 1862, preceding the Battle of Antietam. Preservation of these nine properties cost the State an additional $2.7 million in ISTEA and POS funds to protect 700 acres. Negotiations continue with seven property owners on over 800 acres at the Civil War sites on South Mountain. To date, only three property owners at these sites have rejected the state's offers to purchase easements on their land, resulting in an 82 percent participation rate.

Common Ground between Preservation and Property Rights—Purchased Easements

THE PURCHASE OF DEVELOPMENT RIGHTS (PDR) to preserve historic sites, agricultural land or other natural resources in rural areas provides a common ground for cooperation between private landowners and historic preservation advocates. Some will argue that too much land needs to be preserved for Civil War site protection and interpretation to purchase the development rights on all of it. There just isn't enough money, they will say. Others will argue that governments don't need to buy development rights when they can simply zone them away. Still others are philosophically against purchasing development rights for preservation, because it would set a precedent for compensatory zoning that could inhibit future public efforts to limit development through the police power.

Actual experience in the use of easements would seem to refute some of the arguments against easements as a primary preservation strategy if practical results weigh more than lofty arguments of philosophy. The purchase of conservation easements on private land has a long and successful track record as a preservation strategy. Maryland has the most successful PDR program in the nation for preserving agricultural land. The Maryland Agricultural Land Preservation Fund has protected over 117,000 acres of prime farmland with perpetual easements at a total cost of $125 million, or about $1,068 per acre. They have temporarily protected more than 264,000 additional acres of land in voluntary agricultural district agreements preventing development for five or more years. Participating in an agricultural district is a prerequisite for offering agricultural easements for sale to the state.

The purchase of conservation easements on private land has a long and successful track record as a preservation strategy.

Additionally, the Maryland Environmental Trust has preserved over 50,000 acres of natural, scenic, historical and agricultural land primarily by receiving conservation easements donated by private property owners who want to see their land preserved in perpetuity. These donors receive income, estate and property tax benefits under federal and state laws encouraging land conservation. The Maryland Historical Trust has preserved over 7,500 acres of land with easements.

Several other states have PDR or conservation easement donation programs that result in permanent land preservation, including the following:[18]

State	Acres protected	PDR/Donation
Connecticut	25,042	PDR
Maine	307	PDR
Maryland	**175,000**	**PDR**
Massachusetts	35,907	PDR
New Hampshire	9,148	PDR
New Jersey	27,924	PDR
Pennsylvania	74,500[19]	PDR
Rhode Island	2,428	PDR
Vermont	45,511	PDR
Virginia	100,000	Donation

In the late 1980's Congress authorized more than $130 million to prevent the development of one 540-acre parcel at the Manassas National Battlefield in Virginia. At the current rate that conservation easements are being purchased for protecting Civil War sites in Maryland, this amount of money could preserve more than 52,000 acres of threatened land, nearly 100 times that purchased at Manassas.

Benefits of easements over other techniques

PURCHASING EASEMENTS, RATHER THAN PURCHASING LAND outright, makes good economic sense: easements can be purchased at a lower cost; the property owner retains responsibility for the land's upkeep; the land stays on property tax rolls; and remains in agricultural use. Additionally, conservation easements:

- acknowledge and reward the conservation ethic of many private property owners, especially farmers seeking to protect their industrial base, way of life, and community;
- provide a new source of income to the property owner, to preserve and make liquid the market value of their land, to reinvest in farm improvements, building rehabilitation, or other needs to continue farming, or to pay estate taxes enabling their children to inherit the farm intact;
- are perpetual, running with the title to the land for all future owners, in contrast with the temporary nature of most land-use regulations;
- are tailored to the conservation features of the individual property and the needs of the individual land owner;
- can be negotiated on a voluntary basis one parcel at a time, compared to the "blanket" or uniform coverage of most land-use or historic regulations;
- allow property to stay on the tax roles in private management, in contrast to land purchased in fee for public use which needs to be managed by government;
- avoid conflicts with property owners over the designation of land as historic or over perceived reductions in property values caused by zoning restrictions; and
- are quicker than regulation, because they are typically direct willing-seller, willing-buyer transactions and do not require law changes.

Purchasing easements, rather than purchasing land outright, makes good economic sense.

Summary

THE ENTHUSIASM SHOWN BY LANDOWNERS at Antietam to sell easements on their land confirms that if there is any common ground between the so-called property rights advocates and Civil War heritage groups in preserving battlefields, it lies in the easement approach. Nineteen of 30 owners contacted have sold easements or land, and six more are under contract or are negotiating to sell.

Nearly everyone in the Antietam community saw the benefit of preserving the past; the debate was over how it would be accomplished. When we recognized the invaluable role of private landowners and worked with them, the rural landscape that is an integral part of the Civil War battlefield legacy was preserved for the enjoyment and enrichment of future generations.

The historic preservation movement should continue to defend the public's interest in preserving rural historic resources through land-use regulations when they are appropriate and fairly applied. At the same time, the movement recognizes that private property owners are usually the best stewards of historic resources. Effective preservation will be based on an understanding of and empathy for the needs and motivations of those who are primarily affected by a preservation strategy. Attempts to find common goals or a fair exchange of values will often produce better and longer-lasting results. We should seek to act fairly and cooperatively with property owners and with empathy toward their needs.

However, in the absence of federal help, not every state or local community will be able to come up with the large financial resources needed to purchase all of the development rights sufficient to protect their rural or Civil War resources with easements. Some communities will continue to rely on comprehensive planning, zoning and historic regulation if they care for their heritage. In many cases easements may not be a sufficient preservation technique where public access and historical interpretation may be needed on the property, such as where actual Civil War engagements took place. Most private property owners are reluctant to include public access provisions in easement deeds or to open up their land for public interpretation activities. In these cases, fee simple acquisition should be explored.

We should seek to act fairly and cooperatively with property owners and with empathy toward their needs.

EDITOR'S NOTE: This article was adapted and updated from Preserving Public Interests and Property Rights, An emerging solution to the twentieth-century battle of Antietam, *by H. Grant Dehart and Jo Ann Frobouck, in Historic Preservation Forum, July/August 1993, Volume 7, Number 4. H. Grant Dehart is Director of Program Open Space in the Maryland Department of Natural Resources, and Chairs the Antietam Committee of the Governor's Civil War Heritage Commission. He became involved in Antietam as Director of the Maryland Environmental Trust. He is a Maryland Advisor to the National Trust for Historic Preservation. The views expressed are those of the author, and do not necessarily represent the views of the organizations with which he is associated.*

The Civil War Trust

Nearly 85 percent of America's Civil War battlefields are unprotected from development. To help preserve these historic sites, the Civil War Trust was created in 1991. A private, nonprofit organization, the Trust has donated more than $4.8 million to help community-based organizations purchase land and conservation easements to protect more than 5,600 acres at 24 battlefield sites in 14 states. For example, the Trust contributed $100,000 toward the preservation of 40 acres of the Grove Farm at Antietam.

For more information about the Civil War Trust, write the CWT at 2101 Wilson Blvd., Suite 1120, Arlington, VA 22201. Tel: (703) 516-4944 or 1-800-CW-TRUST.

CHAPTER 7

Community Revitalization

CHAPTER 7

Community Revitalization

This chapter examines efforts in two states—Wisconsin and Arizona—to revitalize older downtowns and neighborhoods. In Wisconsin, the state's Main Street Program has helped the small town of Sheboygan Falls restore boarded-up buildings, recruit new businesses, and rejuvenate its downtown. In Arizona, the state's tax incentives, combined with the designation of a historic district and local volunteer efforts, have helped to stanch the incipient decline of the Fairview Place neighborhood in Phoenix.

JOE RILEY OF CHARLESTON, S.C., MAYOR OF ONE OF AMERICA'S MOST beautiful and vibrant cities, has observed that a community's downtown is its most democratic element: "The downtown belongs to everyone," he says. "People need it. They need the eye contact, the human exchange that occurs in the downtowns of our cities. The downtown is the quintessence of the public realm. You cannot replicate this anywhere else."

But downtowns all over America fell into a decline during the sixties and seventies, as large regional malls shifted the crossroads of communities to the off-ramps of the Interstate. In response to this phenomenon, the National Trust for Historic Preservation established a National Main Street Center in 1980.

The Main Street Program is a comprehensive economic development program that encourages downtowns to retain their unique characteristics, including their historic buildings, and to use these to gain an edge in business markets saturated by sameness. The program helps downtown entrepreneurs, especially small businesses, improve their marketing and other business skills. It emphasizes the value of locally owned businesses, whose dollars stay and recirculate in the community, whose owners have a stake in the town's quality of life because they live there. Finally, the Main Street program emphasizes steady, incremental progress over quick, "big fixes."

The Main Street program is based on comprehensive, incremental work in four broad areas, known as the Main Street four-point approach. Wisconsin's Main Street communities follow the four points, which are:

- *organization*: No downtown revitalization effort can succeed without a strong organization to support and guide it. There must be a Main Street framework that is well-represented by civic groups, merchants, bankers, citizens, public officials, and chambers of commerce. A strong organization provides the stability to build and maintain a long-term effort;
- *economic restructuring*: Main Street revitalization efforts must have a solid economic foundation. This involves analyzing the local market to determine what types of businesses are needed and diversifying the local economic base.

Macon, Georgia's historic Main Street.

Main Street programs recruit new businesses, when appropriate, and sharpen the competitiveness of existing merchants in the downtown;

- *promotion*: Successful business enterprise depends on good marketing. Main Street programs emphasize the importance of organizing special events to draw shoppers, investors, and visitors into the downtown. Street festivals, retail events, and parades are some of the ways Main Street lures people downtown; and
- *design*: Downtown business districts must be attractive and inviting to people. Historic building renovations, street and alley clean-ups, colorful banners, landscaping, and lighting all can improve the physical beauty of the downtown as a quality place to shop, work, walk, invest in, and live.

ERIC OXENDORF

Downtown Revitalization: Wisconsin Main Street

IN THE 16 YEARS SINCE THE NATIONAL TRUST FOR HISTORIC PRESERVATION created the National Main Street Center, 42 states have joined this effort to help local communities reclaim their downtowns. In addition, two cities have launched citywide Main Street programs to help neighborhoods revitalize their commercial districts. One of the strongest state programs is Wisconsin Main Street, which has stimulated the creation of 921 new businesses, 4,726 new jobs, and over $140 million worth of investment in Main Street areas during its first seven years. Both the appearance and the economic vitality of downtowns throughout Wisconsin have improved significantly as Main Street communities have completed over 1,220 building renovation and facade projects.

A look at the changes that have occurred in Sheboygan Falls since 1988 illustrates the important role that a state Main Street program can play in downtown renewal.

Reclaiming Downtown in Sheboygan Falls

SHEBOYGAN FALLS IS A TOWN of about 6,000 people about one hour north of Milwaukee. Until the 1970s, the city had a strong manufacturing base and a strong downtown. But following the construction of a shopping mall and several discount stores in outlying areas, the downtown lost its vitality. By the mid-eighties, physical evidence of the city's tumble from better times was sadly evident. The broken windows of the old Brickner Woolen Mills building on Main Street—used only for storage by a local manufacturer—symbolized the town's decline.

In 1987, the Wisconsin Legislature established the Wisconsin Main Street program to help small towns restore the economic vibrancy of their central business districts. One of Wisconsin Main Street's first steps was to sponsor a competition for towns interested in participating in a demonstration of the Main Street concept. The standard package offered by the state to demonstration communities includes:

- up to five years of free technical assistance with such matters as downtown promotions, business recruitment, fundraising, and other activities aimed at rejuvenating central business districts;
- special training for local Main Street managers in key areas—e.g., program management, marketing, volunteer development and historic preservation;
- quarterly workshops for Main Street managers and their board volunteers;
- front-end training for local program managers when they are first hired; and
- on-site visits by experts providing one-on-one, customized advice on Main Street issues. Staff from both the state and national Main Street programs participate in these consultations.

Main Street in Sheboygan Falls, Wisc.

Having struggled for years to revive their dispirited downtown, the city of Sheboygan Falls entered the competition to become one of Wisconsin's first five demonstration sites.

With guidance from the state, Sheboygan's business and political leaders launched their revitalization effort by recruiting volunteers, incorporating a nonprofit organization, and creating a board of directors to lead "Sheboygan Falls Main Street, Inc." (SFMS) During its first three years, SFMS concentrated on educating merchants about the value of cooperating with each other, building grassroots support, and putting a strong organizational foundation in place. Main Street veterans generally caution communities against taking on too much too soon, for if overly ambitious projects are undertaken prematurely and fail, they can damage an organization's spirit, which is so important to a program's long-term success. SFMS thus focussed first on small, easy-to-complete projects, such as building facade improvements, that had a major visual impact. The improvements were undertaken by local property owners with the help of grants, low-interest loans, and volunteer assistance from the "Falls Facelifters."

The Falls Facelifters grew out of a party, according to Steve Schmidt, a local contractor. "A group of people was just sitting around trying to figure out how they could help the downtown, and someone came up with the idea of recruiting volunteers to help downtown property owners fix up their buildings." The Facelifters would rise early on Saturday mornings and remove unattractive aluminum facades that masked the beauty and distinctive character of downtown historic buildings. As many as 100 people volunteered to work as Facelifters.

As people could see dramatic improvements in the appearance of downtown buildings, their spirits improved, too, and the Main Street program acquired energy and momentum. By 1991, SFMS felt ready to tackle the dilapidated Brickner Woolen Mills building. A special task force recommended rehabilitating the structure and converting it into affordable downtown housing, which Sheboygan Falls badly needed. The SFMS contacted the owner and persuaded him to donate the property to the Main Street organization. SFMS then sold the building to Heartland Properties, a subsidiary of Wisconsin Power and Light with extensive experience in renovating historic buildings. With help from Wisconsin Main Street, Heartland Properties obtained low-income housing tax credits from the Wisconsin Housing and Economic Development Authority and completed the rehabilitation in 1992. The project's 34 apartments were snapped up immediately. Today the building has a 40-person waiting list.

Buoyed by its success in turning a white elephant into a shiny new apartment building, SFMS turned its attention to three more vacant buildings. Another task force recommended converting these structures into small offices for one or two-person operations. Most of the

Need for a Downtown

WISCONSIN MAIN STREET'S ultimate goal, according to its director, Alicia Goehring, is to help communities restore the sense of pride that their downtowns once had and can have again. "It's interesting," she says, "A new community built near Madison, Wisc., without a downtown has realized it doesn't have a center. So the people there are trying to create a downtown for the first time. They realize that downtown is something that pulls an entire community together and that they need that."

Pasadena, California's Main Street, Colorado Boulevard, before and after it was revitalized through the efforts of the local Main Street Program.

city's office space had migrated to the edge of town and spaces smaller than 1,000 square feet were hard to find in the area. The task force thought this new project could fill a market demand for small offices. The project became known as Brickner Square.

Having attended special training workshops sponsored by Wisconsin Main Street, the SFMS staff had learned how to prepare development "pro formas"—economic analyses of the feasibility of buying and rehabilitating properties. These enabled SFMS to persuade six local investors

What Works for Main Street Programs

KENNEDY SMITH, DIRECTOR of the National Main Street Center at the National Trust for Historic Preservation, has analyzed what works and what doesn't for state Main Street programs. Here is her list of "do's" and "don'ts":

- *Plant seeds, then take the time to let them grow.* Efforts to produce big, showy successes may fail if they occur prematurely. It's essential to do the unglamorous, but essential work of laying a solid organizational foundation, building grassroots support, and training the leaders first. States that endorse "big fix" approaches to economic development often fail in the long run. Governors and legislators often want to see tangible results before their term of office ends. This impatience glosses over the value of doing the preliminary groundwork that's so essential.

- *Focus your efforts on just a few model demonstrations rather than on too many communities.* It's a mistake for states to treat the Main Street program as an entitlement for every town in the state. A state is more likely to help its communities as a whole if it concentrates its technical assistance and other efforts on just a few models. The program can develop solid answers to difficult problems. Lessons thus learned can be shared with communities throughout the state later through an information clearinghouse, conferences open to all, and the like. Paying excessive attention to technical assistance may divert attention from other important activities.

- *Work to eliminate or change state actions or policies that work against downtown revitalization.* These may include any of the following: highway bypasses or widening likely to harm a Main Street; subsidies for sprawl-type development in outlying areas; inappropriate or unnecessarily rigid regulations that make it difficult to reclaim downtowns.

- *Select communities to involve for valid program reasons.* Politicizing a Main Street program impugns the program's integrity and, in the long run, will cause bipartisan political support for it to erode.

- *Help communities solve their own problems; don't solve these problems for them.* There is a temptation for states to leap in and try to solve local problems themselves. If a local Main Street program is to have lasting results, the local leaders themselves must work out their problems. The state can act as a broker or facilitator, but it should not be overly intrusive.

Since the National Main Street Center began in 1980, the 1,100 communities that have participated have generated:

- $5.87 billion worth of investment in physical improvements
- 115,000 new jobs (a *net* increase)
- 38,000 new businesses (a *net* increase)
- 36,000 buildings rehabilitated

For every dollar spent on local Main Street programs, an additional $30 have been leveraged.

According to the U.S. Department of Housing and Urban Development, the Main Street program is the most successful *economic development* program in the country.

to invest $25,000 apiece in the Brickner Square buildings. SFMS helped these investors obtain financing to buy and renovate the buildings. The Falls Facelifters saved the building owners about $6,000 by stripping away the old siding on the buildings and carting off the debris.

By November 1994, the Brickner Square buildings were completely rehabilitated. Like the Brickner Woolen Mills building, the Brickner Square project quickly filled up with tenants. Rents went for $4 a square foot more than average downtown rents. Within a year, local investors in the project saw a positive return on their investment.

Results

THANKS TO THESE AND RELATED PROJECTS—including the rehabilitation of four more dilapidated buildings on Main Street—Sheboygan Falls has much to show for its efforts today:
- a drop in the downtown vacancy rate from 30 percent to one percent;
- 38 renovated building facades;
- 53 rehabilitated buildings;
- 89 new jobs, a 19 percent increase in jobs; and
- 42 new businesses (a net increase of 30 percent).

The Falls Firehouse Pizza, a local Main Street business, reports a 42 percent increase in its gross revenues. For every dollar the city put into this effort, private businesses and investors contributed $104 dollars.

"Small towns like ours need to distinguish themselves from what's around us," says Joe Richardson, III, a local business leader. "We need to build on our strengths—on our small

"Small towns like ours need to distinguish themselves from what's around us."

Wisconsin Rules Favor Rehabilitations

WISCONSIN DECIDED IN EARLY 1996 to change the criteria for allocating low-income housing tax credits (awarded by the Federal Government), which are often used in combination with the Federal rehabilitation tax credit.

Under Wisconsin's new system, developers of affordable housing projects that reuse smaller buildings will receive an advantage in the state's scoring system. The new policy favors projects that mix market-rate and low-income apartments. An additional edge is given to projects that contain fewer than 24 units, to projects that rehabilitate historic buildings, and to projects that qualify for both federal and state historic rehabilitation tax credits.

Randall Alexander, a Wisconsin developer who has created many successful low-income housing projects that mix income levels, believes that many state policies sacrifice long-term quality for short-term quantity: "Many projects financed through low-income housing tax credits meet only minimal construction standards and are built on the periphery of cities and towns," he says. "They are contributing to sprawl. Like federally funded public housing, they will be slums by the year 2010."

A consortium of preservation groups and a commercial equity fund are setting up a tax-credit fund that will invest exclusively in small projects involving historic rehabilitation. Communities participating in Wisconsin Main Street will help identify historic buildings that can be used. The fund expects to raise half of its income through affordable-housing tax credits and the balance from state and local housing agencies and banks. Wisconsin has set aside eight percent of its 1996 credits—an allocation worth $504,000—for preservation projects.

town charm, our small shops. If you want to maintain a community, if you want it to grow and attract people, it needs to be good-looking. Otherwise it reflects negatively on everybody in town."

Role of the State

THROUGHOUT THIS EFFORT, Wisconsin Main Street provided assistance of various kinds: a steady stream of advice by telephone, on-site technical assistance, one-on-one consultation with architectural design experts and business consultants, special training workshops, and perhaps most important, access to a network of Main Street managers in other communities. The network is akin to a support group. Managers with similar problems can talk to their peers and get ideas for tackling specific issues.

Matthew Wagner, Sheboygan Falls' Main Street Manager during this period, found the workshops Wisconsin Main Street sponsored on such topics as real estate and market analysis particularly useful: "Without this assistance, we would have had to pay $40,000 to hire experts to perform these tasks. But by receiving training at the workshops, we learned how to do this work ourselves." Richardson sees the town's revitalization effort as building on a program that works: "The state Main Street people help you understand what you need to do in the downtown with the architecture. They help you out with promotions. They give you advice on store hours. They help you raise money, build a volunteer base and then keep it going. We're building on a program that works."

Beyond the Demonstration Projects

"Without this assistance, we would have had to pay $40,000 to hire experts to perform these tasks."

WHILE PROVIDING DIRECT TECHNICAL ASSISTANCE to communities selected as demonstration projects, Wisconsin Main Street also helps other towns revitalize their downtowns through a variety of services that are more broadly available. One of the most popular services is a lending library containing more than 400 books, slide shows, and videos. These publications are indexed according to all different types of projects—fundraising, downtown promotions, upper-floor housing, etc. Communities not involved in the pilot demonstrations are thus able to obtain information generated by the pilots and use it to their advantage.

Other products and services provided by Wisconsin Main Street include:

- *Wisconsin Main Street Project Directory:* a list of 140 different types of projects ranging from consumer surveys to volunteer recognition programs to facade improvement grants. The directory provides names, addresses, and phone numbers of experienced local people to contact with questions about a particular issue.
- *One-day workshops* on topics such as downtown design, new uses for old buildings, and attracting visitors to downtown.
- *Wisconsin Main Street News:* A quarterly newsletter provides case studies on local downtown projects, notices of upcoming workshops and events; a list of local Main Street program managers throughout the state; and other useful information.
- *Governor's Conference on Downtown Revitalization:* This annual conference provides educational workshops, tours, networking opportunities, and exhibit space for businesses to display products and services relevant to downtown revitalization.

Main Street Iowa

A NOTHER SUCCESSFUL STATE MAIN STREET PROGRAM IS MAIN STREET IOWA, which now has 32 towns participating in it.

In Iowa, the state provides 42 days of on-site technical assistance to each participating Main Street town over three years. The "start-up" towns are required to send representatives to four quarterly workshops sponsored annually by the state.

Main Street Iowa provides a full-time architectural design consultant and field assistant to help Main Street towns carry out facade renovations and other rehabilitation projects aimed at improving the overall appearance of the downtown and the profitability of downtown businesses. Towns with more than three years of involvement in the program can receive eight design consultations, but before receiving a ninth, at least one of the eight projects for which advice has already been given must have been completed. This is the state's way of encouraging towns to be serious with property owners.

A Strong Main Street Program

A STRONG STATE MAIN STREET PROGRAM IS ONE:

- whose participating commercial district revitalization programs have a high reinvestment ratio, increasing incrementally each year;
- in which local programs selected to participate remain active;
- which is based on a strong preservation ethic and which has an excellent track record in achieving the preservation of historic Main Street buildings and other relevant historic resources;
- which effectively harnesses existing resources from both the public and private sectors to benefit the revitalization of historic downtowns and commercial districts;
- whose staff can effectively provide basic services to communities;
- which attains a high level of positive visibility and credibility within the state or city;
- which garners bipartisan political support;
- which has adequate and stable funding, from both public and private sources, and a flexible organization structure or network of partners that can accommodate funding from multiple public and private sector sources;
- which positively shapes policies and legislation to assist the revitalization of downtowns and the preservation of historic Main Street buildings; and
- which encourages local revitalization programs to evolve and mature, and which evolves and matures itself, successfully tackling progressively more issues.

The state Department of Economic Development invests $85,000 in technical assistance, training and small grants for each Main Street town under 5,000 during its first three years in the program; $100,000, for each town over 5,000. In return for this financial commitment from the state, Main Street Iowa expects a financial commitment from the participating towns as an indication of their seriousness: Towns under 5,000 must come up with operating budgets of $22,500 a year for three years; towns over 5,000, $45,000 a year for three years.

In 1996, Main Street Iowa celebrated its tenth anniversary. Over 400 people, including Governor Terry Branstad, attended a dinner-dance gala at which $122 million of private investment in local Main Street towns was celebrated and 12 communities received awards. Under Main Street Iowa, the state has witnessed a net gain of 1,303 new businesses employing 3,560 people full time. More than 3,700 building improvement projects have been completed and 253,000 hours of volunteer service have been provided. Downtown Cedar Falls, an Iowa Main Street town, has seen vacancies in its downtown fall from 30 percent to zero. Main Street Keokuk has seen its taxable retail sales increase from $94.5 million in 1986 to over $140 million in 1994.

Main Street Iowa Coordinator Thom Guzman believes the state has been fortunate in having strong support from Governor Terry Branstad: "He has attended nine annual Main Street award ceremonies and given out awards at every celebration. That's pretty important, but it doesn't happen in most states. Our governor knows which communities are Main Street communities."

Asked to describe what he sees as Main Street Iowa's strengths, program director Thom Guzman make these observations:

- Never pick Main Street demonstration sites for political reasons.
- Make sure that local Main Street programs have broad-based community support. In Iowa, local programs include ministers, hospital administrators, industrial plant managers, teachers and others in addition to downtown business leaders.
- States need to give Main Street programs time to succeed. Downtowns took 50 years to decline; they need time to succeed. That can take four or five years. Other states have made a mistake in not giving their Main Street programs enough time to show results.
- State Main Street staffs should come from the trenches. They must have experience in Main Street communities and empathy for business and civic leaders struggling to create a downtown revitalization program.

Neighborhood Revitalization: Fairview Place in Phoenix

Phoenix has used the state of Arizona's preservation tax incentives as a catalyst for the rejuvenation of older neighborhoods. With the help of promotional efforts by neighborhood associations active in local historic districts, the incentives have encouraged homeowners to fix up their houses, but they also have helped to rejuvenate entire neighborhoods.

THE FAIRVIEW PLACE NEIGHBORHOOD IS A SIX-BLOCK AREA NEAR DOWNtown Phoenix. Some of the 342 homes there date to the 1920s, but most were built sometime between 1938 and 1948. Fairview Place is a neighborhood of modest homes that are small, cozy, and unpretentious. Fourteen different architectural styles—including Southwest, Tudor, English stone cottage, Ranch and "French Provincial Ranch" (only in America!)—are represented. The homes average between 900 and 1,200 square feet and sell for between $60,000 and $90,000. People who don't require big houses—retirees and young couples just starting out—make up much of the neighborhood.

In 1990, Richard Fox and other area residents began to notice that the neighborhood was starting to decline. After conferring, they agreed that some action needed to be taken to save the neighborhood. Fox approached his neighbors for their reaction to the concept of forming a neighborhood association. The idea was well received, and the Fairview Place Neighborhood Association was underway.

One of the committee's first decisions was to seek historic designation for the neighborhood. Such designation would stabilize property values, the committee reasoned. It was also a prerequisite for the property tax incentives offered by the state. Although property taxes in Fairview Place were low compared to taxes elsewhere—they averaged about $600 annually—an annual tax saving of about $300 a year would be quite meaningful to retirees and young families.

Arizona Preservation Incentives

ARIZONA ALLOWS A 50 PERCENT reduction in property tax assessments for the preservation of historic houses. Taxpayers who participate in this program must agree to do three things:

- they must renovate their homes according to federal standards intended to ensure the preservation of a property's distinctive architectural features;
- they must agree to maintain the property according to these standards for at least 15 years (or to require succeeding homeowners to do so); and
- they must own and occupy the historic property.

Normally in Phoenix the tasks of preparing a historic district nomination for the National Register of Historic Places fall to the city's historic preservation office. At the time, however, the office's small staff was fully engaged with other work. In order to proceed with its goal, the Fairview Place committee took it upon itself to collect the information and data necessary to justify the designation.

This became an entirely all-volunteer effort, with no architects or other professionals involved. Neighbors divided the tasks. Some photographed houses. Others delved into the history of the neighborhood and the significance of its architecture, and compiled their find-

If you take an hour to get to work, and an hour to get home, that's ten hours a week. It means you are working the equivalent of one extra day just to commute.

Reflections from Gerry McCue

A leader in the revival of Phoenix's Fairview Place neighborhood, Gerry McCue outlines his views on the importance of healthy downtowns below:

THE CITY OF PHOENIX, which is promoting downtown living, sees the revitalization of the Fairview Place neighborhood as beneficial to its effort to revitalize the entire downtown. There are other direct benefits for the residents.

Consider transportation. If you take an hour to get to work, and an hour to get home, that's ten hours a week. It means you are working the equivalent of one extra day just to commute. In our Fairview Place revitalization efforts, we point out that living close in to the city is a more economical way to live. You spend less time traveling and more time at home. You have fewer expenses with vehicle maintenance, and you cause less pollution.

Other benefits of close-in living include access to the entertainment and cultural events that the downtown offers—sports, theaters, libraries, etc. You're closer to all the exciting things going on in the city. Downtown is the heart of a city. The quality of life there should be exciting, enriching, and viable. The core of the city sustains the suburbs. If the downtown dies, suburbs lose their reason to be. Many times, when people see urban decay, not just in physical buildings, but in the quality of life as well, they move further out. The urban perimeter expands. What they may not realize is that the city must extend public services—fire, police, utilities—further and further out. It's very costly for a city to sustain such constant expansion.

From an economic development standpoint, when you visit a major city, you usually don't go to the suburbs. You go from the airport to a downtown hotel. While you're there, you may want to see a few sights. If the downtown neighborhoods are unattractive, you leave the city with the impression that it is not such a nice place. It is important that a city be clean and vibrant. These matters and the overall impression affect the city's ability to attract and keep businesses and homeowners. This is why I think giving tax incentives to people in older neighborhoods, close to downtown, encourages folks to revitalize areas rather than abandon them.

In Fairview Place we are committed to having people know each other and to encouraging personal responsibility for their immediate area—their yard, their house, their neighbor. This is a way to improve our quality of life and to increase our capacity to tackle some of the larger societal problems that otherwise seem so daunting today.

Historic homes in the Fairview Place neighborhood of Phoenix, Ariz.

ings. "We had retirees doing research in the library," recalls Gerry McCue, one of the neighborhood leaders. "One original [house] owner, who is in his eighties, was most helpful. He went around with me to measure houses. In doing all this work, people got to know each other. Other neighborhoods have hired architectural firms to do the work. Here, the residents developed a vested interest in the outcome because they were involved in shaping it. The fact that this was a 'home-grown' effort is what brought the neighborhood together."

The research effort culminated in February 1994 with the National Park Service's placement of the Fairview Place Historic District on the National Register of Historic Places. This meant that individual homeowners in this district could now apply for the tax benefits offered by the state through the city.

In the six years since these revitalization efforts began, the neighborhood has blossomed. It seems friendlier today, according to McCue. The decline in property values noticed a few years ago has stopped. Residents have realized a substantial increase in the value of their homes since the neighborhood achieved historic designation. A Home Tour, sponsored in the spring of 1995, attracted over 800 people. Five neighborhood homes that were for sale, but not part of the tour, were snapped up by people who were won over by the area's warmth and charm. A recent ice-cream social sponsored by the association brought more than a hundred Fairview residents together. The association keeps residents regularly apprised of what's going on through a newsletter, monthly meetings, and frequent events where neighbors can socialize.

The fact that this was a 'home-grown' effort is what brought the neighborhood together.

CHAPTER 8

A Case Study from Rhode Island

CHAPTER 8

A Case Study from Rhode Island

By EDWARD F. SANDERSON

THE RECOGNITION THAT HISTORIC PLACES ARE THE EVERYDAY FABRIC OF OUR communities and neighborhoods has been fundamental to historic preservation in Rhode Island. Rhode Island is the nation's smallest state in land area with just over 658,000 acres, but it is also the second most densely settled state. First occupied by Europeans in 1636, the state's pattern of clustered development was already apparent by the early 1800s. From the 1820s through the 1920s, Rhode Island experienced continuous industrialization, immigration, and urban growth—three trends which intensified settlement densities. Today, the Ocean State boasts more historic buildings per acre than any other state; it is a little state with a big history and a lot of old buildings. Making good use of this building stock really is the only choice we have; it is good planning, good business, good housing, good tourism, good sense.

People have to know about their heritage to care about it. For this reason, surveying approximately 50,000 sites of historical interest has been a major program goal since 1968 when the Rhode Island Historical Preservation & Heritage Commission was created. Every city and town has been professionally surveyed. For each we have published an attractive, illustrated report which describes the community's history and architectural resources. The reports also include inventories of local historic properties, recommendations on which properties meet the criteria for listing on the National Register of Historic Places, and, with local input, suggestions for future historic preservation activities.

These published town historical surveys have strongly encouraged public recognition of historical resources in Rhode Island. Many people take considerable pride in the history of their town or neighborhood. The reports give property owners and prospective property owners access to information about the significance of their own building. In advance of any particular development project, planners and developers have the information they need to know about possible impacts to historic resources. Newspapers and television news desks use the reports as sources of information about local history. In many communities, schools use the reports to teach local history. Local preservation organizations use the report's information in walking tours and brochures. One way or another, a town historical survey report often has helped to lay a foundation for other types of historic preservation activity. Furthermore, connecting specific historic properties with the broader history of the community helps to form a link between current generations of citizens and the buildings which represent their heritage. In building a local base of support for historic preservation, appreciation for distinguished individual landmarks has been important, of course; but equally important has been public recognition of how the visual character of the community—its

Buildings in a historic district in Providence, R.I.

sense of place—is determined by the quantity and quality of old buildings which line its streets.

Rhode Island has developed several different kinds of programs which attempt to help citizens preserve their community. These programs include land-use planning which recognizes historical resources, using public libraries as centers for preservation information, a state income tax credit to encourage preservation and maintenance of historic homes, and joining historic preservation with protection of scenic roads and transportation enhancements.

Getting Preservation into the State Growth Management Act

IN 1987 THE RHODE ISLAND GENERAL ASSEMBLY created a special commission to study new ways to regulate land use and allow (or control) development. The state was in the middle of a building boom. Developers were frustrated by delays of several years or more in order to secure all of the necessary permits at both the state and local levels. Every community had its own set of rules and requirements for development. There was little consistency between towns, and even within the same town permitting could be unpredictable. Planners, environmentalists, and many citizens were upset that so many developments were able to secure permits to subdivide and destroy Rhode Island's small amount of open space. A leading environmental advocate held a news conference to announce that within five years all unprotected open space in Rhode Island would be gone. In this context, historic preservation did not at first seem to be a key issue for the land use commission.

Many people believed that the real problem in Rhode Island land use was the fact that every city and town had different rules for issuing development permits, and most had no apparent standards. Decisions appeared to be individual and ad hoc. This bad situation was made worse by state requirements for a variety of permits, each of which was issued independently of any other permit. The problem had several roots. In the 1970s and 1980s, state level environmental regulations had come into being one at a time, not as integrated components in a rational statewide permitting system. At the local level, state land use law dated from 1921 with not much updating. Lawsuits about land development were common because the laws themselves were unclear. More fundamentally, each city and town in Rhode Island had exercised considerable independence throughout its history, and zoning and subdivision decisions were considered an important local prerogative.

Within five years all unprotected open space in Rhode Island would be gone.

Aware that previous efforts to implement statewide reform of land-use laws in the 1970s had failed to overcome opposition by local governments and developers, the 1987 commission membership included representatives of local government and developers as well as state planners and environmental advocates. Although no official representative of the historic preservation movement was appointed to the commission, there were several members who were friendly. One of these was the chairman, a legislator and professional landscape architect who had worked on several historic preservation projects funded or reviewed by the state historic preservation office. Certainly it would have been preferable if a historic preservation representative had been included among the commission's appointed membership. However, as it turned out, the opportunity for people interested in historic preservation to testify before the commission, and more importantly to work with commission staff drafting reports and legislation, gave preservation interests the voice they needed.

The eventual product of the commission was the Rhode Island Comprehensive Planning and Land Use Regulation Act (R.I. General Laws 45-22.1, 1988). The law requires every city and town to adopt a local comprehensive master plan. At a minimum, the plan must declare local goals and describe specific actions which the town will take to achieve those goals for each of the following issues: land use, housing, economic development, natural and cultural resources, municipal services and facilities, and circulation. State government is given the authority to review the local plan and may reject plans which do not meet the requirements of the Act.

Following adoption of the plan, local government is required to bring its zoning ordinance into conformance with the plan. This provision, which is not included in some other state growth management laws, is intended to give some teeth to the approved plans. More than simply blueprints for the future, in Rhode Island comprehensive master plans are formally adopted as local ordinances, and the plans are the legal foundation for zoning. Another unusual provision in Rhode Island's law is that state agencies are directed to conform their own actions to the local plan once it has been approved by the state.

Getting historic preservation into local comprehensive planning required some ingenuity and good luck. With no representative of historic preservation interests appointed to the commission, preservation was a relatively low profile issue. The general direction taken by the commission was to draft legislation which required a rational and consistent local planning process. The commission did not propose new laws either to restrict or to favor development. The decision whether to limit or encourage new development was left to local government, provided that local land use decisions were the result of the comprehensive planning process. The proposal to include historic preservation ("cultural resources") as well as natural resources in the planning requirements was supported for two reasons. First, the commission strongly wished to have local plans be truly comprehensive. The central tenet of the new legislation was that all relevant land use issues should be included in order to improve upon past planning decisions and in order to give developers and citizens assurance that all of the issues which had to be addressed were included in the local planning and zoning. Once the commission recognized the frequency with which historic buildings are involved in development and zoning issues, no one wanted historic preservation to be a source of unanticipated or unresolved dispute. Local regulation of historic districts already was included in the zoning ordinances of a dozen towns, and it made sense to include historic preservation in local plans.

A second reason for including historic preservation in the land use law was that information about historical resources was readily available. The Land Use Commission members and staff were generally aware that some Rhode Island cities and towns, Newport for example, contain large numbers of historic buildings. Additional information from the town-by-town surveys was supplied to them documenting that every city and town contains substantial historical resources. The very availability of historical survey data became an argument for inclusion of cultural resources as a mandated planning element, in part because of the significance of the resource and in part because commissioners felt it would be unwise to ignore such readily available information. Immediately following adoption of the Land Use Act, state agencies supplied data to a central computerized geographic information system (GIS) which includes all Rhode Island historical resources listed on the National Register of Historic Places or considered eligible for National Register listing (about 20,000 sites). The GIS has been a key data source for local comprehensive planning, and it has had uses for specific studies as well.

Since passage of the Act in 1988, staff at the state historic preservation office have worked with every city and town to develop the historic preservation element of the comprehensive plan. At a minimum, each community has had to answer the following questions:

- What historic resources exist? Where are they located? In what fashion do they relate to the past and future development of the city?
- What preservation activities have already taken place? What activities are in process? How effective have they been?

The very availability of historical survey data became an argument for inclusion of cultural resources as a mandated planning element.

- Have the identified resources been adequately documented and evaluated? Are there resources which have not been identified, documented or evaluated?
- How and in what way are the city's historic resources threatened?
- What are the city's goals for its historic resources?
- How will the city achieve those goals? Through which specific actions? Who are the actors (private/public; local/state)?
- To what extent is preservation part of the city's overall plan for its development? Does the city intend to integrate preservation into other aspects of its planning? (such as housing, taxation, zoning, open space, site plan review, etc.)
- Given the identified resources and the present level of preservation activity, which strategies and actions are most important? Which are most urgent? Which are least important?

The extent to which communities embraced historic preservation as part of their vision for the future varied considerably. However, every city and town plan now includes an official inventory of historic places and to a greater or lesser degree a statement of public purpose to value and attempt to preserve those historic places. At a minimum, when the local planning or zoning board considers zoning variances, subdivision permits, or other actions, it may now be required to include a finding of fact as to whether the proposal under consideration would harm a historic property, and whether there are alternatives which would be less harmful. Beyond the minimum, some towns have added provisions to their subdivision regulations to protect archaeological resources; other towns made adoption of an historic district zoning ordinance a priority in the plan. Many towns identified important historic preservation needs such as the care of historic school buildings, development of affordable housing using historic structures, use of historic rehabilitation tax credits to encourage revitalization of commercial districts, and consideration of heritage tourism. Most towns listed greater public education and understanding of historic resources as a goal.

Every city and town plan now includes an official inventory of historic places.

Few tangible results of Rhode Island's land use planning law are evident yet. Writing new plans took longer than originally expected, and many towns have only recently completed the required zoning revisions or are still in the process. For new development, the slump in the state's economy during the 1990s has been much more decisive than any effect of the Land Use Act. However, the 1988 Act gave historic preservation parity with other, more universally acknowledged planning issues like housing, transportation, and economic development, and it resulted in information about historical resources being incorporated into local data bases. This status is a reflection of the fact that Rhode Island communities contain significant numbers of historic buildings which must be dealt with one way or another, and it is an opportunity for local preservationists to make sure that historic resources are part of their community's future.

Preservation Libraries

EACH YEAR THE STATE HISTORICAL PRESERVATION OFFICE receives many telephone calls from homeowners seeking information and advice about preserving their old house, and local preservation societies receive many more. These are important calls because being able to provide needed information often is the critical first step in a successful restoration project, and for some property owners it is an introduction to the historic preservation movement. In many cases the callers seek basic information which is readily available in published books or magazines and do not need the individual attention of our professional staff. In order to provide a basic reference source for a wide range of commonly requested information, we created the "Preservation Library."

The "Preservation Library" is a collection of 80 books, magazines, and pamphlets about historical preservation which is available for use in 22 libraries throughout Rhode Island. The collection is designed to introduce the reader to historical preservation in Rhode Island and to provide information to the homeowner as he or she carries out the rehabilitation of an old house. General subject areas include: state and local history and architectural styles, diagnosing the needs of your house and planning your project, decorative finishes for the old house, special restoration problems (lead abatement, moving structures, removing graffiti, and access to historic buildings for disabled people), and community-wide preservation issues.

To establish the program, we invited libraries throughout the state to apply for a matching grant to fund the Preservation Library collection. Libraries were selected based in part on their *geographical* location and the level of preservation activity in the communities they serve. Some libraries funded their share of the cost from general acquisition budgets, while others made special requests for funds to their "friends" groups.

One "lead" library was selected to administer the project. Bulk ordering qualified for discounts from publishers. All materials were sent to a single bindery. The lead library prepared catalogue cards and affixed distinctive Preservation Library labels to each item so the collection would be easily identified on library shelves. When the collection was delivered to each participating library, all the usual work of binding, cataloguing, and labeling had already been done. In addition, we supplied brochures which listed every item in the collection and bookmarks which advertised the existence of the Preservation Library. Many libraries organized a reception in honor of the new collection and invited local preservationists.

Now when homeowners or others in Rhode Island are seeking information about historic preservation they are easily referred to one of the 22 libraries statewide which has the Preservation Library collection. Of course not every question can be answered in this way, but the Preservation Library puts core information within everyone's reach. Another benefit of the program was the creation of a new preservation network. The local library is a community institution, and many libraries have active programs of speakers and special events in addition to lending books. Libraries can be excellent sites for the distribution of information or for organized presentations on preservation topics.

State income tax credit

SINCE A LARGE PORTION OF THE HISTORIC PROPERTIES in Rhode Island are houses, it is important to interest homeowners in the benefits of historic preservation. Historic houses are an irreplaceable part of our state's architectural heritage and important for all Rhode Islanders. All across the state, historic preservation has been a means to rehabilitate rundown houses, improve older neighborhoods, and renew aging communities. But private homeowners must bear the entire cost of preserving these buildings, while all Rhode Islanders enjoy the benefits of their preservation efforts. A state income tax credit for preservation of owner-occupied historic houses recognizes the important contributions homeowners make.

Rhode Island's Historic Preservation Residential Tax Credit (RI General Law 44-33.1) allows historic houses listed on the Register of Historic Places to qualify for a state income tax credit equal to ten percent of the cost of restoration work. Only owner-occupied residences are eligible for the credit; rental apartments are not eligible. An owner must spend at least $2,000, and the maximum credit which may be taken in one tax year is $1,000. Unused credits may be carried forward to future tax years until used up as long as the property continues to qualify. Unused credits are forfeited if the house is sold, converted to a

When homeowners or others in Rhode Island are seeking information about historic preservation they are easily referred to one of the 22 libraries statewide which has the Preservation Library collection.

new use, or if the owner makes changes which are not appropriate to the historical character of the house.

The state historic preservation office reviews each project to be sure the work performed is appropriate and issues final tax credit certificates. The credit may be claimed for any type of exterior preservation work, including maintenance-type items such as painting, roofing, and repair of trim elements. New construction (such as a new porch) does not qualify for a credit but must be reviewed along with work which does qualify. On the interior, only structural repairs such as replacement of sills or rebuilding a historic chimney will qualify for a

A historic house in Rhode Island before and after rehabilitation.

CLARK SCHOETTLE, BOTH

credit. Most interior renovation such as building or rebuilding bathrooms, kitchens, and interior remodeling will not qualify for the tax credit, and interior work is not subject to review.

Rhode Island's homeowner tax credit has several distinctive features. It is targeted at owner-occupants in part because the existing federal rehabilitation tax credit excludes this group of property owners who are key to neighborhood renewal. The minimum expenditure is purposefully set low, and periodic maintenance work as well as larger restoration projects may qualify. These provisions are meant to encourage property owners to see preservation of their historic house as a long term commitment rather than a one-time restoration project. Limiting the amount of tax credit which may be taken in any one year to $1,000 has two benefits. First, it lessens the tax revenue impact of the credit. Second, building up unused credits which are carried forward to future tax years discourages inappropriate alterations to historic houses since the unused credits would be forfeited.

Rhode Island's "residential historic preservation tax credit" has been disappointing in one respect. Use of the credit has averaged less than 100 applications per year. This may be the result of relatively modest financial benefits, and it certainly reflects insufficient efforts to publicize and distribute information about the credit. Steps are being taken to address the latter problem, and we remain optimistic that Rhode Island's homeowner tax credit can be the basis for continuing relationships between homeowners and our historic preservation program.

Transportation Enhancements and Scenic Roads

HISTORIC RESOURCES ARE WIDELY DISTRIBUTED across Rhode Island's landscape, and many cross-roads villages are registered historic districts. So it is not surprising that highway construction projects frequently affect historic properties. State highways which once passed through open fields to connect distinct village clusters, now also serve suburban houses and commercial strips and retail malls. Increased use of formerly rural roads by commuters and shoppers puts almost irresistible pressure on the state department of transportation to widen, straighten, and upgrade roads to increase their carrying capacity. Protection of a historic area from the visual intrusion of an expanded highway is sometimes the flash point for public disagreements about transportation policy or the importance of restricting sprawl development.

With the enactment of the federal Intermodal Surface Transportation Efficiency Act in 1991, the Rhode Island Department of Transportation turned to historic preservation among other interests to develop a "transportation enhancements" program. The federal law recognizes that transportation is more than just highways and automobiles and that transportation affects communities in many ways. The Enhancements part of the law sets aside federal funds to be used for projects which protect cultural and natural resources and which integrate transportation into other aspects of the community.

Governor Bruce Sundlun and the Department of Transportation created a "Transportation Enhancement Advisory Committee" to make recommendations on how Rhode Island should spend about $20 million allocated for enhancement projects. The Committee is chaired by the director of the state historic preservation office, and the Committee's eleven members have a broad range of backgrounds, including historical preservation, environmental conservation, local governments, passenger rail service, tourism, planning, and transportation. The Committee developed an open and broad-based process for selecting projects based on objective criteria. A total of 197 proposals was received, representing nearly every city and town, many non-profit organizations, and individual citizens.

Transportation is more than just highways and automobiles.

The projects finally selected by the Committee include a variety of eligible activities. For example, Newport's famous Cliff Walk, part of a National Historic Landmark District, will receive much needed repairs so pedestrians can continue to use our state's most popular walkway in safety. Quite a few projects relate directly to historic preservation, including preservation of two historic railroad stations, purchase of development rights for the land surrounding Rhode Island's oldest house, restoration of several historic structures, and tree planting and streetscape improvements in a number of historic districts. Projects involving greenways, bikeways or pedestrian trails generally run through historic areas.

The Committee was impressed by the energy and creativity which Rhode Islanders showed in proposing ways to improve our transportation system. It is clear that people want the system to be better, and they have good ideas about how to achieve it. The projects recommended by the Committee are an important step toward needed improvements, but there are many more ideas than there are dollars.

In addition to the specific projects which will be funded over the next few years, the enhancement process itself is part of a new dialogue between citizens and the Department of Transportation about what the state's transportation goals should be and how to achieve them. As desirable as landscaping, bike paths, walkways, historic preservation, and the rest of these activities are, they should not be mistaken as the solution to larger transportation problems. However, enhancements do show a variety of ways that transportation projects can be better integrated with the surrounding community and the natural environment. Under the new federal rules, enhancement-type elements are eligible to be included in every transportation project. Preservationists and transportation planners should make good use of this opportunity for constructive cooperation.

Historic preservation also is represented on the Rhode Island Scenic Roadways Board, where the director of the state historic preservation office serves as Vice Chairman. Legislation creating the Board was enacted in 1985 (RI General Law 24-15) partly in response to a particularly controversial highway construction project. The Board has the right to give a road scenic designation upon nomination by local government, and any state highway construction project on a designated scenic road must be reviewed by the Scenic Roadway Board.

Routine road design elements can destroy the geometry and vegetation which give a scenic road its special character.

Currently the Board is carrying out a statewide survey to identify roads which are potentially eligible for scenic designation. Historic and environmental values are incorporated in the designation criteria, and important sources of information for the study are a scenic areas inventory conducted by the Department of Environmental Management, the comprehensive historical surveys conducted by the state historic preservation office, and a statewide historic landscapes survey also conducted by the historic preservation office. During 1996, the Scenic Highway board expects to issue a preliminary inventory of scenic roads throughout Rhode Island. This information will give early warning to the Department of Transportation about which projects may impact scenic resources, and the inventory will be available to be incorporated into local land use plans.

A second study undertaken by the Scenic Highway Board is examining how highway construction standards impinge on scenic aspects of roadways. Routine design elements such as lane widths, radius of curves, alignment of slopes, and design of cleared shoulders can destroy the geometry and vegetation which give a scenic road its special character. By developing a set of alternate design standards for scenic roads in cooperation with the Department of Transportation, the Board will be able to fulfill its mandate to review highway construction projects in a positive manner with a minimum of case-by-case conflict.

The relevance of scenic roadway regulation to historic preservation is two-fold. First, many roads within Rhode Island's historic areas also qualify for scenic designation. Scenic regulation adds a valuable layer of protection, especially for those visual qualities of a historic area which are part of the character of its setting. Second, more tolerant highway construction standards originally developed to protect scenic roads may in the future be applied within historic districts to preserve visual quality, even if they do not contain designated scenic roads.

Conclusion

THE PRECEDING FOUR EXAMPLES show how the recognition of historic resources as widespread and part of the everyday fabric of Rhode Island communities has led to state historic preservation initiatives. For some people there is only one universal measure of what is truly important, however, and that is economic value. Historic preservation is among other things real estate, and as an activity of government historic preservation must compete with other claims upon the public revenue. Recognizing this point of view, in 1993 the state historic preservation office contracted with the Department of Resource Economics at the University of Rhode Island to study the economic effects of historical preservation expenditures from 1971 to 1993.

The study's findings included the following highlights: Expenditures over two decades included $12 million in federal funding, $9 million in state funding, $4 million in local funding, and $216 million in private investment. This is a 9:1 leveraging ratio of private investment to public expenditures. The total value of historic preservation programs was $342 million. This is a 41% overall return on investment, and for public dollars alone the return was fourteen-fold. The effects of preservation investment on jobs and employment were significant. The equivalent of 13,222 one-year jobs were created with wages of $277 million. On an annual basis, historic preservation programs in Rhode Island are creating 1,200 jobs each year with wages of $36.7 million. Tax revenues generated by historic preservation programs totaled $64 million in federal taxes, $13.5 million in Rhode Island taxes, and $8.1 in local taxes. For each dollar Rhode Island appropriated to historic preservation, the state gained back $1.22 in new state tax revenue. The federal government gained $1.30 in new tax revenue for each $1 in tax credits allowed for rehabilitation of historic buildings.

The University of Rhode Island study compared historic preservation with other types of public investments and found that historic preservation stimulates more manufacturing jobs than other public works projects, and the overall economic benefits from historic preservation projects are 25 percent greater than for construction of new highways.

The University of Rhode Island economic analysis demonstrates how the work of rehabilitating and reusing historic buildings has become part of Rhode Island's economic life. The real value of historic preservation clearly goes beyond economics to include safeguarding the landmarks of our heritage, revitalizing neighborhoods, renovating housing, and making communities better places to live. In Rhode Island, land use planning, involving local libraries in preservation education, offering a tax incentive to homeowners to preserve their historic house, and recognizing the impacts of transportation projects on historic areas are some of the ways we are working to preserve historic communities. These state initiated programs supplement federal historic preservation programs administered by our state historic preservation office. The federal program and funding was the critical element in Rhode Island's early program development, particularly the statewide survey. While the federal program and funding continue to be an essential foundation, the development of state initiated programs over the last decade represents a conscious decision to broaden and diversify historic preservation services offered to Rhode Island citizens.

For each dollar Rhode Island appropriated to historic preservation, the state gained back $1.22 in new state tax revenue.

Edward F. Sanderson, the author of this chapter, is executive director of the Rhode Island Historical Preservation and Heritage Commission.

PART II

Transportation
and
Alternatives to Sprawl:
Flip Sides of a Coin

CHAPTER 9

Transportation

NEIL ALEXANDER

Transportation

S
TATE TRANSPORTATION POLICIES CAN DO AS MUCH TO AFFECT THE
character of our communities and the fate of historic resources as any
other single policy.

Examples abound.

A major freeway planned by California through South Pasadena and El
Sereno will, if built, displace 3,000 people and destroy over 1,000 homes, 5,000
trees, and portions of five historic districts.

The setting of Spokane, Washington's most historic high school, Lewis and
Clark, was seriously degraded by the construction of an intrusive elevated freeway
less than a block away. The freeway also made the neighborhood unpleasant for
students living nearby to walk to school.

Residents of Russellville, Ark., pleaded with state highway officials who were
widening a road in 1993 to save the old trees framing their historic main street.
To no avail. The trees came down.

Not only can decisions by state transportation officials affect specific historic
buildings and neighborhoods, but such decisions can also unleash development
forces that undermine whole cities and towns, where historic resources are often
concentrated. A decision to extend a road into the countryside can promote urban
sprawl and siphon away the economic vitality of an older downtown, thereby triggering disinvestment in downtown historic buildings.[1] U.S. Senator Daniel Patrick
Moynihan recognized the impact of transportation projects on our communities
back in 1960, when he wrote, "Highways determine land use, which is another way
of saying they settle the future of the areas in which they are built."[2]

Of course state transportation projects can benefit historic areas and communities, too:

- In West Memphis, Ark., state transportation officials made a down-at-the-
  heels Main Street more inviting to shoppers and pedestrians simply by
  installing new sidewalks and planting new trees.
- In Denver, highway officials removed a highway ramp that once darkened
  a section of the Lower Downtown Historic District, thus enabling the city
  to reunite once severed neighborhoods.
- In San Francisco, the state transportation department helped reestablish
  the gateway to the Ferry Building Depot, one of the city's most popular
  historic landmarks. This project will improve ferry access to the depot and
  enhance the city's waterfront.

How different state transportation policies produce positive or negative results
is the subject of this chapter.

**A new highway
severs the
historic church in
the background
from its context.**

Transportation Choices:
Costs and Potential Savings

THE PRIVATE AUTOMOBILE has conferred many wonderful benefits on American society and will doubtless continue to do so. Most Americans enjoy the convenience and privacy of their cars. While recognizing the automobile's many positive contributions, one must acknowledge that *excessive* dependence on this form of transportation profoundly affects the character and livability of our communities.

"In accommodating the auto," writes Tom Hylton in *Save Our Land, Save Our Towns*, "we have also let it become our only transportation option. This requires that we take our 3,500-pound cars everywhere we go...Virtually every building constructed in the last 50 years is bordered, or even surrounded, by a large parking lot.... No wonder it is impossible to place buildings in attractive settings. No wonder most trips consist of driving from one parking lot to another. No wonder you can't walk from work to shopping to home. Even when buildings are placed within walking distance of each other, multi-lane highways form impenetrable barriers that make it impossible to go even short distances without getting into a car. Cars are so dominant we rarely build streets with sidewalks anymore. In fact, the [Pennsylvania] Department of Transportation has *banned* sidewalks along many of our busiest highways. At many busy intersections, the problem of pedestrian crossing is dealt with simply by prohibiting pedestrians."[3]

Kindred thoughts expressed by Jane Jacobs are as relevant today as they were in 1961, when she observed in *The Death and Life of Great American Cities*: "Today everyone who values cities is disturbed by automobiles. Traffic arteries, along with parking lots, gas stations and drive-ins, are powerful and insistent instruments of city destruction. To accommodate them, city streets are broken down into loose sprawls, incoherent and vacuous for anyone afoot. Downtowns and other neighborhoods that are marvels of close-grained intricacy and compact mutual support are casually disemboweled. Landmarks are crumbled or are so sundered from their contexts in city life as to become irrelevant trivialities. City character is blurred until every place becomes more like every other place, all adding up to Noplace."

Eighty-four percent of all personal travel in the United States occurs by car or by some other privately owned motor vehicle—trucks or mini-vans, for example. Due to sprawling development patterns, insensitive urban design, segregated land uses, and little investment in alternative transportation modes, the opportunity to make short trips by foot and longer trips by public transport or bicycle simply does not exist in much of America. Even the simplest of everyday errands requires getting into a car and driving somewhere. Children can no longer walk to school or over to a friend's house to play; they must depend on their parents to be driven. Elderly people unable to drive cannot walk to a drug or grocery store; they must depend on someone else to take them around. Shoppers often drive across the highway to reach another store or restaurant only a few hundred feet away simply because it is dangerous and unpleasant to cross by walking.

The costs of excessive auto dependence are a burden to state government. In 1994, states spent a total of $59.8 billion on transportation (mostly roads), making transportation the third largest expenditure for states. Only Medicaid and education took bigger bites out of state budgets, and many state education budgets even include substantial sums for busing students because children in many parts of the country can no longer walk to school.[4] The total backlog of unfunded road and bridge repairs facing states is approximately $290 billion nationwide. States devote almost nine percent of their budgets to transportation.[5]

In traditional downtowns (above opposite), people can easily walk to many destinations—to work, restaurants, shops, doctors' offices, etc. Sprawl development such as that shown below discourages walking anywhere, even short distances.

A citizens group known as I-CARE fought this freeway intrusion in Ft. Worth, Texas. Following a long legal battle, I-CARE succeeded in getting plans approved to dismantle the freeway.

JAMES LINDBERG

Because these costs are so high, states and communities across the country are searching for more efficient, less expensive ways of moving people and goods. State governments could achieve several important goals by taking two fairly simple and inexpensive steps:

- encouraging the preservation of traditional downtowns and neighborhoods that are pleasant and easy for people to walk around in; and
- promoting the use of time-honored urban design and land-use principles in new settlements being built today.

By thus preserving or promoting walkable communities, states could reduce the demand for expensive new roads. They could maintain—or create—more attractive, more livable communities. They could improve mobility. (In many densely-populated areas of the country, congested automobile traffic sometimes moves more slowly today than horse-drawn carriages at the beginning of the century.) And they could help to preserve our heritage.

Short Trips and Walking

WHILE MOST AMERICANS ARE NOT SURPRISED by the extent to which they rely on the automobile, they probably would be surprised by two little-publicized transportation statistics. The first is that after driving, *walking* is the next most important form of transportation in the U.S. Many people no doubt assume that public transit or rail or biking is more important as a means of travel than walking. Yet walking accounts for three times more trips than public transit and nine times more trips than biking.[6]

The second surprising statistic is that more than a quarter of all trips in America are under one mile.[7] Many of these short trips, which are the least fuel-efficient and generate the most pollution per mile traveled when made by car,[8] could be easily traversed by foot, bicycle, or bus *if* those who shape our communities, including state traffic engineers, paid more attention to land use and urban design. In his book, *City: Rediscovering the Center*, William H. Whyte gives just one of countless examples of how distances are often made to *seem* much longer than they really are due to the physical surroundings: "It is not linear distance that is critical, but continuity...In Dallas, one of the reasons City Hall Plaza is underused, people will tell you, is how far away it is from downtown. But it isn't; it is in fact quite close—only three blocks from Main Street. But it seems much farther. There is a sharp break in continuity as high rise [buildings] abruptly give way to low-rise [buildings] and to those great separators, parking lots."[9] Others have noted the correlation between the willingness of people to walk and the existence of interesting, pleasant street environments that actually make walking fun.

A Desire for Choices

MANY AMERICANS WOULD LIKE MORE CHOICES when it comes to transportation. The average American household today spends $6,044, or more than $500 a month, on transportation. Most of this money goes toward purchasing, fueling, insuring, parking and repairing cars. Auto-related expenses rival the mortgage in terms of their impact on the household budget and they exceed the costs of food, health insurance, clothing or education.[10] While many people may value their cars next to their homes, others place a higher value on other things—the education of their children or retirement security, for example. These people would appreciate the *option* of spending less on transportation so that they could invest more in other budget areas. According to the 1996 national home buyers' community preference survey, nearly three-quarters of all home buyers said they would prefer to live in a community where they could walk or bicycle."[11]

By preserving walkable communities, states could reduce the demand for expensive new roads.

Historic communities, which are characterized by mixed land uses, compact development, and pedestrian friendly environments, are walkable communities. Consider that in historic Annapolis, Md., 19.2 percent of all commuting trips are made by walking.[12] (Nationally, 73.5 percent of all commuting occurs by automobile.[13]) In the historic "Old Town" section of Key West, Fla., 40 percent of all trips are made by foot; in Key West's "New Town," where commercial sprawl dominates, only four percent of all trips occur by foot.[14] As the chart below suggests, the contribution that walkable historic areas make in alleviating transportation problems is significant.

Percentage of Walk-to-Work Trips between Central City and Central Business District	
Traditional city*	**State**
Harrisburg, Pa.	24.5%
Lancaster, Pa.	39.4%
Portland, Me.	26.5%
Auto City*	**State**
Beaumont, Tex.	1.5%
Lake Charles, La.	1.33%
Warren, Ohio	3.93%

* In each of the more compact traditional cities listed in the above chart, more than 50 percent of the housing stock was built before 1940, and the cities themselves are characterized by relatively compact land-use patterns. Each of the "auto cities" has only a small percentage of housing stock built before 1940 and is more sprawling. Source of figures: 1980 U.S. Census

The potential savings that could be achieved if states encouraged better urban design and land-use principles in newer communities are also significant. In Oregon, for example, a recent study found that if such principles were applied to new development, trips made by foot or bicycle would increase by 22 percent and peak-hour vehicle miles would drop by 13.6 percent.[15]

In short, it is in the self-interest of state government to reduce pressures to build more roads and to give people transportation choices. Full use of older, traditional communities, coupled with the promotion of better land-use and urban design practices in new settlements, would help states cut transportation costs, make neighborhoods more livable, and, in areas where short trips are possible, *improve mobility*.[16]

Why Old and Historic Districts Are Walkable

IN THE OLDER AREAS OF MOST CITIES, and in many historic districts, development is usually compact and tightly-knit. Buildings are close to each other and land uses are typically mixed. Small stores are close to homes. Offices are close to restaurants. Residents are close to workplaces. By limiting the distances one must travel to get from place to place, the mixed land uses and compact development patterns make it feasible to conduct business and carry out essential functions by foot.

Other characteristics make walking safe and pleasant. Sidewalks, often lined with street trees and other amenities separating people from auto traffic, provide a safe haven for the pedestrian. Street "walls" formed by evenly aligned, adjoining buildings make the pedestrian feel safe, as does the narrowness of streets. The architecture is often attractive and interesting. Building facades are not blank and boring, but often feature window displays and architectural details. The presence of trees adds to the charm of the streetscape. Human activity—shoppers, other pedestrians, street cafes—make walking seem fun and interesting. Because many people enjoy walking in such areas, the prospects for chance encounters with friends and associates are enhanced.

Taken together, these land-use, urban-design, and architectural characteristics promote what might be termed "transportation by proximity." When applied creatively, they amount to a transportation "demand-reduction" strategy that reduces pressures to build costly new roads.[17]

One additional benefit of preserving historic districts is that they are conducive to a more active lifestyle. According to the U.S. Surgeon General, more than 60 percent of all American adults do not get enough physical exercise to stay healthy and 250,000 deaths in the U.S. annually are linked to lack of regular physical activity. The sedentary life style now rivals smoking as a contributor to heart disease. For these reasons, physicians recommend at least 30 minutes of walking daily. In sharp contrast to many areas of the country, historic districts are one area in which people *can* walk and enjoy doing so.

A historic area friendly to pedestrians (left) and a sprawl-type development hostile to pedestrians.

Costs Related to Auto Dependence

- Over 100 million Americans live in areas that fail to meet federal clean air standards.[18]
- Sixty-thousand Americans die annually from respiratory illnesses associated with air pollution linked to auto emissions.[19]
- Almost 40,000 Americans die every year from motor vehicle crashes while another three million are injured.[20]
- States face a backlog of $290 billion nationwide in unfunded road and bridge repairs.[21]
- The average American household today spends $6,044, or more than $500 a month, on transportation (mostly auto-related) expenses.[22]

A cemetary dating to the Civil War lies behind this plea for help. A vast but rarely full parking lot for a shopping center degrades this cemetary's setting. To the front, the Virginia Dept. of Transportation built an unnecessarily wide road with no sidewalks so that people living near the shopping center and a nearby metro stop find it hard to walk to these destinations, despite their proximity.

CONSTANCE BEAUMONT

Federal Framework for State Transportation Policies

BEFORE DISCUSSING THE STATE'S ROLE IN TRANSPORTATION, LET'S LOOK BRIEFLY at federal transportation policies, for they establish the financial and legal framework within which states must operate.

From 1956, when the Federal Aid Highway Act was enacted, until 1991, when the Intermodal Surface Transportation Efficiency Act was passed by Congress, the federal government rewarded states financially for building roads while penalizing them for investing in public transit and other alternatives to the automobile. For every $10 a state spent on Interstate highways, the Federal Government would contribute $90. But states received a much smaller percentage of federal funds for the investments they made in public transit. Investments in other modes—pedestrian, transit, bicycle and rail—were scarcely considered at all. The 1956 legislation and the Interstate Highway System it created emphasized high-speed superhighways between and around cities, but did little to enhance mobility *within* cities and towns, especially older ones. Instead, older neighborhoods were bulldozed and replaced by interstate highways. As Kenneth T. Jackson observed in the *Crabgrass Frontier*, "the interstate system helped continue the downward spiral of public transportation and virtually guaranteed that future urban growth would perpetuate a centerless sprawl."[23]

Senator Edward M. Kennedy of Massachusetts expressed the frustration felt by many states with the Federal Government's one-size-fits-all transportation policy when he testified in 1971 in favor of opening up the Highway Trust Fund—at the time wholly dedicated to highways—to mass transit as well:

> I am most familiar with how this funding rigidity has affected the people of my own state. In the Boston metropolitan area, a single expressway forced the displacement of 2,106 households. Daily in the city of Boston, 160,000 cars form a commuter parade into the downtown area which can absorb only 28,000 in offstreet parking. Yet the city can obtain funds for more highways it doesn't need, while it is denied requests for mass transit…[T]he States and cities have a simple choice foisted upon them by Federal legislation: build highways or build nothing.

Given almost four decades of federal financial incentives for states to build highways and little else, it is no surprise that states did exactly that.

Intermodal Surface Transportation Efficiency Act

IN 1991, CONGRESS LOOSENED the financial straightjacket that had skewed state transportation policies in favor of the automobile since the fifties. With the enactment of the

Intermodal Surface Transportation Efficiency Act—"ISTEA," popularly known as "Ice Tea"—federal policy gave the states more freedom to choose how they spend their transportation dollars. For the first time since 1956, states could now invest in something other than highways without being penalized financially. Under ISTEA, states now receive the same percentage of federal matching funds for all transportation projects, whether they be highways, transit lines, sidewalks, bike paths or rail lines. For every $20 a state invests in any mode of transportation, the Federal Government contributes $80.

Besides equalizing the federal share for all transportation projects, ISTEA emphasized three other core principles that are important to historic preservation:

- "intermodalism"—that is, smooth and easy connections between the various transportation modes used by people when they travel, whether for long or short distances;
- a strong local voice in state transportation decisions; and
- a planning process that looks at the land-use and other effects of transportation projects.

Finally, ISTEA authorized a $2.6 billion "enhancements" program through which transportation-related historic preservation projects could be funded. It also provided more flexible road design standards to allow for the preservation of scenic and historic areas.

ISTEA's funding expires on September 30, 1997, so Congress must reauthorize the program before then. Historic preservationists and other livable-community advocates want to see ISTEA's core principles, and especially the Transportation Enhancements Program, continued (see below). The road building industry, however, is already lobbying to do away with these features.

Transportation Enhancements

THE TRANSPORTATION ENHANCEMENTS PROGRAM, authorized as part of the Surface Transportation Program (STP) by ISTEA, is a major source of funds for historic preservation projects. Dozens of small communities participating in the National Trust for Historic Preservation's Main Street Program have competed successfully for transportation enhancement awards to make improvements in their historic commercial districts.

Under the ISTEA legislation, states must set aside ten percent of their STP funds for "enhancement" projects. These include:

- historic preservation projects;
- acquisition of easements on scenic or historic sites;
- rehabilitation and operation of historic transportation structures, such as railroad stations, lighthouses, ships, and canals; and
- landscaping and other scenic beautification.

To qualify for STP funding, most enhancement projects must be related—by function, proximity, or impact—to a transportation element in an intermodal system. An "intermodal" system is one that makes appropriate links between different transportation modes—highways, roads, transit, pedestrian, bicycle, rail, air, bus and water—so these work together smoothly. There is one important caveat to the above requirement for project qualification: On June 6, 1995, the Federal Highway Administration issued a guidance memo stating that historic preservation projects that do not involve a transportation facility—e.g., a historic railroad station—must demonstrate a substantial link to the intermodal transportation system in order to qualify for funding. In other words, mere proximity to a transportation facility is not enough in the case of a preservation project. States may not use enhancement funds to mitigate the environmental impacts of highways, unless the mitigation exceeds what is otherwise legally required.

Residents of South Pasadena, California, protest a freeway planned by the state transportation department.

Intermodal Surface Transportation Efficiency

Transportation planning. The Intermodal Surface Transportation Efficiency Act of (ISTEA) requires states to prepare long-range, comprehensive transportation plans that consider all modes of transportation—transit, rail, pedestrian, bicycle as well as highways. The planning process must also consider national goals—e.g., energy conservation, clean air, traffic congestion relief; social, and environmental impacts of transportation projects; effects of transportation on land use and development; and recommendations made by Metropolitan Planning Organizations (MPOs). MPOs designated for "urbanized" areas (50,000-plus populations) prepare long-range plans as well as Transportation Improvement Programs (TIPs). TIPs also must identify transportation "enhancement" projects recommended for funding. ISTEA requires states to give the public an opportunity to comment on their transportation plans.

National Highway System. ISTEA created the National Highway System, a 159,000-mile network that includes all highways considered important to the country as a whole. These include interstate highways as well as principal urban and rural arterials that link major population centers. Congress approved $21 billion over six years for the system.

Surface Transportation Program. ISTEA created the Surface Transportation Program, through which the Federal Government provides flexible "block grants" to help states pay for the construction and rehabilitation of major roads and bridges. All public roads (except minor collectors or local roads, which must be maintained with state or local funds) can be supported by this program. So can public transit projects, bikeways, walkways, scenic byways, commuter rail, fringe parking, and even traffic congestion relief. Congress earmarked $23.9 billion over six years for the STP program.

Transportation Enhancements. ISTEA requires states to set aside ten percent of their Surface Transportation Program funds for transportation "enhancements." Eligible enhancement projects include any of the following:

- bikeways, walkways, and other facilities for bikers and pedestrians;
- easements on scenic or historic sites;
- scenic or historic byways;
- landscaping or other beautification projects;
- historic preservation;
- rehabilitation and operation of historic transportation structures, such as railroad stations and canals;
- preservation of abandoned rail corridors—or conversion of such corridors to footpaths or bike trails;

Nationally, funding for transportation enhancements will come to $2.6 billion over a six-year period. As of June 1995, 4,504 transportation enhancement projects had received approval from state transportation departments. Of these, 1,197 involved historic preservation. These projects accounted for about $377 million of all enhancement funds awarded as of that time.[24]

Like all STP grants to the states, enhancements grants must be matched on an 80-20 basis: For every $80 of Federal grant funds, the grantee must contribute $20. Enhancement projects must be included in the state's transportation plans and, if proposed for a metropolitan area, in the plan of the Metropolitan Planning Organization.

Examples of enhancement projects carried out with the help of state transportation departments include:

- rehabilitation of the historic Stone Arch Bridge in Minneapolis. The bridge now provides trolley, pedestrian, and bicycle connections between downtown Minneapolis and St. Anthony Falls, Minneapolis' birthplace;

Act of 1991: Major Provisions

- control and removal of billboards;
- archaeological planning and research; and
- mitigation of water pollution due to the runoff of oil and other toxic substances from highways.

Scenic byways. ISTEA also authorized $80 million over six years for scenic byways. The law directed the Secretary of Transportation to appoint an advisory committee to help establish a National Scenic Byways Program and provided technical assistance and grants to states for planning, designing and developing state scenic byways programs. The National Scenic Byways Program was formally established in 1995, and the first designated National Scenic Byways and All American Roads (the best of the best) were designated in the fall of 1996. Scenic byways grants not only help states establish programs to protect and promote scenic roadways, but they also help communities to develop corridor management plans. Nominations of roads to the national program come from the local level. Any road designated as a National Scenic Byway or All American Road must have a plan to manage the scenic corridor and evidence of strong local commitment to achieve the plan's goals.

Funding flexibility: ISTEA permits states to transfer 50 percent of the money they receive from the Federal Government for National Highway System (NHS) projects to their Surface Transportation Program. States may transfer all of their NHS funds to the STP if they do not meet federal Clean Air Act standards. The Clean Air Act requires states to reduce automobile emissions and authorizes the federal government to withhold federal transportation funds from states that fail to do so. One barrier to using the funding flexibility allowed by ISTEA is the existence of some state legal restrictions on the use of state gas tax funds for anything but roads. These states may only use state gas tax revenues to match federally-assisted road projects and not public transit or other modes.

Road Design Standards: All roads that are part of the National Highway System must comply with federal road design standards. These are promulgated by the U.S. Department of Transportation and reflect criteria developed by the American Association of State Highway and Transportation Officials (AASHTO). When the application of AASHTO standards might harm designated scenic and historic areas, ISTEA specifically encourages states to obtain waivers from the U.S. Department of Transportation for these special areas, as long as the road involved is not part of the Interstate system. Roads that are not part of the National Highway System must comply with state standards. The states *may* adopt federal standards but are not required to do so. States thus have the legal flexibility to apply their own standards to non-NHS roads.

- directional and interpretive signs, pull-offs, and parking at four sites along the historic Liberty Trail in Liberty County, Georgia. One of these sites is the Dorchester Academy, where civil rights activists held a planning retreat led by Martin Luther King, Jr., before the Birmingham campaign;
- relocation of a historic train depot in Lafayette, Ind. By moving the depot two blocks, the city of Lafayette has provided a more convenient shelter and staging area for people using the local train and bus services. This project was part of Indiana Main Street's efforts to revitalize downtown Lafayette.[25]

According to a recent survey, the states spending the highest percentage of their "enhancement" funds on historic preservation are: Alabama (32%) Indiana (32%), Kentucky (46%), Mississippi (52%), Texas (53%), and West Virginia (42%). States spending the least for preservation "enhancements" are Alaska (6%), Connecticut (7%), Florida (4%), Hawaii (0%), Idaho (0%), and Washington (3%).

Main Street in West Memphis, Arkansas, before and after a transportation enhancement project was completed.

(For more information about the Enhancements Program, see Building on the Past/Traveling to the Future, *by I Mei Chan. This report is available from the Federal Highway Administration or the National Trust for Historic Preservation. Also see the Case Study on Rhode Island, Chapter 8.)*

Road Design Standards

ROAD DESIGN STANDARDS SIGNIFICANTLY AFFECT HISTORIC RESOURCES AND local community character. The standards determine how wide lanes must be, how sharp street corners are. They determine whether trees are permitted alongside streets, parkways and country roads. They dictate whether intersections have street lights on small poles or tangles of overhead wires with lights dangling from above. They determine whether neighborhoods and downtowns can allow curbside parking, or whether this must be removed to make way for cars speeding through town. They affect whether sidewalks are wide enough (or whether they even exist) to accommodate pedestrians. Road design standards are akin to building codes except they apply to streets and roads instead of buildings. Their influence on community character is profound but poorly understood by the general public and state highway officials.

The Standard Setters

ROADS THAT ARE PART OF THE NATIONAL HIGHWAY SYSTEM (NHS) must comply with guidelines developed by the U.S. Department of Transportation in consultation with the American Association of State Highway and Transportation Officials (AASHTO). If an NHS road segment is in a designated scenic or historic area, however, it can be exempted from AASHTO guidelines if the state obtains a waiver from the U.S. Department of Transportation. Such waivers may be granted to "allow for the preservation of environmental, scenic, or historic values," provided that public safety is not jeopardized.

Roads that are not part of the NHS are subject only to state standards:

> Projects (other than highway projects on the National Highway System) shall be designed, constructed, operated, and maintained in accordance with State laws, regulations, directives, safety standards, design standards, and construction standards.[26]

States thus have the option of applying the AASHTO guidelines to non-NHS roads, such as minor local roads or major roads funded through the Surface Transportation Program. As a practical matter, most states adhere closely to the AASHTO standards even though federal law does not require them to do so. The AASHTO guidelines are found in *A Policy on Geometric Design*, the so-called "Green Book" used as a Bible by traffic engineers.

Design Standards: Source of Confusion and Criticism

ROAD DESIGN STANDARDS ARE A SOURCE OF MUCH CONFUSION and criticism within the historic preservation movement. Citizens who want to preserve historic buildings, old trees, and the pedestrian ambiance of a community are often frustrated with state highway officials who refer to mysterious standards in an arcane manual to which non-transportation personnel have no access. Citizens who become involved in road controversies—and indeed, highway officials themselves—seldom understand the extent to which states may exercise flexibility in applying the guidelines.

Citizens are often frustrated with state highway officials who refer to mysterious standards in an arcane manual.

"The standards are applied as a sort of 'one size fits all' set of rules," says Anne Stillman of the Connecticut Trust for Historic Preservation. "The minimum width requirements for roads and bridges are invariably completely out of scale with many rural and historic communities," she adds. "If a town simply wants to repair an existing road, it often faces a difficult choice: accept a widening that it does not want in order to receive state and federal funds, or pay for the repairs entirely by itself."

"New highways built to these standards are wider, straighter, and flatter than the ones they replace," writes Jim Wick, a Vermonter who became so concerned about a proposed road widening in his home town that he authored a citizens guide on the subject. "The Vermont country road and village street, much revered here and across America," he continues, "are now looked on as substandard and deficient, things that should be changed."[27]

James Lighthizer, former secretary of transportation for the state of Maryland, is an outspoken critic of the standards and their interpretation by traffic engineers: "The AASHTO standards assume that everyone on the road is a drunk speeding along without a seatbelt. Roads are made to conform to what the engineers, not the people, want, and the engineers want to make every road wide enough to land a plane sideways on."

Interpretation of Standards

DESPITE THEIR REPUTATION AS RIGID, immutable rules, the AASHTO "standards" are technically just guidelines. As the Green Book states in its foreword, the guidelines are intended to assist traffic engineers, but they permit "[s]ufficient flexibility...to encourage independent designs tailored to particular situations."[28] The foreword goes on to say:

> The fact that new design values are presented herein does not imply that existing streets and highways are unsafe, nor does it mandate the initiation of improvement projects. This publication is not intended as a policy for resurfacing, restoration or rehabilitation (R.R.R.) projects. For projects of this type, where major revisions to horizontal or vertical curvature are not necessary or practical, existing design values may be retained.
>
> [Traffic d]esigners...are encouraged to consider not only vehicular movement, but also movement of people, distribution of goods, and provision of essential services.

This nod to flexibility notwithstanding, the AASHTO guidelines are generally treated as if they were rigid standards, according to Charles Adams, director of environmental design for the Maryland Highway Division and a transportation official sympathetic to the concerns of preservationists. "But every situation needs to be looked at independently," says Adams. "There are many influences on a transportation project: traffic, the environment, social and preservation issues. All these factors have a bearing on the design of a project. The intent of AASHTO is not that all highways be identical." In explaining the guidelines to others, Adams compares them to a chalkboard in a frame: "You don't have to write everything in the upper-right hand of the chalkboard; you can use the entire board because it all fits within the frame. Some engineers treat AASHTO standards as if they had to fit everything into the upper-right-hand corner of the chalkboard. So they push for the widest, flattest roads. This is not always what we should do."

The first problem with the standards, then, lies with their *interpretation*.

Liability

THE FEAR OF LIABILITY IS THE SECOND PROBLEM. "If you built a project that didn't adhere to the AASHTO standards, then if someone had an accident and took you to court because

Despite their reputation as rigid, immutable rules, the AASHTO "standards" are technically just guidelines.

you deviated from the standards, you'd leave yourself open to a liability suit," explains one state highway engineer. Such fears are widespread, but few engineers are able to cite actual court cases in which someone was held liable due to a highway's design, as opposed to some other factor.

At this writing, the state of Wisconsin, for example, has not been exposed to a single case in which liability for highway design was an issue, according to James Thiel, general counsel for the Wisconsin Department of Transportation and chairman of AASHTO's Legal Committee. "The only way government employees can be held negligent is if they fail to perform a mandatory non-discretionary function. If the action is discretionary, which highway design matters usually are, the employee cannot be held liable for exercising judgment," Thiel says. He believes this standard of care is "fairly prevalent" among the states.[29]

John Heaton, general counsel for the Pennsylvania Department of Transportation, says that mere deviation from the standards is not proof of negligence by a state: "If a [highway] designer deviates from a standard, then he needs to show how he accommodated the safety considerations [that underlie]…the standard in another way. If the designer weighs and balances his decision, acts reasonably, and documents his work, then there is a good chance that his decision can sustain the scrutiny of the court."[30]

In *Take Back Your Streets: How to Protect Communities from Asphalt and Traffic*, the Boston-based Conservation Law Foundation makes these observations on the liability issue:

All the New England states, through legislation, court rulings, or both, have given government bodies immunity from lawsuits relating to road design in all, or nearly all, circumstances.

The imposition of inappropriate road design standards forces developers to bulldoze trees that enhance neighborhoods. In the neighborhood shown above, AASHTO standards were not applied. The result: an attractive, walkable neighborhood.

JAMES LINDBERG

...the rare plaintiff who manages to find a hole in the government's immunity from claims related to design must still prove that the highway department was negligent...If a highway department documents that it considered AASHTO guidelines and made a considered decision to depart from them in certain ways out of concern for pedestrian safety or other community needs, a potential plaintiff is unlikely to take a case far. Failing to follow AASHTO guidelines does not itself constitute negligence, nor does following the guidelines mean that a highway department is not negligent.

...Since liability for failing to keep roads and bridges in good repair is not as sharply limited, and since expensive, poorly designed road reconstruction projects divert funds from road repair work throughout a state or locality, spending limited funds to make a road conform to AASHTO guidelines is likely to be counterproductive from the point of view of exposure to liability. No one should accept potential state or municipal liability as a reason for improperly designing a road in his or her community.[31]

The effect of road design standards can be seen in the nearly treeless neighborhood above.

To be sure, preservation advocates should not dismiss engineers' valid concerns over potential liability. But given the apparent overstatement of this problem, preservationists should probe more deeply and ask state transportation officials to provide citations for actual court cases in which judges held states or their employees liable for exercising judgment on design issues. Liability cases involving other matters—road maintenance, for example—do not fill the bill.

Design Controls

WHILE BOTH FEDERAL LAW and the AASHTO guidelines themselves provide greater flexibility than is often acknowledged, and while the concerns of engineers over liability for exercising flexibility on *design* matters appear to be exaggerated, it would be a mistake to conclude that the AASHTO guidelines are an appropriate model for historic areas or, for that matter, even newer suburbs where human interaction and pedestrian activity are desired. The underlying problem is that the AASHTO guidelines reflect an assumption that most driving occurs on the open road at high speeds. They simply do not consider the fact that in historic districts, urban neighborhoods, main streets and downtowns, roads exist in a different context, amid pedestrians, buildings, trees, and social and commercial activity.

The guidelines' inattention to this reality is often exacerbated by decisions on the part of state transportation officials to set excessively high "design speeds." As Walter Kulash, a prominent transportation expert and a registered professional engineer in Orlando, Florida, who is concerned about protecting the livability of communities, explains:

> The AASHTO guidelines are primarily intended for high-speed rural or suburban settings. Most of their tables don't even relate to speeds under 40 miles an hour, and yet they are widely applied to urban settings. Those of us who advocate livable communities have no quarrel with the AASHTO guidelines for any given speed. That's not the issue with us; the issue is the selection of a design speed of 50 mph for an urban street when it should be 30 mph. Most of the harshness that we experience in our roadside environments relates to these speeds.

The posting of higher speeds often leads to the removal of the very things that give a historic area its charm and sense of security: trees, stone fences, sidewalks, lawns or other buffers for historic houses and buildings. Such speeds dictate ever wider and straighter roads in ever more dehumanizing environments.

The AASHTO Green Book also gives short shrift to the safety of pedestrians in urban areas. It recommends that design speeds "fit the travel desires and habits of nearly all drivers"[32] and, except on local streets, be as high as practicable. To the extent that the book's section on design speeds discusses pedestrians at all, it lumps them together with trees and buildings that "often nullify speed characteristics of a highway with good alignment and flat profiles."[33]

It usually falls to state or local highway officials to set speed limits. They often select the speed within which 85 percent of the traffic travels, because this is what the Green Book recommends, regardless of the speed's appropriateness to a particular setting. As the Conservation Law Foundation observes in its citizens guide on this subject:

> [T]he standard practice is to ensure that only 15 percent of motorists will be exceeding the speed limit, rather than to determine what is safe for residents and responsive to various community needs and to balance motorists' interest in speed against the other considerations…

> Streets and roads do not exist in isolation from their surroundings. They pass through a landscape full of people who *are* somewhere rather than *going* somewhere.

Once the "design speed" is determined, everything else follows. As the Green Book says, "Once selected, all of the pertinent features of the highway should be related to the design speed to obtain a balanced design."[34]

To the extent that the book's section on design speeds discusses pedestrians at all, it lumps them together with trees and buildings that "often nullify speed characteristics of a highway with good alignment and flat profiles."

Encouraging Developments

BECAUSE OF GROWING PUBLIC DISSATISFACTION with the AASHTO standards and their interpretation by state transportation departments, the standard-setters are beginning to respond. An alternative set of standards has been drafted by the Institute of Transportation

Engineers and is supposed to be available soon for public comment. Livable community advocates believe that these standards may be better suited for historic and urban neighborhoods. Maine's Department of Transportation has adopted special standards for lightly travelled roads that are not part of the National Highway System. These standards permit narrower road lanes and shoulders so that the distinctive character of rural areas can be more easily preserved.

Other encouraging developments include the publication of citizen guides that offer practical advice for local communities seeking to preserve their unique character. *Take Back Your Streets*, the Conservation Law Foundation guide mentioned above, is one example. Another is a primer published by the Preservation Trust of Vermont: *A State Highway Project in Your Town? Your Role and Rights.* This guide was authored by Jim Wick, a resident of Tunbridge, Vermont, who simply decided that he would not stand idly by while the state transportation agency destroyed the character of his home town. A new Vermont law enacted in 1996[35] calls for road design standards that respect the state's historic settlement patterns.

In Connecticut, there is mounting resistance to the imposition of community-destroying road standards. In July 1995, plans to widen and straighten Old Saybrook's historic Schoolhouse Road were resoundingly defeated at a town meeting thanks to the vigorous efforts of a local citizens group. A standing-room-only crowd of about 500 people packed a school auditorium and voted down a $379,000 grant for the widening project. Three months later, Guilford, Conn., rejected a $347,000 grant because state transportation officials would not budge when residents asked them to save the historic stone walls and 100-year-old trees lining a local road. "I was stunned at their inflexibility," commented James Portley, the town engineer.[36]

In his citizen's guide, Wick writes, "A town may influence the design of a state highway project if it is active and forceful in pursuing its objectives." Later in this chapter, we will examine how a small town in Maryland did exactly that.

A standing-room-only crowd of about 500 people packed a school auditorium and voted down a widening project.

Maine's Sensible Transportation Policy Act

In 1991, the citizens of Maine approved a state transportation law that provides unusual opportunities for historic preservation. The story behind the enactment of this statute, the Sensible Transportation Policy Act, illustrates what can happen when citizens develop their own vision for transportation policies, organize at the grassroots level, and campaign effectively to get their ideas enacted into law. Maine's subsequent use of a negotiated regulation-writing process demonstrates how consensus-building techniques were used to bring together groups often at odds and to implement this state law.

* * *

IN 1990, THE MAINE TURNPIKE AUTHORITY WAS ON THE VERGE OF RECEIVING THE environmental permits necessary for a $100 million project: the widening of a 30-mile segment of the Maine Turnpike at its southern end, from Kittery to South Portland. Environmentalists had been fighting the widening for years, but they had lost earlier battles with the turnpike authority and the state legislature. They appeared about to lose again when the Natural Resources Council of Maine and Alan Caron, a political and media consultant, came up with the idea of holding a statewide referendum on the turnpike and using the referendum to bring about fundamental changes in state transportation policies.

In Maine, citizens can place questions on the ballot by gathering a certain percentage of signatures based on the previous election's turnout. In this case, 55,000 petition signatures were required. To collect these, advocates of the proposed ballot-box initiative formed a political arm, the Campaign for Sensible Transportation. By Election Day 1990, the Campaign had gathered almost 80,000 signatures, clearly enough to place the initiative on the ballot the following year.

The 1991 initiative posed these questions:

1) Should the turnpike be widened without an evaluation of less costly ways of reducing the traffic congestion?

2) Should a new "Sensible Transportation Policy Act" be enacted?

The act referred to in the initiative included numerous provisions. Among these were:

- A general finding that the decisions of state agencies regarding transportation needs and facilities are often made in isolation, without sufficient comprehensive planning and opportunity for meaningful public input and guidance;
- A statement of general policy requiring "evaluation of the full range of reasonable alternatives to highway construction…and giv[ing] preference to non[road]construction alternatives, such as traffic management and public transit systems;"
- A requirement that the state "incorporate a public participation process in which local governmental bodies and the public have timely notice and opportunity to identify and comment on concerns related to transportation policy decisions…[and that the state] shall take the comments and concerns of local citizens into account and shall be responsive to them;"

In pushing for Maine's Sensible Transportation Policy Act, proponents sought to protect urban amenities such as the one shown opposite.

- A prohibition against the widening of the proposed turnpike unless there was an "affirmative finding that the widening or expansion is consistent with [the new] state transportation policy;" and
- A requirement that the Maine Department of Transportation establish rules to implement the policy enunciated in the "Sensible Transportation Policy Act."

Well-financed business and road construction interests lined up to oppose the initiative, formed their own "Vote No on #1" coalition, and hired a public relations firm from Los Angeles to promote their position. They spent about $1 million—much of it devoted to radio and TV ads—to kill the initiative. Campaign finance reports indicated that virtually all of their campaign contributions came from road construction and paving corporations.[37]

The Campaign for Sensible Transportation raised only about $200,000, mostly from small contributors. It had to rely largely on its coalition partners to get its message out to the public. "We built an alliance between environmentalists and mad-as-hell fiscal conservatives fed up with government spending," explains Caron. "These two groups do not normally work together. We succeeded because we stuck consistently with a message that highlighted wasteful government spending. We understood that if our message were seen as the 'enviros' versus the working people, we'd lose. But if we locked arms with regular folks, we'd win."

Given its paltry financial resources, the Campaign for Sensible Transportation could only stand by while the "Vote No on #1" coalition assaulted the referendum on television for eight weeks. "We saved all our ads for the end," says Caron, "then we ran them like crazy during the last ten days before the vote." The campaign compensated for a lack of funds by getting some free radio and TV ads aired under the Federal Communications Commission's "Fairness Doctrine." Ads depicting the gold-plating of the turnpike proved effective.

The voters had effectively told Maine's Department of Transportation: Stop being just a Department of Highways.

In November 1991, the ballot-box initiative won by a large margin: 59 to 41 percent. Maine voters thus halted the turnpike widening and enacted, *by referendum*, one of the most innovative state transportation laws in the country, the Sensible Transportation Policy Act of 1991. By approving the referendum, the voters had effectively told Maine's Department of Transportation (MDOT): Stop being just a Department of Highways, and start looking at other transportation modes as well for moving people and goods.[38] (Whereas state laws are normally enacted by the state legislature, in this case the voters' approval of the referendum brought about the law.)[39]

Dana F. Connors, Maine's commissioner of transportation at the time, had been an outspoken opponent of the referendum. After it passed, however, he accepted the outcome with grace and statesmanship. "The people have spoken," he said to a television camera in Portland's Regency Hotel on election night. As commissioner, he pledged to do all in his power to make the new law work.[40]

Still, the bitter campaign had left a residue of suspicion and hostility between the opposing sides. Many grassroots citizen activists did not trust MDOT to develop regulations for the new law that would honor its spirit, but they nonetheless thought Connors was sincere in promising to carry out the public's wishes. Within a week of the election, representatives from the Campaign for Sensible Transportation approached Connors and suggested that, instead of writing the rules itself, MDOT should use "neg-reg," a negotiated rulemaking process that involves consensus building and professionally facilitated negotiations among major stakeholders. Connors bought into that idea. By early 1992, MDOT had selected two labor lawyers, Jonathan W. Reitman and Ann R. Gosline, to act as referees for the negotiations.

The Facilitation Process

THE FACILITATORS' FIRST TASK was to figure out whom to invite to the negotiating table. "We went around and talked to dozens of potential stakeholders," says Reitman. "We interviewed everybody about their concerns. We asked them how they thought the process should work." He and Gosline then created a two-tiered structure to write the regulations:

- a steering committee of major stakeholders who could vote on the rules to be developed; and
- an "associate members" group of 40 people. These representatives could not vote but could participate in the discussions and influence the outcome.

Representatives from business, environmental, health, road building, senior citizen, land-use planning, labor and other interests were represented on what became known as the Transportation Policy Advisory Committee (TPAC). The major stakeholders fell into three groups: the environmentalists, business interests, and MDOT officials.

While those who were invited to participate in the process accepted the two-tiered concept, environmentalists complained at the outset that the road building interests, or the "sand and gravel boys," outnumbered them. To address this concern, the facilitators did two things: they expanded the steering committee to include three new members seen as pro-environment, and they recommended a "unanimous consent" approach to the negotiations.

Under the unanimous consent concept, everyone had to agree in advance that no regulations would be issued unless and until *everyone* on the committee signed off and agreed to help implement the regulations. "This unanimity requirement empowers any individual around the table, no matter how weak, to block a consensus that everyone else might buy into," explains Reitman. "But having used it 15 or 20 times in the past, I'm a big supporter of it because I've seen it work so well. Sometimes it takes longer because you have to address the concerns of the dissenter, but in the long run, you come away with an agreement everybody has bought into." Those who felt "underempowered" ultimately accepted this proposal.

The next task was education. The facilitators worked to make sure that everyone on the committee began from a shared baseline by bringing in outside experts—some from Europe as well as the U.S.—to discuss alternative modes of transportation, the Clean Air Act, relationships between land-use and transportation, and other relevant topics. The sessions devoted to education provided a better foundation for future discussions. The sessions also helped the group to identify major issues that needed to be addressed during the negotiations.

Three of the major stakeholders put their recommendations down on paper. The steering committee discussed these and created an evenly balanced "drafting committee" to translate the compromises reached into regulatory language. "It was classic negotiation—word by word, line by line, paragraph by paragraph," says Reitman.

The negotiations were intensive, and it took time before the opposing sides really began to communicate. "There were certain 'breakthrough' moments," recalls Reitman. "When I overheard an environmentalist and a [road-building proponent] discussing their gardens, I felt that this was one of those. When people begin to see each other as human beings, as more than one-dimensional characters, the odds of achieving an agreement increase exponentially."

By September, 1992, the committee had achieved the unanimous agreement desired and submitted its recommendations to MDOT. MDOT held public hearings that fall to get the views of the general public. In December of that year, the agency promulgated the final rules for Maine's Sensible Transportation Policy Act.

When people begin to see each other as human beings, as more than one-dimensional characters, the odds of achieving an agreement increase exponentially.

Reasons for Success

PARTICIPANTS IN THE NEGOTIATING PROCESS attribute its success to several factors. One was the referendum's strong popular support. "What made these negotiations work was the fact that the law was clear as to what had to be done. This was the advantage of the referendum," says Bruce Hammond, a policy analyst at the Natural Resources Council of Maine. "The voters had spoken and we all knew we had to come up with a regulation that implemented the law."

The skills of the facilitators were another major factor. Reitman and Gosline were both trained as attorneys but had extensive experience in dispute resolution and in resolving policy conflicts. Their success in gaining the participants' trust and in breaking through deadlocks proved critical. "They had no vested interest in anything other than in helping us produce an outcome that would work effectively," observes Connors.

Cultural Integrity Section of Maine's

Below is the Cultural Integrity section of Maine's new 20-year state transportation plan. While this section addresses historic preservation issues most directly, other sections of the plan seek to take pressure off of highway demand and thus also alleviate pressures by highways on historic resources.

GOAL 10: CULTURAL INTEGRITY

PROMOTE TRANSPORTATION POLICIES THAT MAINTAIN THE CULTURAL INTEGRITY OF A REGION.

Maine's Transportation System must work to be compatible with the communities which it serves. Wherever possible, road improvements should not damage those historic and scenic areas which are important to a community. Roadway design standards should be compatible with the rest of the community wherever feasible.

The Maine Department of Transportation (MDOT) must work closely with the community, at the earliest stages of project development to become aware of the community's aesthetic and cultural concerns. Community advisory groups should be formed on all significant projects to work with the MDOT to ensure that community values are respected and protected wherever feasible.

Objective 1: Strive to preserve the State's historic, archeological, and scenic resources.

Strategies:
1. Evaluate the potential impacts which transportation projects may have on historic, archaeological and scenic resources.
2. In siting projects MDOT should review town comprehensive plans to identify locally significant sites and areas to be preserved.
3. Work with other State and private agencies to mitigate transportation's impact on critical resources.

A third factor was a commitment by MDOT's upper management to the process. Commissioner Connors' leadership and interest made the participants feel that the time they invested in the process would be time well spent. As an analysis printed in the *Maine Times* observed, "there must be the certain prospect that the product of the group's efforts will be carried out by those who have the power to do so, and a time-certain deadline for the product which is enforced."[41] Tom Reeves, MDOT's chief counsel, dedicated many hours to drafting and redrafting language until it was acceptable to everyone. Reeves, whose background was in law and natural resource policy, and not transportation engineering, understood that it was not enough to write a rule that everyone on the committee found acceptable; the rule also had to be workable for the state transportation department in practice.

Finally, the process itself allowed everybody at the bargaining table to hear the same information, to listen to each other, and to express their concerns so that these were heard by people in a position to respond. "The negotiation process worked splendidly," says Con-

20-Year State Transportation Plan

4. Work with the Travelers Information Advisory Council to enforce Maine's Billboard Law in a manner that preserves the State's scenic character.
5. The MDOT should continue to work with utility companies and private developers in recognizing the aesthetic value of shade trees which border the roads and attempt to preserve that value whenever public safety is not compromised.
6. Continue to work with the utility companies to minimize utility placements which act as barriers to the scenic enjoyment of Maine's countryside.
7. Work with tribal communities to give special consideration to tribal values in planning and implementing transportation projects which might impact Indian lands or areas of important Indian historic or cultural significance.

Objective 2: Consider community character when undertaking transportation improvement projects.
1. Work with communities to identify areas to be protected and methods to do so.
2. Work with the communities in performing a transportation enhancement review as outlined in Section 9 of the Sensible Transportation Policy Rule for all major projects.
3. Work with municipalities to ensure that transportation projects enhance the viability of traditional working waterfronts in coastal communities.
4. Work with communities to maintain the pedestrian scale of central business districts and historic corridors.

Objective 3: Use flexible standards in designing transportation projects outside the national highway system to maintain or improve the natural or built environment of the region.
1. Include local and regional input in the development of project design.
2. Develop standards for constructing on and off road bicycle and pedestrian facilities which are consistent with sustaining natural resources.

nors, who has since moved on to become president of the Maine Chamber-Business Alliance. "And the product of these negotiations has served us well."

An Inclusive Planning Process

THE MOST IMPORTANT FEATURE of the regulations for Maine's Sensible Transportation Policy Act is an inclusive planning process emphasizing early and effective citizen involvement in transportation decisions. Through Regional Transportation Advisory Committees (RTACs), the law gives local citizens a stronger voice than they had before in Maine, a voice stronger than the one most citizens in other states have today. Besides advising the state on transportation policies and projects, the RTACs are given the opportunity to review all MDOT proposals to add new road lanes or replace bridges. The regulations specifically mention historic preservation as one of the interests that should be represented on each of eight RTACs created around the state. The RTACs must also "broadly and fairly" represent environmental, business, planning, elderly, and other constituencies.

"We look to these RTAC citizen boards for advice from a transportation system's point of view," explains Michael Danforth, MDOT coordinator for three of the boards. "The transportation department can handle the technical stuff. The RTACs give us feedback from the 'end users' perspective." More than 500 people responded to MDOT's request for volunteers to serve on the RTACs.

One of the RTACs' first tasks was to help develop the state's 20-year transportation plan, a document required by the federal Intermodal Surface Transportation Efficiency Act of 1991. Published in January 1995, the plan contains a special section on cultural resources. (See sidebar, p. 246.)

The mayor of Fairfax City, Va., supported citizen efforts to improve safety for pedestrians and bicyclists crossing a busy street separating the city's historic district from nearby shopping centers.

CONSTANCE BEAUMONT

It is still a little early to cite other tangible examples of the RTACs' influence on policies and projects, but there are a few:

- the city of Portland's decision to abandon an earlier plan to widen a city street from two to four lanes for more cars only, and to opt instead for a more balanced project that includes just three lanes for cars but two for bikes and a sidewalk for pedestrians;
- a decision to restore a historic trestle bridge linking the downtowns of Lewiston and Auburn, twin cities separated by the Androscoggin River. Local Boy Scouts have already cleaned up the debris-ridden riverbanks while the cities have created a new greenway and installed benches for people to sit and enjoy the river.

Danforth expects the RTACs' fingerprints to be all over the list of capital improvement projects now being prepared for the state as a whole.

Besides emphasizing direct citizen involvement in transportation planning through the RTACs, Maine's Sensible Transportation Policy Act stresses the importance of developing alternatives to highways. Under the rules, MDOT must:

- evaluate reasonable alternatives to new highway construction and give preference to those alternatives before building or expanding roads. In doing so, MDOT must examine ways to reduce traffic congestion and the need for new roads;
- ensure that state transportation investments are consistent with local comprehensive plans prepared by municipalities under Maine's statewide growth management law. These investments must also support state planning goals;
- consider ways to maintain and improve bicycle lanes and pedestrian paths;
- consider, in designing roads: the preservation of historic buildings, landscapes, and districts; the preservation of scenic views and vistas; and the retention of old stone walls and trees; and
- reduce the state's reliance on foreign oil and promote energy efficient forms of transportation.

A State-level "ISTEA"

Redirecting state transportation policies so that they point in the direction of livable, well-preserved communities is akin to turning an aircraft carrier around with a paddle. Not an easy task. The gust of wind provided by Congress' enactment in 1991 of the Intermodal Surface Transportation Efficiency Act has helped considerably. So have the steady strokes of the Surface Transportation Policy Project in Washington, D.C., a broad-based coalition of historic preservation, livable community, public transit, bicycle, pedestrian and other advocates. What needs to happen now is for states to enact "state-level ISTEAs," improving upon ISTEA's concepts as they do so.

In enacting the Sensible Transportation Policy Act, Maine became one of the few states to revamp thoroughly its transportation policy to reflect broader community values, including preservation values. How well these concepts will be implemented remains to be seen. There are institutional and attitudinal forces present at MDOT that may well prevent the Act's positive innovations from blossoming. Indeed, there are people in the department who would just as soon get rid of the Act. Maine has also weakened the comprehensive growth management law it enacted in 1988, thereby backing away from land-use concepts that could help to advance the transportation act's principal goal: reducing auto-dependence.

But Maine has still accomplished something of significance. It has given other states a model to consider in terms of both process and substance. "Maine now has the most 'bottom-up' transportation planning process in the country," says Beth Nagusky, an attorney

Redirecting state transportation policies so that they point in the direction of livable, well-preserved communities is akin to turning an aircraft carrier around with a paddle.

with the Natural Resources Council of Maine during the referendum campaign and reg-writing process. "The simple success of coming up with an operating rule by consensus was quite remarkable," notes Reeves. "The rule provides an open and inclusive process that is tailored to Maine, with its small towns and long winters. Maine has achieved a "first" by developing a comprehensive transportation policy, not by the legislature or the state transportation department, but by a citizen referendum and a professionally facilitated negotiating process that produced a consensus among diverse interests."

**Main Street in
Westminster, Md.**

DAN UEBERSAX, MARYLAND DEPARTMENT OF TRANSPORTATION

A State Transportation Executive in Maryland Listens

BEFORE BUYING A HOUSE IN WESTMINSTER, MD., REBECCA ORENSTEIN USED TO walk up and down the streets of this pretty little town. She quickly fell in love with its small-town charm. Big old trees—some so massive it took three grown men to encircle them with outstretched arms—lined Main Street. Attractive historic buildings dating to the late 19th century dominated the downtown; some went as far back as the 1700s, when the town was laid out. Westminster's central business district, all of which is listed on the National Register of Historic Places, was bustling and friendly. People could walk to Main Street, pop in and out of its small shops, reinforcing old friendships and making new ones along the way.

So Orenstein bought a house in Westminster in 1987. It was an old clapboard located on Pennsylvania Avenue, a side street off Main Street. "The Avenue," as the locals call it, enjoyed a canopy of old trees, three of which stood on Orenstein's new property.

Soon after settling in, Orenstein heard about a road widening project planned for Pennsylvania Avenue by the Maryland Department of Transportation (MDOT). Interested in knowing more, she attended a public information meeting at the local school. There she learned that the state planned to widen the street. Orenstein asked what would happen to the trees. They would all have to come down, she was told. Couldn't the city council object?, she asked. The answer was no. If it did, the city would lose millions of dollars because the project was state-funded and the city couldn't afford to pay for badly needed improvements, such as better storm drains and a new water main.

Some time later, the state's road construction crews showed up and did their job. They widened the street, narrowed the sidewalks, and removed the trees. The three trees on Orenstein's property were bulldozed, as were those in the yard of an elderly woman who had received her trees as an anniversary present 50 years ago.

Orenstein felt like crying. She had bought a neighborhood as much as a house, and now the neighborhood had been damaged. The entire tempo of Pennsylvania Avenue changed following the project's completion. Children played less often on the sidewalks. The casual visiting that used to occur between neighbors on their front porches and people out for walks fell off. The increased traffic encouraged by the wider road and narrower sidewalk had made socializing less easy, less pleasant.

In 1989, Orenstein read a local newspaper report that the state highway department planned to come back, this time to improve East Main Street. The most historic part of Westminster, this area included Shellman House and Cockey's Tavern, where Civil War generals once encamped.

Apprehensive that a replay of the Pennsylvania Avenue experience was about to transpire, Orenstein again marched down to the public information meeting at Westminster City Hall to learn more. There she heard state highway and local officials explain that in order to widen East Main Street from 35 to 40 feet, they would have to remove all the old trees, nar-

Rebecca Orenstein asked what would happen to the trees. They would all have to come down, she was told.

251

JAMES LINDBERG

row the sidewalk, and eliminate 35 on-street parking spaces that local businesses needed to serve their customers.

Wiser now, Orenstein sprang into action quickly. She formed TreeAction, a grassroots citizens organization determined to save the trees on Main Street from destruction. Orenstein and her allies circulated a petition protesting the plan and turned out for public meetings to speak out against it, but they found little sympathy for their point of view on the city council. "Everybody was afraid that Westminster would lose the state money committed to this project if we complained about it," says Orenstein. "There was very little public debate."

So Orenstein took other tacks. She contacted several schoolteachers and asked them to tell school children stories about the history of Main Street. The children then wrote Valentines to the trees, which TreeAction members affixed to the trees. On another occasion, TreeAction tied black ribbons around the trees to let people know they were endangered. "We did everything we could that had a visual impact," says Orenstein. Smelling a good human interest story, the local media began reporting TreeAction's activities. The news coverage increased public awareness, and people began turning out in larger numbers. "We were only three or four people in the beginning," Orenstein recalls. "I could never reveal how small our group was or we would never have been taken seriously."

Although TreeAction had now picked up broader support, it still hadn't persuaded the city council or the state to try to change the plan. So out of desperation, Orenstein called Michael Day, chief of planning at the Maryland Historical Trust. Since she obviously wasn't getting anywhere with lower-level state highway officials, Day suggested that she go right to the top and try to reach James Lighthizer, the newly-appointed secretary of transportation. Day pointed out that Lighthizer had received an award from the Trust for his sensitivity to preservation issues during his tenure as Anne Arundel County Executive.

JOHN EVANS

Orenstein tracked Lighthizer down by phone, explained the problem to him, and asked him please to come to Westminster to look at the area affected by MDOT's plan. A few days later, Orenstein, four other members of TreeAction, Lighthizer and the state highway administrator met in front of the Historical Society of Carroll County to begin a walking tour of East Main Street.

After the tour, Lighthizer left the group to meet with the mayor and public works department and to check with state highway officials. Later that same day, he called Orenstein from his car phone to report that he had stopped everything: "We're going to get more citizen input into this plan. We're going to get the best landscape architect. We're going to do it right," Orenstein recalls Lighthizer telling her.

Lighthizer kept his word. He put an immediate stop to the existing plan. In cooperation with the mayor, he created an East Main Street Reconstruction Task Force comprising 12 or so local business representatives, citizens, highway designers, landscape architects, engineers, and city officials. "We want to take the proper course to ensure that the project reflects the aesthetic, historic, vehicular, pedestrian and functional needs of the community," Lighthizer wrote in his letter to Task Force members. The group met monthly over a period of nine months. This time, instead of coming up with their own plan in a vacuum, the state engineers went back to square one and listened first to the city's representatives and considered what they wanted. "We'd get the citizens' input, develop options, go back to the Task Force and present, discuss and refine these ideas," explains Charles B. Adams, director of environmental design for the Maryland State Highway Administration.

Little attention was given to the comfort of transit users in this "sprawlscape" in Lakewood Springs, Col. (left). Shelter was provided at this bus stop in the historic Browne's Addition in Spokane, Wash. (above).

Reflections of a Transportation Engineer

Walter Kulash is a nationally recognized, registered professional engineer with the Orlando, Florida-based community planning consulting firm, Glatting Jackson. He has worked with dozens of communities across the country on local transportation projects. Over the years he has become a critic of the direction many state transportation policies are taking and is an advocate for better-preserved and more livable communities. Here are some of his thoughts.

STATE TRANSPORTATION DEPARTMENTS provide a prime vantage point to see how miserably our whole system is failing. They are in a better position than anyone to see the insurmountable needs for new roads that are being generated. They understand how we are not even close to funding these needs. They should be much more proactive in letting the public know how unsustainable the current system is.

But our transportation policies have a curious immunity from being considered a failure. Road needs are typically estimated for 20 years into the future. Road improvements are then made to implement those plans. The roads then fill up almost immediately. They are quickly jammed again. In any other business, such immediate obsolescence of a new product would be considered a failure. With roads, they are not. We're just in a hustle to build more.

Why are roads and transportation policies so immune from our standard definitions of failure? Any other products that failed to meet their expectations within a year or two would be considered an incompetent product or service. If my new roof, on which I have a 20-year guarantee, were to start leaking after the first rain, I'd be livid with the whole system that produced that roof. Why aren't we livid with a planning paradigm that says we're going to fix things for the next 20 years, and then they are not even fixed for one year?

State transportation officials are constantly responding to their constituents' clamor for a higher level of service. Is it even reasonable to ask a provider agency, such as a transportation department, to be the one to say this whole system is foolish and wasteful? Many transportation officials don't see themselves as leaders in

After months of back-and-forth dialogue, the group came up with recommendations that completely changed the concept of the road. The new concept emphasized tree preservation, pedestrian enhancements, and the retention of parking spaces for businesses occupying Westminster's downtown historic buildings. The new plans were scrutinized at several well-publicized hearings. These were subsequently approved by the city council, the state highway department, and the U.S. Department of Transportation and the improvements got under way.

To protect the trees during construction, the state brought in a tree expert, Dan Turner, who supervised pruning of the tree roots and creation of larger tree pits to enhance the trees' prospects for survival. The state used seismographs to test the ability of historic structures to withstand vibrations caused by excavation equipment. When the tests indicated a risk of structural damage, the project supervisor directed the road crew to dig by hand.

When the project was completed in 1994, the results pleased everyone. The city got the storm drains, water main, and road repairs it wanted. Westminster retained the old trees lining East Main Street; the state even provided funds to the city to plant 118 new trees. Main Street's pedestrian ambiance was not only preserved but actually enhanced through the installation of masonry pavers, bricks, and other features that set sidewalks and crosswalks off as safe harbors for people on foot. Over half of the on-street parking spaces originally slated for extinction were restored so that downtown businesses could accommodate their customers. Driver safety was improved as well.

the way we "consume travel," just as water and power companies are not concerned with wasteful water or power consumption. They are more concerned about scrambling to keep up with sprawl. The power company is in no position to say, "If you don't stop building so wastefully, we're not going to provide you with power." They would be criticized for being incompetent and would be replaced.

The same thing is going on with roads. We have a lunatic type of development pattern. Instead of challenging this pattern, our road providers just pitch in and make it work as well as they can.

The greatest damage done to neighborhoods comes from the number of road lanes that get tolerated in the first place. Decisions to widen roads to six lanes build in a tremendous amount of unlivability no matter what you do after that.

The culprit is the public that demands more and more lanes. The monster flows from the decision regarding the number of lanes. Once you have a six-lane facility, it is difficult to make it into anything but an ugly monster.

The Florida Department of Transportation's recent decision to limit the size of our roads to no more than six lanes on arterials is an important change of direction. If you assume that the state will be forceful in implementing this, it could become an important determinant of land use. The State of Florida has essentially withdrawn the promise that no matter what property owners and developers do, the state will serve their projects with highway investments.

The great, livable places in this county have always exercised a form of "supply management" in transportation. Portland, Oregon; Madison, Wisconsin; Santa Fe, New Mexico—these cities all have in common the fact that they have simply said no to more road widening.

We are seeing progress in the transportation industry, but much of it is coming from outside the industry, from the "new urbanists." Yet we are also seeing an interesting acceptance of these ideas from the industry once it is confronted with them.

Who says we're better off with higher "level of service" standards promoted by the highway industry when they mean living in a blighted, bleak, ugly and depressing environment?

In the end, the road was not widened to 40 feet; it was simply made a consistent width of 36 feet everywhere. "The widening was not even needed in the first place," says Adams. "We only needed to reconstruct the road. The irony is that by applying a certain standard, we would have widened the road but without achieving any functional benefit, without providing any additional capacity. The road would just have been wider. It would have been a disaster."

"I have to salute Mr. Lighthizer," says Orenstein now. "He really listened to us. He brought an elegance and a grace to the bureaucracy that I had not seen before. In so many towns in Maryland, people can't even find Main Street. In Westminster now, you can still find and enjoy it."

Lessons from Westminster

THE MARYLAND DEPARTMENT OF TRANSPORTATION'S experience with Westminster did not end with Westminster. It served as the catalyst for more far-reaching and fundamental changes in the way the department does business. "The Westminster case opened our eyes to the fact that we needed to take a fresh look at how we designed our road projects," says Adams. "It had a profound effect on our approach to highway design elsewhere. We now routinely work with and involve local citizens in the design of our projects." The Highway

The irony is that by applying a certain standard, we would have widened the road but without achieving any functional benefit. It would have been a disaster.

Development Manual in use when the Westminster project got underway is being rewritten, as are internal guidelines for highway planners.

Several factors accounted for the happy outcome in Westminster.

The first was a local citizen who cared deeply about her community and who, instead of complaining ineffectually about a problem, organized like-minded town residents and persuaded public officials to do something about it. Citizen activism often enlightens state officials and serves as a catalyst for better state policies.

The second key factor was teamwork. Once Secretary Lighthizer removed the artificial deadlines and constraints that had been imposed on Westminster, state highway engineers, the city's public works director, local preservationists, business people, fire department officials and others worked together cooperatively to achieve the best possible outcome.

The third key factor was the governor's appointment of a secretary of transportation who held preservation values and, as he himself said, "likes trees." Had Secretary Lighthizer not been preservation-minded in the first place, it is questionable whether he would have been willing to sacrifice time from his busy schedule to go to Westminster or to instruct his staff afterwards to take another look at their plans. The Westminster case study underscores the importance to preservationists of working to ensure that enlightened secretaries of transportation are appointed by governors in the first place. Few executive branch appointments in state government are more important to historic preservation than this position. "One problem is that most state transportation chiefs are former highway engineers," says Lighthizer. "They don't factor human beings into roadbuilding. If transportation departments would apply common sense and work *with* people, they would be more likely to produce results that everyone likes. This is really what public service is all about, and by the way, transportation planners *are* in the business of public service."

"When you hear someone say, 'It has to be this way,' don't believe it. If people speak out passionately, if they say, 'No, we won't let that happen to our town,' then it doesn't have to be 'this way.'"

—Rebecca Orenstein
Founder, TreeAction, Westminster, Maryland

Elements of a Pro-Preservation State Transportation Policy

IN THE PAST, STATEWIDE HISTORIC PRESERVATION TASK FORCES have seldom addressed mainstream transportation issues that affect historic resources in their reports to governors and state legislators. This must change, for state transportation decisions exert a profound and far-reaching impact on the cultural heritage, social cohesiveness, and livability of our communities.

It is not enough to focus on ISTEA's Enhancement Program. Although the $3 billion earmarked for enhancements represents a major source of money for brick-and-mortar preservation projects, it is pocket change compared to the $119.5 billion set aside for highways by ISTEA. Small enhancement projects, however worthwhile, mean little in the overall scheme of things if the bulk of a state's transportation monies fund highway projects that destroy historic resources. Like "all the King's horses and all the King's men," enhancements can't put communities back together again once they have been damaged by such projects.

A state transportation policy that supports historic preservation and fosters community livability should do all of the following:

CONSTANCE BEAUMONT

A tree-lined street in a residential neighborhood in Arlington, Va. There is talk of widening and straightening this attractive road to meet inappropriate state road design standards.

Goals

- Adopt the physician's maxim and simply "do no harm" to historic and settled communities—that is, avoid causing damage that must be repaired
- Reduce excessive dependence on the automobile
- Offer people choices among different modes of transportation and support public transportation, pedestrian facilities, bikeways and railroads

System Reform

- Involve local citizens, including historic preservationists along with environmental, business, civic and other interests, in the early planning stages of transportation projects
- Require that alternatives to new roads and highways be explored before new lanes are built
- Appoint professionals who have preservation values and a good understanding of the relationships between urban design, land use and transportation to transportation planning and executive positions
- Encourage state universities that train engineers to broaden their curricula to include courses on the relationships between transportation, land use and urban design
- Develop "Drivers Ed" course materials aimed at educating high school students about the costs of *excessive* auto dependence to historic communities, neighborhoods, and the environment
- Make state gas tax revenues available for alternatives to highways, such as mass transit, rail, bus, pedestrian, bicycle modes, and for land-use planning concepts that reduce the demand for new roads and that promote the preservation of walkable communities
- Promote road design standards that make it easier for highway engineers to preserve a community's historic, scenic and pedestrian character

Appoint professionals who have preservation values and a good understanding of the relationships between urban design, land use and transportation.

Connections to Land Use

- Promote land use policies and urban design concepts to reduce automobile dependence, especially for short trips
- Avoid encouraging sprawl-type development that sets the stage for road projects that destroy historic resources and disrupt settled neighborhoods or degrade their settings
- Integrate land-use planning with transportation planning.

CHAPTER 10

Alternatives to Sprawl

CHAPTER 10

Alternatives to Sprawl

I N THIS CHAPTER WE LOOK AT THE ROLE OF STATES IN growth management with a view to advancing several major objectives of the historic preservation movement:

- protecting the economic viability of historic downtowns and neighborhoods;
- preserving the countryside and local community character; and
- maintaining a sense of community.

These objectives are often thwarted by sprawl-type development that causes disinvestment in older communities, destroys the countryside, and creates centerless, faceless settlements.

Because many people are not actually sure what "sprawl" is—this is especially true of young people growing up today who have never seen other types of development—we begin with a definition of sprawl, an explanation of why it creates problems for community livability and historic preservation, and an examination of some economic assumptions underlying sprawl. We then look at specific state growth management initiatives that help to address this issue.

Sprawl.

Sprawl and Its Consequences

LAND-USE EXPERTS HAVE USED DIFFERENT TERMS to define sprawl and to describe its consequences, but most would agree that this type of development has at least four characteristics. It is:

- spread-out, low-density, and land-consumptive;
- located at the outer fringes of cities, towns, or suburbs;
- characterized by segregated land uses;
- dominated by, and dependent upon, the automobile.

These characteristics are all interrelated. "Sprawl is a pattern of physical development characterized by the decentralization of land uses," writes Anton C. Nelessen in *Visions for a New American Dream*. "Sprawl requires the use of a private vehicle to move from one single-use zone to another," he explains. "In the sprawl pattern, goods and services are scattered throughout the region. This arrangement requires elaborate road systems to link all areas…This system, that lacks centers, produces excessive congestion and waste…[T]he automobile is necessary for even the most basic of daily requirements, a quart of milk or a loaf of bread."[1]

"Each shop or office building has to provide its own parking, so each structure is surrounded by asphalt, fragmenting development even more," notes Jonathan Barnett in *The Fractured Metropolis*. "Individual companies or investors seeking relief from traffic and from squalid corridors of continuous parking lots, garish signs, and disorganized, contending architecture seek new sites on the urban fringe."[2]

"A geography of nowhere" is James Howard Kunstler's description of sprawl. In his book entitled with that very phrase, Kunstler observes that "[t]he least understood cost [of sprawl]—although probably the most keenly felt—has been the *sacrifice of a sense of place*: the

MEGAN BELLUE

Sprawl development (left) and a pedestrian-friendly downtown.

idea that people and things exist in some sort of continuity, that we belong to the world physically and chronologically, and that we know where we are."[3]

"In the space of just two generations, sprawl has covered over thousands of acres of prime farmland, despoiled once-beautiful landscapes, and chopped up pristine woodlands," writes Tom Hylton in *Save Our Land, Save Our Towns*. "It has blighted our surroundings with massive highways and parking lots."

One of sprawl's primary flaws, according to Anthony Downs, a Brookings Institution scholar, is that it generates excessive travel. When homes and jobs are spread widely apart, "People have to travel long distances from where they live to where they work, shop, or play," observes Downs in *New Visions for Metropolitan America*. The ubiquity of the private automobile and its needs have compromised the American Dream of open roads and fresh air, Downs adds, but "most Americans do not realize that success in attaining their goals is responsible for other results they abhor."[4]

"Having to drive to every destination and appointment precludes the variety of incident and the potential for casual contacts that traditionally have made downtown districts good business locations: the ability to set up a meeting on short notice, the chance to run into someone you know at lunch, the opportunity to shop on the way to and from work," writes Barnett. He adds: "Suburban gridlock, with a short respite in midmorning before people go out to their lunchtime appointments and another brief interval in the afternoon before everyone starts heading home, is just the most obvious system of what is wrong with current development patterns. The high ratio of parking lots to buildings and the unwalkable distances across highways and service roads make it impossible to design any kind of architectural ensemble, while wasting land and raising infrastructure costs."[5]

Why is Sprawl a Historic Preservation Issue?

SPRAWL AFFECTS HISTORIC PRESERVATION IN THREE MAJOR WAYS:

- Sprawl sucks the life out of older downtowns and neighborhoods, where historic buildings are concentrated. When the economic vitality of a historic area suffers, the buildings in it often become underused or empty. Over time, many of them are "demolished by neglect" or torn down to make way for surface parking lots.
- Sprawl destroys community character and the countryside. Cohesive Main Streets, old stone fences, historic trees, country roads—these and other features of the American landscape are rapidly being destroyed by sprawl development and the vast expanses of asphalt required to accommodate it.
- Sprawl reduces opportunities for face-to-face interaction among people, thereby making it more difficult to create, or retain, a sense of community. By scattering the elements of a community across the landscape in a haphazard way, sprawl provides no town centers and reduces the sense of ownership—and therefore also the commitment—that people have toward their community.
- Sprawl forecloses alternatives to the automobile as a means of transport, thereby adding to pressures to create or widen roads that often result in the demolition of historic resources or the degradation of their settings.
- Sprawl leaves older cities and towns with excessively high concentrations of poor people with social problems, making these places a very difficult environment in which to revitalize communities.

One of the most succinct summaries of the negative consequences of sprawl comes from the Central Puget Sound Growth Management Hearings Board of Washington State. In a ruling on Kitsap County, Washington's land-use plan, which was challenged by the Kitsap Citizens for Rural Preservation on the grounds that the plan would promote sprawl, the Hearings Board held that sprawl causes at least eight major problems:

(1) *it needlessly destroys the* economic, environmental and *aesthetic value* of resource lands;

(2) it creates an inefficient land use pattern that is very expensive to serve with public funds;

(3) it blurs local government roles, fueling competition, redundancy and conflict among those governments;

(4) it threatens economic viability by diffusing rather than focusing needed public infrastructure investments;

(5) *it abandons established urban areas where substantial past investments, both public and private, have been made;*

(6) it encourages insular and parochial local policies that thwart the siting of needed regional facilities and the equitable accommodation of locally unpopular land uses;

(7) *it destroys the intrinsic visual character of the landscape;* and

(8) *it erodes a sense of community*, which, in turn, has dire social consequences.[6]

But sprawl is a tough issue to address, primarily because many people equate sprawl with economic growth. They cannot envision other ways of maintaining the economic vitality of their communities. Let's look closer at the economic issues underlying sprawl.

Economic Assumptions Underlying Sprawl

MOST COMMUNITIES WANT NEW ECONOMIC GROWTH AND DEVELOPMENT. They feel they need it to pay for essential public services and to provide new jobs. But they also want to preserve the economic value of investments they have already made in existing downtowns and neighborhoods. They want to preserve what is beautiful or special about them. They want to remain attractive so that people will want to live and work there, so that new businesses will feel they are making a good investment when they locate there.

The two goals of economic growth and community livability are often pitted against each other in local debates over development. Many real estate developers and political leaders believe that they cannot achieve one objective without sacrificing the other. The fact is, lasting economic growth *depends* on community livability. As Robert M. Solow, a Nobel Prize winning economist at the Massachusetts Institute of Technology, has observed, "Livability is not some middle-class luxury. It is an economic imperative."

Like shoes, growth comes in different styles and sizes. When packaged in the form of urban sprawl, growth can quickly cause a community to lose the very qualities that drew people to it in the first place. The very basis for a community's future economic prosperity can in fact be destroyed. Local economies based on tourism are just one example.

Since the end of World War II, the dominant form of suburban development in the U.S. has been sprawl. While many people have long objected to this type of development for aesthetic, environmental, or quality-of-life reasons, the private sector is beginning to recognize that sprawl is bad for business, too. "[U]nchecked sprawl has shifted from an engine of California's growth to a force that now threatens to *inhibit* growth," observed the Bank of America, California's largest bank, in a January 1995 report entitled "Beyond Sprawl: New Patterns of Growth To Fit the New California."[7]

Developers and business executives who transformed Northern Virginia into a "sprawlscape" during the 1970s and 1980s now regard the area's diffusion and lack of focus

Sprawl destroys the visual character of the landscape and erodes a sense of community.

as a barrier to its future economic health. At roundtable meetings attended by prominent developers and business executives, the area is described as one "without an identity, where few people put down roots and most don't know their neighbors…Even the structure of Fairfax itself—a sprawling, centerless county with no city—no incorporated towns—leads to this sense of rootlessness."[8]

Growth is not the problem; the rate and scale at which it occurs, the shape it takes, and the location it chooses frequently are. A proposed development may be too big for a local economy to absorb without the undue displacement of local businesses that contribute in important ways to the community. A development may be poorly located, requiring state and local governments to spend more tax dollars than they can afford on new roads, schools and other services. A development may destroy historic landscapes and landmarks. It may clash with its surroundings. Or it may simply be dispiritingly ugly.

Growth does not have to be so. It can be well-located, preserve attractive historic buildings, and harmonize with its surroundings. It can be channelled into existing areas that need growth and away from fragile scenic and environmental resources. In this case it becomes a long-term economic asset and often a source of pride to a community as well. The entire historic preservation movement is about preserving *development* that was once "new growth." Regardless of the motivations of its original builders, this development is treasured and even protected today as it is seen as sensitive to people and supportive of community values. There is no reason that new growth today cannot be sensitive to people or reflect community values. One such value is the desire to preserve existing cities and towns and many of the historic and beautiful buildings in them.

The "Fiscalization" of Land Use

> "We're selling our souls just because we don't trust each other."

LOCAL OFFICIALS OFTEN FEAR THAT IF THEY PUSH TOO HARD for alternatives to sprawl by requesting improvements in a development project, the developer or company involved will sue them or move on to the neighboring jurisdiction. The result: Their community gets a project's noise, traffic, and air pollution; the neighboring town gets the tax revenues, jobs, and other benefits.

Given their heavy reliance on property taxes for local revenue, most municipal governments find it extremely difficult to say no to any new development, even if means losing their identity and even their way of life. As a governor's commission in Vermont explains, "Competition over developments that enhance the tax base forces towns to make land-use decisions that very often run counter to their long-term interests." A new term—the "fiscalization" of land use—has even been coined to describe the extent to which tax base concerns drive land-use decisions.

Compounding this problem is the mismatch between the limited jurisdiction of local governments and the regional impact of many large-scale developments. A major mall or a cluster of superstores can easily generate more than 20,000 car trips a day. Such large traffic volumes affect towns for miles around, but those affected may have no say over the new development because it lies outside their borders. Such situations have fostered rivalry among local governments in every state. As a New Englander comments: "One of our biggest problems is what to do when growth in one town has an impact on other towns. What do we do? Do we stand at the line and snarl at each other? Some have been reduced to that. It happens because there is no government structure to mediate the differences." A Northbrook, Ill., planner puts it more bluntly: "We're selling our souls just because we don't trust each other."

CONSTANCE BEAUMONT

JAMES LINDBERG

A "sprawlscape" (above) and a compact historic downtown.

A Role for the States

IT TAKES MORE THAN ONE COMMUNITY acting alone to deal effectively with the problem of sprawl. This is where the states come in, for they can play a critical role in reducing these interjurisdictional disputes.

In an attempt to mediate the intergovernmental rivalry that breeds sprawl and to create a better model for new development in the first place, ten states have enacted statewide growth management laws since 1973: Oregon, Florida, New Jersey, Vermont, Rhode Island, Maine, Georgia, Washington, Maryland and Delaware.[9] (Hawaii, too, has a growth management law, but its statute dates back to 1961.) While these laws vary, virtually all of them attempt to discourage sprawl on the grounds that it wastes the taxpayer's money while destroying cities and the environment alike. At the same time, these laws try to channel new growth into existing urban or town centers. The goal is to use such centers as efficiently as possible before more farmland and other resources are consumed. Consider this introduction to New Jersey's 1985 state planning act:

> It is in the public interest to encourage development...in locations that are well situated with respect to present or anticipated public services and facilities, giving appropriate priority to the redevelopment, repair, rehabilitation or replacement of existing facilities and to discourage development where it may impair or destroy natural resources or environmental qualities that are vital to the health and well-being of the present and future citizens of this State.

Vermont's 1970 land-use law, Act 250, asserts that residential sprawl and strip development alongside highways add to the "cost of government, congestion of highways, the loss of prime agricultural lands, overtaxing of town roads and services and economic or social decline in the tradi-

The department store chain that owns this magnificent historic building in downtown Lancaster, Pa., closed the store and then prevented the city from marketing it to another retailer.

CONSTANCE BEAUMONT

tional community center." Washington State's 1990 growth management law seeks "to reduce the inappropriate conversion of undeveloped land into sprawling, low-density development."

The ten states' growth management laws also "knock heads," as it were, by prodding local communities to talk to each other to resolve—or at least minimize—their conflicts over new growth. "Municipal comprehensive planning must recognize and address land use in contiguous municipalities and encourage cooperative planning efforts by municipalities," states Rhode Island's Comprehensive Planning and Land Use Regulation Act. New Jersey's law seeks "to ensure that the development of individual municipalities does not conflict with the development and general welfare of neighboring communities...." A primary goal of Georgia's growth management act is to "encourage coordinated, comprehensive statewide planning...at the local, regional and state levels of government."

This chapter examines the growth management laws of Vermont, Oregon, and Washington in detail and those of other states around the country in brief. Because many states do not have comprehensive growth management laws and are unlikely to enact them, we also look at growth management efforts in Hailey, Idaho, that were successfully carried out pursuant to a garden-variety state zoning enabling law. These efforts, which were recently upheld by that state's supreme court, demonstrate that communities in states without growth management laws are far from powerless to manage growth. As in so many areas, political leadership is the key.

As we see below, none of these state laws is perfect. Moreover, their implementation is often undercut by powerful cultural, political, and economic forces. Nonetheless, these states stand out from many others in at least two key respects: They have made a deliberate attempt to give cities, towns, and suburbs the tools they need to contain sprawl. And they have required state agencies and local governments to think consciously about and plan for future growth...or given them an incentive to do so. In many states, direction by indirection is still the dominant approach to growth.

An empty superstore. Due to overbuilding, there is now a national glut in retail space.

MEGAN BELLUE

Vermont and Growth Management

ONE OF THE FIRST STATES TO ENACT A COMPREHENSIVE LAND-USE PLANNING law, Vermont sought to contain sprawl as early as 1970.

During the 1960s, Vermonters had grown increasingly anxious as they watched second homes, ski resorts, a new interstate highway and strip development threaten the beauty of their small, rural state. The state's little towns did not have the resources or the professional staff to manage all of this growth. In the late sixties, the International Paper Company proposed a 1,200-unit residential development in southern Vermont. Like a match applied to dry tinder, the proposal sparked a clamor for stronger controls over large construction projects.

At this point Deane C. Davis, Vermont's conservative Republican governor, created a Commission on Environmental Control in May 1969 to examine "how we can have economic growth…without destroying the secret of our success, our environment." Davis asked Arthur Gibb, a respected state legislator, to head the Commission and named a broad cross-section of interests—business people, developers, conservationists, and influential legislators—to serve on it. The group met frequently over a six-month period to map out a program for the 1970 legislature. Within a year, Vermont lawmakers had enacted the State Land Use and Development Bill, popularly known as Act 250.

Vermont has worked hard to preserve its traditional settlement pattern of compact villages and small towns surrounded by beautiful countryside.

JAMES WICK

In *Land, Growth, and Politics*, an insightful analysis of the politics of state growth management, John DeGrove explains how a conservative governor persuaded a conservative legislature to enact what has become known as one of the strongest land-use laws in the country:

> The 1970 Vermont legislature was considered a "landowning legislature," and many feared that it would have little enthusiasm for bills that moved in the direction of regulating the use of land and protecting the environment. The fact that the legislation moved through the legislature with remarkable ease was seen as largely due to the very strong efforts of Governor Davis and his staff. Governor Davis, for example, had one of his assistants systematically move about the state and obtain endorsements from all 14 of the Republican county committees before the legislature was convened.[10]

That the governor made this legislation his number-one priority clearly made a difference. So did his political credentials. As Harvey Carter, a member of the Vermont legislature when Act 250 passed, observes: "For Davis, a Republican, to lead the charge on land use was like former President Nixon's going to China. Only a Republican could have done it. A native Vermonter, Davis respected the outdoors. He had direct contact with farm life. He was a determined environmentalist."

Act 250

THE PURPOSE OF ACT 250 was to protect the state from the costs of substandard, environmentally unsound development. The act originally called for two major elements: a state land-use plan to provide a policy framework for local planning decisions, and a permitting system to control the negative effects of large-scale developments. A land capability and development plan was approved several years later. It resulted in legislative goals for growth and in additional criteria—notably one concerning "scattered development," or sprawl—for evaluating development projects. But ultimately the land-use plan foundered on the shoals of political misjudgments, state agency rivalries, an economic slump, and balance-of-power tensions between state and local governments. The permitting system not only survived but became one of Vermont's most important tools for containing sprawl.

The governor made this legislation his number-one priority.

Act 250 requires that major development projects obtain a permit before being built. "Major" projects are defined as those that involve one or more of the following:

- ten or more residential units;
- ten or more acres of commercial, industrial, or municipal development;
- more than one acre of commercial, industrial, or municipal development if located in towns lacking zoning regulations or subdivision regulations;
- road construction if the road provides access to more than five lots or is longer than 800 feet; or
- mountaintop construction above elevations of 2,500 feet.

Authority to grant Act 250 permits resides in Vermont's "district environmental commissions," of which there are nine for as many regions. To determine whether a project should be approved, rejected, or approved with conditions, the commissions hold public hearings in the town where new development is proposed.

In assessing projects, the commissions apply ten criteria set forth in the law. These criteria ask such questions as:

- Does the proposed development conform with the community's vision for its future, as expressed in an officially adopted municipal or town plan?

- Will the development cause undue harm to an area's scenic or natural beauty? To a town's historic sites? To rare and irreplaceable natural areas?
- Will the development damage the air or water?
- Will the development unreasonably burden a municipality's ability to provide government services?
- Will the development cause unreasonable highway congestion?
- How will the development affect farm and forest lands?
- Will the development create "scattered development"—i.e., sprawl—thereby burdening the taxpayer with added public service costs?

This last question, raised by "Criterion Number 9(H)" in the law, is the one that addresses the issue of sprawl most directly.

Depending on the answers to these questions, the district environmental commission approves or denies a development permit. If the developer or an interested party disagrees with the decision, he may appeal to the nine-member state environmental board, whose members the governor appoints.

Lay citizens, rather than government officials, serve on both the state environmental board and the three-member district commissions. Act 250's creators saw the involvement of ordinary citizens as essential to ensuring a measure of local control in this statewide system.

With the state land-use plan originally envisioned by Act 250 having fallen by the wayside, the law today is not so much a planning tool as a permitting system for developments with regional impacts. It *reacts* to proposals, but it does not provide a planning framework to guide local planning and development in the first place. For that guidance, the state has since turned to Vermont's Growth Management Act of 1988, Act 200.

The Pyramid Case

IN ONE OF THE MOST CELEBRATED ACT 250 DECISIONS pertaining to sprawl, the District 4 Environmental Commission denied a land-use permit to the Pyramid Development Company in 1978. The Syracuse, N.Y.-based developer had proposed the construction of a 490,000-square-foot regional mall in Williston, a small town six miles from Burlington. Local opposition to this project was so strong that the commission had to schedule formal hearings on 43 different days to accommodate everyone who wanted to testify. "So many people were interested in this case," recalls Frank X. Murray, a Burlington lawyer involved in the case. "They set up tables in school gyms and cafeterias, not in a court room. There was nothing stuffy about the atmosphere."

In explaining its reasons for denying Pyramid a permit, the commission said:

The application is denied because the commission finds...that the development does not satisfy the criteria enumerated in the act regarding the following matters: (5) highway congestion, (7) burden on ability of local governments to provide services, (9-G) private utility services, (9-H) costs of public services and facilities as compared with public benefits from a scattered development, (9-J) demands on public facilities and services, (9-K) jeopardizing or interference with the efficiency of existing services, and (10) conformance with the local and regional plan.

John DeGrove, a national expert on land use, later observed that the decision on the Pyramid mall was seen as "a major policy as well as legal milestone for Act 250."[11]

A Governor's Commission on Growth

BETWEEN 1970 AND 1988, the absence of a clear state planning framework to guide new growth encouraged a form of guerilla warfare whenever major developments were proposed. Citizens would say to developers, "Wait a minute. That's not the right place for such-and-such a project." They would then fight these projects using Act 250 criteria. Many people thought this was a bad way to manage growth. Why not avoid such conflicts through better planning in the first place?, they asked.

Seeking to fill the vacuum left by Act 250, Governor Madeleine Kunin created the Commission on Vermont's Future in 1987. The commission's charge: to assess state policies and recommend steps the state should take to prevent the degradation of Vermont's "incomparable heritage of natural resources, scenic landscapes, and liveable communities."

After holding public hearings and meeting with over 2,000 Vermonters, the Commission produced a report in December 1987. In his transmittal letter to the governor, Commission Chairman Douglas M. Costle captured the political mood of the time:

> The people of Vermont care deeply about the future of their state; and, while they are proud of what it is today, they are also very troubled about what it may become…[T]hey see changes occurring at an accelerating pace, and they fear that what makes Vermont so special to them may get lost in the shuffle of those changes. They worry that the Vermont of the future will not look familiar to them—that we will have lost the special sense of community and natural beauty that are the essence of Vermont.
>
> Vermonters are not afraid of change, but they want to shape it. They are not afraid of growth or development, but they want it "done right."

By May 1988, the Vermont legislature had adopted many of the Commission's recommendations by passing Act 200.

Act 200

ACT 200 ESTABLISHED 12 STATE PLANNING GOALS.[12] Those most relevant to this discussion include:

- protection for the historic features of Vermont's villages, towns, cities and landscape;
- a "rational" settlement pattern, the key to which is directing new development into designated "growth centers;"
- preservation of open space; and
- efficient expenditure of public funds and more convenient, efficient patterns of public facilities.

Act 200 strongly encouraged towns to adopt local plans but stopped short of requiring them to do so. Instead, it offered incentives to plan. One was planning grants from the state; another, deference by state agencies to local plans approved by regional planning agencies.

Under Act 200, if towns choose to plan, they are required to play by certain rules: Local plans must address the state's general planning goals; they must include specific elements, such as discrete sections on land use, transportation, and "a statement of policies on the preservation of rare and irreplaceable natural areas, scenic and historic features and resources." Finally, local plans must be compatible with plans of neighboring towns and regions.

Act 200 also encouraged better coordination between and among neighboring towns, regions, and state agencies. One of the loudest complaints heard during the commission's

This "consistency" provision offers potentially significant local control over state projects.

hearings had been that Vermont was threatened by sprawl. Act 200's creators thought that a stronger regional planning mechanism could address this problem. Regional planning commissions predated Act 200, but the new law augmented their power. The regional planning commissions provide a bridge between local and state plans. Vermont looks to these commissions to resolve conflicts between neighboring jurisdictions, or between town and state agency policies, when they arise. If a commission cannot resolve a conflict, a Council of Regional Commissions, whose members are drawn from the 12 regional commissions, state agencies, and the public, arbitrates.

State plans and state agency projects must harmonize with regional plans. In effect, Act 200 says to state agencies: If you want to carry out a certain project, it better be consistent with the approved local or regional plans or you're not going to do it. This "consistency" provision offers potentially significant local control over state projects, roads and highways being a notable example.

C.B. JOHNSON

Vermont's Battle with Wal-Mart: Act 250's Role

ONE OF THE MOST IMPORTANT CHALLENGES OF ACT 250'S METTLE HAS COME from Wal-Mart, the mega-retailer based in Bentonville, Ark. Wal-Mart's push to enter the Vermont market, which began in the early nineties, has provoked a veritable man-on-the-street debate over whether Vermont can retain its "soul" if the kind of sprawl associated with Wal-Mart is allowed to be built.

People feel passionately on both sides of the issue.

"This is the only state into which the retail boa constrictor has failed to expand…People stay here, or move to Vermont, because of the excellent quality of life. The only way Vermont can maintain its small-town spirit is to keep its downtowns vibrant and in business," wrote one Vermonter in a letter to the *Burlington Free Press* in 1994.[13] "They've come to yank rural Vermont into conformity with the rest of suburbanized, macadamized, depersonalized America," wrote a man from Middlebury.[14]

"I think they should allow Wal-Mart to open," a resident of St. Albans told the *St. Albans Messenger*. "It would create more jobs and the competition would be great."[15] A citizen of Concord characterized the opposition to Wal-Mart as just "another calculated strike in the ongoing war waged by downtown business interests and city government to stanch the

In their battle with Wal-Mart, Vermont preservationists sought to preserve the distinctive community character seen in the photo on the left and to prevent the type of sprawl represented in the photo on the right.

BETH HUMSTONE

hemorrhage of their profits and tax base to suburbia...If the preservationists just hang on a little while longer, the potential customers of those new malls and discount stores will have emigrated in search of livelihoods and their fear of (horrors!) human activity will take care of itself."

The Wal-Mart project proposed for St. Albans has undergone the Act 250 process in a caldron of political conflict, passionate emotions, fears of lost livelihoods and profound disagreements over the proper role of government and the best way for communities to grow. As we shall see below, the arguments made for and against this project echo those heard in virtually every state. The outcome of this conflict, however, contrasts sharply with the results many states might have produced. The main reason: Act 250 says public officials should ask questions concerning the broader, longer-term effects of large development projects. These questions often are not even asked elsewhere, let alone answered.

Winchester, Virginia's downtown has seen many businesses that once occupied historic buildings move out to the "Apple Blossom" mall. Vermonters in St. Albans and Burlington sought to prevent this type of disinvestment in their downtowns.

St. Albans

IN APRIL 1993, Wal-Mart announced plans to build a 156,000-square-foot superstore on a former dairy farm outside St. Albans, a small town in Franklin County.[16] The project and its parking lot would spread over an area larger than all of downtown St. Albans. Traffic engineers said it would generate over 9,000 car trips a day. When completed, the new store would equal 40 of St. Albans' average-sized stores in terms of square footage and 75 stores in terms of sales.

John Finn, a former state senator, and other local residents concerned about the health of downtown St. Albans objected almost immediately. "You don't have to be too smart to know that if Wal-Mart is located right off the interstate, nobody's going to come down-

town," Finn commented. "Just look at downtown Platts-burgh, N.Y., and you see what I mean." Ray Firkey, the former mayor of St. Albans City, saw things differently: "I think [Wal-Mart is] key to the economic future of Franklin County...I hope that in the near future they can break ground out there and start building," he told the *Burlington Free Press*.

Finn and other like-minded citizens formed an organization, the Franklin/Grand Isle County Citizens for Downtown Preservation, to oppose the development as proposed. They did not oppose a Wal-Mart store, but rather what they saw as its excessive size and edge-of-town location. "Why couldn't Wal-Mart build a smaller store that fits into our downtown?," Finn asked in an open letter to the *St. Albans Messenger*. "We would all

benefit. People who want to shop at Wal-Mart could. The store would be a great attraction and would help revitalize our downtown."

But this request was rejected. Wal-Mart has a certain formula for its stores and the company's representatives said it could not be modified for St. Albans.

Because the project exceeded ten acres, it was subject to an Act 250 review. This took place in October 1993. After hearing testimony, pro and con, the District 6 Environmental Commission voted, two commissioners-to-one, to give Wal-Mart a permit in December 1993. Finn's group and the Vermont Natural Resources Council appealed this decision to the Vermont Environmental Board almost immediately.

The Trial

THE BOARD HEARD THE APPEAL IN JULY 1994. Both proponents and opponents of the project saw the board's hearings as a high-stakes trial and arranged for expert witnesses to make their case. The arguments presented by each side articulated concerns raised by thousands of American communities embroiled in conflicts over new growth and community conservation.

Speaking on behalf of the preservationists, Arthur Frommer, creator of the famous travel guide series, testified that locating a store on St. Albans' periphery would rob the city of its vitality. If similar development were permitted to occur elsewhere in Vermont, the very basis for the state's two billion dollar tourist industry—its number two source of jobs—would be destroyed:

> The chief reason Americans travel to Vermont is [to see] the charm and historic authenticity of its towns and villages…They find contentment and satisfaction in viewing the picturesque, independently-owned shops, non-chain shops and stores that make up the downtowns of Vermont. They enjoy strolling the streets of a central downtown in which people still socialize [and] travel about on foot…

> It is well-known that the construction of giant malls and cut-rate, warehouselike stores on the outskirts of cities has an immediate, deleterious impact on the continued viability of the downtown shopping areas of compact, traditional towns and cities. The destruction of America's downtowns has occurred all over the country as a direct result of mall development on the outskirts, and especially because of the construction there of mammoth stores of the Wal-Mart variety. In addition to disfiguring those outskirts, they have forced out of business nearly every major category of downtown shop.[17]

Our downtown is no longer a fun place to be.

James Haskell, owner of a small business in Sterling, Ill., reinforced Frommer's points by testifying that after developments similar to that proposed for St. Albans were built outside his home town, a gradual decline took place in the downtown.

> Sterling [used to be] a city with real character…Its downtown sidewalks were alive with lots of people…Retail shoppers intermingled with people in the downtown doing other business…Older people could walk to downtown shops… [People] …had plenty of opportunity to see and communicate with one another. As a result, [they] knew one another better…

> Many of the downtown stores have [now] closed…We [have] lost our department stores, shoe stores, drug stores, jewelry stores, camera store, and a children's clothing store. They have been replaced by less vital uses…a number of lounges, a thrift store, etc…Many of our older downtown buildings have become vacant. The city fathers decided something had to be done about these empty buildings. They were deteriorating. Finally, they decided to take them down. They bulldozed the old downtown buildings in an area the size of four to six city blocks…Our downtown, once the heart of our community, is no longer a fun place to be.

Testifying in behalf of Wal-Mart, Barbara Cole, a Colorado-based consultant, said fears about the economic impact of the proposed store on downtown St. Albans were overblown:

> In my experience no major discounter has ever been responsible for the death of a downtown. In our work with downtown businesses across the country we have found that there are always a number of marginal businesses located in the downtown area. When a Wal-Mart or similar discount retailer enters the market, typi-

cally two things can happen. The stores that are in business to make a profit become more competitive and they adapt.

Also representing Wal-Mart and the developer as an expert witness was RKG Associates, an economic consulting firm based in Durham, N.H. RKG said the project would *help*, not harm, St. Albans' economy and that of surrounding Franklin County: "Wal-Mart will… expand the 'retail pie,'" said RKG. It will "attract additional Canadian consumers to the [St. Albans] market," RKG added.

In response to suggestions that the store would hurt St. Albans' downtown, RKG testified that "the *real* problems with retailing and real estate in downtown St. Albans have very little to do with Wal-Mart." Those problems, according to RKG, are:

- Buildings which are obsolete for modern day retailing;
- The lack of a merchants association, an advertising program and hours of operation which customers expect; and
- The economics of rehabilitating and maintaining older historic buildings.

Without a new anchor store like Wal-Mart, RKG added, retail sales would "leak" from Franklin County to other counties where new retail space was being built. "In summary," RKG concluded, "the evolution of department store retail away from downtowns is as natural as the evolution of the horse and buggy to the automobile. Downtowns are functionally obsolete in their ability to serve the needs of today's consumer…"[18]

RKG's assumptions were challenged by Thomas Muller, a Fairfax, Va.-based economist experienced in analyzing the effects of outlying development on older downtowns, and Beth Humstone, a Burlington, Vt.-based land-use expert. According to the Muller-Humstone report, RKG underestimated Wal-Mart's probable sales by as much as 73 percent by using a secondary source to calculate the company's average sales per-square-foot figure rather than Wal-Mart's own data. As a result, RKG also underestimated the extent to which the superstore would displace existing businesses and jobs. This, in turn, resulted in RKG's overestimating the store's positive effects on job creation and property tax generation, the Muller-Humstone report concluded. Muller and Humstone said that the superstore was likely to displace as much as $22.1 million in existing store sales, or one-third of the total market for department-store-type merchandise.[19]

Persuaded by the Muller-Humstone arguments, the Vermont Environmental Board reversed the district commission's decision and denied the Wal-Mart permit in December 1994. Among the board's principle findings:

- The project would cost the public three dollars for every one dollar it generated in public benefits;
- When business displacement was taken into account, the project would cause a net loss of 130 jobs and hurt the local tax base;
- The project constituted "scattered development," or sprawl, the very type of development Act 250 was created to discourage.[20]

Regarding this last point, the board observed that the project would consume 44 acres of land for just one store containing 100,000 square feet of retail space (the original plan for 156,000 square feet had been scaled down) and its parking. By contrast, almost two million square feet of existing retail, commercial, industrial, institutional, residential and open space managed to fit on a slightly smaller area of land in downtown St. Albans.

Not surprisingly, proponents of the superstore denounced the board's decision while downtown preservation advocates celebrated it. A St. Albans Town selectman said that if left unchallenged, the decision would "set a disturbing precedent of unjustified paternalism, preventing townships across Vermont from increasing their tax bases and improving their

The project would consume 44 acres of land for just one store.

local economies."[21] But John Finn, a leading opponent of the project, observed that "the preservation of the sense of community in Vermont was the [decision's] focus" and applauded the ruling. "The ruling…adds another voice to the valid argument that Wal-Mart stores will suit this state only if they are of Vermont-scale and are located in downtown," editorialized the *Burlington Free Press*.

Although Toys R Us usually builds sprawl-type stores, in downtown Santa Monica, the chain built this well-designed store, which helps to reinforce the urban core.

Lessons

THE ST. ALBANS CONTROVERSY IS NOT OVER YET. In early 1995, Wal-Mart appealed the environmental board's decision to the Vermont Supreme Court, which heard the case in March 1996 and is expected to rule on the case in Fall 1996. It is nonetheless possible to draw some preliminary conclusions from the debate so far.

First, whether one favors or opposes the project, it is clear that Act 250 has forced an examination of the broader, longer-term consequences of large-scale development on St.

DAVID FORBES HIBBERT, AIA

Albans' historic downtown. Such analysis is often absent from the local debates over development in other states, where massive projects capable of undermining public investments in a downtown and of altering a town's way of life often zip through the zoning system with scarcely a question asked about their long-term effects.

Second, Act 250 demonstrated here that it has real teeth—when the environmental board chooses to stand firm. In this respect, Act 250 differs from many state preservation and environmental review acts, which typically offer procedural but not substantive protection for historic and natural resources.

But these achievements of Act 250 have had political consequences. By offending the superstore's proponents, the environmental board stoked a political fire already smoldering in Williston, Vt., where a big developer had been fighting for several years to build another sprawl-type superstore vigorously resisted by the city of Burlington, which feared the project would kill its fragile downtown. (See photo, p. 283) After the St. Albans decision, this developer led a successful campaign in the legislature to oust three state board members in favor of people considered friendlier to new development. An attempt—albeit unsuccessful—was also made to rewrite the Act 250 rules to shut citizens out of the public hearing process.

Throughout the St. Albans controversy, many people were unable to see that there were not just two, but three choices available: (1) the Wal-Mart as proposed, meaning large-scale sprawl on the outskirts of St. Albans; (2) no store at all, leaving those who wanted the store and its jobs unhappy; and (3) a smaller Wal-Mart occupying an underused site in downtown St. Albans. This third choice, which had the potential to satisfy the store's proponents and opponents, never got a real hearing, even though local citizens went to the trouble of commissioning a plan for the downtown site and illustrating it with enhanced photographs. This compromise option was dismissed out-of-hand by the retailer's representatives.

In a promotional flier mailed to households elsewhere around the country, Wal-Mart has written: "There is a concern on the minds of Wal-Mart customers everywhere for the quality of our land, air and water. In order to reach a solution, everyone must make a lot of small contributions. Any step is better than no step at all, and each step takes us closer to making a difference." In a June 1993 press release, Wal-Mart stated that the company "constantly strives to bolster small town historical preservation and environmental standards" and that it "has taken steps in hundreds of communities to maintain the character of the town."[22]

Advocates of well-preserved communities and a healthy environment regret that Wal-Mart would not take such steps in St. Albans.

Massive projects capable of altering a town's way of life often zip through the zoning system with scarcely a question asked.

* * *

Postscript: Bennington and Rutland

THROUGHOUT THE ST. ALBANS CONTROVERSY, the Preservation Trust of Vermont, Governor Howard Dean, and the National Trust for Historic Preservation had been urging Wal-Mart to build smaller, more "community friendly" stores in older downtowns that need new investment. They pointed to vacant or underused sites in downtown Rutland and Burlington, for example, as better places for stores than cornfields outside St. Albans and Burlington. In the fall of 1993, Dean even flew to Wal-Mart's corporate headquarters in Bentonville, Ark., to explain Vermont's longstanding policy against sprawl and to urge the company to cooperate with the state in maintaining the economic viability of its small towns. In the summer of 1994, Wal-Mart executives from Bentonville visited several downtown locations in a tour arranged by the Preservation Trust of Vermont.

These entreaties began to pay off in early 1995. While pressing its standard formula in Williston and St. Albans, Wal-Mart made two major concessions—one in Bennington and one in Rutland—to advocates of healthy downtowns and a better environment. In September 1995, Wal-Mart opened its first Vermont store in a recycled Woolworth's in Bennington. Though not uncontroversial locally, the Bennington store did show a willingness on Wal-Mart's part to bend. This store's smaller size—only about 50,000 square feet instead of the 90,000- to 200,000-square-foot stores Wal-Mart is building elsewhere—is more in keeping with Bennington's small size. Instead of putting a store on prime farmland, Wal-Mart has moved into an existing commercial strip on the edge of town.

In May 1996, Wal-Mart announced plans to re-use an old Kmart site in downtown Rutland. At 76,000 square feet, this store, too, is more suitable for a small city than the much larger stores being built elsewhere. Rutland Mayor Jeff Wennberg and other local officials celebrated the announcement, with Wennberg saying he was "hopeful that [Wal-Mart's] presence in our downtown will lead to a revisiting on a national level of the value of downtown locations for 1990s department stores."[23]

"From the beginning, we and most other Vermonters have not been against Wal-Mart," explains Paul Bruhn, executive director of the Preservation Trust of Vermont. "We have, however, strongly opposed mega-stores that sprawl into the countryside and undermine the strength of our downtowns. We think these stores are a good-faith response to our concerns of location and scale. At approximately 50,000 square feet, the Bennington store is less than half the size the company normally builds. It will not create new sprawl. And the Rutland store will be located right downtown, which needs new economic investment."

Governor Dean has said he appreciates Wal-Mart's willingness to look at downtown sites for the company's Vermont operations: "Revitalizing downtowns is an essential ingredient for economic growth that respects and enhances the unique charm of Vermont."[24] Richard Moe, president of the National Trust for Historic Preservation, publicly commended Wal-Mart for both projects as steps in the right direction.

Without Act 250, it is doubtful that Vermont would have had the leverage to bargain with Wal-Mart.

Soon after the Bennington store opened, the *Addison County Independent* reminded people that the battle against Wal-Mart in Williston and St. Albans has not been an effort to keep the company's name out of the state: "Rather, the effort has been to tailor Wal-Mart's presence to a scale reflecting Vermont's small and rural environment." Calling it instead a "battle to tame the behemoth and scale it down to Vermont's size," the *Independent* declared that "Bennington has scored the first victory." Rutland scored the second.

Without Act 250, it is doubtful that the state of Vermont or its cities would have had the leverage to bargain with Wal-Mart and achieve these victories.

Analysis of Act 250

THE EXTENT TO WHICH ACT 250, now a quarter-century old, has acted as a deterrent to sprawl defies precise measurement. It is undoubtedly significant. As Greg Brown, deputy commissioner of Vermont's Department of Housing and Community Affairs, observes, "I'd be willing to bet that developers outside Vermont have considered building developments here that would have been approved elsewhere. They've looked at our procedures, and said, 'We won't mess with those.' That's not bad; it's good. These criteria in Act 250 say: Here's what we deem important. People complain. They say the process is complicated and expensive. That's true. But for large, complicated projects, it should be."

People do indeed complain. John McClaughry, president of the Ethan Allen Institute in Concord, Vt., has called the Vermont State Environmental Board "an anti-growth Frankenstein monster…ignoring the wishes of local government, and setting itself up as an elite, unelected taxing body."

As a matter of record, Act 250 permits are granted to most applicants who seek them. In 25 years, the district environmental commissions have denied only two percent of the more than 14,000 applications filed.[25] Many permits have been subject to special conditions,

Burlington Loses as Sprawl in Williston Wins

BURLINGTON, VERMONT, had fought since the late 1970s to prevent sprawl from gaining a beachhead in Williston, a small town six miles outside the city. But after the state supreme court ruled in late 1995 that construction of a sprawling Wal-Mart could go forward, the bulldozers moved in immediately. One of the fears of historic preservationists had been that if a precedent allowing new sprawl were established, more such development would move in, too. This is exactly what is happening. In addition to the Wal-Mart, other sprawl-type stores have already moved in as well. The Home Depot store shown under construction in this photo will be surrounded by acres of asphalt and radically departs from the traditional settlement patterns espoused in Vermont's land-use law. Historic preservationists and Citizens for Responsible Growth of Williston were not opposed to the superstores; they just wanted them to be located and designed so as to reinforce Vermont's existing communities and to protect investments taxpayers have already made in existing infrastructures. The city of Burlington had urged Wal-Mart to locate on vacant urban renewal land in the city, but that suggestion was rejected.

C.B. JOHNSON

however. A few highly controversial projects, such as those in St. Albans and Williston, have dominated the political debate.

Many would disagree with McClaughry's description of the environmental board as an "anti-growth Frankenstein monster." The involvement of lay people on this board and the district commissions is widely credited with having sustained political support for some rather far-reaching conditions placed on development.[26] Doug Costle, former dean of the Vermont Law School, makes this observation in a handbook explaining Act 250:

> [Act 250] is not a court of law where trained attorneys argue their case for or against a permit application. It's not a bureaucratic regulatory process, where engineers argue technical points with state civil servants…Permits are reviewed by lay people who serve on…commissions around Vermont. They are not government employees. They are local citizens who have agreed to spend time each week reviewing permit applications. Receiving only token payment for their work, commissioners must support themselves, like everyone else, through regular jobs.
>
> While some would argue that there's a faster way to run a permit process, few would say there is necessarily a better way…Like democracy itself, the process often appears inefficient, but how many of us would be willing to trade it for something else?[27]

The Act 250 process has helped to redress, but has hardly eliminated, the imbalance of power between volunteer citizens operating on shoestring budgets who are not professionally involved in zoning or real estate matters, and large corporations or deep-pocketed developers whose attorneys are not only well-versed in land-use arcana but also backed up by significant financial resources. Act 250 puts a brake on massive developments that might barrel forward elsewhere like a freight train, to the consternation of citizens who learn about these projects too late to do anything about them. "I wish very much that Connecticut had a law like Vermont's Act 250," says Laura Clarke, director of the Connecticut Trust for Historic Preservation. "Their law puts local debates over growth in a larger context. People are becoming increasingly aware of the fact that their communities are affected by large developments in neighboring towns."

Developers cannot say to one town, "If you don't let me build this mammoth project here, my way, I'll just go next door."

Vermont preservationists differ over whether Act 250 has mitigated the problem of developers pitting one small town against another. Some believe that with a statewide development review process such as Act 250, developers cannot simply say to one town, "If you don't let me build this mammoth project here, my way, I'll just go next door;" they face the same rules next door. But Harvey Carter, a former state legislator, thinks Act 250 does little to ameliorate this problem: "Developers still have enormous leverage in bargaining with communities. They are able to persuade selectboards to bend rules for development, arguing that it will broaden the tax base. If states were to equalize the property tax burden on a statewide basis, this would do more to protect historic and environmental resources than virtually anything else. Communities could then make intelligent land-use decisions."

Act 250 remains a reactive system that deals with individual projects on a case-by-case basis. It does not create a positive vision for a state's future growth and development. It is only invoked when a specific development proposal is on the table, somebody has money on the line, and the clock is ticking. These are not ideal conditions for making planning decisions affecting a community's long-term future.

Act 250 also is a net with big holes. In general, it catches the big fish while permitting many small ones to pass through unexamined. Yet the cumulative effect of many small, sprawl-type developments can be as damaging in the long run as that of a few large ones. South Burlington's Shelburne Road, which is awash in sprawl, illustrates this very point.

Efforts to weaken Act 250—whether by appointing opponents of land-use planning to the state environmental board, by reducing funding for its operations, or by truncating opportunities for citizen participation—have been and no doubt will continue to be made so long as the law continues to do its job. But in spite of Act 250's shortcomings and complaints about it, the law appears to retain widespread public support. Whenever opponents have made a run at the act, they have failed—so far, at any rate.

In the final analysis, Act 250's effectiveness depends on local citizen involvement. Frank Murray, the attorney who handled the St. Albans case for the downtown revitalization advocates, says that Act 250 gives citizens an opportunity to influence projects affecting their lives, but only if they take advantage of it: "Just like anything else, if you don't have people who participate, the law isn't worth anything. Here in Vermont, people do participate. They come out to public hearings and they care." Greg Brown reinforces this point: "The places in Vermont that have succeeded are those where citizens were involved. This is where the power resides to stand up to the greedy in our culture and say, 'No, dammit, you're not going to do that here.'"

Townsend Anderson, the state historic preservation officer for Vermont and a former developer with extensive experience in rehabilitating historic buildings, sees Vermont's battle against sprawl as critical to the state's preservation of historic communities. "Sprawl rarely brings about a net increase in economic growth. If there is not real growth, there is simply displacement of economic activity. This triggers a whole cycle of deterioration in older communities, affecting both historic resources and the public investment in existing infrastructure. Historic buildings lose their tenants; building owners, in turn, lose their income and thus the capacity to maintain the resource.

"When businesses are looking to expand or relocate, one of the first things they do is to look at the attractiveness and cohesiveness —i.e., at the overall integrity—of a community. The vibrancy of our small towns and their relationships with the open spaces and working farms that surround them are qualities that we roll out in Vermont when we market ourselves to the outside world. If these qualities are destroyed by sprawl, we lose the Number One asset we have for economic growth."

If these qualities are destroyed by sprawl, we lose the Number One asset we have for economic growth.

KEVIN KASOWSKI

Oregon and Urban Growth Boundaries

LIKE VERMONT, THE STATE OF OREGON HAS ESTABLISHED ITSELF AS A LEADER in the movement to contain sprawl. Indeed, Oregon is a veritable exporter of creative growth management concepts. Major players in Oregon's land-use planning program, such as 1000 Friends of Oregon, a statewide environmental advocacy organization, have even become mentors to groups fighting sprawl all over the country.

As in Vermont, it was a Republican governor, Tom McCall, who assumed the mantle of leadership and persuaded the Oregon legislature to enact a comprehensive land-use law to protect what was special about the state.

In 1972, Oregonians could see already how insensitive development was destroying the beauty of California, their neighbor to the south. Closer to home, cheap construction was beginning to deface Oregon's own spectacular coastline. As Charles E. Little wrote in his account of Oregon's land-use legislation, the coastal town of Lincoln City "had become the paradigm for the reduction of this magnificence to a shambles of condominiums, high rises, amusement parks, industrial and municipal pollution, and shocking highway clutter."[28] Oregon's Willamette Valley had lost some 34 percent of its fertile farmland to urban encroachment during the sixties. Clackamas County had lost 10,000 farm acres in one year alone.[29]

In a retrospective on Oregon's land-use history, Robert Liberty, executive director of 1000 Friends of Oregon, recalls that in the late sixties and early seventies:

- Scattershot development was allowed virtually anywhere.
- Towns and cities were allowed to spread endlessly outward, with nothing to stop them.
- Zoning could be changed overnight by a vote of the county commission, leaving neighborhoods and farm and forest land vulnerable to sudden change.[30]

"If you travel outside of Oregon, to Massachusetts, Missouri, or Montana, you'll realize this is still the way things are in most places," says Liberty.[31]

In introducing his program to the 1973 legislative session, Governor McCall spoke passionately:

> There is a shameless threat to our environment…and to the whole quality of life, the unfettered despoiling of the land. Sagebrush subdivisions, coastal 'condomania' and the ravenous rampage of suburbia in the Willamette Valley all threaten to mock Oregon's status as the environmental model for the Nation. We are in dire need of a state land-use policy, new subdivision laws, and new standards for planning and zoning by cities and counties. The interests of Oregon for today and in the future must be protected from the grasping wastrels of the land.[32]

Senate Bill 100, which became the Oregon land-use planning act, had bipartisan support. It was cosponsored by Senator Hector Macpherson, a conservative Republican dairy farmer, and Senator Ted Hallock, a Portland Democrat, in early 1973. Within five months, the pro-

Development stops at the Urban Growth Boundary in Oregon.

posal had made its way through the legislature to the desk of Governor McCall, who signed it into law on May 29, 1973.[33]

Urban Growth Boundaries: The Centerpiece of Oregon's Land-Use Law

OREGON'S LAND-USE PROGRAM SETS FORTH 19 STATE planning goals to guide new growth and development. The centerpiece of Oregon's sprawl-containment program is the "urban growth boundary" requirement of Goal 14. With a stated objective of "provid[ing] for an orderly and efficient transition from rural to urban land use," Goal 14 requires every local government to create an "urban growth boundary…to identify and separate urbanizable land from rural land." In determining this boundary, local governments calculate the amount of land needed to accommodate new housing, economic development, open space and other needs for 20 years. They then draw a line around that land. The objective is to avoid the environmental and fiscal costs of sprawl.

Complementing Goal 14 are five other goals:

- Goal 3, which requires that all land outside the urban growth boundary be zoned exclusively for farm use if it is classified as prime farmland by the Soil Conservation Service;
- Goal 4, which requires protection of land for timber production;
- Goal 10, which requires land-use patterns that allow for adequate housing;
- Goal 11, which calls for an orderly and efficient arrangement of public facilities to serve urban and rural development; and
- Goal 12, which requires local transportation plans to consider alternatives to the automobile and to avoid reliance upon any single transportation mode.

Taken together, these goals seek to prevent sprawl from carving up Oregon's farm and forest lands and to encourage new development in urban centers that have the infrastructure and capacity to support it.

Portland, Oregon, transformed an ugly parking lot into a vibrant urban space in the downtown. (Close-up and aerial views).

MARTHA CASSADY

The 19 planning goals have the force of law and are not merely advisory. State agencies must adhere to them in carrying out their programs. Local governments must address them in the policies set forth in their local comprehensive plans. Zoning laws and capital improvement programs must support them.

Oregon's land-use program provides for two administrative bodies and one judicial agency to oversee the system. The Land Conservation Development Commission (LCDC), a seven-member body of lay persons appointed by the governor, is charged with developing state planning goals, promoting citizen participation, and reviewing local comprehensive plans for conformance with the goals. The Department of Land Conservation and Development (DLCD) provides administrative and staff support for the Commission. The Land Use Board of Appeals (LUBA), which consists of three hearing officers appointed by the governor, acts as a referee when disputes arise between neighboring jurisdictions or between cities and the state.

Under the Oregon system, every local government in the state must prepare a binding comprehensive plan consistent with state planning goals. These plans are submitted to the commission for review and approval. If the commission approves the plan, state actions as well as local land-use activities must comport with its policies.

The law also allows citizens, businesses, and nonprofit organizations to participate in the development and review of the plans and regulations. 1000 Friends of Oregon has reviewed about two-thirds of all county plans and parts of the plans for about 40 cities.

The 19 planning goals have the force of law.

Drawing the Line in North Plains

H OW, AS A PRACTICAL MATTER, does the Urban Growth Boundary concept work? A recent attempt by North Plains, Ore., to nearly double its boundary provides a real-life illustration of this growth management tool in action.

North Plains is a small town of about 1,000 people west of Portland. Located five miles outside the boundary for the Portland metropolitan area, North Plains sits in the middle of productive farmland. The area produces grains, corn, beans, and other crops, but it is struggling economically.

In 1992, the town decided it needed to do something about its downward economic spiral. Town fathers saw North Plains' proximity to a nearby freeway interchange as one of their greatest economic assets. If this area were made available for large-scale commercial development—a retail outlet mall or a big-box retailer, perhaps—the local tax base might improve, they reasoned. At the urging of local property owners, one of whom had obtained enough land purchase options to create a major development opportunity, North Plains amended its local comprehensive plan in 1993 to embrace another 306 acres in its boundary. This expansion included the land around the freeway interchange.

In Oregon, the Department of Land Conservation and Development (DLCD) must review such plan amendments. In this case, the department objected to the boundary expansion on the grounds that it would jeopardize the efforts of the Portland metropolitan region to contain sprawl. The elected regional government for the three counties that make up this region—Multnomah, Clackamas, and Washington—have been working for several years on an innovative plan, "Metro 2040 Frameworks," which directs new growth into high-density "nodes" that a light rail system will serve. The compact, transit-oriented development promoted by this plan is considered essential to achieving the state's goal of reducing sprawl and excessive automobile dependence. The North Plains plan conflicted squarely with this goal.

The Oregon Department of Transportation (ODOT) objected to North Plains' boundary expansion because it violated the state's transportation plan. State officials feared that the expansion would simply attract new auto-dominated development to the area. Large volumes of auto traffic would inevitably follow, thereby overloading the interchange and eventually forcing the state to pay for an interchange expansion. As Richard Benner, director of the DLCD, explains:

> The interchange is on a state highway. North Plains isn't going to come up with the money to improve that interchange. The town will knock at the state's door to improve it. In this case ODOT said, "No, that's not in our transportation plan. If you expand the boundary, you will grow. Pretty soon the state will be forced to invest in the interchange expansion because the area will become congested."

Another concern of the state was that the North Plains population could not have supported land uses planned for the interchange site without drawing traffic from the broader metropolitan area, thereby necessitating more and longer car trips for people throughout the region. "This thing was being promoted as a way to make North Plains more livable at the expense of the neighboring jurisdiction's livability," says Jim Sitzman, a DLCD representative.

If a city adopts a plan amendment that the DLCD considers to be in violation of state law, the department is obligated to appeal to the Land Use Board of Appeals (LUBA). Together with the state transportation department and 1000 Friends of Oregon, the DLCD did just that in April 1994. On June 24, 1994, LUBA rejected the city's request for a boundary expansion.[34]

Tim Ramis, attorney for the city of North Plains, was disappointed by the decision: "It says that if you're a big city like Portland, you can deprive smaller towns of the opportunity to attract their share of the growth."

Sitzman acknowledges that North Plains' economic woes need attention, but he believes there are less damaging ways to address them: "We felt that North Plains had other development options that could have occurred within its existing boundary. These would have had a less damaging impact on farmlands." The state has offered the assistance of its economic development agency to help North Plains overcome its problems.

1000 Friends' executive director Robert Liberty saw the LUBA ruling as a boost to the state's effort to contain sprawl:

> This decision says "nothing doing" to those who want to pave increasingly scarce farmland for more L.A.-style sprawl. As Oregon grows, we need to be increasingly conservative with our use of land. In this case, LUBA agreed that North Plains has ample room to grow inside its existing boundary without expanding onto excellent farmland. As a region, we need to make the best use we can of land that is already in or near existing developed areas. We can't afford to sprawl out endlessly onto the farmland that feeds us.

The city appealed LUBA's decision, but on October 5, 1994, the Oregon Court of Appeals affirmed it.

The Role of Advocacy

WHEN OREGON'S LAND-USE LAW was enacted in 1973, Henry R. Richmond, then a young attorney at the Oregon Student Public Interest Research Group, foresaw that the law's implementation would inevitably engender controversy if it were to do its job. An environmental watchdog organization could help make sure the state stayed with the program, he

Pretty soon the state will be forced to invest in the interchange expansion because the area will become congested.

figured. With encouragement from Governor McCall, Richmond founded 1000 Friends of Oregon in 1975 to play the watchdog role.

In the 20 years since, 1000 Friends has gone to court many times to ensure state and municipal compliance with Oregon's land-use law. As part of this effort, 1000 Friends has formed the Cooperating Attorneys Program (CAP), a network of *pro bono* attorneys who help cities, towns, farmers, planners, preservationists and environmentalists defend the law's principles in court. Since 1982, CAP has worked on more than 100 cases. In about 75 percent of them, the CAP client has won a whole or partial victory.

Results

OREGON'S STRONG LAND-USE LAW, coupled with aggressive and strategic advocacy by 1000 Friends, has produced impressive results.

Some 16 million acres of farmland have been protected by Oregon's exclusive farm use zoning. This is almost three times the area of Vermont and more than 200 times as much farmland as has been protected through the purchase of development rights in the Northeastern states and Maryland as of 1990, according to 1000 Friends.[35]

Oregon now has an entire body of case law upholding key elements of the state's land-use program. Among the more important decisions is a 1977 ruling by the Oregon Supreme Court that a city's land-use policies, including annexations, must include sprawl control standards.[36]

A 1991 study by the Land Conservation and Development Commission revealed that the Portland area urban growth boundary, which had expanded by only two percent in the previous 17 years, had contained 95 percent of the area's residential development in the tri-county area. "Those are statistics no other urban area in the country can match," says 1000 Friends.[37] While comparable western cities that have allowed sprawl to proliferate on their outskirts have seen their historic downtowns decline—Spokane, Wash., is a good example—Portland is a vibrant urban center today and continues to grow. The urban growth boundary has helped Portland remain an attractive magnet to businesses and homeowners throughout the West. Developers as well as preservationists recognize the system's benefits: "In a city like Phoenix," observes David K. Bell, executive vice-president of Portland's's GLS Properties, Inc., "where one developer after another develops progressively cheaper subdivisions in concentric circles all the way out to the farmlands, it's hard to create value."[38]

On the other hand, some of the newer development near the edges of Oregon's cities resembles the same kind of homogenizing sprawl seen anywhere in the country. The only difference it that it is located inside, rather than outside, the boundary. Oregon's Urban Growth Boundary policy does nothing to improve the quality of urban design. The state's best guidance on design issues comes from the "Transportation Planning Rule" issued in 1991. This rule, which seeks to implement Oregon's Goal 12, requires developers to orient their buildings to transit stops, provide pedestrian amenities that promote walking, and reduce the asphalt lagoons that often surround new development.[39] National chains have been particularly resistant to the state's pleas for better-designed new development inside the boundaries.

With state help, Portland removed this intrusive highway from its beautiful waterfront and converted it into a park, where local residents enjoy free concerts in the summertime.

COURTESY BOB STACEY

Challenges

WHILE OREGON REMAINS THE POSTER CHILD for good land-use planning in the United States, its program continues to be challenged and its historic preservation component has suffered a major setback. Three attempts to repeal Oregon's land-use law have been made: one in 1976, another in 1978, and a third in 1982. Each of these ballot-box initiatives went down to defeat. It is noteworthy that such major business interests as Tek-tronix, Hewlett-Packard, and the Metro Home Builders Association opposed efforts to repeal the law in 1982.[40] In 1995, further assaults on the program were made by members of the state legislature, but most of these were defeated. Those that were not were later vetoed by Governor John Kitzhaber.

However, all is not rosy in Oregon. "Despite the ballyhoo surrounding Oregon's program and its tremendous successes," observes Henry Richmond, "the program is barely hanging on. Even here we don't have an adequate constituency for good land use planning. There is still a vocal minority that fulminates against it. In 1995 the governor had to veto four bills that chipped away at our program. So when you look at all 50 states, you see that even the program deemed most successful is still politically insecure."

Indeed, during the 1995 legislative session, the state legislature overrode former Governor Barbara Roberts' veto of an owner consent proposal (see p. 36) that allows owners of historic properties to block the designation of their properties as historic. As a result, property owners have had the ability since September 9, 1995 to veto a community's designation of property as historic. And in 1996, the DLCD rewrote the regulations for Oregon's Goal 5, which hitherto had protected historic resources, in such a way as to gut the state's historic preservation program. After the legislature made the designation of historic properties a voluntary decision for property owners, the DLCD went on to make the community protection of such resources a voluntary decision for local governments as well.

The boundary is what has kept our communities here vital. This vitality is essential to the preservation of historic buildings.

The same arguments, heard in every state, that land-use controls will stifle economic growth and infringe upon private property rights, are repeatedly advanced by those hacking away at the Oregon program. But there is much evidence that these controls have helped, not hurt, economic growth and improved the quality of life in this state. The *Wall Street Journal*, for example, recently noted that "[t]he number of downtown jobs [in Portland] has doubled since 1975 without the city adding a single parking space, widening roads or building new ones."[41] The Oregon economy is generally healthy today, with unemployment in many parts of the state as low as four percent.[42] The state's population has doubled since 1950 and is still growing almost 50 percent faster than the national average.[43]

Despite setbacks resulting from the state's owner-consent law and the DLCD's weakening of Goal 5 regulations, historic preservation has benefitted greatly from Oregon's Urban Growth Boundary policy. "I believe the Urban Growth Boundary is the reason we have a healthy city," says Lisa Burcham, executive director of the Historic Preservation League of Oregon. "Because of the boundary, we see more reuse of existing buildings downtown. People can envision the reuse of historic warehouse buildings for new housing and other purposes. The boundary is what has kept our communities here vital. This vitality is essential to the preservation of historic buildings. It is what has kept our communities livable. It has contributed significantly to the sense of community that exists in Oregon's cities and towns."

With its land-use law, Oregon remains one of the most attractive, livable states in the nation. Statewide public opinion polls make clear that the citizenry as a whole wants to preserve Oregon's beauty and livability.

Washington's Growth Management Act

Oregon's has exerted a major influence on the land-use planning efforts of other states. While many people think it would be difficult today to enact the type of law that Oregon has had since 1973, elements of the Oregon program have surfaced in several state growth management laws enacted since 1985. Moreover, the Oregon statute continues to serve as a model for legislative proposals under consideration elsewhere. Here we examine a variation on the Oregon model: Washington State's Growth Management Act.

W ASHINGTON IS JUST BEGINNING THE SPRAWL-CONTAINMENT PROCESS that its neighbor to the south began in the seventies. Following a period of public alarm over the state's "Californication"—clogged freeways, disappearing farmland, leap-frog development pushing all the way out to the mountains—the Washington legislature enacted the Growth Management Act (GMA) in 1990. "…[U]ncoordinated and unplanned growth," declared the legislature, "together with a lack of common goals expressing the public's interest in the conservation and the wise use of our lands, pose a threat to the environment, sustainable economic development, and the health, safety, and high quality of life enjoyed by residents of this state."[44]

Reducing sprawl is one of the law's 13 primary goals. As in Oregon, the centerpiece of Washington's sprawl-prevention program is the urban growth boundary. Here, however, the term used is "Urban Growth Area" (UGA). Under the law, 29 of the state's 39 fastest growing counties must draw a line to put rural lands off-limits to new urban-style development. As the law explains:

> Each county…shall designate an urban growth area [UGA]… within which urban growth shall be encouraged and *outside of which growth can occur only if it is not urban in nature* [emphasis added]…An urban growth area may include territory that is located outside of a city only if such territory already is characterized by urban growth or is adjacent to territory already characterized by urban growth.

As in Oregon, in determining the urban growth boundary, local governments must determine how much land they will need for new housing, businesses, open space and other purposes during the next 20 years. If areas outside a boundary have already been developed, they need not be brought within the boundary; a local government may simply choose not to permit additional urban growth there. A local government may not annex land or allow new urban development outside the boundary. The policy favors existing cities and towns as the focal points of growth.

The faster-growing counties, and the cities within them, must prepare local comprehensive plans that address the state's major planning goals.[45] Plans must include discrete elements for land-use, transportation, capital facilities and other needs. Although the growth management act lists historic preservation among the state's top 13 planning goals, it does not require municipalities to include preservation elements in their plans. Consequently,

Reducing sprawl is one of the law's 13 primary goals.

less than half of the plans adopted so far have included an optional historic preservation element. In this respect, Washington's law contrasts with that of Rhode Island, which not only requires such elements but also the identification of historic resources.

Within a year of adopting a plan, municipalities must enact zoning rules and capital improvement programs consistent with the plan. Amendments to local plans must be batched and handled all at the same time—no more than once a year—so that communities can assess their cumulative impacts. This provision discourages the sort of individual "spot-zonings" that often unravel the best of plans. A local zoning decision may be challenged in court if it contradicts local planning policies. This feature highlights the importance of ensuring that local plans support community preservation goals in the first place. State agencies must comply with county and city planning policies.

The law encourages cooperative, coordinated planning by local governments within a given region. County plans must harmonize with the plans of cities within the county, and the plans of neighboring jurisdictions must comport with each other. So-called "critical areas"—e.g., wetlands, wildlife habitats and floodplains—and "resource lands"—e.g., farms and forests—must be identified and protected. Lands may not be designated as "resource lands" inside an Urban Growth Area unless a program is available to buy or transfer development rights (TDRs) of landowners. (*See p. 40 for a discussion of TDRs.*) Such programs are designed to ensure that property owners do not suffer economic hardship as a result of restrictions that might be placed on their land. Historic resources are *not* included in the law's definition of critical areas.

Unlike Oregon, Washington opted for stronger local autonomy and does not require state approval of local plans. However, jurisdictions that refuse to plan—or whose plans fail to address key issues—lose eligibility for state infrastructure grants and loans. In extreme cases, the governor may withhold sales, liquor, and gas tax revenues.

Local plans are presumed to be valid by the state, but if they are challenged, they may be ruled invalid. If citizens, private organizations, or public agencies believe that a city or county has approved an inadequate plan or drawn an inappropriate urban growth boundary, they may appeal to one of three state growth management hearing boards established to resolve disputes. There is one board each for the western, eastern, and Puget Sound areas of the state. Each board has three members appointed by the governor. These decentralized, regional forums contrast with the centralized Land Conservation and Development Commission chosen by Oregon to oversee the implementation of its law.

Only six years old, Washington's growth-management law is still being debated, refined, challenged and applied. As in Oregon, the state is trying to navigate through a turbulent channel of political and cultural crosscurrents. These include:

- conflicts between the obligation of government to protect the common good and the rights of individual property owners to use their land;
- tensions between the state's desire to protect its quality of life and the wishes of local government to maintain their autonomy; and
- concerns about the state's legacy for future generations and here-and-now temptations for individuals to make large sums of money.

Nothing less than a revolution in the way people treat land is being fought in Washington State today. Whether business-as-usual or a longer view of the state's future will win out remains unclear. But nowhere is it clearer that a revolution is under way than in the recent decision by the Central Puget Sound Growth Management Hearings Board on the comprehensive plan of Kitsap County. This decision strikes a blow against sprawl about as forceful as one could imagine. Not surprisingly, it has provoked a firestorm.

Whether business-as-usual or a longer view of the state's future will win out remains unclear.

A Strike Against Sprawl in Kitsap County…and A Reaction

KITSAP COUNTY IS A FAST-GROWING COUNTY a ferry ride away from Seattle on Puget Sound. While much of the county is still rural in character, its rural lands are rapidly disappearing as new development, both residential and commercial, claims one acre after another.

"Our county has a history of making land-use decisions that favor sprawl," says Beth Wilson, former president of Kitsap Citizens for Rural Preservation. "This type of development has devastated our cities and caused the abandonment of their central business districts. To the extent that our cities have any economic activity left, they are just filled with antique stores." Wilson cites Bremerton, a city of 38,000, as an example. Already enervated by strip development on its edges, Bremerton's downtown suffered badly following the county's approval of Silverdale, a 95-acre, 700,000-square-foot shopping mall. After Silverdale opened in 1985, much of the downtown, including such anchors as J.C. Penney's and Sears, moved out to the mall within about two years, according to Mike Phillips, editor of the *Bremerton Sun*. "This kind of thing has happened everywhere in the country," Phillips observes, "but it happened here with remarkable speed. It was a bitter pill psychologically. It caused a real crisis in terms of community leadership."

In late 1994, the county approved a new comprehensive plan that, critics say, essentially reinforced the very kind of sprawl development that the Growth Management Act was passed to discourage. In early 1995, 19 different organizations filed formal challenges of the plan. These groups included Kitsap Citizens for Rural Preservation, the state's Department of Community, Trade, and Economic Development, and 1000 Friends of Washington, a forceful proponent of better land-use planning. In complaints filed with the Central Puget Sound Growth Management Hearings Board, these organizations faulted the plan for, among other things:

- drawing urban growth boundaries that were far too large, leaving much of the county exposed to sprawl;
- enabling all rural areas to be developed in one or two-acre lots, thereby perpetuating land-use patterns of the past that the law sought to discourage; and
- failing to show how the county would pay for capital facilities—roads, water and sewer extensions, etc.—needed to serve new growth allowed by the plan.

Sprawl has devastated our cities and caused the abandonment of their central business districts.

The Hearing Board Decision

IN A REMARKABLY HARD-HITTING DECISION issued October 5, 1995, the hearings board essentially agreed with those challenging the plan. The board declared the plan invalid because it failed to comply with the GMA:

> In effect, all of Kitsap County has been made into one giant suburban growth area which the Act prohibits…Although the county may be able to have [low-density] zoning in limited areas under certain specified circumstances, the Board holds that it cannot zone the entire unincorporated area of the county outside of Urban Growth Areas at such [low-density] levels…. [T]he county cannot base its future planning for new growth on its past development practices if those past practices,

as here, do not comply with the Growth Management Act. What was once permissible is no longer so…Although past practices cannot be ignored, they also cannot be the template for the future.

* * *

The County's designated UGAs [Urban Growth Areas] do not comply with the requirements of…[the Growth Management Act]. They are far too large…[T]the Plan is internally inconsistent…The County's Plan is not comprehensive…because it is not complete…[T]he lack of a fully completed capital facilities plan is more than a conceptual shortcoming—it is a fatal legal defect in the County's plan. [46]

The board ordered the county to bring its plan into compliance with the Growth Management Act by April 3, 1996.

Not surprisingly, the order provoked a reaction. "The Growth Management Act is biased and favors a city-based type of development," says Dan Baskins, a member of both the Kitsap County Landowners Coalition and the board of the Kitsap County Home Builders Association.[47] "Our organizations are extremely frustrated and are working to repeal the law." Ron Perkerewicz, the county's planning director, disagrees with those who have characterized Washington's growth management program as a "bottom-up," rather than "top-down," system. "The state has taken away local control," he says. A coalition of elected officials from ten or so counties disaffected by state hearings board decisions seeks to repeal parts of the GMA.

Kitsap County's three-member Board of Commissioners has been criticized for inviting the confrontation with the hearings board. "The commissioners are acting like a stubborn child who refuses to go to bed at 10:00," says Phillips. "They dug in their heels early. The resolution of this conflict will require a different style of community leadership than the one we have now. It will require the kind of consensus-oriented leadership you're seeing all over America in a new generation of local leaders, but not here."

At this writing, the county says it is working to revise the plan, as ordered by the hearings board, but will need an extension. Meanwhile, the county has "downzoned" rural lands—i.e., it has reduced the extent to which these lands may be developed—thereby upsetting many landowners. On the other hand, new property tax assessments were recently mailed out. They portend tax increases of between 15 percent and 30 percent, according to Wilson, who believes people are finally beginning to see the connection between sprawl and higher taxes.

The county commissioners' handling of the situation and the board's decision have become election issues, and Wilson has decided to run for one of the three commission seats. "We can fight these issues out in court, but that does not really bring about the changes that are needed," she says. "The only way to achieve positive changes is through leadership."

> *People are finally beginning to see the connection between sprawl and higher taxes.*

Analysis

IS WASHINGTON'S Growth Management Act working?

No one appears to have had the time to tally up the number of acres actually protected by the law, but Tracy Burrows, planning director of 1000 Friends of Washington, believes that "tens of thousands of acres of farm and forest lands" have probably been saved already by virtue of the statute's requirement that "critical areas" and "resource lands" be identified and protected. And this does not even count the acres protected as a result of their exclusion from designated Urban Growth Areas.

One shortcoming of the system is that the state has no practical incentives to get counties to comply. The state has the legal authority to withhold taxes from municipalities that refuse to cooperate, but using this sanction is considered such a political lightning rod that the authority has been exercised only once. Washington distinguishes "consequences" in the act from "sanctions." The legislature established both. The loss of eligibility for state infrastructure grants and loans is a consequence of non-compliance and is not discretionary. Sanctions are the withholding of tax revenues by the governor, and sanctions are discretionary. In May 1996, Governor Mike Lowry announced his intention to impose economic sanctions against Chelan County if the county continued to flout the growth management law. "Your continued non-compliance with the law leaves me no alternative but to notify you of my decision to impose sanctions unless you come into compliance with the law…Your delays and refusal to comply with state law are extraordinary and particularly so in comparison to the hard work and commitment elsewhere in the state. You cannot expect the governor or the people of this state to apply the law fairly to all, save those who refuse to comply," the governor wrote county commissioners in a letter dated May 21, 1996. He said that if the county failed to meet specified deadlines, he would direct the State Treasurer to withhold state motor vehicle fuel tax revenues to which the county was otherwise entitled.

Historic resource protection in a city with no economic activity is almost meaningless. If the Growth Management Act should succeed in redirecting new investment into older urban areas, as is the goal, it should help historic property owners find new, economically viable uses for historic buildings. But as such investment returns to these areas, it will become increasingly important for municipalities to have strong historic preservation and design review ordinances in place to ensure the preservation of historic buildings and the good design of new ones. Without such ordinances, it is entirely possible, even likely, that

Downtown Poulsbo in Kitsap County, Washington.

MEGAN BELLUE

the same kind of insensitive development that homogenizes the countryside will diminish the quality of cities and towns.

While some business interests, especially in the logging and real estate sectors, vigorously disapprove of the act and are actively working for its repeal, other business interests value the certainty and protection of land values that the law provides. "Seven of the nine major corporations locating in Washington in 1995 have committed investments to areas with growth management plans in effect, and these businesses say they made their decisions in part because of the certainty for land values that these plans provide," says Steve Wells, assistant director of Washington's Department of Community, Trade and Economic Development. The general public also continues to be concerned about the problem of disappearing farms, forests, and open spaces and to press for the protection of Washington's legendary beauty.

Gary Pivo, board president of 1000 Friends of Washington, thinks the state should examine the incentives its tax structure creates for development and make sure they support sprawl-containment objectives. "Sprawl's economic and competitive advantages over cities must be eliminated," he says. Among the keys to success in managing growth better, he includes the strength of Washington's growth management hearing boards, the capacity of citizens groups to appeal sprawl-promoting growth policies, and political leadership backed up by citizen activism.

Our landscape has been devastated during the last 50 years by the type of land development Kitsap County was promoting.

The aggressiveness of 1000 Friends of Washington in "watchdogging" the law's implementation has clearly influenced the decisions of the three growth management hearings boards, which have told local governments in no uncertain terms that the state meant business when it passed the law. The board's ruling on Kitsap County is extraordinary for its boldness in drawing a line in the sand between sprawl-promoting practices of the past and the new vision for Washington's future. David Bricklin, the Seattle attorney who represented Kitsap Citizens for Rural Preservation in this case, thinks the decision was warranted: "Clearly our landscape has been devastated during the last 50 years by the type of

Eight Consequences of Sprawl

IN ITS RULING ON KITSAP COUNTY, the Central Puget Sound Growth Management Hearings Board stated that there are at least eight major negative consequences of sprawl:

(1) it needlessly destroys the economic, environmental and aesthetic value of resource lands;

(2) it creates an inefficient land use pattern that is very expensive to serve with public funds;

(3) it blurs local government roles, fueling competition, redundancy and conflict among those governments;

(4) it threatens economic viability by diffusing rather than focusing needed public infrastructure investments;

(5) it abandons established urban areas where substantial past investments, both public and private, have been made;

(6) it encourages insular and parochial local policies that thwart the siting of needed regional facilities and the equitable accommodation of locally unpopular land uses;

(7) it destroys the intrinsic visual character of the landscape; and

(8) it erodes a sense of community, which, in turn, has dire social consequences.[48]

land development Kitsap County was promoting. We need to reverse that trend. We need some wrenching statements to bring the ship about. For decades we've been nudging and cajoling without much impact. A good dose of medicine from time to time makes sense." Bricklin notes that the 1996 state legislature that just adjourned did not succeed in weakening the act, even though some members tried. "Even this supposedly 'pro-development' legislature did not have the political backing to take the heart out of the GMA," he says. "What the legislature did *not* do speaks volumes."

During the previous 1995 legislative session, no fewer than 30 bills were introduced to weaken the growth management act. Although these were all defeated, the legislature did approve a "takings" bill—known as I-164—requiring state and local governments to compensate private property owners for any reduction in property values due to land-use regulations. Passed at the behest of timber, real estate, and development interests angered by the state's enforcement of wetlands protection as well as the growth management law, the bill was seen as the most extreme "takings" measure in the country and drew a strong response from a broad-based coalition that included environmentalists, historic preservationists, the League of Women Voters, senior citizens, churches, labor groups and others. With the help of citizen-volunteers, the coalition collected an astonishing 231,122 petition signatures to put an initiative on the ballot to repeal the takings law. This was a record number for any referendum in Washington's history and more than twice as many as needed to place an ini-

Tacoma v. Pierce County

IN 1993, THE CITIES OF TACOMA, Sumner, Milton and Puyallup challenged the urban growth boundary of Pierce County for being too big. They feared that if so much raw land were made available for new development, their tax bases would erode while sprawl would flourish. On July 5, 1994, the Central Puget Sound Growth Management Hearings Board ruled that the county had not provided a valid basis for its boundary and directed county officials to reevaluate the basis for their boundary.[49]

Randy Lewis, government relations officer for the city of Tacoma, explains the cities' perspective on this case:

> If new development permitted on raw land in the county is less expensive to build, it will take place there rather than in the city. The relationship between suburban sprawl and urban disinvestment is all too clear: The historic downtown withers as retailers move out to the strip malls on the outskirts of town. The downtown is left with boarded-up stores. Property values drop. The outlying sprawl deprives the city of sales and property tax revenues. This occurs not necessarily because anything is wrong with the city's central business district, but simply because land is cheaper and development standards are easier to meet in the county.

> The city imposes sign controls and requires landscaping, sidewalks, street lights, and other things that make a community livable. Developers can put up anything in the county—shopping centers with ten acres of asphalt, not a single tree, and signs 200 feet high.

> If I can build 200 units on cheap county land because I don't have to install curbs, gutters, street lights, and sidewalks, I can price houses $10,000 to $20,000 cheaper than in the city. All this affects the older city of Tacoma.

> People rail about their property rights, but they also rail about their taxes. We could cut their taxes if we managed growth better.

tiative on the ballot. Newspapers across the state blasted I-164 for its extremism. The *Seattle Times* called the measure a "stink bomb [that] could bankrupt local governments." The *Tacoma News Tribune* declared I-164 "the single worst thing the 1995 legislature did." "Why should the public pay corporations for not damaging neighborhoods…[and] not building high-volume stores on streets too small to carry the traffic?" asked the Spokane's *Spokesman Review*. "Corporations don't pay the public for property value depreciated when a damaging project goes through."

Arrayed on the other side were homebuilders, developers, realtors, logging interests and farmers. Recognizing the need for traditional zoning and land-use planning laws to protect water, air, wildlife and historic resources, businesses such as Boeing and Weyerhaeuser remained neutral.

On November 7, 1995, Washington voters repealed the "takings" law by a 60–40 margin.

Growth management issues will undoubtedly figure prominently again in the November 1996 election.

The success of Washington State's Growth Management Act in curbing urban sprawl will depend largely on the snugness of the urban growth boundaries. So far, most jurisdictions have drawn excessively loose boundaries, according to 1000 Friends of Washington. Citizens groups and others are appealing the boundaries—and often winning—but pressures for business-as-usual by development and real estate forces remain strong. Success will also depend on the willingness of people living inside the Urban Growth Areas to permit more dense development there. Whether such development will be accepted will depend largely on the ability of local citizens to get directly involved and help shape it.

"Why should the public pay corporations for not damaging neighborhoods? Corporations don't pay the public for property value depreciated when a damaging project goes through."

Idaho: Protecting a Downtown from Sprawl

While Vermont, Oregon, Washington, New Jersey, Georgia, Maine, Rhode Island, Maryland, Florida and Delaware have enacted comprehensive growth management laws, most states have not and are unlikely to do so. Although comprehensive growth management statutes provide certain tools unavailable in other states—notably the ability to engage in regional planning and to resolve inter-jurisdictional conflicts over new growth—communities lacking such laws are by no means powerless to prevent sprawl and preserve historic resources. This was made clear in the recent decision rendered by the Idaho Supreme Court, Sprenger, Grubb & Associates v. City of Hailey. *As the following case study illustrates, a state enabling law for planning and zoning that is typical of the laws in most states can, and in Hailey, Idaho, did, support local efforts to maintain the old downtown as the heart of the community and to prevent sprawl from sucking the life out of the city center.*

AILEY IS A SMALL CITY OF ABOUT 4,500 PEOPLE AND THE SEAT OF BLAINE County (pop: 9,000) in Idaho. Founded in 1881, Hailey began as a center for hard rock mining during the gold rush. After the Union Pacific Railroad built a resort in 1936 in nearby Sun Valley, tourism became the area's most important source of income. Preserving the natural beauty of the land surrounding Hailey is important to the town's success in retaining tourism-related jobs and businesses.

In the seventies and eighties, several events occurred that cast a shadow on Hailey's future ability to maintain the economic health of its historic downtown.

In 1973, McCulloch Properties, Inc., developer of Lake Havasu City in Arizona, purchased 654 acres of land on the south side of Hailey and persuaded the city council to annex this land into the city and rezone most of it from agricultural to residential purposes. A small tract of 12.6 acres was zoned for general business. The entire area became known as the Woodside Subdivision. In 1977, McCulloch sold the property to Sprenger Grubb & Associates (SGA), a local developer. In 1979 and 1988, SGA asked the city to "upzone" two parcels of Woodside for more intense development. On both occasions the city did so, and SGA benefited financially from the city's actions. Meanwhile, another developer persuaded the city council that it was in Hailey's best interest to annex and rezone land on the north side of town. Here, too, the city went along.

Fearful that these and other lands on the periphery of Hailey were now ripe for exploitation as sprawl-type development, Keith Roark, then prosecuting attorney, decided to run for mayor. "Based on my own personal experience living elsewhere in the country, I felt that if we permitted this type of development, it would be the deathknell for downtown Hailey. I have seen this happen time and again elsewhere," says Roark. He ran on a pro-downtown, anti-sprawl plank and won in 1989.

If we permitted sprawl-type development, it would be the deathknell for downtown Hailey.

A Downtown Plan

AS THE NEW MAYOR, Roark persuaded the city council in 1990 to amend Hailey's comprehensive plan to make it clear to everyone that the city would henceforth encourage new development in the downtown but discourage sprawl on the outskirts. The plan revisions adopted that year:

- limited new commercial activity to the central business district downtown;
- established a firm annexation policy whereby land already annexed must be developed and settled before new annexations would be considered;
- called for the creation of a historic district to protect the city's past; and
- required fiscal impact studies for new developments to determine whether they would generate sufficient revenues to defray public costs necessary to support them.

The 1990 plan amendments sought to preserve the downtown's aesthetic qualities and economic vitality.

In 1993, the same developer who had persuaded the city earlier to rezone the land on Hailey's north side now came forward with a second request: Would the city "upzone" 13 of those acres for large-scale retail development? The developer, from California, wanted to build a 95,000-square-foot Kmart.

A local resident who felt that Hailey should preserve its small-town way of life reacted quickly. Concerned that large-scale retail sprawl on the outskirts of Hailey would make it impossible to maintain the downtown's vibrancy, she initiated a petition drive to urge the city council to reject the upzoning request. Within a week or so, she gathered 1,000 signatures.

As the mayor and city council now saw the situation, Hailey's downtown was threatened by the likelihood of sprawl and strip development on both the south and north sides. At Mayor Roark's recommendation, the council held a public hearing in July 1993 to consider two actions:

- a proposed "downzoning" of the 12.6-acre Woodside tract from "Business" to "Limited Business." This would allow small-scale retail development that would serve the needs of neighborhood residents but rule out large-scale, "big box" retailing; and
- the requested "upzoning" from residential to "Business" of the Northside tract. This would accommodate the Kmart.

Since both zoning actions related to the downtown's future, the council thought it made sense to consider them together.

The public hearing held in July 1993 was one of the most heavily attended in the history of Hailey. Annette Frehling, a local resident who had moved to Hailey from Florida because Hailey did *not* look like every other town in America, and other concerned citizens had alerted residents to the importance of showing up and speaking out. Several hundred people turned out and the hearing lasted for six hours. Local residents spoke out overwhelmingly in favor of the downzoning and against the upzoning. Most of those who testified emphasized the importance of preserving the aesthetic and financial viability of the downtown core and of preventing strip development removed from the core.

The council voted unanimously that night to approve the downzoning and to reject the upzoning. In taking these actions, the council concluded that "the existence of a large retail commercial property outside the Hailey Business Core…is not in accordance with the current Hailey Comprehensive Plan…"

But under the local zoning code, the council's action required a "third and final reading" before the rezonings could become law. This was set for September 13, 1993.

Downtown Hailey, Idaho.

Threat of a Lawsuit

ON THE EVE OF THE FINAL READING, SGA sent a letter to every household in Hailey stating that if the downzoning were to go forward:

> We will be forced to file a lawsuit against the City of Hailey and ask for one of two outcomes, either to have the business zoning returned to us or to be compensated for the difference in land value between the two zones…

> What does this mean to you, the person who will foot the bill for this action of your elected officials? If the Court decides to allow the City to change the zoning and says they need to compensate SGA at the rate of $2,000,000, assuming the City can get a bond issued for 20 years at 4% interest, the total charge to the City would be $2,940,000. There are an estimated 1600 households in Hailey. That equates to a monetary judgment of $1,838 per household. If the awarded figure is $3,000,000, under the same terms, the total amount financed is $4,414,905. That amounts to $2,759 per household…

> What you need to decide right now is whether you are willing to pay to keep affordable shopping out of Hailey and then drive to Twin Falls or Boise to find it. It is your decision. Monday, September 14 at 6:00 p.m. may be your last chance to speak up for yourself. Come to the City Council at the County Courthouse, state your opinion and voice your concerns. The City Council's decision will have a direct impact on you, your pocketbook and your leisure time.[50]

The citizens of Hailey did turn out, in large numbers, for the September 14 hearing to speak their minds. But their minds favored a very different future for Hailey than the one envisioned by the developer.

Again, several hundred residents turned out for this hearing and spoke overwhelmingly in favor of downzoning Woodside.

SGA had argued that the downzoning would reduce the value of its property. The city acknowledged this was true, but SGA and the city disagreed by how much. The city said $800,000; SGA, $3 million.

The citizens of Hailey favored a very different future for Hailey than the one envisioned by the developer.

On the other hand, homeowners living near the controversial land felt that *their* property values would be lowered if the rezoning were *not* approved. "Anyone who lives close to the store would be adversely affected," said a local mortgage banker. The value of residences near the proposed retail outlet would suffer, and homes would be tough to sell, he testified.

Local residents also pointed out that SGA could still develop its land under the downzoning. Indeed, the "Limited Business" classification permitted a variety of commercial land uses: motels, apartment buildings, personal service establishments, gas stations, drug stores, etc.

One city council member said at the hearing that allowing business zones in the periphery of the city "pulls the rug out from under those businesses who have invested their hearts and their wallets in our downtown." The city was mindful of what had already happened in nearby Twin Falls, where outlying retail sprawl had deprived the city's central core of its economic viability.

At the end of the hearing, the city council voted unanimously to stick with its earlier decisions to downzone Woodside and to reject the upzoning for Kmart.

In describing the hearing the next day, the *Wood River Valley* observed: "Monday night's testimony was truly compelling. Residents described Hailey as one of the last great small towns in America. To keep it that way, the majority argued, the city needs to do what other towns didn't: block developers' attempts to build mega-mall stores outside the existing commercial district."

The next month SGA sued the city, alleging that the downzoning was "arbitrary and capricious," an "invalid exercise of the police power," tantamount to "protectionism" for downtown merchants from competition, and an unconstitutional "taking" of private property without just compensation.

But a district court upheld the city's rezonings in July 1994. SGA appealed this ruling to the state supreme court.

In responding to SGA's new complaint, the city noted that since acquiring the Woodside property in 1973, SGA had requested, and been granted, several "upzonings" that increased the value of its property. "It appears that SGA's position is that some zoning changes within the Woodside Subdivision can take place, but they may not include any rezones with which SGA disagrees," the city stated in its brief.

In answer to SGA's complaint that the city's action represented "protectionism" and an unlawful restriction of competition with existing merchants in the downtown, the city said that the new ordinance:

> does not prevent new retail, restaurant, and entertainment businesses from coming into existence and competing with existing businesses in these fields; it merely prevents such future businesses from being established over one and one-half miles removed from the downtown core in an area surrounded by residences. Determination of the *location* of various uses is what land use regulation and planning is all about. Numerous vacant parcels of property in the vicinity of Hailey's downtown core remain available for new restaurants, retail stores and entertainment facilities. The Hailey City Council simply made a determination, supported by the *vast* majority of the residents in attendance at the hearing on July 26, 1993, that a use such as a major retail development…should not be allowed in an outlying area of the City.

If SGA's position were adopted, the city added, local governments in Idaho would be "severely restricted" in making planning decisions to address new situations that arise, including ones, as here, where the majority of local residents and their elected representatives wanted to preserve both the aesthetic quality and economic viability of their community.

Another Battle to Save a Downtown

IN 1991, THE U.S. COURT OF APPEALS for the Tenth Circuit upheld a policy similar to Hailey's in Lawrence, Kansas. In this case, the city of Lawrence had enunciated a policy of supporting downtown revitalization and discouraging development in outlying areas in its comprehensive plan of 1982. A large shopping mall developer then proposed to build a "cornfield mall" on the outskirts of Lawrence. After the city denied the developer's request to rezone the land from agricultural to commercial purposes on the grounds that such a rezoning ran counter to Lawrence's comprehensive plan, the developer sued the city for violating its "due process" rights and for breaking the federal Sherman Act by using the comprehensive plan to protect downtown merchants from competition.

But in 1991, both the District Court of Douglas County, Kansas and the federal court upheld the city's actions. In a memorandum decision dated April 4, 1991, the state court held that the goal of retaining the downtown's vitality "constitutes a legitimate concern of the governing body…Declining to rezone property in a manner that would threaten the vitality of the downtown area is rationally related to that purpose." The appellate court affirmed the district court ruling: "We believe the district court correctly concluded that retaining the vitality of the downtown area was a legitimate interest of the city commission."[51]

A Legal Victory

ON SEPTEMBER 25, 1995, the Idaho Supreme Court upheld the city's actions, just as the district court had done a year earlier. In affirming the lower court's ruling, the higher court issued an unusually clear and strong opinion upholding the right of a community to protect its downtown core from the enervating effects of outlying development.

Idaho's Supreme Court Ruling: A Pro Downtown

Below are excerpts from *Sprenger Grubb & Associates v. City of Hailey*, 903 P.2d 741 (Idaho 1995). This decision buttressed Hailey's effort to protect its downtown against sprawl.

Constitutional Violations

IT CAN BE PLAUSIBLY ARGUED that the rezoning deprives [the developer] of the highest and best use of its land. However, "[o]nce again, we hold that a property owner has no vested interest in the highest and best use of his land, in the solely monetary sense of that term."…This Court has repeatedly declared that a zoning ordinance which downgrades the economic value of property does not constitute a taking of property in violation of the United States Constitution, where some residual value remains in the property…

The rezoning from Business to Limited Business places further restrictions on SGA's use and enjoyment of the land, but not so much as to constitute a taking. The permitted and conditional uses allowed in the Limited Business zone still provide [the developer] with adequate options for commercial enterprises….

SGA contends that a regulation can be a taking if it "interferes with distinct investment-backed expectations," *citing Penn Cent. Transp. Co. v. New York City*, 438 U.S. 104, 124 (1978). However, United States Supreme Court decisions sustaining land use regulations which are reasonably related to the promotion of the general welfare "uniformly reject the proposition that diminution in property value, standing alone, can establish a 'taking.'"…Moreover "[t]he inquiry into whether a taking has occurred is essentially an 'ad hoc, factual' inquiry," and a regulation's "interference with reasonable investment-backed expectations" is but one of several factors that should be considered.

We hold that the rezoning of SGA's land from Business to Limited Business constitutes no taking of property without just compensation, as prohibited under the United States and Idaho Constitutions.

Validity of Exercise of Police Powers

SGA CLAIMS THE REZONING ACTION was an invalid exercise of police powers to protect downtown merchants from retail competition. SGA contends the City Council members had protectionist motives, and sought to regulate competition…[and] that a desire to prevent competition for the benefit of Hailey's downtown merchants is not a proper application of zoning law and police power principles.

"The zoning power is not unlimited; the power to zone derives from the police power of the state, and zoning ordinances must therefore bear a reasonable relation to goals properly pursued by the state through its police power."…Assuming *arguendo*…that protecting downtown merchants from competition is not a goal that may be "properly pursued" by the City through its police power, the record indicates other legitimate purposes supporting the rezoning.

In its findings of fact and conclusions of law…the City Council articulated various reasons for its decision to rezone the property. Finding of fact number 6 cites the Hailey Comprehensive Plan, which states

The court specifically rejected the developer's arguments that a mere reduction in property values caused by the downzoning amounted to an unconstitutional "taking" of private property. The court pointed out that even under the downzoning, SGA could still develop its land. The court dismissed SGA's argument that the city's action was a "protectionist" move to shield downtown merchants from competition. "Determining *where* particular business uses shall be allowed to expand in a community is normally an appropriate exercise

Decision for Hailey

that the Business and Limited Business Districts are to be expanded around the existing business core. Likewise, finding number 12 states that the Hailey Comprehensive Plan requires the City Council to encourage a central business core that will be conducive to economic growth and will contain a concentration of community services, shopping, entertainment and cultural facilities so as to optimize the use of the existing infrastructure and decrease dependency on automobiles. Finding number 14 refers to a statement by the Hailey Police Chief that the Hailey Police Department does not currently have the law enforcement personnel necessary to patrol two business districts within the City of Hailey. Finding of fact number 15 says the overwhelming weight of public comment was that the existence of a large business zone located nearly two miles from the central core of the City was extremely detrimental to the welfare of the public and the integrity of the community. The Council's Conclusions of Law state that "the existence of a large retail commercial property outside the Hailey Business Core...is not in accordance with the current Hailey Comprehensive Plan, adopted in 1983," and "...will create excessive additional requirements at public cost for public facilities and services."

Determining *where* particular business uses shall be allowed to expand in a community is normally an appropriate exercise of the police power. Preserving aesthetic values and the economic viability of a community's downtown business core can be a proper zoning purpose. Moreover, SGA's protection from competition argument is defective because nothing in the rezoning ordinance prevents new retail, restaurant, and entertainment businesses from locating in or around the City's downtown core and competing with existing businesses. On this record, we cannot agree with SGA that the *only* reason for the rezoning was to protect downtown merchants from competition. "Where there is a basis for a reasonable difference of opinion, or if the validity of legislative classification for zoning purposes is debatable, a court may not substitute its judgment for that of the local zoning authority"...We hold that the rezoning ordinance bears a reasonable relation to goals property pursued by the City through its police power.

Consistency of Rezoning with Comprehensive Plan

SGA CLAIMS THE CITY COUNCIL acted arbitrarily and capriciously in rezoning the 12.6 acres in light of other zoning decisions.

A presumption of validity is accorded to the decisions of a municipal zoning board...The burden of proof is placed upon the party attacking the zoning decision to show that the zoning ordinance, as applied to the property in question, was confiscatory, arbitrary, unreasonable and void...

[T]he City...responded asserting that...[its] actions were consistent with the comprehensive plan, and specifically, with the City's goal to expand the retail business uses around the downtown core, while avoiding the expansion of large retail businesses in outlying areas of the city.... We hold that the record supports the City's response that its actions were decided in accordance with its comprehensive plan. Accordingly, we conclude that the rezoning of the 12.6 acres was not arbitrary or capricious.

of the police power," the court said. "Preserving aesthetic values and the economic viability of a community's downtown business core can be a proper zoning purpose." Finally, the court disagreed with SGA's complaint that the city had acted "arbitrarily and capriciously," noting that the rezonings *were* "in accordance with its comprehensive plan."

The Idaho opinion is so clear and well-written that it could prove to be a seminal decision offering courts in other states a strong model for buttressing the efforts of communities to preserve downtowns in the face of sprawl. (See sidebar, p. 308.)

"What we accomplished with this case," Roark reflected afterwards, "was to provide 'breathing space' for some of the things that people were able to enjoy 50 years ago: a vibrant and active downtown, locally owned shops, a Main Street that looks like a Main Street…What we have in Hailey is what I consider to be a safe harbor, one last good place where people who care about each other and care about their community can express themselves."

* * *

Postscript

On March 25, 1996, the City of Hailey approved a 36,000-square-foot cap on the size of retail stores to ensure that they would be more in keeping with the character of a small town.

"Preserving aesthetic values and the economic viability of a community's downtown business core can be a proper zoning purpose."

Reflections from Keith Roark

Asked what he thinks state governors and policymakers could do to support local efforts to preserve communities and make them livable, Keith Roark, former mayor of the city of Hailey, Idaho, made these comments:

- The concept of "community" is everything, whether this exists in a neighborhood in a large metropolitan area or in a small town like Hailey. Policymakers must first understand that a strong community is an antidote to so much of what ails America: drugs, crime, gangs, etc. If you have a community that's cohesive, if you have a sense of community, these and other problems can be controlled. If you don't, if you just have anonymous, impersonal settlements, it becomes much more difficult to solve these problems.

- It is true that the big national chains that typically build huge outlets on the outskirts of our towns can offer a price structure on most of the goods that the average American uses that independent businesses can't match. You can't argue with this. On the other hand, if you're concerned about the other values of a community, you must recognize that you pay a cost for these low prices. You may have to pay more for socks at local businesses than you would at a mega-mart or similar outlet, but you will also have a community worth living in.

- If you are committed to the idea that communities are more than buildings—but they involve buildings and the businesses inside them and the people who run those businesses as individuals, rather than huge, amorphous corporations where people don't matter at all—then you're going to do what it takes to preserve and reinvigorate them. You will have to make political decisions.

- I don't know what can be done at the state level unless you have this same kind of commitment. But what I see today is very much the other side of the coin. I see this terrible business of states competing against each other to create the biggest tax incentives to lure huge manufacturing plants and corporations with lots of jobs without any understanding of what those companies are going to do to our communities. The emphasis is all on getting those jobs, creating that growth. But then later, after you've got all that growth, you also have a lot of sprawl, a stressed infrastructure, things are breaking down everywhere, and you look around and wonder: Why is crime so high? The next response is to build more prisons.

- In the West at least, economic growth is measured just in terms of jobs and numbers. This, I think, is a potential disaster. If you measure your success as a governor in terms of the number of jobs created, the mega-marts are wonderful because they hire lots of people. You can tell the people: Look at all the jobs created under my administration. But this says nothing about the smaller businesses snuffed out along the way.

Around the Country

A Costs-of-Sprawl Study in New Jersey

NEW JERSEY'S STATE PLANNING ACT, YET ANOTHER STATE ATTEMPT TO channel new growth into existing communities and to steer it away from the countryside, went into effect in 1985. Major features of this legislation included:

- a "cross-acceptance" process that requires adjoining municipalities and state agencies to talk to each other and coordinate their plans for growth; and
- creation of a state planning commission, which was directed to formulate a comprehensive state plan to guide development in New Jersey.

One of the first acts of the planning commission established by this law was to conduct a Gallup poll to find out how New Jerseyites felt about growth and development issues. Eighty-seven percent of those surveyed said they wanted New Jersey's cities to be revitalized. Seventy-five percent said development regulations should be strict or very strict, and only 22 percent felt that existing land-use controls were already adequate.[52]

Rutgers found that the plan's policies would save the state's taxpayers over a billion dollars by the year 2010.

With these survey results in mind and with heavy involvement from citizens throughout the state, the commission developed a preliminary state plan in 1989. This was attacked by New Jersey homebuilders and real estate developers, who felt that the plan would stifle growth and cause a loss of jobs and businesses. At their behest, the state legislature ordered the planning commission to examine the plan's economic effects. Rutgers University's Center for Urban Policy Research, which conducted this examination, found that not only would the plan's policies *not* hurt business and job creation, but they would actually save the state's taxpayers over a billion dollars by the year 2010. Between 1990 and 2010, Rutgers estimated the plan's implementation would also save:

- $740 million in road costs;
- $440 million in water supply and sewer infrastructure costs;
- $400 million annually in operating costs for municipalities and school districts; and
- $1.3 billion in capital infrastructure costs overall.[53]

The New Jersey State Planning Commission released a final State Development and Redevelopment Plan in 1992. The plan noted that if the state continued to grow in the same pattern it had followed in the past, it would face a $20 billion shortfall in revenues needed for infrastructure improvements by the year 2010.[54] Borrowing heavily from concepts inherent to many historic districts, the plan advocates compact urban centers in which land uses are mixed, transit and pedestrian travel are accommodated along with the automobile, and social interaction is facilitated through the creation of attractive public spaces. The plan advocates "community development boundaries" to define these centers. Like Oregon's Urban Growth Boundaries, the boundaries direct new growth inside the boundary and discourage it outside. Unlike Oregon's, New Jersey's boundaries are not mandatory.

Advocates of historic preservation and urban revitalization considered the plan enlightened, but the extent to which it will be implemented remains a question. If the plan has any teeth at all, they lie in the requirement that state agencies follow the planning principles espoused by the state plan. These are supposed to influence state agency decisions regarding the location of roads and other public investments. Areas designated as "growth" centers are supposed to receive priority in the allocation of various state funds. Development in environmentally or historically sensitive areas designated for preservation is not supposed to be encouraged by state agencies.

In a recent test of the state's commitment to the plan, New Jersey Future, a citizen-based organization that advocates affordable housing and good land-use planning, recently sued the state's Council on Affordable Housing in May 1996 for approving a sprawling housing development on 748 acres of farmland in Hillsborough. "Ninety-five percent of the development site is on farm and environmentally sensitive lands that were deemed least suitable in the State Plan cross-acceptance process, making this a critical test of the effectiveness of the State Development and Redevelopment Plan," New Jersey Future observed.[55] "We will not solve the problems of New Jersey unless we stop throwing away people and land," said New Jersey Future Director Barbara Lawrence at a press conference explaining her organization's decision to file the lawsuit.

The court's disposition of this case, which is now pending, will greatly affect the seriousness with which New Jerseyites take the state plan in which citizens invested hundreds of hours of time.

Veto of Road Access in Delaware

GOVERNOR THOMAS R. CARPER signed Delaware's comprehensive growth management act into law on July 19, 1995. Known as the "Shaping Delaware's Future Act," the new measure contains several provisions that benefit historic preservation:

- Historic preservation elements are now mandatory, rather than optional, elements of county comprehensive plans for land use;
- Counties are authorized to amend their land-use plans to provide the creation of districts from which—and to which—development rights may be transferred as a means of protecting sensitive areas;
- The state is explicitly not obligated to provide financial assistance or infrastructure improvements to support development projects that are inconsistent with pre-approved state plans and policies.

"We will not solve the problems of New Jersey unless we stop throwing away people and land."

This last provision addresses a national problem: political pressures exerted by powerful development and business interests on state agencies to subsidize sprawl. In a nationally significant, but largely unnoticed application of this provision, Delaware's Department of Transportation (DelDOT) refused on May 21, 1996 to grant a highway access permit to a developer seeking to build a Wal-Mart store outside the small historic town of Lewes. In an editorial praising the department's decision, *The News Journal* commented, "If the department sticks to its guns, Delaware may well break the back of mindless sprawl."

As Delaware residents watch their small state being carved up by helter-skelter, ugly development, they are clamoring for stronger controls over the use of land. One bill now pending in the state Senate would require DelDOT highway impact studies before major rezonings could be approved. Counties could disregard the study findings only by super-majorities and under special circumstances.

Governor Carper has exercised strong leadership in the area of growth management. "It is becoming increasingly clear to most Delawareans that if we don't begin to do a better job of planning for future development in our state," says Carper, "we risk losing some of the very things that make the quality of life here so special."

A Bottom-Up Approach in Georgia

THE GEORGIA PLANNING ACT OF 1989 grew out of a 35-member "Growth Strategies Commission" established by Governor Joe Frank Harris in 1988. In passing this law, the legislature sought to maintain Georgia's "home rule" tradition and to respect local autonomy over local matters. Georgia does not require local governments to prepare local comprehensive plans, but if a community refuses to plan, or if it fails to address state planning goals, it may not apply for state water and sewer grants, community development funds, or other forms of financial assistance. In effect, the Georgia law says to localities: You don't have to plan or think about how you grow. But if you don't the state is not going to waste its resources on you.

Communities that choose to plan must include sections in their plans that address historic preservation issues, and these sections must provide an inventory of historic resources. In this way, the state planning law addresses a widespread frustration of historic preservationists: the failure of municipalities to identify historic resources that warrant protection.

Small towns, many of which lack the financial resources to plan, may receive technical assistance from a network of 17 Regional Development Centers (RDCs) established by the state planning law. The RDCs are not controlled by the state, but rather by their own boards of directors. Every local government is represented on an RDC board. The centers sponsor educational workshops on planning issues, provide information to local governments, and mediate intergovernmental disputes over planning issues.

Karen Easter, deputy director of Georgia's Historic Preservation Division, says that many towns fail to grasp the relationships between land use, transportation, and economic development policies on the one hand and historic preservation goals on the other: "Preservationists often think that if they just focus on the historic preservation element of a plan, they've done a great job. You can have a wonderful preservation program, but if everything else in the local plan works against it, you haven't achieved much." She cites the example of a Georgia county whose plan called for protecting a Civil War battlefield but whose zoning ordinance would cause the battlefield's obliteration. Georgia's historic preservation division understands the connection between historic preservation and growth management and has tried to provide planning assistance to local governments on preservation issues.

Withdrawal of Subsidies for Sprawl in California

MANY PEOPLE BELIEVE THAT THE SPRAWL-TYPE development patterns dominant in America are simply the result of private market forces. In fact, many state governments actually subsidize sprawl. One way to encourage the preservation and revitalization of historic resources and older downtowns, therefore, is simply to withdraw subsidies for sprawl. This is exactly what the state of California did in 1993, when it passed the "Community Development Reform Act."

"It simply makes no sense to spend hundreds of millions of dollars on new infrastructure and facilities while we allow existing, under-utilized investments to deteriorate...If the growth patterns that have been in place [in Maryland] over the past 25 years do not change, consider what will happen during these next 25 years: we will have virtually abandoned our great and historic urban centers, we will consume hundreds of thousands of acres of farmland, we will consume hundreds of thousands of acres of forests..."

— Maryland Governor Parris N. Glendening [56]

This legislation grew out of widespread complaints that local redevelopment authorities were declaring farmland and open spaces "blighted," then turning this land over to big box retailers and auto malls. "These agencies were persuading local governments to give them sales tax kickbacks, which the agencies would then use to subsidize the big boxes," explains Tony Symonds, a former consultant to the California Assembly. "There were more and more bidding wars among the agencies for large-scale developments that generated a lot of sales tax revenue. Some of these stores were getting their land from redevelopment agencies for only a dollar a year. Others were getting agencies to use their bonding authority to raise money for parking facilities to serve them." These agencies were also subsidizing the malls and big boxes, including Price Clubs, Home Depots, Kmarts and the like, through low-interest loans, land write-downs, tax-increment financing, eminent domain, and off-site improvements. This activity was very different from the support for blighted urban areas that the state envisioned as the mission for these agencies when it created them.

At a time when state agencies were fighting over budgetary crumbs, redevelopment agencies were giving away millions of tax dollars to large corporations, according to Peter Detwiler, a consultant to the State Senate's housing and land-use committee. The big box retailers were not generating a net increase in economic activity statewide, even though they might increase revenues for individual communities. In California, redevelopment agencies are state agencies operating at the local level.

In 1993, the legislature approved a measure sponsored by Assemblyman Phil Isenberg (D-Sacramento) to stop the practice of giving away public dollars to large corporations on raw land. Governor Pete Wilson signed the legislation and it went into effect on January 1, 1993. As enacted, the Community Redevelopment Act of 1993:

- prohibits a local redevelopment agency from providing any form of direct assistance to retail projects located on more than five acres of land that has not previously been developed for urban uses; and
- prohibits local governments from dedicating a portion of sales tax revenues generated by big box retailers to redevelopment agencies. This was intended to prevent the agencies from using these revenues to benefit the retailers.[57]

In a recent challenge of the new law, the Redevelopment Agency of Chula Vista approved a $1.9 million subsidy for a sprawl-type superstore in November 1994. In March 1995, two city residents sued the agency and the Chula Vista City Council for violating the law. In December 1995, the Superior Court of California for the County of San Diego ruled in favor of the plaintiffs who objected to the subsidies.

Visualizing—and Studying—Sprawl in Pennsylvania

ONE OF THE MOST EFFECTIVE EDUCATIONAL TOOLS on the subject of sprawl is the book by Tom Hylton, *Save Our Land, Save Our Towns*. Sponsored by Preservation Pennsylvania, a statewide historic preservation advocacy organization, and published in 1995, the book has ignited the debate over sprawl in Pennsylvania in a way that more academic, technical reports have failed to do. Designed to be read by the lay person in less than two hours, this richly photographed book relates the subject of sprawl to the lives of ordinary people. Some sample passages:

- [T]he sprawling nature of postwar suburban development has destroyed our sense of community. We no longer build places that include people of all ages and incomes. We no longer experience the informal meetings and greetings on Main Street that earlier generations took for granted.

We no longer experience the informal meetings and greetings on Main Street that earlier generations took for granted.

■ In the first half of the century, most children walked to neighborhood schools and came home for lunch. Today, children rarely walk anywhere on their own. We don't want them to! They might get run over. So they ride to school on buses, and must be chauffeured everywhere else by their parents. Meanwhile, the elderly dread the loss of their driving privileges, because when that happens, they lose their independence.[58]

After explaining the effects of sprawl on the everyday lives of people, the book goes on to offer solutions.

Distributed to every member of the state legislature, the book is having an impact in Pennsylvania. Pennsylvania State Senator David J. ("Chip") Brightbill, a senior Republican, introduced a Senate resolution in January 1996 calling for a task force to study ways to encourage community building and to discourage suburban sprawl. The Brightbill Resolution reads as follows:

A RESOLUTION

Committing the Senate to the formation of a task force to study the problem of unplanned sprawl and to recommend changes in state policy to combat sprawl.

WHEREAS, land development patterns that began roughly 60 years ago and that continue currently have consumed excessive amounts of this Commonwealth's agricultural and other land;

WHEREAS, Current development patterns have threatened or altered the essential character of many communities; and

WHEREAS, Current development patterns have contributed to the decline of this Commonwealth's cities and towns; and

WHEREAS, Current development patterns have contributed to an excessive increase in automobile traffic and resulting air pollution; and

WHEREAS, Current development patterns have damaged the waters of this Commonwealth by contributing to pollution from runoff and from faulty on-lot septic systems; and

WHEREAS, Current development patterns have required wasteful public expenditures to reproduce infrastructure that has been abandoned in this Commonwealth's established communities; and

WHEREAS, Current development patterns have harmed society as a whole by contributing to the separation of society along lines of income and race; and

WHEREAS, public frustration concerning unplanned sprawl has sometimes caused inappropriate efforts to block all growth and development, thereby endangering economic development and the rights of property owners; and

WHEREAS, Efforts to combat sprawl must take into account the need for economic development in this Commonwealth, particularly in areas of this Commonwealth where such development has not occurred or has not occurred recently; therefore be it

RESOLVED, That the Senate commit itself to the formation of a task force to study the problem of unplanned sprawl and to recommend changes in State policy to combat sprawl, including, but not limited to, consideration of changes involving increased public education and providing incentives to local government to perform comprehensive planning; and be it further

RESOLVED, That the task force shall consist of five members of the Senate, three of whom shall be appointed by the majority Leader of the Senate and two of whom shall be appointed by the Minority Leader of the Senate, and that the Majority Leader of the Senate shall designate the chairman of the task force; and be it further

RESOLVED, That the task force shall conduct hearings and report to the Senate in due course.

[For states concerned about the problem of sprawl but uncertain as to how to proceed, a study such as the one outlined above for Pennsylvania may be a useful first step.]

The elderly dread the loss of their driving privileges, because when that happens, they lose their independence.

A Resource for Growth Management in the Northeast

THE NORTHEAST REGIONAL OFFICE of the National Trust for Historic Preservation has developed a program to help small communities in the seven Northeastern states (CT, ME, MA, NH, NY, VT, RI) respond to development pressures. This program, known as Project PREPARE (Preservation Resources: Planning and Responsibility) offers information to communities on growth management policies in the seven states and suggests ways each town can assess its ability to manage change, plan for the future, and protect its community character.

This project grew out of a suggestion by former Vermont Governor Tom Salmon, who recognized the impact that growth policies, economic development, natural resource protection and historic preservation have on local community character. Under the direction of Philip B. Herr, a land-use planning expert and professor at the Massachusetts Institute of Technology, the regional office has also prepared a self-diagnostic approach to historic preservation and planning. Entitled *Saving Place: A Guide and Report Card for Protecting Community Character*, this publication helps local preservation organizations, planners, real estate developers, and public officials identify the steps they need to take in order to protect the historic and scenic character of their communities.

(*Several other Project PREPARE publications are also available from the National Trust. See Appendix.*)

Postscript

RHODE ISLAND ALSO HAS A STATEWIDE GROWTH management law, which requires local governments to include sections on cultural resources in their local comprehensive plans. For more information on the law's application to historic preservation, see the case study by Ted Sanderson in Chapter 8.

CONSTANCE BEAUMONT

Downtown Ephrata in Lancaster, Pa., where a historic Main Street is now threatened by superstore sprawl.

CONSTANCE BEAUMONT

Reflections from Three Experts

Some people have been thinking about the problem of sprawl for a long time. Below are the thoughts of three growth management experts.

Henry R. Richmond, Chairman, National Growth Management Leadership Project

In 1975 Richmond founded 1000 Friends of Oregon, the statewide environmental advocacy organization created to "watchdog" implementation of the Oregon land-use law. Richmond founded and now chairs the National Growth Management Leadership Project.

THE CHALLENGE OF STOPPING SPRAWL is not so much a technical problem as a political one. There is a general lack of public understanding about the connection between society's many social problems and its patterns of development. To stop sprawl, people must understand that many problems they face are rooted significantly in these land-use patterns. Families, business owners, and public officials just don't see the relationships between their daily problems and these issues. We must persuade people concerned about sprawl to work with constituencies with which they have communicated little in the past. It takes a majority coalition to succeed in this area.

The solutions will not be found in government. Government won't ever do what needs to be done with land-use policies until there is private-sector leadership to generate the public support that will allow the political people to act.

Oregon's Governor Tom McCall succeeded in this area because he educated and pushed and made better land-use planning a priority. But he was an exception. He was ahead of the public. He was constantly teaching, educating, moving the public to get Oregon's land-use law enacted. This was his Number One priority for four years. No other governor has done that.

What can we do now?

Remind states of their central role in land-use planning. State policymakers should know that the machinery currently being operated by municipalities throughout the country is at least a century out of date. It is that machinery that generates the development patterns we have now. State legislatures are the only forums in which these problems can be addressed. Moreover, the states have a fiscal stake in addressing them.

Many people assume there is something organically local that creates land-use patterns. That's not true. Our local land-use systems were put in place by the state legislatures decades ago. States must recognize that land-use planning is a state issue, just like transportation, electrical utility rate-setting, and education.

The signs in the window reflect the views of many Lancaster County residents concerning the large-scale sprawl that has moved in aggressively during the last several years.

Larry Orman, former executive director of Greenbelt Alliance

The Greenbelt Alliance is a regional citizens group based in San Francisco. Orman is a seasoned expert on land-use planning issues.

JUST SAYING, "SPRAWL IS A PROBLEM," doesn't get any action. In California now, nobody is clamoring for legislative action on this issue. A major reason is that many political constituencies don't realize how their interests are damaged by these development patterns.

In the report that Greenbelt Alliance co-authored with the Bank of America, "Beyond Sprawl: New Patterns of Growth to Fit California," we tried to describe how sprawl hurts different groups. We pointed out that a variety of specific interests—including downtown property owners such as churches, hospitals, and utilities—are hurt because they can't leave the cities. We pointed out that businesses suffer from higher costs and a loss in worker productivity due to long commutes necessitated by sprawl. We noted that the average Californian spends one dollar out of every five to buy and maintain cars. We discussed the hardships created for poor and working-class citizens who can't afford cars and who therefore find it difficult to get to jobs located in the suburbs, where good public transportation isn't available.

My advice for growth management advocates in other states is to look closely at who is hurt by current development patterns and at who can be helped by an alternative. To these people, say, "Let's get organized." Build a political alliance against sprawl on direct self-interest, not just general impacts or ideology.

As for sprawl-containment tools, the best one is the urban growth boundary (UGB). If you can get people to support this concept and establish a policy of keeping development inside the boundary, you can make progress. UGBs are hugely popular, once they're in place. Without the boundary, growth management efforts just don't have much effect on halting sprawl.

> *Build a political alliance against sprawl on direct self-interest, not just general impacts or ideology.*

Greg Brown, Deputy Commissioner, Vermont Housing and Community Affairs Department

WHAT WORKS in growth management?

- You must empower and encourage citizens to participate actively in planning. Local citizen involvement is critical, but this requires a substantial public education campaign.
- You must show people alternatives to sprawl. Help them visualize how their towns will look if they make certain land-use decisions.
- Talk about *managing change*, not stopping growth. Otherwise you make a fatal mistake. You become irrelevant. You provide a foothold for your opponents. But it's not just a matter of managing *growth*. We need to plan for a state's economic *contraction* as well. Any good planning program needs to be able to deal with a recession as well as a boom in the economy.

ELEMENTS OF A PRO-HISTORIC PRESERVATION GROWTH MANAGEMENT POLICY

- Begin by educating the public and developing the political consensus and public support necessary to sustain a strong growth management policy.
- Establish a broad-based commission to conduct an investigation into the state's land-use and preservation problems and to make recommendations for their solution. Include state legislators as well as others on the commission.
- Include the protection of historic, cultural, and scenic resources and the containment of sprawl among the state's major planning goals.
- Use slides, photographs, videos, and other visual materials to help people visualize alternatives to sprawl and how their towns will look if they make certain land-use decisions.
- Require local governments to plan for their future growth and development, or at least provide incentives for them to do so.
- Ensure broad-based citizen involvement in the preparation of local plans.
- Require Urban Growth Boundaries to show where new growth should go and where it should not.
- Require that local plans include a cultural resources element that helps to protect historic and scenic areas.
- Require consistency between and among local planning policies, zoning decisions and capital improvement programs to ensure that planning goals are not undermined.
- Withhold state transportation, water, sewer, and other grants from local governments that refuse to plan for their future growth or to protect historic and other resources.
- Repeal state policies that promote sprawl.
- Require or encourage adjoining municipalities to coordinate their local plans and to resolve conflicts between them.
- Establish appropriate forums and criteria to review developments with regional impacts.
- Require state agencies to comply with local planning policies that adequately address state planning goals, including historic preservation and sprawl containment.
- Provide adequate funding and technical assistance to support local and regional planning efforts and follow up quickly after growth management legislation is enacted.
- Review the effects of state taxation policies and modify them, if necessary, to support historic preservation and other planning goals
- Appoint competent people with vision and consensus-building skills to agencies responsible for growth management and give them the staff and resources they need to do the job.
- Make sure those in charge of implementing growth management laws understand and support the legislation's objectives.
- Exercise leadership.

PART III

The Property Rights Issue
and Strategies

CHAPTER 11

The Property Rights Issue

CHAPTER 11

Private Property Rights, Government Regulation, and the Constitution: Searching for Balance

By Jerold S. Kayden

"...nor shall private property be taken for public use, without just compensation."
—United States Constitution, Fifth Amendment

THE CLOSE OF THE 20TH CENTURY BEARS WITNESS TO INCREASING TENsions between private property rights and government regulation. Landowners complain that, under the guise of environmental laws and land use regulations, public officials too often display gross insensitivity to constitutionally protected private property. If an endangered species, wetland, farmland, historic landmark, or similar asset located on private property is worth protecting, argue some owners, let the public pay for it. Equally assertive voices from environmental and planning camps frame the exercise of property rights in the context of broader public interests. They emphasize that the right to private property is not—indeed has never been—absolute, and that owners should use their property in ways that respect the needs of neighbors and society.

The battle cry of both sides has reverberated in all three branches of government, at national and state levels. After 50 years of relative quiescence, the Supreme Court of the United States revisited this debate with its 1978 opinion in *Penn Central Transportation Company v. New York City*,[1] and has not let up since.[2] Through the 1980s and 1990s, the Court has attempted to resolve what constitutes a taking of private property by government regulation, whether compensation must be paid for regulatory takings, when and where property owners must bring their lawsuits, and similar issues. During its 1986 and 1991 terms, the Court granted review in no less than three land use cases each, an unprecedented foray into the arena; and in 1994, the Court decided yet another land use dispute pitting owner against government (*Dolan v. City of Tigard*).[3] Most knowledgeable observers expect the High Court to maintain an active presence, if only to answer some of the questions posed in its

Grand Central Station, a historic landmark in downtown Manhattan, was at the center of the legal battle resulting in the U.S. Supreme Court's upholding of New York's local preservation ordinance.

own opinions. Lower federal and state courts have taken their cues from the Supreme Court's frenetic pace and issued their own statements on constitutional doctrine governing the land use debate.[4]

Never content to be left out in the cold, the U.S. Congress and numerous state legislatures have joined the fray, enacting or considering laws granting statutory protection to landowners well beyond that secured by the Constitution. Under so-called takings impact assessment laws, government administrators have to conduct assessments of their regulations before enactment to ensure that they do not transgress the constitutional line. These laws mirror Executive Order 12630, adopted in the waning days of the Reagan Administration in 1988, requiring federal executive agencies to conduct such reviews.[5] Under so-called compensation/diminution laws, government agencies pay monetary compensation to property owners whenever government actions decrease by more than a specified percentage the value of private property.

As development creeps steadily outward from central cities to environmentally sensitive places in the countryside, the conflict between property rights and government regulation will only accelerate. This article explores the constitutional framework for the property rights-regulation conflict, with special attention paid to two recent U.S. Supreme Court opinions. As the Court continues its century-long struggle to define an acceptable balance between individual and societal rights, it is apparent at least to the justices that this constitutional riddle is not susceptible to bright-line solutions and glib answers.

The Constitution's Compensation Requirement

LODGED IN THE FIFTH AMENDMENT of the United States Constitution as part of the Bill of Rights, the Just Compensation Clause commands, "nor shall private property be taken for public use, without just compensation."[6] The purpose of the clause is to assure individuals do not bear public burdens that, in all fairness and justice, should be borne by the public as a whole.[7] With roots reaching as far back as King John's Magna Carta of 1215, this just compensation edict has protected property owners against arbitrary and uncompensated government seizure of property while implicitly endorsing government's authority to take property for the public good.

With roots reaching as far back as King John's Magna Carta of 1215, this just compensation edict has protected property owners against arbitrary and uncompensated government seizure of property.

Indeed, in its most straightforward application, the clause has generated little controversy. To make possible the construction of highways, dams, and other public facilities, governments at national, state, and local levels have frequently exercised their power of eminent domain to seize land from private owners, even if they object. Disputes have involved questions about the amount of compensation offered, and occasionally about whether the purpose sought to be achieved by government is sufficiently "public,"[8] rather than about government's basic authority to take private property.

As America became more industrialized in the late 1800s, government found it increasingly necessary to impose regulations, especially on industrial activities, to protect the public's health and safety. Sometimes, such regulations severely impinged on an owner's use of property, and the question arose whether such restrictions contravened some aspect of the Constitution. During the late 1800s and early 1900s, the Supreme Court faced several of these conflicts and ruled in favor of the government. For example, in *Mugler v. Kansas*,[9] the Court upheld a regulation prohibiting the manufacture of alcohol, even though the effect of the law was to terminate the operation of a brewery. In *Hadacheck v. Sebastian*,[10] the Court approved a city law prohibiting operation of an existing brickyard in downtown Los Angeles, even though the law allegedly diminished the value of the property from $800,000 to $60,000, a decrease of more than 92 percent. In these and similar cases, the challenged land uses could easily be classified as common law nuisances, and landowners for centuries had understood that their property rights were subject to the nuisance maxim, "*sic utere tuo ut alienum non laedes*," translated "use your own property in such a manner as not to injure that of another."

The question whether a government regulation could ever contravene the just compensation clause, especially where it severely interfered with the owner's use of his or her property, nonetheless persisted. In 1922 the legendary Justice Oliver Wendell Holmes seemingly resolved this mystery when he announced in *Pennsylvania Coal Co. v. Mahon*[11] that, if a "regulation goes too far it will be recognized as a taking."[12] Justice Holmes fully understood the precarious balance between the needs of government and the rights of individuals. He observed that "[g]overnment hardly could go on if to some extent values incident to property could not be diminished without paying for every such change in the general law."[13] Indeed, he rationalized under his theory of "average reciprocity of advantage"[14] that, while an owner loses through restrictions on his or her property, the same owner gains from restrictions placed on neighboring owners. Still, Justice Holmes could not allow this principle to swallow the clause itself, and thus found himself enunciating a test that, with all its inexactness, made clear that there was, after all, a constitutional line not to be crossed.

For many years after the *Mahon* case, the courts, governments, and property owners operated under the "Model T" technology of Justice Holmes' "goes too far" aphorism. After several cases in the 1920s reviewing the constitutionality of zoning and its application under the Due Process clause,[15] the High Court effectively absented itself from the field for 50 years, leaving the lower courts and the parties themselves to tinker with the bare words of the Just Compensation Clause and Justice Holmes' gloss to govern property rights versus government regulation disputes. In 1978, however, the Supreme Court made up for lost time when it issued the most comprehensive judicial treatise ever on the Just Compensation Clause, in *Penn Central Transportation Company v. New York City*.[16] There, the Court upheld against a takings claim the constitutionality of New York City's landmarks preservation law and its application to the privately owned Grand Central Terminal. In so doing, the Court spelled out standards that guide to this day the constitutional analysis for takings challenges against land use and environmental regulations.

New York City enacted its landmarks law in 1965, authorizing a landmarks preservation commission to designate landmarks and historic districts having "a special character or special historical or aesthetic interest or value as part of the development, heritage or cultural characteristics of the city, state or nation."[17] Under this authority, the city's landmarks commission designated the 1913 Beaux Arts-style Grand Central Terminal a landmark, thereby requiring its owner to seek the commission's permission before altering or demolishing it. Penn Central, the railroad company and owner of Grand Central Terminal, applied to the commission to develop a 55-story or 53-story commercial office building directly above the terminal proper, requests denied by the commission in its belief that this would harm the landmark qualities of the terminal itself.

The Court prefaced its constitutional analysis with the candid admission that determining what constitutes a taking "has proved to be a problem of considerable difficulty"[18] and that "no set formula" exists to make such determination.[19] Instead, the Court announced an "essentially ad hoc, factual inquir[y]" focusing on three factors: first, "the economic impact of the regulation on the claimant"; second, "the extent to which the regulation has interfered with distinct investment-backed expectations"; and third, the "character of the governmental action."[20] Applying this three-factor inquiry to the facts of the case, the Court concluded that Penn Central's claim did not rise to the level of a taking.

First, the commission's actions did not interfere with Penn Central's long-standing "primary expectation"—operation of the terminal.[21] By inference, the expectation, if any, that

"Government hardly could go on if to some extent values incident to property could not be diminished without paying for every such change in the general law."

Penn Central may have had in developing the air rights above its terminal held less weight. Second, Penn Central conceded that it earned a "reasonable return" on its investment.[22] Third, the landmarks law gave Penn Central the possibility of transferring the restricted development rights and utilizing them on eight adjacent parcels of land, an opportunity that produced some economic value to the company.[23] *Penn Central* thus makes clear that landowners are not entitled as a matter of constitutional law to the highest and best, most profitable use of their property. Although the landmark designation denied the railroad company millions of dollars in foregone revenue and dramatically diminished the value of its property, the constitutional line was not crossed.

Two years after delivering the *Penn Central* magnum opus, a unanimous Supreme Court composed a linguistic variation on the *Penn Central* theme, framing the analysis as an outcome-determinative test rather than an impressionistic inquiry. In *Agins v. City of Tiburon*,[24] the Court rejected a takings challenge to a local zoning ordinance limiting an owner to the development of one to five units of housing on a five-acre parcel. The justices pronounced that a regulation effects a taking if it "does not substantially advance legitimate state interests…or denies an owner economically viable use of his land [citing *Penn Central*]."[25] Because zoning for open space preservation represented a substantial advancing of legitimate state interests, and because on the facts before the Court it was not apparent that the property owner had been denied economically viable use, the Court upheld the zoning provision.

Both the *Penn Central* "ad hoc," "no set formula," three-factor inquiry and the *Agins* two-pronged disjunctive test have been cited, mantra-like and interchangeably, by literally thousands of federal and state court opinions. As applied, the constitutional hurdle for the property owner remains high. First, owners are not entitled to the most profitable use of their land. Second, substantial diminutions of value caused by government regulations are uniformly tolerated. Third, virtually all public interests sought to be achieved by typical land use and environmental laws are legitimate in the eyes of the Constitution. Fourth, the mechanisms embodied in such laws are usually found to substantially advance the articulated public interests.

What happens, however, if and when the constitutional line is crossed? Is the regulation merely invalidated, or must government pay compensation to the landowner? For many years, property owners and government regulators debated this point in and out of court. Public officials asserted that the existence of a compensation remedy would chill the proper exercise of authority on behalf of worthy public goals, and that judicial invalidation of the government action should suffice. Landowners countered that the nonexistence of a compensation remedy allowed government to violate the constitutional mandate without penalty, and to return time and again with new regulations to replace those invalidated by court action. The Supreme Court finally ended this argument in its 1987 *First English Evangelical Lutheran Church v. County of Los Angeles*[26] decision, holding that compensation must be paid to the landowner, but only for the period of time the regulation effects a taking.

Owners are not entitled to the most profitable use of their land.

Doctrine Elaborated: The Lucas and Dolan Decisions

TWO 1990S OPINIONS FROM THE SUPREME COURT have provided additional insights into the constitutional approach without altering the fundamental direction suggested by the *Penn Central-Agins* framework. In *Lucas v. South Carolina Coastal Council*,[27] the Court burnished the "economically viable use" test, while in *Dolan v. City of Tigard*,[28] it put flesh on the "substantial advancing" bones. David Lucas, a residential developer, purchased in 1986 two vacant parcels of land on the South Carolina coast for $975,000, with the intention of constructing two single-family homes permitted as a matter of right under then applicable regulations. In 1988, the South Carolina Legislature enacted the Beachfront Management

Act, in part based on legislative findings that the "beach/dune system along the coast of South Carolina…protects life and property by serving as a storm barrier which dissipates wave energy and contributes to shoreline stability in an economical and effective manner," and that development along the coast "has jeopardized the stability of the beach/dune system, accelerated erosion, and endangered adjacent property."[29] The Act authorized the South Carolina Coastal Council, a state administrative agency, literally to draw a line in the sand, seaward of which new development of all types would be prohibited. Unfortunately for Lucas, his two lots fell on the seaward side of the line drawn by the council, allowing him use of his lots for beachcombing, campfires, and construction of a deck and walkway, but preventing him from building his houses.[30]

In court, Lucas conceded that the purpose of the South Carolina law to protect the beaches was perfectly legitimate, but argued that he was nonetheless entitled to compensation for the law's draconian effect on the value of his parcels. A state trial judge agreed, finding that the law reduced the lots' total value from $975,000 to $0, and that this effected a taking requiring payment of compensation in an amount of $1,232,387.50.[31] The South Carolina Supreme Court reversed, holding that when a regulation is designed "to prevent serious public harm," as this one concededly was, then no compensation is owed to the affected owner even where application of the regulation results in an economic wipeout.[32] It is worth remembering that the claim of serious public harm is hardly chimerical. Hurricane Hugo swept into South Carolina causing substantial loss of life and property in 1989.

In a closely divided 5–4 opinion, the U.S. Supreme Court overturned the South Carolina decision, strongly suggesting, without formally holding, that application of the Beachfront Management Act to Lucas' property effected a taking.[33] First, the Court reaffirmed the *Agins* formulation that, where a regulation denies an owner "all economically viable" use of his or her property,[34] then it amounts to a "categorical" taking.[35] For purposes of this analysis, a denial of "all economically viable use" is synonymous with a complete wipeout of value, that is, from $975,000 to $0. Second, the majority embellished its "categorical" takings rule by undercutting it with an exception. As the Court explained, when "background principles of the State's law of property and nuisance" would have authorized neighbors or other affected parties to bring a judicial action against the landowner to stop certain uses of property, then the State may accomplish the same result through, for example, newly enacted laws like the Beachfront Management Act.[36] After all, the new law could not be said to be "taking" anything at all, because the landowner was never entitled to conduct nuisance or other such uses on the property in the first place. Put in terms familiar to lawyers, the newly prohibited uses were never part of the metaphorical "bundle of sticks" that law professors are fond of conjuring to define "property" during the first year of law school.

In Footnote 7, the Court muddied what many considered settled waters when it pondered aloud the correct unit of "property" to be evaluated for purposes of determining whether a regulation denies all economically viable use. Should courts focus exclusively on that portion of the property burdened by the regulation, or should they look instead to the parcel as a whole? In *Lucas*, the matter had resolved itself: both of Lucas' parcels were fully restricted. What would happen, however, when a regulation prohibited an owner from building anything on the proverbial "back 40," but allowed development of the "front 60"? Should courts find a "categorical" taking of the back 40, or consider the regulation in the context of its effect on all 100 acres? Think about the commonplace zoning ordinance that requires that buildings be set back 15 or 20 feet from the street. Should a property owner be able to claim a *Lucas* categorical taking on the basis that 100 percent of his or her land parcel in the 20-foot setback area is sterilized from development?[37]

It is worth remembering that the claim of serious public harm is hardly chimerical. Hurricane Hugo swept into South Carolina causing substantial loss of life and property in 1989.

In Footnote 8, the Court explored the flip side of the "denial of all economically viable use" coin, asserting that a taking may be found even when an owner has not been denied all economically viable use. In such a case, the majority suggested that property owners clothe their takings claim in two of the *Penn Central* factors, the economic impact of the regulation on the claimant and the effect on distinct investment-backed expectations. Property owners thus enjoy two bites at the economic apple: the first to prove a total wipeout; the second, if needed, to prove serious economic impact less than a total wipeout. Lower courts have already heeded this call, suggesting takings even where some economic value remains.[38]

In *Dolan v. City of Tigard*,[39] the Court reviewed a commonplace land use regulatory practice that requires property owners who want to develop new projects to set aside portions of their land for streets, parks, and other public infrastructure in return for government approval. The question in such cases frequently turns on whether the burden being imposed on the landowner reasonably addresses a harm or need generated by the proposed development, or whether it disproportionately burdens the landowner.

Mrs. Dolan owned a 9,200-square-foot plumbing and electric supply store on a 1.67-acre plot along the main street of Tigard, a suburb of Portland, Oregon. Part of her land fell within the 100-year floodplain for Fanno Creek, a waterway cutting through and bordering the parcel. Mrs. Dolan wanted to expand her store to 17,600 square feet and add a 39-space paved parking lot. The city agreed to grant development permission, as long as she dedicated to the city land falling within the floodplain and an additional 15-foot-wide strip adjacent to the floodplain for a pedestrian/bicycle pathway. The cumulative land dedication represented approximately 10 percent of her land parcel. The city rationalized these conditions on the basis that the expanded store and parking lot would create negative impacts on legitimate state interests—increased storm water runoff from the increase in impervious surfaces, and extra automobile traffic—and that the proposed conditions of the floodplain and pathway dedication could mitigate these impacts.

Seeking to build the expansion without these conditions, Mrs. Dolan challenged the city under the Just Compensation Clause and won in the U.S. Supreme Court. At its core, the Court's 5–4 decision asked whether it was fair to demand that Mrs. Dolan set aside parts of her property for public use. Because the conditions would deprive her without compensation of one of the most essential sticks from her property bundle—the right to exclude the public[40]—the city would have to demonstrate more to the justices than the simple importance of floodplains and pathways to the public interest. The Court announced two requirements to assure fairness: first, there must be an "essential nexus" between legitimate public purposes and the conditions imposed on the development permit;[41] second, there must be "rough proportionality" between the nature and extent of the conditions and the impact of the proposed development.[42]

The city easily met the "essential nexus" requirement, because the floodplain and pedestrian/bicycle pathway conditions were clearly related to the legitimate public purposes of preventing flooding and lessening traffic congestion. The city flunked the "rough proportionality" test, however, failing to show how the public access provision of the floodplain dedication would contribute to flood impact mitigation,[43] and demonstrating only that the pedestrian pathway "could" offset some of the traffic generated by the larger store.[44] "No precise mathematical calculation is required," observed the majority, "but the city must make some sort of individualized determination that the required dedication is related both in nature and extent to the impact of the proposed development."[45] For the pathway, the "conclusory statement that it could offset some of the traffic demand generated" would not suffice.[46] The Court's message to cities should not discourage land use planning and regulation. Indeed, the majority remarks on the "commendable task of land use planning, made

There must be an "essential nexus" between legitimate public purposes and the conditions imposed on the development permit.

necessary by increasing urbanization."[47] But the Court does serve notice on public officials that special burdens imposed on landowners must be demonstrably justified on the basis that such burdens proportionately address impacts springing from the new development. In short, cities must do their homework.

Conclusion

STEPPING BACK FROM THE TWO-PRONGED DISJUNCTIVE TESTS, the three-factor inquiries, and the important details that delight lawyers but elicit glassy stares from everyone else, one conclusion stands out about the Court's constitutional approach to the Just Compensation Clause. While the Court's rhetoric may from time to time burnish the mantle of private property rights,[48] its actual rulings give ample breathing room to government regulations in furtherance of land use and environmental goals. In its view, the clause was not fashioned with a jeweler's hammer to protect landowners against every downward fluctuation in value caused by government action, any more than it was designed to recoup from owners increments of value resulting from public investments and favorable regulatory actions. In the regulatory context, the clause is meant to safeguard owners against government beyond the pale, acting as a check on actions having an extreme impact on property use and value. For the rest, the political forces affecting the interaction between public officials and private property owners will have to suffice.

And where does this constitutional jurisprudence leave the property rights versus government regulation debate? Apparently not far enough along for the property rights side. In search of more generous deference, property owners have sought and received hearings in Congress and many state legislatures on behalf of two species of statutes. Under the takings impact assessment laws, government agencies are required to assess in advance whether their future actions and regulations may unconstitutionally impinge on property rights. This idea mimics the "environmental impact statement" assessment pioneered in the National Environmental Policy Act of 1969,[49] which in theory does not stop government from acting, but in practice can slow down or kill actions. Among the states that have enacted such laws are Delaware, Idaho, Indiana, Kansas, Louisiana, Missouri, Montana, North Dakota, Tennessee, Texas, Utah, Virginia, West Virginia, and Wyoming.[50] The second type of legislation, compensation/diminution statutes, requires payment of compensation for government actions that diminish the value of property beyond a specified amount. Four states—Florida, Louisiana, Mississippi, and Texas—have adopted such laws.[51] The Texas statute grants to property owners the right to elect invalidation of the regulatory action rather than compensation.

If takings impact assessment and compensation/diminution statutes become the rule, rather than the exception, at national and state levels, then the constitutional jurisprudence painstakingly elaborated by the Supreme Court will become temporarily irrelevant. Whether citizens over the long haul support ideologically and monetarily the practice of paying someone not to fill a wetland, develop a natural habitat, or tear down a historic landmark will in the end determine whether the Court's 70-year effort becomes historical backdrop or continues as vital law.

The Court's actual rulings give ample breathing room to government regulations in furtherance of land use and environmental goals.

Jerold S. Kayden, a lawyer and city planner, is Associate Professor at the Harvard University Graduate School of Design. He is a key legal advisor to the National Trust for Historic Preservation on constitutional matters and an internationally recognized expert in the field of land use and property rights law. He has a law degree from Harvard Law School and served as a law clerk to Supreme Court Justice William Brennan from 1980–81. Mr. Kayden is co-author, with Harvard Law School Professor Charles Haar, of Landmark Justice *(Preservation Press, 1989), a treatise on Justice Brennan's judicial decisions in the field of land use.*

Private Property Rights: Economic and Political Issues

NOTWITHSTANDING STRONG AND CONTINUING JUDICIAL SUPPORT FOR historic preservation and other quality-of-life laws, it is not enough for such laws to pass constitutional muster. They must also be seen as *fair and reasonable* by the general public. As a member of the Virginia General Assembly said following an eloquent defense of historic preservation laws by a prominent legal scholar, "I don't care what's legal. I'm concerned about what is *fair*."

Now that the courts have spoken, the "takings" debate has shifted to the political arena. In addressing the political questions, one must understand that behind the property rights controversies lies a web of apprehensions regarding the economic effects of land-use restrictions and the role of government.

GERALD MOORHEAD

Economic Effects of Land-Use Restrictions

THE ECONOMIC CONCERNS ARE THE MOST IMPORTANT. Much of the legal fire over property rights is stoked by fears that land-use regulations will lower property values. Whether such fears are well-founded depends on one's point of view. Consider the following situations:

- Mr. Smith lives in Michigan but owns and rents an $80,000 house in a quiet residential neighborhood in Spokane, Wash. He asks the Spokane City Council to rezone his land from residential to commercial use so that he can sell his land to a fast-food chain for a large profit. Neighboring homeowners oppose the rezoning on the grounds that a traffic-generating fast-food outlet would lower the value of their homes and destroy the neighborhood's attractiveness as a place to raise families. The city council denies the rezoning. Mr. Smith accuses the city of destroying the value of his property and violating his rights. His neighbors breathe a sigh of relief. *Their* property values and the equity they've invested in their homes have been protected. In this situation, Mr. Smith did not actually lose any money; he simply failed in his bid to make a lot more.

- The Joneses have owned and maintained a farm on the outskirts of Lawrence, Kan., for 25 years. Their land is zoned for agricultural uses and valued at $600,000. As they approach retirement age, they want to build up their nest egg. A developer offers to buy their land for $2 million if the county will rezone the farmland for a regional shopping mall. The Joneses accept this offer and request the rezoning. At public hearings, neighboring farmers who want to continue farming protest the rezoning on the grounds that a mall would start a land rush that would lead to higher property taxes. They can't afford higher taxes and still farm. Local business and civic leaders involved in a major effort to revitalize Lawrence's downtown object on the grounds that the mall would suck the life out of the central business district, ultimately lowering the value of downtown commercial properties. These leaders point out that taxpayer-funded projects in the downtown that are aimed at making the community as a whole more attractive to new businesses would be wasted. Others testify that if the mall goes forward, the taxpayers, not the Joneses and not the developer, will have to foot the bill for new roads needed to accommodate all the new traffic. The city council denies the rezoning. Like Mr. Smith, the Joneses have not lost any money or equity in their property, but they have failed to make the $1.4 million profit they wanted. The developer did not lose anything because his option-to-buy was conditional and the condition wasn't met. Investments in the downtown made by local businesses and Lawrence taxpayers, on the other hand, have been protected.

CONSTANCE BEAUMONT

In both of these examples, property owners have confused their inability to make maximum profits from land *speculation* with a *loss* in property value. While they *entertained* hopes of getting rich through rezonings, *they never actually possessed that right*. In effect, they equated a lost bet with a deprived right. Addressing this rather common problem, the U.S. Supreme Court observed in *Penn Central Transportation Co. v. City of New York*:

> the submission that [property owners] may establish a "taking" simply by showing that they have been denied the ability to exploit a property interest that they heretofore had believed was available for development is quite simply untenable.[52]

Private property owners often turn to government and land-use laws to protect them against ruinous devaluations of property caused by insensitive actions or development undertaken by other property owners.

The fact that a property speculator gets mad when government refuses to go along with his or her dreams of getting rich does not justify land-use activities that create economic hardships for neighboring property owners or added tax burdens for the whole community. As Henry R. Richmond, a noted land-use expert, asked after New Jersey developers argued against a state land-use plan that would prevent them from realizing $353 million in profits but would save the taxpayers $1.3 billion, "Should these [property owners] be able to insist on getting a $353 million benefit if it means imposing a $1.3 billion problem...on everyone else? This is not a lawyer's problem or the arcanities of the Constitution or some sort of jurisdictional complexity. It is a simple question of fairness."[53]

"Should these property owners be able to insist on getting a $353 million benefit if it means imposing a $1.3 billion problem on everyone else?"

Enhancement of Property Values by Regulation

IF LAND-USE REGULATIONS SOMETIMES LOWER THE VALUE of individual properties—or prevent the value from increasing as fast as the property owner wants—more often, such regulations protect and enhance property values. In fact, the *absence* of restrictions on property can and frequently does lower property values. Developers of suburban subdivisions and regional shopping malls know this to be true, for they routinely impose strict rules on

Protecting Property Values with Restrictions

The following language is taken from a homeowners association covenant in Fairfax City, Va. The rules embodied herein are representative of thousands of privately-imposed restrictions on property that homeowners look to to protect their property values against the actions of neighboring property owners.

Maintenance of Property: Each [homeowner] is obligated...to maintain his dwelling and grounds in a manner consistent with good property management. Appropriate external care of all buildings and improvements is expected. Proper upkeep of the yard includes seeding, watering, mowing, pruning, mulching and weeding. Each homeowner has a responsibility to assist in controlling weeds...Homeowners are reminded that the architectural committee has the right to apply the remedy rule (i.e., if the property owner fails to comply, the architectural committee can hire someone to correct the problem and bill the homeowner.)...No clothing or any household fabric shall be hung in the open.

Architectural Control: To continue harmony of external design and location in relation to surrounding structures and topography, the [covenant] gives the architectural committee the responsibility for reviewing, approving, or disapproving prior to implementation proposed plans and specifications for construction of any structure of any kind, or alterations to any structure, exterior additions, changes or modifications of any nature.

Remedies for Violation: Violation...of any restriction gives the architectural committee the right upon 15 days notice to enter upon the land as to which such violation or breech exists and summarily abate and remove at the expense of the owner any erection, thing or condition that may exist thereon contrary to the intent and meaning of the [covenant].[54]

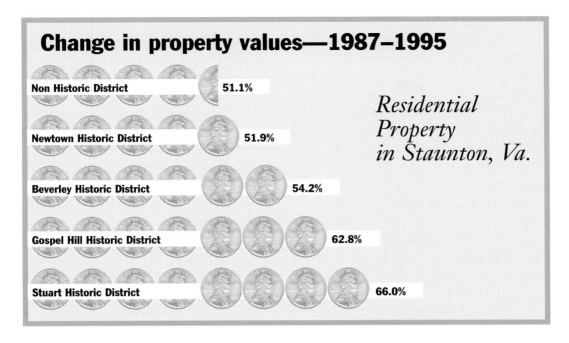

As these two charts indicate, land-use controls
embodied in local historic preservation
ordinances can serve to enhance property values.

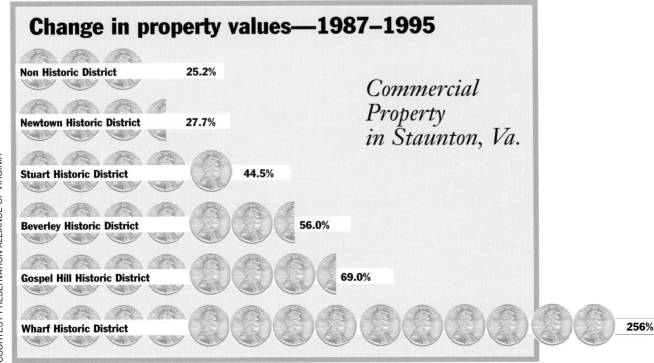

the use of property. These privately imposed rules are Draconian compared to government land-use regulations. (See sidebar p. 336.)

These rules happen to come from the private sector, but they make the point that developers and homebuilders recognize the importance of restrictions on private property to the maintenance of property values. Suburban subdivisions with tight controls often rank among the highest priced, highest tax-revenue-generating areas in America. The reason is simple: People who invest in a town or a neighborhood want certainty. They want assurance that other property owners will not destroy their investments by building something ugly or intrusive or otherwise inappropriate next door. As a property owner in Denver's Lower Downtown Historic District who originally fought local design controls observes, "The regulations protect my buildings from what my neighbors might do to adjoining properties. If you make an investment here, you have a sense it will be in good company." Land-use regulations, including historic preservation regulations, enable government to provide certainty for investors and to stabilize property values.

Advocates of legislation ostensibly aimed at protecting property rights often act as if the economic values of land were generated entirely by individual landowners. In doing so, such advocates overlook the extent to which external forces affect property values. Government funded roads, schools, and utilities; private investments in the renovation of historic buildings that attract tourists to a town; time and labor spent by homeowners painting their houses and mowing their lawns—these are just a few of the many ways in which governments and other property owners add economic value to communities in general and private properties in particular. Some people call these contributions to economic value "givings," suggesting that if government must pay property owners every time its regulations diminish their property values in any way, perhaps property owners should be required to reimburse the government or others for these "givings."

The regulations protect my buildings from what my neighbors might do to adjoining properties.

In an insightful article entitled "Property Rights/Property Values: The Economic Misunderstandings of the Property Rights Movement," Donovan D. Rypkema explains the importance of forces outside the boundary of a landowner's property:

> Consider two five-acre parcels of desert land—one in the middle of the Sahara and the other in the middle of Las Vegas. Within the lot lines both have the same physical characteristics: flat, dry, and, in their natural state, incapable of supporting human habitation. Do they have the same economic value? Obviously not. But the differences between the two lie entirely outside the boundaries of the property.

* * *

> It is not the land but the activity surrounding the land that gives considerable value to one parcel and next to none to the other. In other words, the millions of dollars the Las Vegas site is worth stems not from the investment of the deed holder of the site but almost entirely from the investment of *others*—the City of Las Vegas, employers, owners of other properties, residents of Las Vegas. The creation of value in real estate is to a large extent *external* to the property itself.[55]

So the value of private property comes not only from the investments and labor of the individual property owner, but also from the activities of adjoining property owners, the community, and the government.

The Role of Government

IT IS POPULAR THESE DAYS TO DENOUNCE government for stepping on the rights of "the little guy" and for generating excessive, sometimes mindless regulations. Few among us could not cite examples of governmental mindlessness and heavy-handedness. Like the people who make them up, governments blunder, sometimes seriously.

Unfortunately, individual property owners, too, can be heavy-handed and intrusive. Property owners, like other citizens, often turn to historic preservation and land-use laws to protect their property rights, property values, and neighborhoods from the heavy-handedness of some private property owners and developers who do not share their long-term interest in the community's livability. Sometimes these laws are the *only* thing standing between these people and ruinous reductions in the value of their property.

So property rights conflicts do not erupt only between government and property owners; more often than not, they occur between one property owner and another. When they do, property owners need a disinterested party to mediate the dispute. Under our system, the government and land-use rules serve as mediators. The government may not be perfect, but it is *our* government and the democratic system gives us ways to improve it.

The "Takings" Movement

A NATIONAL MOVEMENT afoot seeks to repeal or weaken state and federal laws that enable communities to promote the general welfare and protect their heritage through land-use laws. While this movement describes itself as the "property rights" or "wise use" movement, many of its activities actually threaten private property rights, property values, and the wise use of land. In this chapter we refer to this movement as the "takings" movement because this term more accurately characterizes what it is all about: claiming that land-use rules enacted by democratically elected representatives of American citizens to benefit the public are "takings" of private property.

Who is behind the "takings" movement? Much of the movement's financial support comes from agribusiness and wealthy mining, timber, and grazing industries, especially in the West. These industries poured thousands of dollars in 1995 alone into state legislative and political campaigns aimed at weakening land-use laws. The cynically named "Wise Use" movement's published agenda calls for anything *but* the wise use of land. For example, it advocates opening up ancient forests, national parks, and other public lands to new development and exploitation by mining and other extractive industries, foreign and domestic.

Other partners in the "takings" movement include organizations with a government-is-bad philosophy, idealogues opposed to almost any governmental activity, and property owners who got caught abusing land and who are now lashing back at the government for requiring them to respect the rights of others.

Partners in the movement that deserve more sympathy include working farmers who do indeed face hard financial times and some individual property owners who have been mistreated by government. Historic preservationists, along with others, should help find solutions to the problems and legitimate concerns of working farmers and individuals treated unfairly by government.

Sometimes land-use laws are the only thing standing between people and ruinous reductions in the value of their property.

Two Kinds of "Takings" Bills

IN 1995, LEADERS OF THE "TAKINGS" movement instigated no fewer than 99 bills in 48 states to curtail the ability of government to protect historic and natural resources and the livability of neighborhoods. These bills tend to fall into one of two categories:

- *assessment* bills requiring government agencies to analyze the financial effects of land-use regulations on property owners *before* such regulations may be implemented; and

■ *compensation* bills requiring taxpayers to reimburse property owners for reductions in property values attributable to government regulations.

A look at two recent battles—one in Arizona, one in Washington—illustrates the pitfalls of "takings" legislation and strategies citizens can use to prevent the distortion of property rights from actually destroying private property and community values.

Property values in historic districts such as this one are protected by local preservation ordinances.

ANN GARRISON

The Battle Over Proposition 300: A War Story from Arizona

W ITH LITTLE DISCUSSION, THE ARIZONA LEGISLATURE PASSED A "takings assessment law" near the end of its 1992 session. Like similar bills in other states, this measure said that before state government could enforce any regulations, it must stop and assess the financial impact of the regulations on private property owners.

Realtors, developers, agribusiness and other advocates of Arizona's assessment legislation saw this measure as a way to make sure government "looked before it leaped." They cited environmental laws as an example of government-gone-awry. They talked about the plight of small businesses struggling to make a living but frustrated by insensitive government bureaucrats. The assessment bill would make government treat people fairly, they said. "If government officials are forced to study the financial impact of their actions on property owners, they are less likely to waste our tax dollars," said their literature.

Others saw the assessment bill as a threat to the public's health, safety, and welfare and to the preservation of neighborhoods. "The state public-health sanitation chief fears the law will make it harder for state officials to condemn food products or revoke health permits," editorialized the *Arizona Daily Star*. "If proponents [of the assessment bill] have their way, this proposal will be extended to local zoning ordinances and make it harder to protect the value of our homes and neighborhoods," said the legislation's opponents. The assessment legislation was a "Developers Protection Act" that would create a nightmare for Arizona taxpayers, in their view.

Opponents of the assessment legislation regarded this measure as so disastrous that they quickly formed a coalition to work for its repeal through a ballot-box initiative. The coalition included neighborhood associations from Phoenix and Tucson, the Audubon Society and other environmental organizations, the American Association of University Women, the League of Women Voters, historic preservationists, public health advocates, and others.

The assessment legislation was a "Developers Protection Act" that would create a nightmare for Arizona taxpayers.

A Campaign Strategy

COALITION LEADERS DEVELOPED A CAMPAIGN BUDGET, outlined a battle plan, and formed the Arizona Community Protection Committee to orchestrate various activities. These included: fundraising, voter attitude polls, message development, brochure printing and distribution, letters-to-the-editor, a speakers' bureau, participation at public events and debates, radio ads, TV spots, and meetings with newspaper editorial boards and reporters.

Arizona law permits citizens to seek to overturn state legislation by popular referendum if they can gather a certain number of signatures within a certain time. In this case, 52,771 signatures were needed within a 90-day period. Working over the summer of 1992, the coalition collected some 71,000 signatures, thereby securing the assessment legislation's suspension and a question on the November 8, 1994 ballot asking voters to reconsider the "takings" measure. At this point the legislation was being referred to as "Proposition 300." In order to repeal the assessment measure, voters had to vote against Prop 300.

To refine its campaign strategy and develop a message that would resonate with the public, the "No on Prop 300" coalition turned to professional political and media consultants. (Prop 300's proponents did the same thing with a much larger budget.) Using focus groups as sounding boards, the consultants recommended a message stressing that Prop 300 would cost taxpayers millions of dollars and increase, not decrease, government bureaucracy. Such a message would put the measure's proponents on the defensive and in the awkward position of arguing that the assessments would not cost the taxpayers much money.

Having settled on the message, the coalition worked with its consultants to provide "message training" to campaign volunteers and political candidates opposed to Prop 300. This coaching helped opponents of the "takings" measure to make their case more effectively to the public.

Media

RECOGNIZING THE IMPORTANCE OF MEDIA SUPPORT, the coalition spent many hours with news reporters, columnists, and editorial boards explaining the consequences of Prop 300. This investment of time paid off. Most of the state's major newspapers, including the influential *Arizona Republic*, came out against Prop 300. Opponents of the "takings" legislation were encouraged to write letters-to-the-editor, and many did. A speakers' bureau was also created so that the "No on 300" coalition's views would be well represented at public forums and debates.

As people thought through the implications of Prop 300, they envisioned a number of potential public health disasters. Here are two held up as examples:

- A hazardous waste landfill is prohibited on a site or the owner is required to purchase better technology to meet a new standard. Under this bill, the landfill owner could argue a government "taking" has occurred and that he is entitled to be paid tax dollars to comply.
- If a meat inspector conducts a random check of grocers and discovers meat stored at higher temperatures than allowed by regulation, he may not be able to remove the meat from the shelves. Under Prop 300, an inspector cannot act to avoid a *potential* public health problem; the meat may be taken "only in response to real and substantial threats to public health."

Three state agencies estimated their administrative costs of compliance with Prop 300 at about $457,000 a year. Since Arizona has over 100 agencies, the total cost of administration would clearly be much higher, even without the inclusion of expenses likely to result from the increased lawsuits the law would undoubtedly invite. These costs began to concern people, as did the specter of new layers of bureaucratic review before the state could act to protect the public. "A state regulatory agency that wants to avoid entangling itself in costly (to the taxpayer) legal battles would be wise to become a rubber stamp. That doesn't sound like good government," editorialized the *Arizona Republic*.[56] "If you like lawyers, confusing law, spending the state's money, open-pit mines, and pesticides, you're bound to love this law," wrote the *Tribune Newspapers*.

While supporting the idea of government compensation for "regulatory takings," Grady Gammage, a Phoenix zoning lawyer who works with both preservationists and developers, suggested that it made more sense to conduct "takings" impact assessments by looking at

"If you like lawyers, confusing law, spending the state's money, open-pit mines, and pesticides, you're bound to love this law."

the impact of a *specific* regulation on a *specific* piece of property, which is the way the courts have traditionally evaluated "takings" claims:

> You do not engage in a hypothetical inquiry as to whether or not a regulation *might* potentially impact property. But that was precisely what Prop 300 mandated. Instead of having a judge dealing with someone's specific property and the impact of a specific regulation on that property, you would have an Assistant Attorney General charged with thinking about whether or not regulations...might negatively impact private property. Well, that's an easy question to answer—yeah, they might! But it is a fruitless and silly exercise to set up a bureaucracy to do that. The goal was to stop regulation.[57]

Financial support for the campaign to rescind Prop 300 was critical. After the pro-Prop 300 forces came out with a "$300 for Prop 300" pitch in their fund-raising solicitations, their opponents countered with a plea for "$3 Against 300." This underscored the "little guy," grassroots support for the opponents of Prop 300 and the big-money support for the "takings" legislation. It generated $20,000 in small contributions of $25 or less.

Opponents of Prop 300 fell short of their original goal to raise $722,000, but they did raise a respectable $371,000. The opposition raised almost twice as much, $718,000, but also fell short of its original goal of $2 million. Moreover, it did not appear to use this money effectively.

Since many organizations involved in the "No on Prop 300" coalition each had their own members, the coalition was able to tap them for campaign volunteers. Some 200 volunteers helped distribute campaign fliers and other literature in precincts identified as critical. Volunteers also handed out short fliers summarizing the arguments against Prop 300 on Election Day.

By the day of the vote, November 8, 1994, Arizonans were concerned enough about the negative consequences of Prop 300 to reject it soundly. Prop 300 failed, with 600,000 votes against it, 400,000 votes for it. Recognizing that the assessment requirement could harm private property owners and communities in unintended ways, the voters of this politically conservative state handed the "takings" movement its first major defeat.

What worked in Arizona

FOLLOWING ITS VICTORY, the Arizona Community Protection Alliance summarized the reasons for its success so that quality-of-life advocates in other states might benefit from Arizona's experience. Here are some of the most important reasons:

- *An early decision to fight Prop 300 with a focused, well-organized, and adequately funded campaign.*
- *A broad-based coalition.* Proponents of Prop 300 tried to portray their opponents as "radical environmentalists," but the involvement of the League of Women Voters and other groups known to be thoughtful citizens made this difficult.
- *An emphasis on fundraising.*
- *A strong message that focused on Prop 300's cost to taxpayers and the specter of an entangled bureaucracy...and discipline on the part of campaign workers in sticking with the message.*
- *Good research.*
- *Message training for campaign volunteers on how to talk about Prop 300 to the public.*
- *A well-organized and mobilized grassroots.*
- *Strong media support.*
- *Paid media.* The coalition spent $260,000, or 70 percent of its total budget, on the media. This purchased two and a half weeks of radio time in Phoenix and Tucson and a week of television time in Phoenix, Tucson, and Flagstaff.

The voters of this politically conservative state handed the "takings" movement its first major defeat.

Round Two of the "Takings" Battle: A War Story from Washington State

I F ARIZONA WAS THE FIRST STATE TO DELIVER THE "TAKINGS" MOVEMENT ITS first major defeat, Washington State was the second.

In 1994, building, real estate, and timber industry groups spent some $200,000 to collect signatures petitioning the state legislature to enact a "takings" bill. Using a professional signature-gathering firm, these groups collected 184,340 valid signatures in support of their proposal, "Initiative 164." Under Washington law, the state legislature is required to act on measures initiated by citizen petitions that receive support from a certain percentage of voters. Washington lawmakers acted on this initiative by passing the Private Property Regulatory Fairness Act on April 18, 1995.

Like Arizona's Proposition 300, the new law required "takings" assessments before any state regulations could be implemented. The Washington proposal went much further, however, by requiring taxpayers to compensate landowners for *any* reduction in property values attributable to land-use regulations. Moreover, the government could not require a private property owner to pay for—or even provide—any studies, maps, plans or reports used in decisions that might restrict the use of land.

The legislation threatened neighborhoods with a loss in protection against polluters and land speculators.

"Takings" advocates hailed the Washington law as the strongest property rights bill in the nation. It would put a damper on "top down, arrogant governing, and the autocratic interpretation of law by regulatory agencies," according to a "takings" legislation advocate who felt that land use regulations were "crippling the counties' ability to provide basic services to residents, destroying the economic base of the state and stripping property owners of their constitutional rights."[58]

The law's easy passage amazed historic preservationists, environmentalists, and good-government advocates who had considered it so extreme they could not imagine its being considered by committees of the Washington legislature, let alone enacted. In their view, the legislation threatened neighborhoods with a loss in protection against polluters and land speculators. It also endangered state and local budgets for education, police and fire protection, and other public services.

A Coalition

AS IN ARIZONA, a broad-based coalition of interests formed quickly with the goal of overturning I-164 through a ballot-box initiative. The coalition included the League of Women Voters, environmentalists, historic preservationists, churches, municipal governments, labor unions, senior citizens, and others.

The coalition began by devising a comprehensive campaign strategy. Major elements of this included: research (including voter attitude polling), communications and press relations, paid media advertising, fundraising, direct mail, and a field network to conduct a voter petition drive, identify supporters, man a phone bank and get voters out when the time came.

The coalition then undertook its second major task: the collection of 90,834 signatures, the number required to put a question on I-164 to the voters on the November 7, 1995 ballot. If the coalition failed to gather these signatures by July 23, 1995, I-164 would go into effect.

Using a paid phone bank to recruit volunteers, the coalition lined up some 10,000 people around the state who were willing to work on the "No On 164" campaign, as it was initially called. Starting in May, these local volunteers collected signatures, spoke at local events, hosted house parties, and wrote letters to the editor explaining how I-164 would hurt the public. Operating under the pressure of a 77-day time frame, the volunteers collected 231,122 petition signatures, a record number for a referendum in Washington and more than twice as many as needed to get I-164 on the November ballot. When it became known that the question regarding I-164 would be framed on the ballot as "Referendum 48," the coalition changed its name and became the "No On 48" campaign. In order to repeal I-164, Washington voters had to vote no on Referendum 48.

In mid-August, the No On 48 coalition conducted eleven training sessions for participants in a speaker's bureau it had created. Key speakers and county campaign coordinators gathered in Spokane, Ellensburg, Seattle and other cities to practice their public speaking skills on the "takings" issue and hone their arguments against Referendum 48. "Neighbors Say No" parties were hosted as a way to raise money from small contributors. Activities aimed at generating "free" media coverage—letters to the editor, calls to talk radio, and contacts with local press—were carried out. Ads in local newspapers, booths and tables at fairs, yard signs, and door-to-door distribution of campaign fliers all helped to generate public visibility for the coalition.

Although Boise Cascade and other timber companies had contributed heavily to the Yes on 48 campaign, the No On 48 coalition got a lift when Murray Pacific, a large timber company, withdrew its support for the "takings" legislation and Weyerhaeuser announced its neutrality. Both companies considered the measure too extreme.

Recognizing that Referendum 48's passage would effectively gut local preservation ordinances in some 30 Washington communities, historic preservation leaders signed a letter in September 1995 urging Washingtonians to support the No on 48 Coalition. "Imagine Spokane without the historic Browne's Addition...Tacoma without the [historic] Pantages Theater or Warehouse District...Ellensburg without its Downtown Historic District...Seattle without the Pike Place Market or Pioneer Square, and your own community without the buildings that give it distinction and character," the letter read. The "takings" legislation "purports to be a 'property rights' measure," the letter continued. "It is not...Taxpayers will be forced to pay developers and landowners top speculative value as 'compensation' for just following the rules that have protected our communities for the last generation."

The No on 48 coalition emphasized that Referendum 48's passage would result in expensive government studies, additional bureaucracy, and endless litigation. If Referendum 48 passed, taxpayers would have to pay for state safeguards to protect water quality, food, and worker safety, coalition fliers said.

But the compensation requirement drew the most fire. "Why should the public pay corporations for not damaging neighborhoods...[and] not building high-volume stores on streets too small to carry the traffic?", asked Spokane's *Spokesman Review*. Newspapers across the state blasted the initiative. The *Seattle Times* called I-164 a "stink bomb [that]

"Imagine your own community without the buildings that give it distinction and character."

could bankrupt local governments." The *Tacoma News Tribune* called it "the single worst thing the 1995 legislature did." Virtually every major paper in the state came out against Referendum 48.

An Expensive Proposition

IN LATE SEPTEMBER, the University of Washington's Institute for Public Policy released an independent study estimating that it would cost taxpayers between $305 million and $986 million annually to implement just the assessment requirements of the law plus $3.8 billion to $11 billion more annually to meet the compensation requirements, depending on how the measure was implemented. The minimum cost per household would be $230.91 a year, according to the Institute. These figures got the taxpayers' attention. So did the numerous examples illustrating I-164's potential harm to neighborhoods and, yes, property owners. Local governments could be prevented from stopping a shopping mall or chemical plant from building next door to a homeowner's bungalow, one flier suggested.[59]

Supporters of the "takings" legislation had tried to paint themselves as a grassroots movement working to support the "little guy" against Big, Bad, Bureaucratic Government. Campaign contribution records revealed a different picture. Four major industry groups—builders and developers, realtors, agribusiness and timber—contributed over 85 percent of the Yes On 48 coalition's money. These contributions included $206,676 from the Building Industry Association of Washington, $107,800 from the National Association of Home Builders, $116,904 from the Washington Association of Realtors, $100,000 from the National Association of Realtors, $278,000 from timber interests, and $174,057 from the Washington State Farm Bureau, county farm bureaus, and other agriculture interests. Only three percent of the Yes on 48 coalition's money came from contributions of less than $100.

In contrast, the No On 48 coalition derived a total of only $141,631 from major interest groups, the largest being the League of Conservation Voters, which contributed $55,000. Other major contributors included the Portland, Oregon-based Western States Center

R e f e r e n d u m   4 8

STOP Initiative 164

The Washington State Legislature passed Initiative 164 on April 18, 1995. This measure becomes law on July 23, 1995, unless we can collect more than 90,000 signatures to place Referendum 48 on the November 7th ballot. Once on the ballot, voters must REJECT Referendum 48 to repeal Initiative 164.

✓ **Initiative 164 could result in the largest tax increase in state history**

✓ **Initiative 164 will create more government, red tape and endless lawsuits**

✓ **Initiative 164 will put our neighborhoods, health and environment at risk**

Referendum 48: Official Ballot Title

"The Washington State Legislature has passed a law that restricts land-use regulations and expands governments' liability to pay for reduced property values of land or improvements thereon caused by certain regulations for public benefit."

Referendum 48: Ballot Measure Summary

This measure would prohibit regulation of private property without prior analysis of the regulation's economic impact and would require such regulation to have the least private impact necessary to the regulation's purpose. Government liability would extend beyond constitutional requirements, requiring payment for reduction in private property values caused by certain regulations adopted for public benefit. Private property includes land, improvements, water rights, crops, and forest products. Successful plaintiffs would be awarded attorneys' fees for enforcement.

($31,750), the Sierra Club ($20,000), and two private philanthropists who contributed $25,000 and $20,000, respectively. Over 50 percent of the No on 48 coalition's money came from contributions under $100.

The big-money, special-interest backing for the "takings" legislation itself became a campaign issue.

Four weeks before the vote, the No On 48 coalition swung into high gear, launching a publicity blitz with radio and TV ads in major media markets. Some 500,000 brochures and fliers were distributed through the coalition's volunteer network. On the eve of the vote, volunteers made some 150,000 phone calls urging citizens to get out and vote.

On November 7, 1995, the No On 48 coalition won big. Washington voters rejected Referendum 48 by a margin of 60 to 40 percent.

Interpreting the vote, No On 48 Campaign Director Dee Frankfourth commented, "Senior citizens, environmentalists, working men and women, neighborhoods, the religious community and thousands of citizens have stood up and shouted…. Vested interests can't buy their way into our neighborhoods. They can't take over our governments. And they can't turn our governments into an enemy of the people. We the people *are* the government."

Vested interests can't buy their way into our neighborhoods. They can't take over our governments. And they can't turn our governments into an enemy of the people. We the people are the government.

Better Remedies

WHILE CRITICIZING THE "TAKINGS" MOVEMENT FOR SO TWISTING THE FIFTH Amendment's meaning as to jeopardize the very general welfare that the Constitution itself seeks to promote, historic preservationists feel strongly that property rights must be respected and that property owners must be treated fairly. Governments *do* blunder and overreach.

State policymakers can help state and local officials do a better job of preserving communities *and* protect private property rights in a number of ways. Here are some particularly important ones:

1. *Encourage local governments to plan better for growth, development, and conservation.* A thoughtful, local comprehensive plan that outlines strongly supported community goals, identifies sensitive areas in need of protection, and establishes a rational basis for land-use regulations lets property owners know in advance how and where a community wants growth to occur.[9] Such plans may not eliminate preservation-development conflicts, but they can help to minimize them. Municipalities that have adopted solid, well-reasoned plans help property owners avoid making bad investments in inappropriate areas. When backed up with consistent zoning ordinances and capital improvement programs, such plans also put local governments in a better position to defend their land-use decisions when conflicts do arise.

2. *Make sure that state enabling laws for historic preservation set forth clear criteria for designating historic properties and provide adequate standards for the local review of alterations and demolitions.* If these standards are reasonable and objectively applied, they are more likely to be seen as *fair* by property owners.

3. *Ensure that enabling laws include adequate public notice and public hearing requirements.* Such laws must establish reasonable time frames and standards for the review of property demolition or alteration requests.

4. *Ensure that property owners are given the opportunity to appeal decisions they consider unreasonable or arbitrary to either the courts or higher government authorities.*

5. *Provide "economic hardship" or zoning variance provisions to ensure equitable treatment of property owners if and when economic hardship cases do arise. (See Protection Chapter).*

6. *Support education and training efforts for local planning, historic preservation and other boards by state agencies.*

7. *Authorize and encourage local governments to offer tax, financial, and regulatory incentives, when appropriate, to encourage property owners to preserve historic structures and to provide a safety valve when land-use regulations would otherwise create economic hardships. (See Tax Incentives Chapter).*

8. *Encourage congressional lawmakers to examine the effects of the federal tax code on farmers with a view to eliminating land conservation disincentives and pressures on farmers to sell out to development.* Inheritance and estate taxes are a special problem and warrant special attention. So do highway projects that devalue farmland as farmland while creating pressures and opportunities for land speculation and development.

What Others Say about "Takings" Legislation

Newspapers

Tuscaloosa News (January 30, 1994):

> [Proponents of the "takings" bill] want the state—and who is the state, other than taxpayers such as you?—to pay them for not abusing their own land and infringing upon their neighbors' rights.

Columbus Ledger-Enquirer (January 27, 1994):

> The absurd ramifications of [a "takings"] law can only be imagined: property owners near churches and schools paid for *not* opening liquor stores or nude dancing clubs; rural landowners paid *not* to install nuclear waste dumps; suburban developers paid *not* to put neon-lit convenience stores in the middle of residentially zoned subdivisions. The possibilities are endless—and bottomless.

Republicans

New Hampshire State Senator Richard L. Russman (testifying for the National Conference of State Legislatures on federal "takings" legislation on February 10, 1995)

The Fifth Amendment
A Shield, Not a Weapon

IN HIS FOREWORD to *Takings Law in Plain English*, a primer on "takings" law, Indiana Supreme Court Chief Justice Randall T. Shepard summarizes the current tension between quality-of-life and "takings" advocates:

> Over the generations, Americans have joined forces time and time again to build clean, safe and prosperous communities and to protect our enjoyment of them. The fishermen who seek to save a river full of great bass, the neighborhood association which works to revitalize the area's historic homes, and the activists who strive to give us cleaner air—all have the need and the right to use the legal tools which can keep our nation a decent and healthy place.

> In modern times, these common efforts at building better communities are often under assault from those who seek only individual advantage. Most Americans see the Fifth Amendment as a shield protecting us from government overreaching. Others seek to use it as a sword, a weapon against efforts to conserve what is special about this land.[60]

Compensation-type "takings" bills represent expensive "budget-busters." Their purpose is to give taxpayer subsidies to those who have to comply with requirements designed to protect *all* property values, and the health and safety of average Americans. After all, we all live downstream, downwind, or next door to property where pollution and other harmful activities have been restrained to protect *all* of our property values and our collective interest in a safe, healthy and enjoyable community.

[B]eyond a few isolated instances, there are no studies or evidence to support the notion that the judicial branch of government has abdicated its role in protecting private property owners from overreaching government regulation. If anything, recent court decisions such as *Dolan v. City of Tigard*, *Nollan v. California Coastal Commission* and *Lucas v. South Carolina Coastal Council* demonstrate a willingness by the U.S. Supreme and the lower federal courts to find "takings" of property value when governmentally imposed land-use restrictions go too far.

Co-Chairpersons of Washington State's "No On 48" Campaign, Nancy Bagley, League of Women Voters, and Robert Mack, Esq.:

Governments should not be the guarantor of maximum speculative land value. And governments should not start paying either corporate interests or small landowners to follow basic health, safety and environmental regulations when commonsense regulatory relief could provide remedy.

Governments should not be the guarantor of maximum speculative land value.

Former Washington Governor and U. S. Senator Daniel J. Evans (on Referendum 48, a "takings" measure requiring financial assessments and compensation):

…Moody's Investors Service, the Wall Street firm that rates the credit-worthiness of municipal bond issues, delivered unsettling news regarding Referendum 48 [the takings legislation]…Their assessment is that, if 48 passes, many local governments around the state would be put into a position of financial inflexibility. As governments attempt to balance the huge costs of compliance with 48 against normal local government operating costs for things such as schools, fire stations and garbage collection, Moody's will be forced to carefully reconsider the ability of these localities to meet their debt obligations. Bond ratings could suffer accordingly, costing local taxpayers millions.

I am immensely proud of this state. I won't apologize for wanting to keep Washington a great place to live. We share common values here: a commitment to our children, to our communities, to civility and cooperation. Our strength is in our ability to resolve differences and solve problems together.

Referendum 48 strikes at the heart of those values, and is based on the false premise that the interests of the individual always outweigh those of the community.

Democrats

Colorado Governor Roy Romer and Vermont Governor Howard Dean (In a May 19, 1995 letter to President Bill Clinton):

Many states have considered takings bills, but the vast majority have rejected any legislation on this subject. The reasons are simple. These bills impose unnecessary new costs on the taxpayers; they create more bureaucracy when we are trying at all levels to trim the size of government; and they undermine basic zoning and environmental protections.

Oregon Governor John Kitzhaber (at his July 13, 1995 ceremony vetoing a "takings" bill):

> The effect of the bill will be to make it impossible to implement any law or rule which protects Oregon's environment. In short, we would be trading narrow private interests at the expense of protecting our common heritage of a beautiful Oregon.
>
> [As an example of the kind of regulation that would have been prohibitively expensive to enact had the "takings" legislation become law, Kitzhaber drew attention to the view from the Rose Garden of Mount Hood—a view protected by the city of Portland Regulation through its "viewshed" regulations.] We can all enjoy this view because it has been protected. No building can be built so as to obstruct it. There is no doubt that comes at a private cost. But the public benefit is overwhelming—and it is overwhelmingly supported by Oregonians....Those who believe Oregonians are willing to walk away from 30 years of thoughtful and successful environmental protection are simply wrong.

Washington Governor Mike Lowry (in a June 29, 1995 letter to President Bill Clinton):

> We, as government leaders, must begin articulating the importance of community values and commitment to the communal welfare. We have heard a great deal lately from those who would allow the private sector to determine what serves the community. But we know that the history of this nation has been shaped by people banding together to achieve larger goals that cannot be met on the individual level...Takings legislation at both the federal and state levels seems to me to pit the individual against the community in a way I hoped we had left behind decades ago.

Ralph S. Tyler, Deputy Attorney General, State of Maryland: [On a "takings" assessment bill proposed in Maryland]:

> The wisdom of delaying governmental action by adding an additional layer of legal review, and as a result increasing both the public and private costs of governmental programs, is highly questionable....[61]

Organizations

National League of Cities and U.S. Conference of Mayors (in a joint letter signed July 18, 1995 opposing federal legislation requiring compensation whenever government regulations reduce property values by a specific percentage):

> The bill's compensation provisions would be to create a new federal entitlement spending program with unforeseen consequences for the federal deficit. Our mutual constituents, average taxpayers, would be forced to pay for these new government expenditures, as well as the burgeoning bureaucracy and cumbersome paperwork that would ensue...[This takings legislation] is a blunt instrument that would exacerbate rather than solve the major issues with federal government overregulation and would be likely, in the end, to lead to more mandates on local governments, thus making the problem worse, not better.

The wisdom of delaying governmental action by adding an additional layer of legal review is highly questionable.

CHAPTER 12

Strategies

CHAPTER 12

Strategies

FOR THE MOST PART, WE HAVE FOCUSSED ON THE *CONTENT* OF STATE policies and programs up until now. Here we talk about strategy. How can historic preservation and livable community advocates persuade state policymakers to put enlightened policies in place? What are the best strategies for influencing public policy? Are there common pitfalls to be avoided?

Here three seasoned experts share their insights into the process of shaping policies and offer advice on how to influence it.

Wisconsin State Senator Brian Rude

A Republican from LaCrosse, Brian Rude has served as president of the Wisconsin Senate and has sponsored most of the important historic preservation laws to pass in his state during the last decade. In 1985, Senator Rude served on the Wisconsin Task Force on Historic Preservation, whose recommendations led to the enactment of a comprehensive package of historic preservation measures. The successes of this task force later became a model for other states. Senator Rude has worked for the enactment of Wisconsin's 25 percent rehabilitation tax credit, a major heritage tourism initiative, legislation encouraging cities to enact historic preservation ordinances, and other measures. He serves on the National Trust for Historic Preservation's Board of Advisors.

Pick your battles.

- Establish a presence with your elected officials. This presence must be ongoing. People have a tendency to call for help only when the fire bell is ringing. They need to be working at building good relationships all the time, not just during an emergency.
- Create a public policy arm for your statewide historic preservation organization. We did this in Wisconsin and it worked well. A public policy task force should be constantly reviewing state legislation and its impacts on historic preservation.
- Pick your battles. Some fights are worth taking on; others are losers. Don't waste time fighting a battle you are sure to lose, a battle that could damage your long-term effectiveness.
- Develop a realistic agenda and compromise when it makes sense to do so. In Wisconsin we originally proposed that all municipalities be required to enact historic preservation ordinances. This requirement was later compromised to apply only to cities with properties on the National Register of Historic Places. Although we didn't get everything we wanted, we still achieved a victory by having dozens of new communities pass preservation ordinances.
- Get involved in political campaigns. It's more than simply contributing money to a candidate. You can equalize the influence of political action committees (PACs) in other ways. It can be something as simple as writing a letter to the editor. As a legislator, I often begin reading the paper by looking at the letters to the editor. Writ-

The historic Lit Brothers building in downtown Philadelphia. Once threatened, this landmark has been restored thanks to the advocacy and efforts of many historic preservationists.

ing a letter costs nothing and is easy to do. Five or ten letters in the local paper saying that Senator Joe Smith cares about the community mean a lot to a legislator. Or, recognize your legislator with a plaque or appropriate recognition. One state representative once told me, "I'd rather have a plaque than a $300 contribution."

- Educate your state and local officials about historic preservation. Don't assume that they know everything. They have dozens of other issues on their plate. When I got into this field, two local historic preservationists took me on a tour of LaCrosse, Wisconsin, where they showed me successful preservation projects as well as barriers to preservation. They talked about the economic benefits of preservation. Showing people real projects is very effective.

- Use visuals. In Wisconsin, we had tried for years to get legislation enacted that would ban sandblasting of historic buildings because this technique is so damaging to them. But we were getting nowhere until George Meyer, a preservationist with experience in rehabilitating historic buildings, came up with the idea of showing state legislators what sandblasting really meant. He had 132 bricks sandblasted. One half of each brick was sandblasted; the other half wasn't. He then had these bricks delivered in little boxes to all 132 members of the legislature. When the legislators opened the boxes and looked at the bricks, they immediately understood the issue for preservationists. The impact was phenomenal. People said, "Oh, now I see the problem with sandblasting." The ban then sailed through and the governor signed it.

Senator Brian Rude on the Value of Historic Preservation

THE HISTORIC PRESERVATION MOVEMENT is concerned about the livability of communities and the revitalization of downtowns as well as the preservation of historic resources. When I look at the Main Street program in Viroqua, Wisconsin, where I was born, I see that the people there took what had been a dying area and turned it into a vibrant, attractive downtown. Efforts like these make people feel good about their community. They unite people in a way that nothing else does. A downtown is the core of a community. It's what keeps people together.

When people unite around historic preservation, it improves their quality of life, but it also improves the economy. If people see vibrancy in a downtown or a neighborhood, they feel better about investing in it. Having seen what citizens did in Viroqua, I would be inclined to start a small business there before I'd invest elsewhere. It is better to put money into an attractive area that has developed a good client base.

I believe in historic preservation because I have a great love of things that are old. I respect tradition and many of the values it embodies. I recognize that not everything old is worth saving, but a lot of things are. We must remember, however, that ultimately, historic preservation must make good economic sense or it cannot succeed. Preservation projects must be able to stand on their own. Rehabilitation tax credits and other preservation incentives are helpful, but a historic preservation project must be fundamentally viable. We cannot let romance dictate our decisions.

What we are trying to do in state government is to give citizens the tools they need to make historic preservation happen in their communities.

Betty M. Chronic

Betty Chronic is a leader in the Colorado historic preservation movement and has lobbied in a volunteer capacity for Colorado's rehabilitation income tax credit and other measures. She has formerly served as a state legislator, director of the Colorado Elections and Licensing Division, Department of State, chair of the City of Boulder Landmarks Preservation Advisory Board, and president of Historic Boulder. She has also been a charter board member and president of the Colorado Mental Health Association. She now serves as the regional chair for the National Trust for Historic Preservation's Board of Advisors.

- Establish a good relationship with your state legislators. This is best done in the home district. Appear at public events. Let your representatives know when they've done something right. Send thank-you notes when appropriate. Work to establish a sense that you and your organization are trustworthy and credible. Try to build this relationship before the legislative session begins. If the session has already started, it is too late.

- Have a sense of humor and be able to accept defeat. On one occasion following our loss of a major battle, I dressed in black the next day to attend the final demise of the bill. I told my legislator friends that I was attending a wake. They laughed. This is important in politics. We must never come on as adversaries.

- Use common courtesy. This is one of the things that is missing the most from some of the contacts that I witness at the state capitol. Be patient and understand that state legislators are busy people with a lot on their minds.

- Be truthful, even if it hurts. Level with people. The lobbyists whom legislators look to for information are the ones who are credible and who tell the truth.

Level with people.

James Mann

James Mann is director of the National Trust for Historic Preservation's Midwest Regional Office in Chicago and Associate General Counsel for State Policy. He has extensive experience in state policy advocacy and land-use planning issues. He represented both local governments and private parties over the past 15 years on legislative issues and served as general counsel to the Metropolitan Planning Council, the Chicago area's most influential private regional planning organization. He has been active with various community development projects, both as a volunteer and staff.

- Make historic preservation a mainstream issue. Unless preservation is taken seriously, as seriously as transportation or economic development, it will not have a seat at the table where the important policy decisions are made. Preservation issues should not be put off onto the margins, but rather should be structured in such a way as to gain the support and attention of the state legislative and executive branch leadership.

- Figure out which of the various preservation incentives or policies would work best for your state. Do the hard economic analysis to determine which ones would provide the biggest payback. Then go after these incentives or policies in the order of their importance.

- Achieve early and symbolic victories to energize the preservation troops and build morale. Winning is important to building the capacity of organizations and to their future.

The utilities are just one example of a good non-traditional ally.

- Identify allies with whom you can work to achieve your policy goals. After identifying traditional allies, look for non-traditional allies as well, groups with which you may not have worked in the past but who might share your concerns about a particular problem. Public utility companies are an example of a non-traditional ally that clearly has interests in common with historic preservation, but with which preservationists have rarely worked in the past. Like historic preservation, the utility companies are hurt by urban sprawl. The utilities are just one example of a good non-traditional ally.

APPENDIX

Helpful Publications

Preservation Law Reporter

The best source of current developments on historic preservation law and policy is the *Preservation Law Reporter* *(PLR)*, a monthly publication available through the Law Department of the National Trust for Historic Preservation. Edited by Julia Hatch Miller, Esq., *PLR* covers recent court decisions and legislative developments at the state as well as the federal and local levels of government. *PLR* also provides special reports on critical issues. Under separate cover, the *PLR* publishes a reference volume that provides a comprehensive summary of statutory materials, tax credit information, sample easements, and model ordinance provisions. Three reports of particular interest to those concerned with state policy include:

- "Takings and Preservation: A Survey of State Decisions," *PLR*, Vol. 10, Nos. 7–8, July/August 1991.
- "Special Analysis: Owner Consent Provisions in Historic Preservation Ordinances: Are They Legal?" *PLR*, Volume 10, Number 2, February 1991.
- "Coordination of Historic Preservation and Land-Use Controls: New Directions in Historic Preservation Regulation," Volume 5, No. 4, Winter 1986/87.

The *PLR* is available by subscription ($90 for regular subscribers; $50 for members of the National Trust for Historic Preservation's Forum Program, the National Main Street Network, or staff or board members of a local preservation commission). Contact the NTHP at 1785 Massachusetts Ave., N.W., Washington, D. C. 20036. Tel: 202/588-6000 or -6035.

Information Series on Historic Preservation Issues

The National Trust for Historic Preservation regularly publishes a series of special reports on various preservation issues. *"Information Series"* reports of special relevance to those involved in state policymaking include the following:

- *1996 Directory of Private Nonprofit Statewide Preservation Organizations* (Order No. 2181)
- *Safety, Building Codes and Historic Preservation* (Order No. 2157)
- *Successful State Advocacy*, with case studies from Colorado, Florida, Kansas and Wisconsin (Order No. 2152)
- *Regional Heritage Areas: Approaches to Sustainable Development* (Order No. 2188)
- *Preservation Revolving Funds* (Order No. 2178)
- *Coping with Contamination: A Primer for Preservationists* (Order No. 2170)
- *The Economics of Rehabilitation* (Order No. 2153)
- *Establishing an Easement Program to Protect Historic, Scenic and Natural Resources* (Order No. 2125)
- *A Survey of State Statutes Protecting Archaeological Resources* (Order No. 2ARC)
- *Focus on Property Rights* (Order No. 2V74)
- *The Protection of America's Scenic Byways* (Order No. 2168, 1996)

For any of these reports, contact the National Trust for Historic Preservation.

Special Reports on Planning Issues

The American Planning Association (122 South Michigan Ave., Chicago, Ill. 60603. Tel: 312/431-9100) publishes a series of reports known as "Planning Advisory Service reports (PASs)." Among the PAS reports of special relevance to those in state policymaking are:

- Transferable Development Rights Programs: TDRs and the Real Estate Marketplace. May 1987. No. 401
- Preparing a Historic Preservation Plan. March 1994. No. 450
- Preparing a Historic Preservation Ordinance. February 1983. No. 374
- Aesthetics and Land Use Controls. December 1986. No. 399
- Innovative Tools for Historic Preservation. Sept. 1992. No. 438

Books and Other Publications

Arendt, Randall, *Rural by Design*. (Chicago: Planners Press/American Planning Association, 1994).

Beaumont, Constance E., *How Superstore Sprawl Can Harm Communities—And What Citizens Can Do About It* (Washington, D.C.: National Trust for Historic Preservation, 1994).

Carlson, Daniel; Lisa Wormser; and Cy Ulberg, *At Road's End: Transportation and Land Use Choices for Communities* (Covelo, Calif.: Island Press, 1995).

Chan, I Mei, *Building On the Past/Traveling to the Future* (Washington, D.C.: Federal Highway Administration and National Trust for Historic Preservation, 1995).

Dawson, Alexandar D., "Transportation Enhancements Under ISTEA: A Once-In-A-Lifetime Chance for Planners," *Zoning and Planning Law Report*, Vol. 19, No. 1. January 1996.

Davis, Margaret, *State Systems for Designating Historic Properties and the Results of Designation* (Washington, D.C.: National Trust for Historic Preservation/Public Policy Department, 1987).

DeGrove, John M., *Land Growth and Politics* (Chicago: Planners Press/American Planning Association, 1984).

Diamond, Henry L., and Patrick E. Noonan, *Land Use in America* (Washington, D.C. & Covelo, Calif.: Island Press, 1996).

Diehl, Janet, et al., *The Conservation Easement Handbook* (San Francisco: Trust for Public Land, 1988).

Downs, Anthony, *New Visions for Metropolitan America* (Washington, D.C.: The Brookings Institution, 1994).

Duerksen, Christopher J., et al., *A Handbook on Historic Preservation Law* (Washington, D.C.: The Conservation Foundation and the National Center for Preservation Law, 1983). [NB: Out of print but often available in libraries of state and local historic preservation organizations. See statewide organizations listed in Appendix B.]

Duerksen, Christopher J., and Richard J. Roddewig, *Takings Law in Plain English* (Washington, D.C.: National Trust for Historic Preservation/Clarion Associates, 1994).

Harr, Charles M., and Jerold S. Kayden, *Landmark Justice: The Influence of William J. Brennan on America's Communities* (Washington, D.C.: Preservation Press/National Trust for Historic Preservation, 1989).

Harr, Charles M., and Jerold S. Kayden, *Zoning and the American Dream: Promises Still to Keep* (Chicago: Planners Press/American Planning Association, 1989).

Herr, Philip B., *Saving Place: A Guide and Report Card for Protecting Community Character.* (Boston: Northeast Regional Office, National Trust for Historic Preservation, 1991).

Hylton, Thomas, *Save Our Land, Save Our Towns* (Harrisburg, Pa.: Richly Beautiful Books, 1995). Also available through Preservation Pennsylvania (See Appendix B).

Jackson, Kenneth T., *The Crabgrass Frontier* (New York & Oxford: Oxford University Press, 1985).

Kunstler, James Howard, *The Geography of Nowhere* (New York: Simon & Schuster, 1993).

Langdon, Philip, *A Better Place to Live: Reshaping the American Suburb* (Amherst: University of Massachusetts Press, 1994).

Marriott, Paul Daniel, *Saving Historic Roads: A Guidebook for Their Identification, Preservation, and Management* (Washington, D.C.: National Trust for Historic Preservation, 1996).

Myers, Phyllis, *Lessons from the States: Strengthening Land Conservation Programs through Grants to Nonprofit Land Trusts* (Washington, D.C.: Land Trust Alliance 1992).

Nelessen, Anton Clarence, *Visions for A New American Dream* (Chicago: Planners Press/American Planning Association, 1994).

Rypkema, Donovan D., *The Economics of Historic Preservation* (Washington, D.C.: National Trust for Historic Preservation, 1995).

Rypkema, Donovan D., *Virginia's Economy and Historic Preservation: The Impact of Preservation on Jobs, Business and Community* (Staunton, Va.: Preservation Alliance of Virginia, 1995).

Slater, Philip, *The Pursuit of Loneliness* (Boston: Beacon Press, 1970 [revised 1976]).

Stipe, Robert E., and Antoinette J. Lee, *The American Mosaic: Preserving A Nation's Heritage* (Washington, D.C.: US/ICOMOS, 1987).

Stokes, Samuel N., A. Elzabeth Watson, and Shelley S. Mastran, *Saving America's Countryside*, second ed. (Baltimore: The Johns Hopkins University Press, forthcoming [1997]).

Take Back Your Streets: How to Protect Communities from Asphalt and Traffic (Boston: Conservation Law Foundation, 1995).

U.S. Department of Transportation, Federal Highway Administration. *Community Guide to Planning and Managing a Scenic Byway.* [Order from the National Scenic Byways Clearinghouse, 1440 New York Ave., N.W., Suite 202, Washington, D.C. 20005 (1-800-4BYWAYS).]

White, Bradford J., and Paul W. Edmondson, *Procedural Due Process in Plain English: A Guide for Preservation Commissions* (Washington, D.C.: National Trust for Historic Preservation, 1994).

Wick, Jim, *A State Highway Project in Your Town? Your Role and Rights: A Primer for Citizens and Public Officials.* Available from Preservation Trust of Vermont, 104 Church St., Burlington, Vermont 05401. ($10 plus $3 for shipping)

Young, Dwight, *Alternatives to Sprawl* (Cambridge, Mass.: Lincoln Institute of Land Policy, 1995). Also available from the National Trust for Historic Preservation and The Brookings Institution in Washington, D.C.

Helpful Organizations

NATIONAL TRUST FOR HISTORIC PRESERVATION

Headquarters:
1785 Massachusetts Avenue, N.W.
Washington, DC 20036
(202) 588-6000

Regional Offices:

Mid-Atlantic Regional Office
One Penn Center at Suburban Station
1617 John F. Kennedy Boulevard, Suite 1520
Philadelphia, PA 19103-1815
(215) 568-8162
DE, MD, NJ, PA, PR, VI, VA, DC, WV

Midwest Regional Office
53 West Jackson Boulevard, Suite 1135
Chicago, IL 60604
(312) 939-5547
IL, IN, IA, MI, MN, MO, OH, WI

Mountains/Plains Regional Office
910 16th Street, Suite 1100
Denver, CO 80202
(303) 623-1504
CO, KS, MT, NE, ND, SD, WY

Northeast Regional Office
Seven Faneuil Hall Marketplace
4th Floor
Boston, MA 02109
(617) 523-0885
CT, ME, MA, NH, NY, RI, VT

Southern Regional Office
456 King Street
Charleston, SC 29403
(803) 722-8552
AL, AR, FL, GA, KY, LA, MS, NC, SC, TN

Western Regional Office
One Sutter Street
Suite 707
San Francisco, CA 94104
(415) 956-0610
AK, AZ, CA, Guam, HI, ID, Micronesia, NV, OR, UT, WA

Southwest Regional Office
500 Main Street
Suite 606
Fort Worth, TX 76102
(817) 332-4398
TX, NM, OK

National Main Street Center
1785 Massachusetts Avenue, N.W.
Washington, DC 20036
(202) 588-6219

NATIONAL ORGANIZATIONS

Advisory Council on Historic Preservation
1100 Pennsylvania Avenue, N.W., Suite 809
Washington, DC 20004
(202) 606-8503

American Farmland Trust
1920 N Street, N.W., Suite 400
Washington, DC 20036
(202) 659-5170

American Institute of Architects
1735 New York Avenue, N.W.
Washington, DC 20006
(202) 626-7300

American Planning Association
122 S. Michigan Avenue
Chicago, IL 60603
(312) 955-9100

American Society of Landscape Architects
4401 Connecticut Avenue, N.W.
Washington, DC 20008-2302
(202) 686-2752

Civil War Trust
2101 Wilson Boulevard, Suite 1120
Arlington, VA 22201
(703) 516-4944

Conservation Fund
1800 North Kent Street, Suite 1120
Arlington, VA 22209
(703) 522-8008

Countryside Institute
Glynwood Center
P.O. Box 157
Cold Spring, NY 10517
(914) 265-3338 and
(202) 234-4773

Land Trust Alliance
1319 F Street, N.W., Suite 501
Washington, DC 20004
(202) 638-4725

Lincoln Institute of Land Policy
113 Brattle Street
Cambridge, MA 02138
(617) 661-3016

National Alliance of Preservation Commissions
c/o School of Environmental Design
609 Caldwell Hall
University of Georgia
Athens, GA 30602
(706) 542-4731

**National Conference of State
Historic Preservation Officers**
444 North Capitol Street, N.W., Suite 342
Washington, DC 20001-1512
(202) 624-5465

National Conference of State Legislatures
1560 Broadway, Suite 700
Denver, CO 80202
(303) 830-2200

National Park Service
18th and C Streets, N.W.
Washington, DC 20840
(202) 208-4621

National Register of Historic Places
Interagency Resources Division
National Park Service
U.S. Department of the Interior
P.O. Box 37127
Washington, DC 20013-7127
(202) 343-9536

Preservation Action
1350 Connecticut Avenue, N.W., Suite 401
Washington, DC 20036
(202) 659-0915

Rails-to-Trails Conservancy
1400 16th Street, N.W., Suite 300
Washington, DC 20036
(202) 797-5400

Scenic America
21 Dupont Circle, N.W.
Washington, DC 20036
(202) 833-4300

Surface Transportation Policy Project (STPP)
1400 16th Street, N.W., Suite 300
Washington, DC 20036
(202) 939-3470

ENVIRONMENTAL ORGANIZATIONS

Environmental Defense Fund
257 Park Avenue South
New York, NY 10010
(212) 505-2122

National Audubon Society
700 Broadway
New York, NY 10003-9501
(212) 979-3088

National Wildlife Federation
1400 16th Street, N.W.
Washington, DC 20036
(202) 797-6800

Natural Resources Defense Council
40 West 20th Street
New York, NY 10011
(212) 727-2700

Sierra Club
730 Polk Street
San Francisco, CA 94109
(415) 776-2211

The Wilderness Society
900 17th Street, N.W.
Washington, DC 20006
(202) 833-2300

Trust for Public Land
116 New Montgomery Street
4th Floor
San Francisco, CA 94105
(415) 495-4014

STATE MAIN STREET COORDINATORS

Alabama
The Alabama Historical Commission
468 South Perry Street
Montgomery, AL 36130-0900
(334) 242-3184

Arizona
Arizona Main Street Program
Department of Commerce & Community Development
3800 North Central
Suite 1400
Phoenix, AZ 85012
(602) 280-1350

Arkansas
Main Street Arkansas
1500 Tower Building
323 Center Street
Little Rock, AR 72201
(501) 324-9880

California
California Main Street Program
California Trade & Commerce Agency
801 K Street, Suite 1700
Sacramento, CA 95814
(916) 322-3536

Connecticut
Connecticut Main Street Program
Northeast Utilities Service Company
107 Selden Street
Berlin, CT 06037
(203) 665-5168

Delaware
Delaware Main Street Program
Delaware Development Office
P.O. Box 1401
Dover, DE 19903
(302) 739-4271

Florida
Florida Main Street Program
Bureau of Historic Preservation
Division of Historical Resources
500 South Bronough Street
4th Floor, Rm. 411
Tallahassee, FL 32399-0250
(904) 487-2333

Georgia
Georgia Main Street Program
Center for Business and Economic Development
Georgia Southwestern College
Americus, GA 31709
(912) 931-2124

Hawaii
Main Street Hawaii
Department of Land and Natural Resources
33 South King Street, 6th Floor
Honolulu, HI 96813
(808) 587-0003

Illinois
Illinois Main Street Program
612 Stratton Building
Springfield, IL 62706
(217) 524-6869

Illinois Main Street Program
Office of Lieutenant Governor
100 W. Randolph, Suite 15-200
Chicago, IL 60601
(312) 814-8760

Indiana
Indiana Main Street Program
Indiana Department of Commerce
One North Capitol
Suite 700
Indianapolis, IN 46204-2288
(317) 232-8912

Iowa
Main Street Iowa
Iowa Department of Economic Development
200 East Grand Avenue
Des Moines, IA 50309
(515) 242-4733

Kansas
Kansas Main Street Program
Kansas Department of Commerce and Housing
700 S.W. Harrison Street
Suite 1300
Topeka, KS 66603-3712
(913) 296-3485

Kentucky
Kentucky Main Street Program
Kentucky Heritage Council
300 Washington Street
Frankfort, KY 40601
(502) 564-7005

Louisiana
Louisiana Main Street Program
Division of Historic Preservation
P.O. Box 44247
Baton Rouge, LA 70804
(504) 342-8160

Maryland
Maryland Main Street Center
100 Community Place, CAA
Crownsville, MD 21032
(410) 514-7265

Massachusetts
Downtown Revitalization Program
The Commonwealth of Massachusetts
Executive Office of Communities & Development
100 Cambridge Street
Boston, MA 02202
(617) 727-7180 ext. 426

Mississippi
Mississippi Downtown Development Association
P.O. Box 2719
Jackson, MS 39207
(601) 948-0404

Missouri
Missouri Main Street Program
Missouri Department of Economic Development
P.O. Box 118
Truman Bldg., Rm. 770
Jefferson City, MO 65102
(314) 751-7939

New Hampshire
New Hampshire Main Street Center
NH Community Development Authority
14 Dixon Avenue
Suite 2170
Concord, NH 03301
(603) 226-2170

Nebraska
Nebraska Main Street Program
University of Nebraska
309 Architecture Hall
Lincoln, NE 68588-0149
(402) 472-0718

New Jersey
Main Street New Jersey
New Jersey Department of Community Affairs
CN 806
Trenton, NJ 08625
(609) 633-9769

New Mexico
New Mexico Main Street Program
Economic Development and Tourism
1100 St. Francis Drive
Santa Fe, NM 87503
(505) 827-0200

New York Main Street Alliance*
35 W. Main Street
Mt. Kisco, NY 10549
(914) 242-5950
*Not part of National Trust's Main Street Program

North Carolina
North Carolina Main Street Center
NC Department of Commerce
Div. of Community Assistance
P.O. Box 12600
Raleigh, NC 27605-2600
(919) 733-2850

Oklahoma
Oklahoma Main Street Program
Oklahoma Department of Commerce
P.O. Box 26980
Oklahoma City, OK 73126-0980
(405) 841-5115

Oregon
Oregon Main Street Program
Oregon Downtown Development Association
Livable Oregon, Inc.
921 S.W. Morrison Street
Suite 508
Portland, OR 97205
(503) 222-2182

Pennsylvania
Pennsylvania Main Street Program
Department of Community Affairs
504 Forum Building
Harrisburg, PA 17120
(717) 772-1578

Puerto Rico
Corazon del Pueblo
P.O. Box S 4275
San Juan, PR 00905
(809) 728-5585

South Carolina
South Carolina Downtown Development Assoc.
P.O. Box 11637
Columbia, SC 29211
(803) 256-3560

Tennessee
Tennessee Main Street Project
Department of Economic and Community Development
320 6th Avenue, North
6th floor
Nashville, TN 37243-0405
(615) 741-2373

Texas
Texas Main Street Center
Texas Historical Commission
P.O. Box 12276
Austin, TX 78711
(512) 463-6092

Utah
Utah Main Street Program
Department of Community & Economic Development
324 South State Street
Suite 500
Salt Lake City, UT 84111
(801) 538-8638

Vermont
Vermont Downtown Program
Department of Housing and Community Affairs
109 State Street
Montpelier, VT 05609-0501
(802) 828-3217

Vermont Downtown Program
Department for Historic Preservation
135 State Street, Drawer 33
Montpelier, VT 05633-1201
(802) 828-3226

Virginia
Virginia Main Street Program
Department of Housing and Community Development
Third Floor
501 North Second Street
Richmond, VA 23219
(804) 371-7030

Washington
Washington Downtown Revitalization
P.O. Box 48300
Olympia, WA 98504-8300
(360) 586-8977

West Virginia
West Virginia Main Street Program
Capitol Complex, Building B531
Charleston, WV 25305
(304) 558-0121

Wisconsin
Wisconsin Main Street Program
Department of Development
P.O. Box 7970
Madison, WI 53707
(608) 267-3855

Wyoming
State of Wyoming
Department of Commerce
Division of Economic and Community Development
517 West Loucks Street
Sheridan, WY 82801
(307) 777-6436

STATE HISTORIC PRESERVATION OFFICES

Alabama
Alabama Historic Commission
468 South Perry Street
Montgomery, AL 36130-0900
(334) 242-3184

Alaska
Division of Parks
Office of Hist. & Archeology
3601 C Street, #1278
Anchorage, AK 99503-5921
(907) 269-8721

Arizona
Arizona State Parks
1300 West Washington
Phoenix, AZ 85007
(602) 542-4174

Arkansas
Arkansas Historic Preservation Program
323 Center Street, Suite 1500
Little Rock, AR 72201
(501) 324-9880

California
Office of Historic Preservation
Department of Parks & Recreation
P O. Box 942896
Sacramento CA 94296-0001
(916) 653-6624

Colorado
Colorado Historical Society
1300 Broadway
Denver, CO 80203
(303) 866-3395

Connecticut
Connecticut Historical Commission
59 So. Prospect Street
Hartford, CT 06106
(203) 566-3005

Delaware
Division of Historical and Cultural Affairs
Hall of Records
P.O. Box 1401
Dover, DE 19903
(302) 739-5313

District of Columbia
Historic Preservation Division
614 H Street, N.W.
Suite 305
Washington, DC 20001
(202) 727-7120

Florida
Division of Historic Rscs,
Department of State
R.A. Gray Building
500 S. Bronough Street
Tallahassee, FL 32399-0250
(904) 487-2333

Georgia
Historic Preservation Division
57 Forsyth Street, N.W.
Suite 500
Atlanta, GA 30303
(404) 656-2840

Guam
Guam Historic Preservation Office
Department of Parks & Recreation
490 Chasan Palasyo
Agana Heights, Guam 96919
011-671-477-9620

Hawaii
Department of Land & Natural Resources
P.O. Box 621
Honolulu, Hl 96809
(808) 587-0401

Idaho
Idaho State Historical Society
1109 Main Street
Suite 250
Boise, ID 83702-5642
(208) 334-2682

Illinois
Illinois Historic Preservation Agency
1 Old State Capitol Plaza
Springfield, IL 62701-1512
(217) 785-1153

Indiana
Department of Natural Resources
402 West Washington Street
Indiana Govt. Center South, Room W256
Indianapolis, IN 46204
(317) 232-4020

Iowa
State Historical Society of Iowa
Capitol Complex
East 6th and Locust Street
Des Moines, IA 50319
(515) 281-8824

Kansas
Kansas State Historical Society
6425 Southwest 6th Avenue
Topeka, KS 66615-1099
(913) 272-8681 x.205

Kentucky
Kentucky Heritage Council
300 Washington Street
Frankfort, KY 40601
(502) 564-7005

Louisiana
Department of Culture
Recreation & Tourism
P.O. Box 44247
Baton Rouge, LA 70804
(504) 342-8200

Maine
Maine Historic Preservation Commission
55 Capitol Street, Station 65
Augusta, ME 04333
(207) 287-2132

Marshall Islands, Republic of the
Secretary of Interior and Outer Islands Affairs
P.O. Box #1454, Majuro Atoll
Republic of the Marshall Islands 96960
011-692-625-3413

Maryland
Director of Historical and Cultural Programs
Department of Housing and Community Development
100 Community Place, Third Floor
Crownsville, MD 21032-2023
(410) 514-7600

Massachusetts
Massachusetts Historical Commission
The Massachusetts Archives Building
220 Morrissey Boulevard
Boston, MA 02125
(617) 727-8470

Michigan
State Historic Preservation Office
Michigan Historical Center
717 West Allegan Street
Lansing, MI 48918
(517) 373-0511

Micronesia, Federated State of
Office of Administrative Services
Div. of Archives and Historic Preservation
FSM National Government
P.O. Box PS 35
Palikir, Pohnpei, FSM 96941
011-691-320-2343

Minnesota
Minnesota Historical Society
345 Kellogg Boulevard West
St. Paul, MN 55102-1906
(612) 296-2747

Mississippi
Mississippi Department of Archives & History
P.O. Box 571
Jackson, MS 39205-0571
(601) 359-6850

Missouri
State Department of Natural Resources
205 Jefferson
P.O. Box 176
Jefferson City, MO 65102
(573) 751-4422

Montana
State Historic Preservation Office
1410 8th Avenue
P.O. Box 201202
Helena, MT 59620-1202
(406) 444-7715

Nebraska
Nebraska State Historical Society
P.O. Box 82554
Lincoln, NE 68501
(402) 471-4787

Nevada
Historic Preservation Office
101 South Stewart Street
Capitol Complex
Carson City, NV 89710
(702) 687-6360

New Hampshire
State Historic Preservation Office
P.O. Box 2043
Concord, NH 03302-2043
(603) 271-6435

New Jersey
Dept. of Environmental Protection
CN-402, 401 East State Street
Trenton, NJ 08625
(609) 292-2885

New Mexico
Historic Preservation Division
Office of Cultural Affairs
228 East Palace Avenue
Santa Fe, NM 87503
(505) 827-6320

New York
Parks, Recreation & Historic Preservation
Agency Building #1, Empire State Plaza
Albany, NY 12238
(518) 474-0443

North Carolina
Division of Archives & History
109 East Jones Street
Raleigh, NC 27601-2807
(919) 733-7305

North Dakota
State Historical Society of North Dakota
612 E. Boulevard Avenue
Bismarck, ND 58505
(701) 328-2667

**Northern Mariana Islands,
Commonwealth of the**
Dept of Community & Cultural Affairs
Northern Mariana Islands
Saipan, Mariana Islands 96950
011-670-664-2120

Ohio
Ohio Historic Preservation Office
567 East Hudson Street
Columbus, OH 43211-1030
(614) 297-2470

Oklahoma
Oklahoma Historical Society
2100 North Lincoln Boulevard
Oklahoma City, OK 73105
(405) 521-2491

Oregon
State Parks & Recreation Department
1115 Commercial Street, NE
Salem, OR 97310-1001
(503) 378-5019

Palau, Republic of
Ministry of Community & Cultural Affairs
P.O. Box 100
Koror, Republic of Palau 96940

Pennsylvania
Pennsylvania Historical & Museum Comm.
P.O. Box 1026
Harrisburg, PA 17108
(717) 787-2891

Puerto Rico, Commonwealth of
Office of Historic Preservation
Box 82, La Fortaleza
San Juan, Puerto Rico 00901
(809) 721-2676

Rhode Island
Rhode Island Historical Preservation Comm.
Old State House, 150 Benefit Street
Providence, RI 02903
(401) 277-2678

South Carolina
Department of Archives & History
P.O. Box 11669
Columbia, SC 29211
(803) 734-8609

South Dakota
State Historical Preservation Center
Cultural Heritage Center
900 Governors Drive
Pierre, SD 57069
(605) 773-3458

Tennessee
Dept of Environment and Conservation
401 Church Street, L&C Tower 21st Flr
Nashville, TN 37243-0435
(615) 532-0109

Texas
Texas Historical Commission
P.O. Box 12276
Austin, TX 78711-2276
(512) 463-6100

Utah
Utah State Historical Society
300 Rio Grande
Salt Lake City, UT 84101
(801) 533-3500

Vermont
Vermont Division of Historic Preservation
135 State Street, Drawer 33
Montpelier, VT 05633-1201
(802) 828-3056

Virgin Islands
Dept of Planning and Natural Resources
Suite 231, Nisky Center, No. 4SA Estate Nisky
St. Thomas USVI 00802
(809) 774-3320

Virginia
Department of Historic Resources
221 Governor Street
Richmond, VA 23219
(804) 786-3143

Washington
Ofc. of Archeology & Historic Preservation
111 West 21st Avenue, KL-11
Olympia, WA 98504
(360) 753-4011

West Virginia
WV Division of Culture & History
Historic Preservation Office
1900 Kanawha Boulevard East
Charleston, WV 25305-0300
(304) 558-0220

Wisconsin
State Historical Society of Wisconsin
816 State Street
Madison WI 53706
(608) 264-6500

Wyoming
Wyoming State Hist. Pres. Ofc.
2301 Central Avenue, 4th Floor
Cheyenne, WY 82002
(307) 777-7697

STATEWIDE PRESERVATION ORGANIZATIONS

Alabama
Alabama Preservation Alliance
P.O. Box 2228
Montgomery, Alabama 36102
(334)434-7281

Alaska
Alaska Association for Historic Preservation
Old City Hall
524 W. 4th Avenue, Suite 203
Anchorage, Alaska 99501
(907) 333-4746

Arizona
Arizona Preservation Foundation
P.O. Box 13492
Phoenix, Arizona 85002
(602) 280-1350

Arkansas
Historic Preservation Alliance of Arkansas
P.O. Box 305
Little Rock, Arkansas 72203
(501) 372-4757

California
California Preservation Foundation
405 14th Street, Suite 1010
Oakland, California 94612
(510) 763-0972

Colorado
Colorado Preservation, Inc.
P.O. Box 843
Denver, Colorado 80201-0843
(303) 893-4260

Connecticut
Connecticut Trust for Historic Preservation
940 Whitney Avenue
Hamden, Connecticut 06517-4002
(203) 562-6312

Delaware
Preservation Delaware
Goodstay Center
2600 Pennsylvania Avenue
Wilmington, Delaware 19806
(302) 651-9617

District of Columbia
D.C. Preservation League
1511 K Street, N.W., Suite 739
Washington, D.C. 20005
(202) 737-1519

Florida
Florida Trust for Historic Preservation
P.O. Box 11206
Tallahassee, Florida 32302
(904) 224-8128

Georgia
Georgia Trust for Historic Preservation
1516 Peachtree Street, N.W.
Atlanta, Georgia 30309
(404) 881-9980

Hawaii
Historic Hawai'i Foundation
P.O. Box 1658
Honolulu, Hawaii 96806
(808) 523-2900

Idaho
Idaho Historic Preservation Council
P.O. Box 1495
Boise, Idaho 83701
(208) 386-9124

Illinois
Landmarks Preservation Council of Illinois
53 West Jackson Boulevard, Suite 752
Chicago, Illinois 60604
(312) 922-1742

Indiana
Historic Landmarks Foundation of Indiana
340 West Michigan Street
Indianapolis, Indiana 46202-3204
(317) 639-4534

Iowa
Iowa Historic Preservation Alliance
P.O. Box 814
Mount Pleasant, Iowa 52641-0814
(319) 292-4593

Kansas
Kansas Preservation Alliance
P.O. Box 129
Ottawa, KS 66067-0129
(913) 242-9561

Kentucky
Commonwealth Preservation Advocates, Inc.
P.O. Box 387
Frankfort, Kentucky 40602-0378
(502) 926-4444

Louisiana
Louisiana Preservation Alliance
P.O. Box 1587
Baton Rouge, Louisiana 70821
(504) 928-9304

Maine
Maine Citizens for Historic Preservation
P.O. Box 1198
Portland, Maine 04104
(207) 775-3652

Maryland
Preservation Maryland
24 West Saratoga Street
Baltimore, Maryland 21201
(410) 685-2886

Maryland Association of Historic District Commissions
2801 Barker Street
Silver Spring, Maryland 20910
(301) 495-7340

Massachusetts
Historic Massachusetts, Inc.
45 School Street
Boston, Massachusetts 02108
(617) 723-3383

Michigan
Michigan Historic Preservation Network
P.O. Box 398
Clarkston, Michigan 48347
(810) 625-8181

Minnesota
Preservation Alliance of Minnesota
International Market Square
275 Market Street, Suite 54
Minneapolis, Minnesota 55405-1621
(612) 338-6763

Mississippi
Mississippi Heritage Trust
P.O. Box 577
Jackson, Mississippi 39205-0577
(601) 354-0200

Missouri
Missouri Alliance for Historic Preservation
P.O. Box 895
Jefferson City, Missouri 65102
(314) 635-6877

Montana
Montana Preservation Alliance
P.O. Box 1872
Bozeman, Montana 59771-1872
(406) 585-9551

Nebraska
Nebraska Preservation Council, Inc.
2245 A Street
Lincoln, Nebraska 68502
(402) 438-5979

Nevada
<NONE>

New Hampshire
Inherit New Hampshire, Inc.
P.O. Box 268
Concord, New Hampshire 03302-0268
(603) 224-2281

New Jersey
Preservation New Jersey, Inc.
The Proprietary House
149 Kearny Avenue, 2nd Floor
Perth Amboy, New Jersey 08861-4700
(908) 442-1100

New Jersey Historic Trust
CN 404, 506-508 East State Street
Trenton, New Jersey 08625
(609) 984-0473

New Mexico
New Mexico Preservation Heritage Alliance
1677 Cerro Gordo Road
Santa Fe, New Mexico 87501
(505) 983-2645

New York
Preservation League of New York State
44 Central Avenue
Albany, New York 12206-3002
(518) 462-5658

Municipal Art Society
457 Madison Avenue
New York, New York 10022
(212) 935-3960

North Carolina
Preservation North Carolina
P.O. Box 27644
Raleigh, North Carolina 27611-7644
(919) 832-3652

North Dakota
Preservation North Dakota
#221 Jamestown Mall
Jamestown, North Dakota 58401
(701) 251-1855

Ohio
Ohio Preservation Alliance, Inc.
65 Jefferson Avenue
Columbus, Ohio 43215
(614) 221-0227

Oklahoma
Preservation Oklahoma, Inc.
P.O. Box 25043
Oklahoma City, Oklahoma 73125-0043
(405) 232-5747

Oregon
Historic Preservation League of Oregon
P.O. Box 40053
Portland, Oregon 97240
(503) 243-1923

Pennsylvania
Preservation Pennsylvania
257 North Street
Harrisburg, Pennsylvania 17101
(717) 234-2310

Puerto Rico
Sociedad para la Preservacion Historica de Puerto Rico
c/o Nestor Murray Irizarry
Casa Paoli
Calle Mayor 14
Ponce, Puerto Rico 00731
(809) 840-4115

Rhode Island
<NONE>

South Carolina
The Palmetto Trust for Historic Preservation
P.O. Box 12547
Columbia, South Carolina 29211
(803) 771-6132

South Dakota
Historic South Dakota Foundation
P.O. Box 2998
Rapid City, South Dakota 57709
(605) 394-6842

Tennessee
Association for the Preservation of Tennessee Antiquities
110 Leake Avenue
Nashville, Tennessee 37205
(615) 352-8247

Tennessee Heritage Alliance
Upper Cumberland Institute
Box 5183
Tennessee Tech University
Cookeville, Tennessee 38505
(615) 372-3338

Texas
Preservation Texas, Inc.
c/o Galveston Historical Foundation
2016 Strand
Galveston, Texas 77550
(409) 765-7834

Utah
Utah Heritage Foundation
Memorial House in Memory Grove Park
P.O. Box 28
Salt Lake City, Utah 84110-0028
(801) 533-0858

Vermont
Preservation Trust of Vermont
104 Church Street
Burlington, Vermont 05401
(802) 658-6647

Virgin Islands
St. Croix Landmarks Society
P.O. Box 2855
Frederiksted
St. Croix, Virgin Islands 00840
(809) 772-0598

St. Thomas Historical Trust
28 Havensight
St. Thomas, Virgin Islands 00802
(809) 776-3000

Virginia
Association for the Preservation of Virginia Antiquities
204 West Franklin Street
Richmond, Virginia 23220-5012
(804) 648-1889

Preservation Alliance of Virginia
P.O. Box 1407
Staunton, Virginia 24402-1407
(540) 886-4362

Washington
Washington Trust for Historic Preservation
204 First Avenue, South
Seattle, Washington 98104
(206) 624-7880

West Virginia
Preservation Alliance of West Virginia
P.O. Box 3371
Charleston, West Virginia 25333-3371
(304) 345-3707

Wisconsin
Wisconsin Trust for Historic Preservation
646 West Washington Avenue
Suite D
Madison, Wisconsin 53703
(608) 255-0348

Wyoming
<NONE>

NATIONAL GROWTH MANAGEMENT LEADERSHIP PROJECT

Suite 716, Willamette Building
534 SW Third Avenue
Portland, OR 97204
(503) 228-9462

PROJECT COORDINATING COMMITTEE:

Alabama
Cahaba River Society
2717 7th Avenue South
Suite 205
Birmingham, AL 35233
(205) 322-5326

California
Greenbelt Alliance
116 New Montgomery Street
Suite 640
San Francisco, CA 94105
(415) 543-4291

Colorado
Colorado Environmental Coalition
1000 Friends of Colorado
2323 20th Street
Boulder, CO 80304
(303) 443-5931

Florida
1000 Friends of Florida, Inc.
P.O. Box 5948
Tallahassee, FL 32314
(904) 222-6277

Georgia
The Georgia Conservancy
1776 Peachtree Street, N.W.
Suite 400 South
Atlanta, GA 30309
(404) 876-2900

Hawaii
Hawaii's Thousand Friends
305 Hanai Street, #282
Kaihua, HI 96734
(808) 262-0682

Illinois
Openlands Project
220 South State Street
Suite 1880
Chicago, IL 60604
(312) 427-4256

Kentucky
Bluegrass Tomorrow
465 East High Street
Suite 208
Lexington, KY 40507-1941
(606) 259-9829

Maine
Natural Resources Council of Maine
271 State Street
Augusta, ME 04330
(207) 622-3101

Maryland
Chesapeake Bay Foundation
162 Prince George Street
Annapolis, MD 21401
(410) 268-8816

Massachusetts
1000 Friends of Massachusetts
44 Bromfield Street
Room 615
Boston, MA 02108
(617) 338-6400

Minnesota
1000 Friends of Minnesota
2200 Fourth Street
White Bear Lake, MN 55110
(612) 653-0618

Montana
Greater Yellowstone Coalition
P.O. Box 1874
Bozeman, MT 59771
(406) 586-1593

New Jersey
New Jersey Future
204 West State Street
Trenton, NJ 08608
(201) 222-6800

New Mexico
1000 Friends of New Mexico
320 Galisteo Street
Suite 203
Santa Fe, NM 87501
(505) 983-3445

New York
New York Planning Federation
488 Broadway
Albany, NY 12207
(518) 432-4094

Land Trust Alliance of New York
R.R. 2, Box 13
Millbrook, NY 12545
(914) 677-0084

Open Space Institute
666 Broadway
New York, NY 10012
(212) 505-7480

North Carolina
Western North Carolina Alliance
P.O. Box 182
Asheville, NC 28802
(704) 258-8737

Ohio
EcoCity Cleveland
2841 Scarborough Road
Cleveland Heights, OH 44118
(216) 932-3007

Oregon
1000 Friends of Oregon
534 SW Third Avenue
Suite 300
Portland, OR 97204
(503) 497-1000

Pennsylvania
Pennylvania Environmental Council
1211 Chestnut Street
Suite 900
Philadelphia, PA 19107
(215) 563-0250

Rhode Island
Save the Bay, Inc.
434 Smith Street
Providence, RI 02908
(401) 272-3540

South Carolina
South Carolina Coastal Conservation League
P.O. Box 1765
Charleston, SC 29402-9940
(803) 723-8035

Vermont
Vermont Natural Resources Council
9 Bailey Avenue
Montpelier, VT 05602
(802) 223-2328

Virginia
Piedmont Environmental Council
28-C Main Street, Box 460
Warrenton, VA 22186
(540) 347-2334

Washington
1000 Friends of Washington
1305 4th Avenue
Suite 303
Seattle, WA 98101
(206) 343-0681

Anatomy of New Jersey's Grant and Loan Program

New Jersey's Historic Preservation Bond Program, discussed in Chapter 2, provides grants and loans for the rehabilitation or stabilization of historic sites and structures. Since its inception in 1988, the program has helped many organizations preserve and restore a wide variety of historic places.

With over eight years of experience in administering this grant-and-loan program, the New Jersey Historic Trust has ironed out the many kinks that inevitably arise in such an effort and has devised a system for weeding out incompetent from capable grantees. No program is perfect, including this one. But because the thinking behind New Jersey's Historic Preservation Bond Act program may benefit preservationists in other states, the program guidelines are summarized below.

What kind of help does the program offer?

The program awards matching grants on a competitive basis to assist in the rehabilitation or stabilization of designated historic sites and structures. Grants range from $20,000 to $1.25 million. The program also provides low-interest loans to help rescue imminently endangered historic places.

Who administers the program?

The New Jersey Historic Trust, a state-chartered, private nonprofit organization located in Trenton. The Historic Trust is "in but not of" the state Department of Environmental Protection and Energy.

Who can apply?

Units of state, county, and local government as well as private nonprofit organizations. Applicants must demonstrate that they have control over the property to be rehabilitated, either through possession of a fee-simple title or a lease. For public agencies, the lease must be for at least five years; for nonprofits, at least 20 years.

What criteria are used in selecting projects?

- relative importance of the historic resource and its physical condition. Only properties listed on, or determined eligible for, the State or National Register of Historic Places are eligible.
- visibility of the project to the public
- likelihood of the project's stimulating other preservation projects in the area
- benefits to the community as a whole
- project timetable and budget (are they realistic?)
- applicant's experience and qualifications
- geographic and ethnic diversity, as well as diversity of historic periods and resources

- applicant's ability to administer and finance the proposed project and to maintain the project once it is rehabilitated
- evidence of broad community support for the project. Each grant must be matched in cash. Other state funds may not be used for the match
- specific plans showing how the architectural and historic quality of a structure will be preserved
- public accessibility to the structure or site

What kinds of rehabilitation work can be funded?

Rehabilitation, stabilization, mechanical equipment improvements, building code compliance, and features to improve a building's accessibility to persons with disabilities. Up to 25 percent of a grant may be used for certain non-construction activities. These include architectural plans and specifications; engineering studies undertaken to ascertain whether it's feasible to save a building; and historic structure, landscape, archaeological and engineering reports, as well as signage.

Activities expressly prohibited include: property acquisition; new construction (unless it's minor and necessary, such as the replacement of missing decorative or structural elements); project administration; contingency reserves; charges in excess of the lowest bid on a project (unless the Historic Trust approves them); interest and finance charges; cost overruns; fundraising; lobbying; and routine building maintenance.

How does the state make sure historic structures are properly rehabilitated?

Applicants must submit evidence that all grant-funded rehabilitation work will preserve the distinctive features of a historic structure when they apply. All projects must comply with the rehabilitation guidelines published by the U.S. Department of the Interior through the National Park Service.

Who selects projects?

The staff of the New Jersey Historic Trust reviews grant applications to ensure that they are complete and that the applicants and proposed projects meet the program criteria. An expert advisory panel evaluates the applications and recommends the best ones to the Historic Trust's board of trustees, which makes the final selections. Selected projects are forwarded by the Trust as an appropriation bill to the state legislature, which provides a final stamp of approval.

How does the Historic Trust ensure that grant funds are properly spent and that projects actually get completed?

All grant recipients must sign grant agreements with the Historic Trust before receiving any funds. These include "easements" that place legally enforceable limitations on future changes to a historic structure's use or appearance, thus guaranteeing its long-term preservation after funds are expended. Easement terms vary, from five years for grants of $20,000 to $50,000, to 20 years (or more, depending on negotiations) for grants over $250,000. Grant applications require proof that the applicant organization's chief executive officer approves of the project and is authorized to enter into a grant agreement with the Historic Trust.

How does the Historic Trust ensure that the public will benefit from funded projects?

All projects funded must provide for public access to the grounds of the historic site. Interior access is required only if the grant underwrites changes to a structure's interior. The minimum requirement for public access to site grounds is six hours a day, 12 days a year, for the life of the easement. Grant recipients must notify the public through newspaper ads or some other means when sites are open to the public.

Are there deadlines for completing projects?

Yes. These vary according to the terms of a grant agreement, but all work on a project must begin within two years of a grant's approval. The Historic Trust withholds five percent of all grants pending final audits on completed projects.

How does the Historic Trust promote the program's visibility?

Every grant recipient is required to erect a sign indicating that the project was carried out with financial assistance from the Historic Preservation Bond Program.

How is the program's use promoted?

The New Jersey Historic Trust sponsors workshops around the state to inform interested groups about the program and to help them with grant applications. The Historic Trust also publishes a number of attractive publications that describe the program and its benefits.

ENDNOTES

Endnotes

Preface

1. Alex Achimore, "Putting the Community Back into Community Retail," *Urban Land* (Washington, D.C.: Urban Land Institute, August 1993), p. 34.

Introduction

1. The $5 million in the Massachusetts Preservation Projects Fund will be distributed over a five-year period.

Chapter 1: Protection

1. Telephone interview with Otis Pratt Pearsall, a key figure in the movement to create the Brooklyn Heights Historic District.

2. Arthur Frommer, "Historic Preservation and Tourism," *Preservation Forum*, National Trust for Historic Preservation. Fall 1988.

3. Edward D. Fowler, "Construction and Demolition Wastes: The Neglected Challenge of the 90's." A paper presented to the Legislative Commission on Solid Waste Management, New York City. January 21, 1991.

4. *North Carolina Law Journal*, Vol. II, No. 1, 1980.

5. Charles Hillestad, "Let's 'Honor' the Vandal of the Year," *Preservation News*, November 1990.

6. *Penn Central Transp. Co. v. City of New York*, 438 U.S. 104, 98 S. Ct. 2646 (1978).

7. *Berman v. Parker*, 348 U.S. 26 (1954).

8. *City of New Orleans v. Pergament*, 198 La. 852, 5 So. 2d 129 (1941).

9. *Village of Hudson v. Albrecht, Inc.*, 458 N.E. 2d 852 (Ohio 1984).

10. *Penn Central Transportation Co. v. City of New York*, 438 U.S. 104, 130 (1978).

11. *United Artists' Theater Circuit, Inc., v. City of Philadelphia*, 635 A.2d 612 (Pa. 1993).

12. *Agins v. City of Tiburon*, 447 U.S. 265 (1980). *Lucas v. South Carolina Coastal Council*, 112 S. Ct. 2886 (1992).

13. 438 U.S. at 108, 129.

14. 438 U.S. at 124.

15. 438 U.S. at 126. See also *Maher v. City of New Orleans*, 516 F.2d 1051 (5th Cir. 1975) (owner failed to show "the ordinance so diminished the property value as to leave Maher, in effect, nothing").

16. *Pittsburgh Historic Review Commission v. Weinberg*, No. 24 W.D. App. Docket 1995 (May 21, 1996).

17. For a useful summary of state court decisions on the "taking" issue, see "Takings and Preservation: A Survey of State Decisions," by Julia Hatch Miller, in the *Preservation Law Reporter*, Vol. 10, Nos. 7–8, July/August 1991.

18. Foreword by Robert E. Stipe to *Procedural Due Process in Plain English: A Guide for Preservation Commissions*, by Bradford J. White and Paul E. Edmondson. National Trust for Historic Preservation, 1994.

19. *Ibid.*

20. A useful summary of state court decisions upholding local preservation laws appears in the August 1991 issue of the *Preservation Law Reporter* (Volume 10, Nos. 7–8), available from the National Trust for Historic Preservation's Law Department.

21. See Historic Landmark and Historic District Protection Act, D.C. Code §5-1002 (10–11) and §5-1004 (e). For case law interpreting the District's special merit provision, see generally *Preservation Law Reporter* (National Trust for Historic Preservation, 1982–1996).

22. For more information on the issue of "demolition by neglect," see Oliver A. Pollard, III, "Minimum Maintenance Provisions: Preventing Demolition by Neglect," *Preservation Law Reporter*, Volume 8, 1989 Annual Report.

23. Allison Dyches, "Demolition by Neglect: What the Experts Say," *Preservation Progress*, (The Preservation Society of Charleston), vol. 35, no. 5, November 1991, p. 3. Cited in a master's thesis, "Demolition by Neglect: A Loophole in Preservation Policy," by Andrea Merrill Goldwyn. Presented to the University of Pennsylvania.

24. Va. Code Ann. §15.1-486.

25. In a 1995 case in which a church in Ypsilanti challenged the Michigan law on the ground that its application of the demolition-by-neglect provision constituted a "taking" of private property, the Circuit Court for the County of Washtenaw held that the city's denial of the church's request to demolish a historic structure for a parking lot was not an economic hardship of constitutional proportions. *City of Ypsilanti v. First Presbyterian Church of Ypsilanti*, decision by Circuit Court for County of Washtenaw. File No. 94-2253-C2.

26. 516 F.2d 1051, 1066–67 (5th Cir.), *cert denied*, 426 U.S. 905 (1975).

27. *Eubank v. City of Richmond*, 226 U.S. 137 (1912).

28. *Brodner v. City of Elgin*, 96 Ill. App. 3d 224, 420 N.E.2d 1176 (1981).

29. *East Bay Asian Local Development Corp. v. State of California*, No. 95-ASO2560 (Cal. Super. Ct. May 15, 1996).

30. The *Preservation Law Reporter* covers current developments in preservation law and is published by the Law Department of the National Trust for Historic Preservation.

31. Julia Hatch Miller, "Special Analysis: Owner Consent Provisions in Historic Preservation Ordinances: Are They Legal," *Preservation Law Reporter*, Volume 10, Number 2, February 1991. National Trust for Historic Preservation.

32. *Penn Central, op. cit.*

33. 24 Ill. Rev. Stat. §11-48.2–5.

34. Robert H. Freilich and Terri A. Muren, "Growth Management and Historic Preservation," a Critical Issues Fund Paper presented to the City of Atlanta in 1988, pp. 18–19. Available from the National Trust for Historic Preservation.

35. See Richard J. Roddewig and Cheryl A. Inghram, *Transferable Development Rights Programs*, PAS Report No. 401 (Chicago: American Planning Association, 1987), pp. 29–30.

36. *Ibid.*

37. "Historic Preservation Legislation in Wisconsin," a useful summary of the state's laws, is available from the State of Wisconsin Legislative Reference Bureau. Ask for Informational Bulletin 96-2, February 1996.

38. Iowa's law states: "No change in the use of any structure or property within a designated historical district shall be permitted until after an application for a certificate of appropriateness has been submitted to and approved by the commission…If the commission determines that the…proposed change in use would be incongruous with the historical, architectural,

archaeological or cultural aspects of the district, a certificate of appropriateness shall not be issued."

39. For a good discussion of these issue, see "Coordination of Historic Preservation and Land Use Controls: New Directions in Historic Preservation Regulation," by Julia Hatch Miller, in the Winter 1986/87 issue (Volume 5, No. 4) of *Preservation Law Reporter.*

40. R.I. Gen. Laws. §45-22.1-1 et seq. (1988).

41. 85-55, Laws of Florida; Part II, Ch. 163. F.S.

42. Julia Hatch Miller, "Coordination of Historic Preservation and Land Use Controls: New Directions in Historic Preservation Regulation," *Preservation Law Reporter*, Volume 5, No. 4, Winter 1986/87, National Trust for Historic Preservation.

43. Robert E. Stipe and Antoinette J. Lee, *The American Mosaic: Preserving A Nation's Heritage*, (Washington, D.C.: US/ICOMOS, United States Committee/International Council on Monuments and Sites, 1987), p. 14.

44. N.J.S.A. 13:1B-15.128 et seq.

45. Kan Stat. Ann. §75-2715 to 75-2725.

46. The states with environmental policy acts are: Arkansas (Ark. Stat. Ann. §8-1-101 [1987]); California (Cal. Pub. Res. Code §21000 et seq. [West 1982]); Connecticut (Conn. Gen. Stat. Ann. §22a-14 to 22a-20 [West Supp. 1974–75[); District of Columbia (D.C. Code Ann. 1981 §6-981 et seq.); Florida (Fla. Stat. §380.92 et seq.); Hawaii (Hawaii Rev. Stat. §343-1 to 343-8 (1985); Indiana (Ind. Code Ann. §13-1-10-1 to 13-1-10-8 [West 1987]); Maryland (Md. Nat. Res. Code Ann. §1-301 to 1-305 [1983 and Supp. 1987]); Massachusetts (Mass. Gen. Laws Ann. ch. 30. §61-62H); Minnesota (Minn. Stat. Ann. §116B.01 et seq. [West 1977 and Supp. 1981]); Montana (Mont. Code Ann. §75-1-101 to -105; §75-1-201 [1981]); New York (N.Y. Envtl. Conserv. Law §8-0101 to 8-0117 [McKinney 1984]); North Carolina (N.C. Gen. Stat. §113A-1 to 10 [1978]); South Dakota (S.D. Codified Laws Ann. §34A-9 to 34A-9-12); Virginia (Va. Code §10.1-1200 through 10.1-1212); Washington (Wash. Rev. Code §43-21C.010-43.21C.910 [1974]); Wash. Admin. Code R. 197-11); Wisconsin (Wis. Stat. §1.11 et seq.); Dept. of Natural Resources WEPA rules are found in Wis. Admin. Code NR 150.01-40.

47. Some experts have pointed out that the cumulative effect of many "minor" building alterations can be quite major, but most state environmental policy acts do not invoke reviews of such alterations.

48. N.Y. Envtl. Conserv. Law §8-0101 to 8-0117 (McKinney 1984).

49. *Ibid.*

50. Wash. Rev. Code Ann. §43.21C (Supp. 1982).

51. Minnesota Environmental Rights Act, Minn. Stat. §116B.01 *et seq.*

52. For another important case involving the Minnesota Environmental Rights Act, see *Minnesota v. County of Hennepin*, 495 N.W. 2d 416 (Minn. 1993). This case is also reported at 12 PLR 1025 (Feb. 1993) in the *Preservation Law Reporter*.

Chapter 2: Money for Preservation

1. "Virginia's Economy and Historic Preservation: The Impact of Preservation on Jobs, Business, and Community," Preservation Alliance of Virginia, 1995, p. 1.

2. Kohm Associates of Morristown is now called DKB and Partners.

3. Campaign flier, "The Arizona Heritage Fund: An Economic Development Opportunity."

4. *Ibid.*

5. Arthur Frommer, "Historic Preservation and Tourism," *Preservation Forum*, Fall 1988, p. 10.

6. *Ibid.*, p. 11

7. *Historic Preservation Legislation in Wisconsin*, State of Wisconsin Legislative Reference Bureau, Informational Bulletin 96-2, February 1996.

8. *Foundations*, A Report to the Governor and the 94th Legislature of the State of Nebraska by the Nebraska Task Force on Historic Preservation, May 1995.

Chapter 3: State Tax Incentives

1. Twenty-seven of these programs specifically target historic properties; ten of them provide incentives of older buildings generally under certain conditions.

2. Richard J. Roddewig, "Preservation Law and Economics," *A Handbook on Historic Preservation Law* (Washington, D.C.: The Conservation Foundation and the National Center for Preservation Law, 1983), p. 432.

3. *Ibid.*, p. 447.

4. *Ibid.*

5. Bureau of the Census Statistical Briefs, SB/93-4, Bureau of the Census, U.S. Department of Commerce, April 1993.

6. Donovan Rypkema, *The Economics of Historic Preservation* (Washington, D.C.: National Trust for Historic Preservation, 1994).

7. Georgia actually has two abatement programs. The one mentioned here is applied statewide, but a second, little-used program is a local option.

8. On the other hand, Utah allows "mid-stream" approvals: Even if a property owner began work before getting his plans approved, he might still claim the credit if the work completed meets the Department of Interior rehabilitation standards and other program criteria.

9. A report authored by Floyd Argersinger for the Washington State Department of Revenue and the Washington State Department of Community Development, "Washington State Special Valuation for Improvements to Historic Property," January 1993.

10. Initially the Wisconsin Dept. of Revenue required land values to be considered part of the basis as well. In our example, then, the homeowner would have had to incur $120,000 in rehabilitation expenses.

11. The original cap was $50,000, but this was later lowered to $10,000.

12. Wisconsin State Budget Office.

Chapter 4: Removing Regulatory Barriers

1. See Terry J. Tondro, "Reclaiming Brownfields to Save Greenfields: Shifting the Environmental Risks of Acquiring and Reusing Contaminated Land," *Connecticut Law Review*, Volume 27, Number 3, Spring 1995, p. 789.

2. Minnesota's Voluntary Investigation and Clean-up Program (VIC) built on an earlier program known as Property Transfer Assistance, created by the state legislature in 1988. This program was enacted at the request of the Minnesota Attorney General and the Minnesota Pollution Control Agency (MPCA) in an effort to expedite the reclamation of polluted land. The legislature authorized MPCA to charge fees to parties who voluntarily participate in the program for the cost of technical services.

3. Thomas Oliphant, "Out of the Superfund Muck," *The Boston Sunday Globe*, October 2, 1994.

4. Chris Barrish, "Recycled Sites Are Back in Business," *Delaware News Journal*, November 30, 1995.

5. *Guide for Planning Educational Facilities* (1991 edition), Council of Educational Facility Planners International, Scottsdale, Arizona. p. F-13.

6. Glen I. Earthman, Ed.D., *School Renovation Handbook* (Lancaster: Technomic Publishing Co., Inc. 1994).

7. July 26, 1991 Memorandum from Yale Stenzler, Executive Director, State of Maryland Public School Construction Program, to All Superintendents of Schools and Facility Planners.

8. "Rebuild It And They May Stay," an editorial by the *Baltimore Sun*, May 6, 1996.

9. January 20, 1994 letter from Walter T. Ruark, Director, Division of School Business Services, Maine Dept. of Education, to Robert G. Pelletier, Superintendent, Winthrop School Department.

10. See Melvyn Green, "Building Codes and Historic Preservation," *Forum*, National Trust for Historic Preservation, Spring 1988, p. 11.

11. Telephone interview with Randall Alexander, president of The Alexander Co.

12. See California Statutes, Health and Safety Code 18950–18961; California Code of Regulations, Title 24, Part 8; and *Precedents* (Appeal Rulings and Formal Interpretations).

13. Appendix F in the Massachusetts State Building Code was originally known as Appendix 11.

Chapter 5: State Agency Investments

1. Thomas Hylton, *Save Our Land, Save Our Towns*, (Harrisburg, Pa: Richly Beautiful Books, 1995).

2. *Ibid.*, p. 6.

3. Address by Governor Parris N. Glendening to Preservation Maryland, November 3, 1995 in Frederick, Md.

4. Executive Order 134, "Promoting the Economic Revitalization of Downtown Centers of Cities and Towns by Establishing a Process for Locating Appropriate State Offices and Buildings in Such Areas." Issued by Massachusetts Governor Michael S. Dukakis in 1977.

5. Executive Order 15, promulgated by Vermont Governor Madeleine M. Kunin on Sept. 6, 1985.

6. Executive Order 94-07, "Siting State Offices in Oregon's Community Centers," issued June 7, 1994 by Governor Barbara Roberts.

Chapter 6: Rural Preservation

1. Foreword by Stewart L. Udall to *Saving America's Countryside* (Baltimore: The Johns Hopkins University Press, 1989), p. xviii.

2. Dwight Young, *Alternatives to Sprawl* (Cambridge: Lincoln Institute of Land Policy & Washington, D.C.: National Trust for Historic Preservation, 1995), p. 5.

3. "Michigan Farmland and Agriculture Development Task Force: Policy Recommendations and Options for the Future Growth of Michigan Agriculture," December 1994, p. 4.

4. Samuel N. Stokes, *Saving America's Countryside* (Baltimore: The Johns Hopkins University Press, 1989), pp. 3–4.

5. *Pennsylvania Agricultural News*, Vol. 74, No. 1, January 1990, p. 1.

6. Usually the township acts favorably on landowner petitions to create Agricultural Security Areas (ASAs). However, in 1996, Paradise Township in Lancaster County refused to designate an ASA requested by landowners.

7. Bureau of Farmland Protection, Pennsylvania Dept. of Agriculture, "Agricultural Security Areas Formed Under Act 43," March 29, 1996.

8. See Robert E. Coughlin, "The Adoption and Stability of Agricultural Zoning in Lancaster County, Pennsylvania."

9. *Ibid.*, p. 5.

10. See letter by Robert Freeman transmitting to the state legislature the "Final Report of the 1991–92 House Select Committee on Land Use and Growth Management," June 30, 1992.

11. David Schneider, *Foundations in a Fertile Soil* (Lancaster, Pa.: Historic Preservation Trust of Lancaster County, 1994), p. 38.

12. Letter from Governor Howard Dean in "Report to the General Assembly" of the Vermont Housing and Conservation Board, 1995, p. 1.

13. "Pathways to Posterity," A Report by the Governor's Commission on the Economic Future of Vermont, 1989.

14. Quoted by Phyllis Myers in *Lessons from the States: Strengthening Land Conservation Programs through Grants to Nonprofit Land Trusts* (Washington, D.C.: Land Trust Alliance, 1992), p. 32.

15. *Ibid.*, p. 33.

16. Report to the General Assembly of the Vermont Housing and Conservation Board, 1995, p. 16.

17. H. Grant Dehart, *Rural Historic Village Protection in Maryland*, National Trust for Historic Preservation, Public Policy Series, October, 1990.

18. American Farmland Trust, April 1996, *Purchase of Agricultural Conservation Easements, Status of Programs as of April 12, 1996.*

19. Pennsylvania's total for acres protected has recently risen to 80,000, an increase that took place following the release of the American Farmland Trust's report.

Chapter 9: Transportation

1. See Kenneth T. Jackson, *The Crabgrass Frontier* (New York: Oxford University Press, 1985), p. 270.

2. Daniel Patrick Moynihan, "New Roads and Urban Chaos," *The Reporter*, April 14, 1960.

3. Tom Hylton, *Save Our Land, Save Our Towns* (Harrisburg: RB Books, 1995), pp. 25–26.

4. In Maine, for example, 85 percent of all public school students are bused to schools. Maine taxpayers pay $31.6 million annually for school busing services. Source: Telephone interview with Bill Millar, School Support Services Team, Maine Dept. of Education.

5. See "1994 State Expenditure Report," National Association of State Budget Officers, April 1995, pp. 11 and 62.

6. See John Pucher, "Urban Passenger Transport in the U.S. and Europe: A Comparative Analysis of Public Policies, Part 1, Travel Behaviour, Urban Development and Automobile Use," *Transport Reviews*, 1995, vol. 15, no. 2, p. 103.

7. FHWA Final Report: The National Bicycling and Walking Study, Publication No. PD 94-023, 1994, p. 23.

8. *Ibid.*, p. 18.

9. William H. Whyte, *City: Rediscovering the Center* (New York: Anchor Books/Doubleday, 1988), pp. 312–313.

10. "Consumer Expenditures in 1994," U.S. Dept. of Labor, Bureau of Labor Statistics, Report 902, February 1996, p. 3. Note: Only six percent, or $381, of the average annual expenditure of $6,044 spent on transportation goes for public transportation.

11. Survey conducted by the San Francisco-based consumer research firm, American Lives, Inc., and cited by Kenneth R. Harney in "Home Buyers Want Modern Towns With Lots of Old-Fashioned Charm," *The Washington Post*, June 1, 1996.

12. FHWA Interim Report: The National Bicycling and Walking Study, Report No: FHWA-PD-92-003, November 1991, p. 4.

13. *Ibid.*, p. 4.

14. July 19, 1996 telephone interview with Dan Burden, Pedestrian and Bicycle Coordinator for State of Florida.

15. LUTRAQ UPDATE: Making the Land-use, Transportation, and Air Quality Connection, Vol. 1, No. 4, January 1993, p. 2.

16. See Kenneth R. Harney, "Home Buyers Want Modern Towns With Lots of Old-Fashioned Charm," *The Washington Post*. June 1, 1996.

17. See Constance E. Beaumont, "The Critical Need for a Sensitive—and Sensible—National Transportation Policy," *Historic Preservation Forum*, July/August 1991, Vol. 5, No. 4, pp. 43–44.

18. See James J. MacKenzie et al, *What It Really Costs to Drive* (Washington, D.C.: World Resources Institute, 1992).

19. *Ibid*. See also *The Washington Post*, May 9, 1996, p. A4.

20. *Ibid.*, p. 19.

21. See 1994 State Expenditure Report, National Association of State Budget Officers, April 1995, pp. 11 and 62.

22. See "Consumer Expenditures in 1994," U.S. Dept. of Labor, Bureau of Labor Statistics, Report 902, February 1996.

23. Kenneth T. Jackson, *The Crabgrass Frontier* (New York/Oxford: Oxford University Press, 1985), p. 249.

24. I. Mei Chan, *Building on the Past, Traveling to the Future: A Preservationist's Guide to the ISTEA Transportation Enhancement Provision*, (Washington, D.C.: Federal Highway Administration/National Trust for Historic Preservation), p. 19.

25. *Ibid.*, pp. 44–45, 38–39, 40–41.

26. Title 23, U.S.C. §109(p).

27. Jim Wick, *A State Highway Project in Your Town?*, Burlington: Preservation Trust of Vermont, 1995.

28. *A Policy on Geometric Design*, American Association of State Highway and Transportation Officials.

29. Keith C. Miller makes a similar point: "[C]laims based on negligence in the design of a roadway are the least successful of all those actions based on alleged defects in roadways…[T]his is because of the general rule that flaws in highway design are within the scope of governmental immunity for planning and related discretionary functions." See Keith C. Miller, *Automobile Accident Law and Practice* (New York: Matthew Bender, 1988), p. 8-8.

30. John Heaton, "Liability," A Paper Submitted at the Federal Highway Administration's Workshop on Highway Design, March 24, 1994.

31. Stephen H. Burrington and Veronika Thiebach, *Take Back Your Streets: How to Protect Communities from Asphalt and Traffic* (Boston: Conservation Law Foundation, 1995), pp. 17–18.

32. *A Policy on Geometric Design*, op. cit., p. 64.

33. *Ibid*, p. 67.

34. *Ibid*, p. 63.

35. 19 V.S.A. §10c.

36. Andi Rierden, "Towns Just Saying 'No' to Federal Funds," *New York Times*, October 1, 1995.

37. Mary Catherine Snyder, "Maine's New Rules," Surface Transportation Policy Project Resource Guide.

38. See Richard Barringer & Sondra Bogdonoff, "An Essay on Human Understanding," *Maine Times*, January 8, 1993.

39. The full text of the Maine Sensible Transportation Policy Act had been attached to the petition but not to the ballot. When presented with petitions, the state legislature has the option of enacting the proposed legislation or of sending it along to the voters to be considered in a referendum. In this case the legislature chose the latter course.

40. Barringer & Bogdonoff, *op cit.*

41. *Ibid.*

Chapter 10: Alternatives to Sprawl

1. Anton C. Nelessen, *Visions for a New American Dream: Process, Principles, and An Ordinance to Plan and Design Small Communities* (Chicago: American Planning Association/Planners Press, 1993), pp. xii and 49. Nelessen also notes that it is ironic that "[t]he many cars traveling to and from the separated [land] uses now cause the same kind of pollution that single-use zones were created to eliminate."

2. Jonathan Barnett, *The Fractured Metropolis* (New York: HarperCollins, 1995), p. 6.

3. James Howard Kunstler, *The Geography of Nowhere* (Simon & Schuster, 1993), p. 114.

4. Anthony Downs, *New Visions for Metropolitan America* (Washington, D. C.: The Brookings Institution, 1994), p. 7.

5. Barnett, *op. cit.*, p. 25.

6. *Bremerton, et al., v. Kitsap County*, 95-3-0039 Final Decision and Order, Central Puget Sound Growth Management Hearings Board, State of Washington. Oct. 5, 1995, p. 28.

7. "Beyond Sprawl: New Patterns of Growth to Fit the New California," a report by the Bank of America, the California Resources Agency, the Greenbelt Alliance, and the Low-Income Housing Fund. January 1995.

8. Eric Lipton, "Business Elite Fret About Northern Virginia," *The Washington Post*, February 5, 1996.

9. Hawaii enacted its State Land Use Law (Chapter 204, Hawaii Revised Statutes) in 1961, but this statute is omitted from our discussion here.

10. John M. DeGrove, *Land Growth and Politics*, (Chicago: American Planning Association/ Planners Press, 1984) p. 70.

11. *Ibid.*, p. 93.

12. The original Act 200 included 32 goals, but the legislature saw these as confusing and unattainable and later cut them to 12.

13. Readers Forum, July 3, 1994, *Burlington Free Press*.

14. Ron Powers, "Tug of War for the Soul of Vermont," *Middlebury Magazine*, Spring 1995.

15. *St. Albans Messenger*, December 24, 1994.

16. The size of the proposed Wal-Mart store, which would have been built in two phases, was later reduced from 156,000 square feet to 100,780 square feet.

17. Prefiled Testimony by Arthur Frommer In Re Wal-Mart Stores, Inc. and St. Albans Group submitted by Franklin/Grand Isle County Citizens for Downtown Preservation to the State of Vermont Environmental Board, June 13, 1994.

18. Prefiled testimony of Richard K. Gsottschneider & Lawrence E. Cranor, Jr., In Re St. Albans Group and Wal-Mart Stores, Inc., submitted to the State of Vermont Environmental Board, June 9, 1994.

19. Thomas Muller and Elizabeth Humstone, "Phase One Report: Retail Sales Impact of Proposed Wal-Mart on Franklin County," October 15, 1993.

20. Findings of Fact, Conclusions of Law, and Order on St. Albans Group and Wal-Mart Stores, Inc., Application #6F0471-EB, State of Vermont Environmental Board, December 23, 1994.

21. Richard Cowperthwait, "Town Fights Wal-Mart Ruling," *Burlington Free Press*, July 25, 1995.

22. "Wal-Mart Bolsters Small Town Historic Preservation," Wal- Mart Press Release, June 23, 1993.

23. Frederick Bever, "Wal-Mart Seals Plaza Deal," *The Rutland Herald*, April 26, 1996

24. "Wal-Mart Wins Over Its Critics," *Addison County Independent*, September 25, 1995.

25. Candace Page, "Landmark Act 250 Ended 'Anything Goes' Era," *Burlington Free Press*, May 25, 1995.

26. John DeGrove, *op. cit.*, p. 79.

27. Foreward by Doug Costle to *Vermont Act 250 Handbook*, by Cincy Corlett Argentine. Brattleboro, VT: Putney Press, 1993.

28. Charles E. Little, *The New Oregon Trail: An Account of the Development and Passage of State Land-Use Legislation in Oregon* (Washington, D.C.: The Conservation Foundation, 1974), p. 11.

29. John DeGrove, *op. cit.*, pp. 236–237.

30. Robert Liberty, "The Way It Was, The Way It Is," *Landmark*, 1000 Friends of Oregon, January 1995, p. 3.

31. *Ibid.*

32. Governor McCall quoted by Charles E. Little in *The New Oregon Trail* (Washington, D.C.: The Conservation Foundation) 1974, p. 7.

33. 1973 Or. Laws ch. 80 (codified as amended at OR. REV. STAT. §197.005-.860 (1991)). See Robert L. Liberty, "Oregon's Comprehensive Growth Management Program: An Implementation Review and Lessons for Other States," *Environmental Law Reporter*, Vol. XXII, No. 6, June 1992.

34. The Oregon Land Use Board of Appeals (LUBA) can reverse or remand a plan amendment only if it finds that the amendment violates state laws, the goals or the local plan or regulation. LUBA cannot make or interpret state policy, so its reviews tend to be narrower and more legalistic.

35. Robert Liberty, *op. cit.*, p. 3.

36. *Petersen v. City of Klamath Falls*, 279 Or. 249, 566 P.2d 1193 (1977).

37. *Landmark*, *op. cit.*, p. 25.

38. See Michael J. Major, "Containing Growth in the Pacific Northwest," *Urban Land*, March 1994, pp. 16-17.

39. For more information about Oregon's Transportation Planning Rule, contact the Oregon Dept. of Land Conservation and Development, 1175 Court St., N.E., Salem, Ore. 97310. Tel: 503/373-0050.

40. DeGrove, *op. cit.*, p. 290.

41. Bob Ortega, "Portland, Ore., Shows Nation's City Planners How to Guide Growth," *Wall Street Journal*, December 26, 1995.

42. Robert L. Liberty, "Citizens' Voice Needed to Assure Quality Growth," *Landmark*, 1000 Friends of Oregon, January 1996, p. 2.

43. *Landmark*, Anniversary Issue, 1000 Friends of Oregon, January 1996, p. 4.

44. Revised Code of Washington 36.70A.020.

45. Ninety-five percent of the Washington population is planning under the Growth Management Act, according to Michael McCormick, former assistant director of Washington's Department of Community Development.

46. *Bremerton v. Kitsap County*, Final Decision and Order, Central Puget Sound Growth Management Hearings Board, Consolidated Case No. 95-0039, October 6,1995, pp. 70–72.

47. Telephone interview with Dan Baskins, May 14, 1996.

48. *Bremerton v. Kitsap County*, op cit., p. 28.

49. *City of Tacoma, City of Milton, City of Puyallup, and City of Sumner v. Pierce County*, Final Decision and Order by the Central Puget Sound Growth Management Hearings Board, State of Washington. Case No. 94-3-0001, July 5, 1994.

50. Letter from Sprenger, Grubb & Associates, Inc., Woodside Developers, to the citizens of Hailey.

51. *Jacobs, Visconsi & Jacobs v. City of Lawrence, Kansas*, 927 F 2d 111 (10th Cir. 1991).

52. Barbara L. Lawrence, "New Jersey's Controversial Growth Plan," *Urban Land*, January 1988, p. 19.

53. Executive Summary, "Impact Assessment of the New Jersey Interim State Development and Redevelopment Plan," by Rutgers University (Principal Investigator, Robert W. Burchell), February 28, 1992.

54. "Communities of Place: The New Jersey State Development and Redevelopment Plan," New Jersey State Planning Commission. June 2, 1992, p. 125.

55. New Jersey Future newsletter, March/April 1996, p. 1.

56. Speech by Governor Parris N. Glendening at the Revitalization and Preservation Conference in Frederick, Maryland, November 3, 1995.

57. AB 1290 was codified at California Health and Safety Code §33426.5.

58. Tom Hylton, *op. cit.*, pp. 26–27.

Chapter 11: Private Property Rights

1. 438 U.S. 104 (1978).

2. *See, e.g., Preseault v. ICC*, 494 U.S. 1 (1990); *Pennell v. City of San Jose*, 485 U.S. 1 (1988); *MacDonald, Sommer & Frates v. County of Yolo*, 477 U.S. 340 (1986); *Williamson County Regional Planning Comm'n v. Hamilton Bank*, 473 U.S. 172 (1985); *Loretto v. Teleprompter Manhattan CATV Corp.*, 458 U.S. 419 (1982); *San Diego Gas & Elec. Co. v. City of San Diego*, 450 U.S. 621 (1981); *Kaiser Aetna v. United States*, 444 U.S. 164 (1979).

3. *Dolan v. City of Tigard*, 114 S. Ct. 2309 (1994); *Lucas v. South Carolina Coastal Council*, 112 S. Ct. 2886 (1992); *Yee v. City of Escondido*, 503 U.S. 519 (1992); *PFZ Properties, Inc. v. Rodriguez*, 503 U.S. 257 (1992) (writ dismissed as improvidently granted); *Nollan v. California Coastal Comm'n*, 483 U.S. 825 (1987); *First English Evangelical Lutheran Church v. County of Los Angeles*, 482 U.S. 304 (1987); *Keystone Bituminous Coal Ass'n v. DeBenedictis*, 480 U.S. 470 (1987).

4. *See, e.g., Loveladies Harbor, Inc. v. United States*, 28 F.3d 1171 (Fed. Cir. 1994); *Florida Rock Industries, Inc. v. United States*, 18 F.3d 1560 (Fed. Cir. 1994), *cert. denied*, 115 S. Ct. 898 (1995); *Seawall Associates v. City of New York*, 74 N.Y.2d 92, 542 N.E.2d 1059, *cert. denied*, 493 U.S. 976 (1989).

5. Executive Order No. 12630, 53 Fed. Reg. 8859 (1988).

6. U.S. Const. amend V.

7. *Armstrong v. United States*, 364 U.S. 40, 49 (1960).

8. *See Hawaii Hous. Auth. v. Midkiff*, 467 U.S. 29 (1984); *Poletown Neighborhood Council v. City of Detroit*, 410 Mich. 616, 304 N.W.2d 455 (1981).

9. 123 U.S. 623 (1887).

10. 239 U.S. 394 (1915).

11. 260 U.S. 393 (1922).

12. *Id.* at 415.

13. *Id.* at 413.

14. *Id.* at 415.

15. *Nectow v. City of Cambridge*, 277 U.S. 183 (1928); *Gorieb v. Fox*, 274 U.S. 603 (1927); *Zahn v. Board of Public Works*, 274 U.S. 325 (1927); *Village of Euclid v. Ambler Realty Co.*, 272 U.S. 365 (1926).

16. 438 U.S. 104 (1978).

17. *Id.* at 110.

18. *Id.* at 123.

19. *Id.* at 124.

20. *Id.* at 124. As an example of the application of the "character" factor, the Court stated that a regulation authorizing a "physical invasion" would more likely constitute a taking than a regulation "adjusting the benefits and burdens of economic life to promote the common good." *Id.*

21. *Id.* at 136.

22. *Id.*

23. *Id.* at 137.

24. 447 U.S. 255 (1980).

25. *Id.* at 260.

26. 482 U.S. 304 (1987); *see also San Diego Gas & Electric Co. v. City of San Diego*, 450 U.S. 621 (1981) (Brennan, J., dissenting) (influential four-justice dissent presaging *First English* outcome).

27. 112 S. Ct. 2886 (1992).

28. 114 S. Ct. 2309 (1994).

29. 112 S. Ct. at 2896 n.10.

30. *Id.* at 2889-90.

31. *Id.* at 2890.

32. *Id.*

33. The Supreme Court sent the case back to the South Carolina Supreme Court, which consistent with the *Lucas* decision found a taking. *Lucas v. South Carolina Coastal Council*, 309 S.C. 424, 424 S.E.2d 484 (1992). Lucas and the South Carolina Coastal Council subsequently settled the case, with Lucas receiving over $1.6 million in direct compensation, interim interest, attorneys fees, and costs.

34. The Court inserted the word "all," and sprinkled the opinion with additional adjectives—"beneficial," "productive," and "feasible"—to join "viable," without any express indication that the supplemental words added new meaning to the test. 112 S. Ct. at 2893, 2899.

35. *Id.* at 2893.

36. *Id.* at 2900.

37. For a recent journey down this road, see *Loveladies Harbor, Inc. v. United States*, 28 F.3d 1171 (Fed. Cir. 1994).

38. *Florida Rock Industries, Inc. v. United States*, 18 F.3d 1560 (Fed. Cir. 1994), *cert. denied*, 115 S. Ct. 898 (1995).

39. 114 S. Ct. 2309 (1994).

40. Under the Just Compensation Clause, the Court has invalidated regulations authorizing uninvited "permanent physical occupations" of private property by strangers, be they human or a half-inch cable wire and box. *See e.g., Loretto v. Teleprompter Manhattan CATV Corp.*, 458 U.S. 419, 441 (1982) (striking down New York City law authorizing television cable company to lay cable on private property against owner's will).

41. 114 S. Ct. at 2317. This requirement was originally announced in *Nollan v. California Coastal Comm'n*, 483 U.S. 825 (1987).

42. 114 S. Ct. at 2319.

43. In dissent, Justice Souter criticized this conclusion on the basis that, if anything, it described a failure of "essential nexus" rather than "rough proportionality." *Id.* at 2330 (Souter, J., dissenting).

44. 114 S. Ct. at 2321-22.

45. 114 S. Ct. at 2319-20 (footnote omitted).

46. 114 S. Ct. at 2322 (emphasis added). Justice Stevens' dissent tweaked the majority for its apparently decisive reliance on a single letter—a "c" for *c*ould rather than a "w" for "*w*ould"—to reach its conclusion. *Id.* at 2326.

47. 114 S. Ct. at 2322.

48. *See id.* at 2320; *Nollan v. California Coastal Comm'n*, 483 U.S. 825, 833-35 nn. 2, 3 (1987).

49. 42 U.S.C. Sections 4321, 4332(C) (1970).

50. *See* 5 CQ Researcher 513, 520 (1995).

51. *Id.*

52. *Penn Central Transportation Co. v. City of New York*, 438 U.S. 104 (1978).

53. See Dwight Young, *Alternatives to Sprawl* (Cambridge, Mass.: Lincoln Institute of Land Policy, National Trust for Historic Preservation, and the Brookings Institution, 1995), p. 17.

54. "Great Oaks Homeowners Association Handbook," City of Fairfax, Virginia.

55. Donovan D. Rypkema, "Property Rights/Property Values: The Economic Misunderstandings of the Property Rights Movement," *Historic Preservation Forum*, July/August 1993, p. 25.

56. "Proposition 300: No," an editorial by *The Arizona Republic*, October 24, 1994.

57. Grady Gammage, "Arizona's Prop 200: A Winning Battle," *Historic Preservation Forum*, Winter 1996, p. 46.

58. Barbara Mossman, "Washington State Legislature Passes Sweeping Property Rights Bill," *Land Rights Letter*, May 1995.

59. Eric Scigliano, "Quick and Dirty," *Seattle Weekly*, June 28, 1995.

60. See Foreword by Randall T. Shepard to Christopher J. Duerksen and Richard J. Roddewig, *Takings Law in Plain English* (Washington, D.C. American Resources Information Network and Clarion Associates, 1994). See also p. 41.

61. February 2, 1993 letter from Ralph Tyler to The Honorable Walter M. Baker.